M

Majoring in Psychology

About the Authors

Dr. Helms is an Associate Professor of Psychology at Kennesaw State University where he joined the faculty in 2003. Prior academic appointments included teaching not only at the undergraduate level but also at the master's, specialist, and doctoral levels. His publications, research, and practice interests are predominantly in the areas of forensic psychology and the scholarship of teaching. He was an associate editor of the *Journal of Forensic Psychology Practice* (2002–2009) and presently serves on its editorial board. Currently, he holds licensure as a psychologist in Georgia and maintains a small private forensic and clinical consulting practice. His clinical experience includes work in the community mental health arena, inpatient psychiatric facilities, and multiple forensic environments. He has previously practiced and taught in California and Kentucky. Dr. Helms is a member of the American Psychological Association and the American Psychology-Law Society.

Dr. Rogers is an Assistant Professor of Psychology at Kennesaw State University where he joined the faculty in 2005. His research and practice interests are in the areas of personality assessment, measurement, interpersonal and psychodynamic theories, and the scholarship of teaching and learning. Currently, he holds licensure as a psychologist in Georgia. He previously practiced and taught in Michigan. His clinical experience includes work across the age spectrum and across levels of impairment, with emphasis on psychological assessment and psychodynamic interventions. Dr. Rogers is a member of the American Psychological Association; the Division of Evaluation, Measurement, and Statistics; the Society for the Teaching of Psychology; and the Society for Personality Assessment.

Majoring in Psychology

Achieving Your Educational and Career Goals

Jeffrey L. Helms and Daniel T. Rogers

WILEY-BLACKWELL

A John Wiley & Sons, Ltd., Publication

This edition first published 2011
© 2011 Jeffrey L. Helms and Daniel T. Rogers

Blackwell Publishing was acquired by John Wiley & Sons in February 2007.
Blackwell's publishing program has been merged with Wiley's global Scientific,
Technical, and Medical business to form Wiley-Blackwell.

Registered Office
John Wiley & Sons Ltd, The Atrium, Southern Gate, Chichester, West Sussex,
PO19 8SQ, United Kingdom

Editorial Offices
350 Main Street, Malden, MA 02148-5020, USA
9600 Garsington Road, Oxford, OX4 2DQ, UK
The Atrium, Southern Gate, Chichester, West Sussex, PO19 8SQ, UK

For details of our global editorial offices, for customer services, and for information
about how to apply for permission to reuse the copyright material in this book
please see our website at www.wiley.com/wiley-blackwell.

The right of Jeffrey L. Helms and Daniel T. Rogers to be identified as the author of this
work has been asserted in accordance with the Copyright, Designs and Patents Act 1988.

Library of Congress Cataloging-in-Publication Data

Helms, Jeffrey L.
Majoring in psychology : achieving your educational and career goals / Jeffrey L. Helms and
Daniel T. Rogers.
    p. cm.
   Includes bibliographical references and index.
   ISBN 978-1-4051-9064-0 (hardcover : alk. paper) – ISBN 978-1-4051-9063-3 (pbk. : alk. paper)
   1. Psychology–Vocational guidance.   2. Psychology–Study and teaching.   I. Rogers, Daniel T.
II. Title.
BF76.H45 2010
150.71'1–dc22

                                                                                    2009041433

A catalogue record for this book is available from the British Library.

Set in 10.5/13pt Minion by Graphicraft Limited, Hong Kong
Printed and bound in Malaysia by Vivar Printing Sdn Bhd

1   2011

Brief Contents

Table of Contents

Part II   The Subfields of Psychology   135

Boxes

Tables

Preface

This book grew out of our experience teaching and working with psychology students on issues related to academic and career success. Whether in the classroom of our Careers in Psychology course that addresses these topics, or in the midst of advising a student, we have developed a deep appreciation for how simultaneously exciting and overwhelming the process of pursuing academic and career goals can be. Students are passionate about discovering the options available to them and identifying their unique goals. Instructors relish the opportunity to guide students through this process and watch them succeed. However, students and instructors alike can at times feel lost given the range of complex issues involved in academic and career development. In fact, some of the most helpful information, strategies, and resources for meeting these goals go unused simply because students or their instructors are unaware of their existence. Our appreciation for this mixed experience from both the student's and instructor's perspectives led us to write this book.

This book provides students interested in psychology, and the instructors who work with them, with information that is vital to academic and career success in the field. As such, the book is an ideal text for courses that address aspects of majoring in psychology (e.g., academic strategies, career and graduate school preparation) and/or aspects of career planning (e.g., learning about the careers of psychologists in various subfields and their education and training). Students who are seeking to clarify their academic and career goals and develop knowledge and skills to support achieving these goals will find the book most helpful.

There are other texts available that concentrate on one or two of the areas covered in this book, such as selecting a career, navigating your academic path, or preparing for graduate school. Many of these texts are excellent resources, and we encourage students and instructors to examine them according to interest and need. However, our goal was to bring these and other related topics together in one place. In doing so, we compile sound, research-based information and strategies on succeeding as a psychology major and communicate them in an interesting and compelling way.

We hope that the book answers questions about the major and its career paths while supporting the pursuit of academic and career goals.

This book is divided into two sections. Part I concentrates on student success in achieving general educational and career goals. In this section we examine such issues as the utility of a psychology degree, strategies for academic success, career decision making, and employment and graduate school preparation. In addition to content, the chapters offer suggested exercises, readings, and resources to enhance understanding of the issues at hand. Part II of the book concentrates on student success in achieving specific educational and career goals. In this section we examine the various career options within psychology and issues related to these careers. Each chapter addresses a major area within psychology and provides valuable information about the focus, training, and work of individuals with careers in these areas. The chapters also include information about relevant career options at both the graduate *and* bachelor's levels. In addition to suggested exercises, readings, and resources, each chapter offers a glimpse into the careers and perspectives of two nationally recognized psychologists working in their respective subfield.

It is our belief that success as a psychology major cannot simply be defined as earning good grades, securing a job after graduation, or gaining acceptance into graduate school. Instead, success involves becoming a strong student who is well informed not only about the field but also about her or his relationship to it. As such, we hope that this book serves as a reliable and trustworthy guide both for students curious about the field and their place within it and for instructors who are assisting them in their pursuit.

Acknowledgments

As with any undertaking of this size, many people contributed to its realization. Among these are the individuals at Wiley-Blackwell Publishers and the reviewers of the manuscript at various points. The feedback provided throughout the process was invaluable. We also thank the contributors to the Professional Spotlights and short topical articles included throughout the book. Their contributions bring the book to life. These individuals are:

Marie Balaban, Eastern Oregon University
Christopher M. Carr, St. Vincent Sports Performance Center
John Chan, Success Factors
Christine Dunkel Schetter, University of California, Los Angeles
Regan A. R. Gurung, University of Wisconsin, Green Bay
Kate F. Hays, The Performing Edge
Matthew T. Huss, Creighton University
Russell E. Johnson, University of South Florida
Kimberlyn Leary, Cambridge Hospital
Rebecca S. Martinez, Indiana University
Laura L. Mayhew, University of South Florida
Robert McGrath, Fairleigh Dickinson University
William Pfohl, Western Kentucky University
Cynthia L. Pickett, University of California, Davis
Antonio E. Puente, University of North Carolina, Wilmington
Maria Teresa Schultheis, Drexel University
Randolph A. Smith, Lamar University
Gina M. Vincent, University of Massachusetts Medical School
Janie H. Wilson, Georgia Southern University

We thank our colleagues at Kennesaw State University. Without the supportive environment for teaching, teaching excellence, and this type of scholarly activity, this book would not have been realized. We also thank our students for their enthusiasm and curiosity about this wonderful field of study. Last but not least, we thank Mary E. Schnorf for her assistance with the index development. In short, thank you all.

JLH: I would like to thank my coauthor for accepting my offer to work on this project. I could not have chosen a better collaborator. On a more personal note, I thank my mother, father, and brother for their support throughout my education, career, and life. It is to them that I dedicate this work. Thank you for everything.

DTR: To my coauthor, thank you for planting the seeds for this project and inviting me to help bring it to fruition. To my family, April and Noah, thank you for your tremendous support throughout this project, the ones before, and those yet to come.

Part I

Majoring in Psychology

Why Major in Psychology?

Introduction

Psychology is a fascinating and diverse field of study. It attracts students with varied backgrounds, interests, and abilities, all of whom come to the field hopeful that psychology is a good fit for them. In addition to pursuing topics that they find compelling, these students stand to benefit from devoting themselves to the study of such a broad field. Psychology's breadth is what makes it possible for students to acquire a wide range of knowledge and skills that are applicable to a variety of careers. In other words, psychology offers many different things to many different types of individuals. Consider for a moment three such students, all undergraduates majoring in psychology.

Valerie is 19 years old and always knew she would go to college. Since middle school she had planned to become a teacher, so she first chose education as her major. However, after taking several introductory courses and talking with faculty members in the education department, Valerie decided that teaching was not for her. She next considered majoring in nursing, but the admission standards for the local nursing programs are highly competitive. Valerie feared that the grades she earned in two courses required for the nursing program would make her acceptance unlikely. One day last semester, Valerie's roommate described an interesting demonstration her psychology professor had presented in class. This reminded Valerie of her interest in psychology in high school, and she decided to take a course to see what psychology was like at the college level. Valerie enjoyed the course and performed well, so she decided to change her major to psychology. When she recently mentioned the change to her parents, they were not especially positive. They asked questions about what she could do with the degree and how her career options would compare to those of education or nursing majors. Valerie was unsure how to answer their questions because she had not yet given much thought to what she can or will do with her degree. But, she figures that if so many other people major in psychology, there must be employment options for her.

Katrina is 37 years old and has attended college at several points in the past at two different institutions. Most recently she stopped attending after the birth of her first child. She then resumed working full-time and was unsure if she would ever return to school to complete her degree. Now that her children are older and her financial status is more secure, she has decided to return to college part-time in order to get back into the academic routine. Ever since she was young, Katrina has had a desire to become a clinical psychologist. She was involved in family therapy as a child and individual therapy as an adolescent. She has fond memories of the psychologists she interacted with and the benefits of these treatments. Since then she has taken it upon herself to read psychological theory and some of the latest research in the field. Now that she is returning to school again, Katrina has committed herself to taking her education seriously and staying focused on her career goal. She knows meeting this goal will require completing her bachelor's degree and then moving on to complete her doctorate. Although Katrina is excited to begin moving forward along this path, she is also concerned about starting what feels like a long road ahead.

Ajay is 25 years old. He began college two years ago after working for several years in his family's business. His first major was computer science, an area of interest for him since high school. His teachers, family, and friends encouraged him to pursue this major given his talents and technological skills. He enjoyed the courses at first, but later realized that he did not feel passionate about the topics or the prospects of future careers in the field. Due to his growing apathy, and his working 30–40 hours a week, Ajay's grades suffered. Then he took a psychology course several semesters ago and started a dialogue about his interests with the professor. As a result, Ajay decided to switch majors to psychology. Since that time he has invested himself in his coursework and excelled academically. After serving as a research assistant in one of his professor's labs over the past year, Ajay is now planning to pursue a research career in cognitive psychology. He intends to merge his computer science skills with his developing interest in human memory. Although changing majors extended his graduation date for another year, Ajay now knows exactly what it is he wants to do in his career and has worked diligently to learn about the field, improve his academic skills, and gain valuable experience.

Valerie, Katrina, and Ajay represent typical undergraduate psychology majors. Some of you will identify with one or more aspects of their histories and experiences. Others of you may not see parts of yourself in these particular students, but there are still several things you all have in common. Each of you has decided to major in psychology, or seriously consider it, as a result of intertwining experiences and life circumstances. Each of you has found something intrinsically interesting about the field. Each of you is hoping that this major will be the one that satisfies your interests and allows you to accomplish your goals. In essence, each of you hopes that you have found a home in psychology.

As professors of psychology who have taught, advised, supervised, and mentored thousands of undergraduate students in all areas of their academic and career pursuits, we have worked with many students like Valerie, Katrina, Ajay, and you. We are highly invested in helping all students succeed in the ways that best match their goals. In doing this, we encounter students on a daily basis who could have benefited from having certain questions answered and guidance provided when they were first navigating the psychology major. Our sense that this important need exists, coupled with our desire to help students succeed, has led us to write this book. It is our hope that you find elements of it informative and instructive in pursuing your academic and career goals.

In this opening chapter, we first offer some brief suggestions on how to use the book effectively. The remainder of the chapter considers a question that may be looming large in many of your minds – why psychology? Some of you have already committed to the major while others are still trying to make a decision. This section will help all students formulate and explore their specific interests in the field regardless of their certainty in their major.

How to Use This Book

This book seeks to cover issues relevant to psychology majors in a comprehensive manner. As a result, you will likely find that certain chapters appeal to you immediately because they address your current situation (e.g., deciding if psychology is the right major, preparing a résumé, trying to gain research experience). However, we want to encourage you not to neglect chapters simply because they do not feel relevant at this particular moment in your education. The information contained in these chapters will be helpful to you in the near future, and it may challenge your current thinking about the career options available to you. For example, those of you who are freshmen and sophomores may feel like the chapters on preparing for employment and graduate school address distant concerns. You are in part correct in that the point at which you submit résumés and applications may be a few years away, but most of the steps and strategies that will allow you to succeed in these endeavors must be put into place right now. Many students applying to jobs and graduate schools wish they would have prepared better, including taking important steps in their first year of college. Also, those of you who feel certain of your career interests should keep in mind that careers are selected for many reasons. But choosing not to pursue a certain area simply because you are not well informed about it might ultimately cheat you out of a rewarding career. By the same token, writing off graduate school because of a misconception you have about it, or leaving psychology as a major because you believe you cannot work in your area of interest with a bachelor's degree, would be mistakes that are preventable only if you are well informed.

Why Major in Psychology?

Majoring in Psychology for What Psychology Is

One of the primary goals of this book is to have students who are majoring in psychology do so with a clearer sense of their specific interests in the discipline and how these interests will translate into career goals and plans. This would involve students majoring in psychology for reasons that have to do with the discipline itself and how a program of study in this field will support their future endeavors. To facilitate this process, it is vital to consider first what psychology is.

Psychology is the scientific study of behavior and mental processes in both human and nonhuman animals. The field focuses on outward, easily observable behavior as well as more covert experiences and processes such as emotions, memory, nervous system activity, and attitudes. Psychologists study typical and atypical behavior and mental processes at both the individual and group levels. Given this focus, psychologists often engage in generating new research and applying research findings to real world problems and situations. Some have careers that concentrate exclusively on research or applied endeavors, but many psychologists are involved in both activities.

The field's scientific foundation leads many psychologists to actively gather new knowledge about behavior and mental processes. This knowledge is generated in systematic ways, typically building on previous knowledge in a steady march towards greater understanding. Psychologists generate questions about various aspects of behavior and design methods of collecting data to help answer these questions. This process leads to new questions and additional research. The field's applied foundation means that many psychologists work to address problems in behavior and mental processes. This work involves developing new techniques and tools for addressing these problems as well as putting interventions into practice. The applied endeavors of psychologists serve the needs of human and nonhuman animals while simultaneously generating new ideas and opportunities for research.

The mixture of research and applied endeavors is evidence that psychology is an incredibly diverse field. This diversity in part results from the field's focus on the broad topic of behavior and mental processes. In fact, psychologists who may appear to have little in common in terms of their day-to-day work still understand and operate within the basic foundations of the discipline. For example, consider the following three psychologists:

- Dr. Rivera is an industrial/organizational psychologist. She works for a large consulting firm that contracts with major businesses to provide services related to their workforce and the workplace. Dr. Rivera's specialty is employee selection and leadership training. She travels extensively when training new clients on the implementation of her firm's techniques and software.
- Dr. Johnson is an experimental psychologist who studies stress reactions in nonhuman animals. She is a faculty member at a large state university where she teaches undergraduate and graduate courses, supervises graduate students' research, and operates a research lab. Dr. Johnson recently secured grant funding to conduct a new study on the effects of stress on caffeine tolerance in mice.
- Dr. Janowitz is a school psychologist who works for two districts in a rural county. He is assigned to two high schools, three middle schools, and four elementary schools. He works directly with students by conducting psychological evaluations, creating educational plans, coordinating mental health and academic services, and facilitating prevention programs on substance abuse.

The daily activities of these psychologists appear so diverse that one might believe they were trained in different fields of study. But closer examination reveals that each is engaged in the study of behavior and mental processes. It is also evident that the research and applied areas of the field are relevant to all three. Although only Dr. Johnson appears to be actively conducting research, Dr. Rivera's and Dr. Janowitz's work is closely tied to the scientific aspects of the field. Both use assessment tools and techniques that are products of extensive research. In addition, both utilize research and statistical methods to gather and analyze data on the effectiveness of their work. Although Dr. Rivera and Dr. Janowitz are clearly involved in applied activities, Dr. Johnson's research on stress responses has potential applications that she considers when writing about her work and attempting to secure funding. In addition, her involvement in the teaching and supervision of students is an applied endeavor. As these three psychologists illustrate, the breadth of the psychology discipline provides room for people with diverse interests and talents to make a contribution to the field.

Despite the commonalities among all psychologists, there are some stark differences in the specific focus of their work. Most psychologists specialize in a particular subfield of the discipline. They acquire this expertise in graduate school where their training focuses intently on a few specific areas. In contrast to this specificity of training at the graduate level, training in psychology at the undergraduate level is similar at most institutions. The objectives for student learning are analogous across programs, as reflected in the guidelines for undergraduate majors provided by the American Psychological Association (APA; 2007). These guidelines emphasize knowledge of and capacity to use:

- the major concepts, theories, and findings in the field;
- research methods, research design, and statistical analyses;
- critical thinking and scientific inquiry;
- applications of psychological principles;
- key values in the field (e.g., ethics, ambiguity tolerance);
- informational and technological literacy skills;
- effective communication skills;
- awareness, understanding, and respect for sociocultural and international diversity;
- understanding of personal behavior and strategies for improvement;
- information about career options.

Undergraduate programs in psychology emphasize this core set of learning objectives in order to prepare students for the next phase of their careers. Students who graduate with this knowledge and skills set are prepared to move into a variety of careers or enter graduate school for specialized training in the field.

Popularity of the Degree

For decades psychology has been among the most popular majors on college and university campuses. According to a report from the National Center for Educational Statistics (NCES; Snyder, Dillow, & Hoffman, 2008), in the 2005–2006 academic year,

88,134 students earned a bachelor's degree in psychology in the United States. The only three categories with more graduates were business, social sciences and history, and education. Unlike psychology, these categories in the NCES data contain more than one major (e.g., "business" might include management, accounting, marketing, etc.). Therefore, the actual popularity of psychology as a major may be even higher. Clearly students are gravitating to the psychology major in large numbers. Odds are that on your campus a substantial number of your peers are pursuing the psychology major. This popularity has some general advantages for you.

Consider first that when departments have large numbers of majors, institutions must provide adequate resources to facilitate the education of these students. As a psychology major, you may have access to resources that students in smaller, less popular departments do not. Second, because psychology has attracted large numbers of undergraduate majors over time, the field has established a rich tradition of developing and researching effective ways to teach students. In fact, psychology is often viewed as a leader among disciplines in teaching and providing a quality undergraduate education. This means that many of your psychology professors will be devoted to helping students succeed. Third, although the popularity of a major does not always closely follow the job market for its graduates, if a large portion of the 88,000 graduates were struggling to find employment, the popularity of psychology over time would likely decrease. Therefore, these graduates must be having reasonable success securing employment.

A Multipurpose Degree

Part of the popularity of psychology, and other similarly structured degrees, is that it can serve two basic purposes. Some psychology majors will use their degree to seek employment and perhaps begin their careers. These students are often described as pursuing a liberal arts degree. Others will use their degree to enter graduate school and complete additional training prior to beginning their careers. These students are often described as pursuing a preprofessional degree. The path you choose is largely based on your career objectives and plans. Although students pursuing the liberal arts or preprofessional degrees typically fulfill the same requirements, they are on different trajectories within the major. They should all be focused on gathering the types of knowledge, skills, and experiences that will be most beneficial to their particular path.

The preprofessional degree path is discussed in greater detail in a later chapter, but for now it is important to understand that all careers as psychologists require extensive graduate education and training. The bachelor's degree alone does not prepare you to work as a psychologist. Instead, it can prepare you to seek certain types of graduate education, many of which are covered in detail in the chapters on the various careers in the field. The liberal arts degree path is also discussed in depth in a subsequent chapter. In the meantime keep in mind that if you plan on pursuing employment or beginning your career after earning your bachelor's degree in psychology, this degree will not equip you with a specialized set of skills in the same way that a degree in nursing, engineering, accounting, or computer science would. As a liberal arts degree, your degree in psychology will provide you with general knowledge about the field as well as skills necessary to engage in lifelong learning (e.g., critical thinking, information gathering, and analysis).

Majoring in Psychology for Reasons Unrelated to Psychology

If you talk to your peers about their reasons for majoring in psychology, you will likely hear a wide variety of experiences and explanations. Some of these reasons will pertain to the nature of the psychology discipline and what it has to offer students. However, many of your peers, and perhaps even you, will give reasons that are unrelated to psychology as a field of study. Students repeatedly cite three such reasons as motivating factors.

The "path of least resistance" reason.   Students sometimes choose to major in psychology because they believe it provides a more favorable route to earning a bachelor's degree compared to other majors. For example, these students sometimes confess that a factor in their selection of the major was that the psychology curriculum at their institution does not require a course they wanted to avoid. Common examples include foreign language, higher-level math, or natural science courses. Other times these students assert that they simply need to finish a bachelor's degree in something in order to obtain a job or advance in their current position. Some of these students believe that the focus of their degree will not have bearing on their career choices and plans. They pursue a degree, but they do not look for a discipline that will enhance their skills and knowledge in their chosen career. Other students acknowledge selecting psychology as a major because it seems to be an easier or more popular path, but those students are unlikely to be reading this book with any seriousness. However, some of you may have originally come to psychology because it seemed like the path of least resistance and now you are beginning to wonder if it can be something more. You should aggressively pursue this thought. Whatever your ultimate career plans, major in psychology with clear objectives and understand how the major will help you accomplish your goals.

The "one course and I was sold" reason.   Students often choose to major in psychology because they had a positive experience in their first psychology course (Rajecki, Williams, Appleby, Jeschke, & Johnson, 2005). Many claim that the material was so interesting that they simply felt this was the major for them. Others assert that the concepts in their first course came so easily to them that psychology just seemed like common sense. Still others note that they tried other majors first, but upon taking one psychology course they knew what they wanted to do. Typically these students are referring to courses such as Introductory Psychology or perhaps Advanced Placement Psychology in high school. These courses provide a broad overview of the field as a whole. In highlighting major points and themes, they often address the most interesting and compelling topics and research. The fact that students have positive learning experiences in these courses is great news, but it is actually quite a common experience. Their enjoyment of this experience can be the result of many factors such as having excellent teachers, being motivated to study, earning a good grade, and being interested in the subject matter. None of these factors alone, especially in the context of a single course, should be a deciding factor in determining one's major and future career. Consider for a moment what would have happened had these same students taken a different section of the course with a less engaging teacher or perhaps enrolled in an introductory course in another major? Could the entire fate of their college and professional lives have been altered by this slightly different experience? If they based the selection of their major and career on a single course, then the answer is yes.

If this all sounds a bit concerning, it should. However, do not be alarmed if you are currently a psychology major in large part because of a positive experience in an introductory course. Be honest with yourself that it was this single event that stimulated your interest in the field and treat it as a starting point for a thoughtful decision-making process. The fact that you are excited about some aspect of psychology is great, and it will be important to preserve this passion and follow your interests. But you still need to determine whether the major is right for you and whether your career objectives are in line with what the degree offers.

The "I'm destined to be a helper" reason. A large proportion of students chose psychology as their major because they "want to help people" or have "always been fascinated by human behavior." Research suggests this is a significant factor identified by freshmen and senior psychology majors alike (Stewart, Hill, Stewart, Bimler, & Krikland, 2005). By claiming they want to help others, these students are often referring to career goals that have to do with providing mental health services to patients. When pressed for additional details, many of these students assert that they have always had a talent for listening to or "reading" people and helping them with their problems. For example, some students state that they are the one in their family or circle of friends who is the most compassionate and supportive when others are in need, and that the people around them routinely seek out their advice and comfort. These are certainly worthy goals and important personal experiences. But the truth is most people have a strong curiosity about human behavior, and many of us possess high levels of empathy and good listening skills as part of our makeup. In addition, many people desire to have careers in which they can positively impact the lives of others. Were we to ask, we would find these same interests and desires among teachers, civil servants, attorneys, researchers, business owners, politicians, physicians, and artists, to name a few. Many of them chose their career paths in part because they saw an opportunity to use their talents and pursue their interests in ways that would help others or contribute to society. Therefore, a desire to help others, and even some possible inherent skill at doing so, is not a sound reason on its own to major in psychology. Those of you who possess this interest must work to learn about whether psychology is the right vehicle for you to accomplish your specific career goals.

Determining if Psychology Is for You

Determining whether psychology is the best major for you can be difficult. The decision can in part be made easier by answering three questions in relation to the major. First, do you understand and appreciate psychology as a scientific discipline? Answering yes to this question means that regardless of your career interests in the field, you understand the purpose and value of having your undergraduate education rooted in both the research and applied foundations of the field. Second, are you and psychology a good fit? An affirmative answer to this question means that what psychology offers at the undergraduate level matches your interests, skills, abilities, values, and ways of thinking about the world. Third, is psychology the right vehicle to help you accomplish your career goals, even if they are not well defined at the moment? In answering yes to this question, be sure that majoring in psychology at the least will not impede your goals and at the most will give you the best foundation for achieving them.

Determining whether psychology is right for you is going to require effort on your part. You will need to examine thoroughly the field and what it has to offer. This means investigating the field in general and investigating the specifics of the major as it is offered at your institution. The remainder of this book will provide extensive information to guide you in this process. We encourage you to engage the information with an open and critical mind, thinking carefully about your choices in your academic and career pursuits. Whether along the path you decide psychology is right for you or you determine that your interests and career goals are best pursued in another discipline, the process of exploring the field and yourself will have been well worth the effort.

Suggested Exercises

1. If you are still undecided about your major, talk with one faculty member in each of the areas you are considering to gain their perspectives on the advantages and limitations of the major at your institution. Also talk with individuals in the community who are working with a degree in the field to gain their perspective on majoring in psychology.

2. Talk with junior and senior-level psychology majors about their experiences and any suggestions they have for students in your position. If you do not know any advanced students, contact a psychology student organization (e.g., Psi Chi) to ask for names of students who would be willing to talk to you. The officers of these groups are often an excellent resource.

3. Talk with peers in your classes about why they are pursuing psychology. Listen for reasons that you think match yours as well as any different or novel reasons you may not have considered. Notice which of your peers seem to have given this more or less thought than you.

4. Ask the department of psychology at your institution if they have contact information for recent alumni. Many departments maintain databases of recent alumni, and many of alumni are willing to take the time to talk with current students. If your department has such information, contact a recent graduate to ask about their experiences as a student and see if they have any advice for you.

Suggested Readings by Topic Area

Selecting a Major

Andrews, L. L. (2006). *How to choose a college major* (2nd ed.). Boston: McGraw Hill.

Fogg, N. P., Harrington, P., & Harrington, T. (2004). *College majors handbook with real career paths and payoffs: The actual jobs, earnings, and trends for graduates of 60 college majors.* St. Paul, MN: Jist Publishing.

The College Board. (2008). *Book of majors 2009.* New York: Author.

Introduction to Psychology

Myers, D. G. (2006). *Psychology* (8th ed.). New York: Worth Publishers.

Weiten, W. (2007). *Psychology: Themes and variations* (7th ed.). Belmont, CA: Thomson Wadsworth.

References

American Psychological Association. (2007). *APA guidelines for the undergraduate psychology major.* Washington, DC: Author. Retrieved from http://www.apa.org/ed/resources.html.

Rajecki, D. W., Williams, C. C., Appleby, D. C., Jeschke, M. P., & Johnson, K. E. (2005). Sources of students' interest in the psychology major: Refining the Rajecki-Metzner Model. *Individual Differences Research, 3,* 128–135.

Snyder, T. D., Dillow, S. A., & Hoffman, C. M. (2008). *Digest of education statistics: 2007* (NCES 2008-022). Washington, DC: National Center for Education Statistics, Institute of Education Sciences, U.S. Department of Education. Retrieved from http://nces.ed.gov/pubsearch/pubsinfo.asp?pubid=2008022

Stewart, R., Hill, K., Stewart, J., Bimler, D., & Krikland, J. (2005). Why I am a psychology major: An empirical analysis of student motivations. *Quality & Quantity, 39,* 687–709.

2

Succeeding in College

Transitions, Strategies, and Resources

Introduction

The number of individuals choosing to attend college has grown substantially in recent years. According to data from the National Center for Education Statistics (Snyder & Hoffman, 1991), in 1980, 51.9% of all high school graduates enrolled in some type of postsecondary education the following year. By 2005, this number increased to 67.2% (Snyder, Dillow, & Hoffman, 2008). A similar trend occurred among students who returned to college years after completing high school. Between 1980 and 2005, the percentage of college students who were over the age of 35 increased from 11.7% to 17.7% (Snyder et al., 2008).

How did you decide to become a part of these growing numbers of college students? Some students wrestle with the decision over time, weighing the pros and cons of continuing their education beyond high school. But in recent years, more students are simply assuming that attending college will be a part of their life. A major contributing force in this trend has been the changing job market. Data indicate that the occupations with the highest salaries ("Highest Paying," 2001), as well as those with the projected fastest growth ("Fastest Growing," 2000), usually require at least a bachelor's degree. As a result, increasing numbers of individuals view a college degree as essential to having a successful career. More are feeling pressure to attend college, often without adequate preparation to handle college-level work (Wirt et al., 2004). At some point in their undergraduate education most of these students discover their career interests and goals, but many begin college without a clear sense of focus and motivation. As a result, some will experience academic difficulties, and some of these will carry serious consequences. Fortunately, a large portion of these academic difficulties can be prevented.

This chapter highlights several important steps students can take to help ensure success in college. Although none of these are quick fixes for serious academic problems, they are not difficult to integrate into your educational life. The first section describes some common elements of students' experiences in adjusting to college. Understanding how college differs from high school, and how these changes can impact your academic performance, is an important first step in taking control over your education. The second section explores strategies for academic success and suggests ways for incorporating them into your academic efforts. The final section describes resources that are available to most college students at their own institutions and how these resources can enhance the academic experience. You may find that you already are aware of some aspects of these steps. However, few students are aware of them all, and even fewer are routinely implementing them into their academic life. Therefore, this chapter should be beneficial whether you are highly successful, struggling, or just getting started in your college experience.

The Experience of Adjusting to College

What was your overall experience of coming to college? Perhaps you can count back to the start of your college career in terms of decades or just a few short months. Regardless, how has the college path progressed for you since that time? Box 2.1 provides questions to help you reflect for a moment on some of the key aspects of your transition experience.

College can be one of the most exciting and formative periods of your life. But adjusting to college can be difficult because so many factors in your life change. One of the biggest adjustments that must be made is to the academic environment. Compared to most students' high school experiences, the information that is learned in college, and the degree to which it is learned, is largely dependent upon their own initiative. This section of the chapter provides an overview of several academic changes that occur in the transition from high school to college. Each is directly related to the active role students must adopt in their learning at this level. The section concludes by examining common problems students experience as a result of these changes. Having a clear understanding of these changes is an important part of ensuring that

---

Box 2.1   Reflecting on the Transition to College

- What messages did you receive from others about going to college?
- How did you make your decision to apply?
- What were you most excited about?
- What were you most fearful of?
- What was your very first college class like?
- How did the academic environment and work change from high school to college?
- What aspects of the academic work did you struggle the most with?
- What, if anything, would you do differently if you could start over?

you have realistic expectations for your college experience and are prepared to handle the inevitable difficulties by taking an active role in your education.

College students provide an important source of information about the academic changes occurring in the transition to college. Appleby (2005) conducted a study in which he polled freshmen about their perceptions of the differences between academic life in high school and college. Certainly any one student's perceptions are unique to them, but Appleby distilled several themes from the responses that likely resonate with most students' experiences. Many of these themes have also been echoed in previous research, and they are summarized here into four characteristics of the college academic environment: the academic work, students' responsibility for their learning, the structure of courses, and interactions with others.

The Academic Work

The difficulty of the academic work increases significantly in college. This is unlikely to come as a surprise to anyone. However, many students are unclear as to the ways in which the work becomes more difficult. Often they assume that the increased difficulty will be comparable to the changes that occurred when advancing a grade in high school. But the academic work of college is different in quantity and quality. The amount of material that is assigned in readings, covered in lectures, and expected to be learned, can be extensive. If you are taking four to six courses per term, the workload can be all consuming. Changes in the quality of the academic work are the direct result of professors assigning and expecting work to be completed at an advanced level. Many college courses overlap with subjects you have already completed in high school, but taking the course at the college level requires understanding the material in greater depth as concepts and topics are explored in more detail. You will also be expected to demonstrate purposeful and reflective thinking about the material in addition to the memorization of facts and mastery of skills.

With the shifts in the quality and quantity of the academic work, students must increase the amount of time they devote to assignments. At the same time, many report a decrease in the amount of time that is given to complete this work. The assignments are more labor intensive because they often have multiple steps or components. In high school these steps are often broken into discrete assignments. But professors in college tend to assign larger projects as a whole, even if they provide feedback at each stage. Writing assignments also tend to be broader in scope, requiring greater reviews of existing literature and integration of material. With students enrolling in multiple courses, completing them in only a few months, and already experiencing increased workload in terms of the material assigned, these more involved assignments contribute to the dramatic increase in time that must be invested in academic work.

Students' Responsibility for Their Learning

High school teachers bear much of the responsibility for their students' learning. In college, professors take a less involved role in ensuring that you learn the course material. As a college student, you must take on a substantial portion of the responsibility for your learning. Professors carry some of this responsibility, but they fulfill this duty by organizing and facilitating the course and promoting student engagement. The actual engagement in the learning process is up to you to initiate and sustain. One indication that the responsibility for learning shifts in college can be seen in the amount of time that students spend in class. High school students are physically at school 6–8 hours each weekday. In contrast, many full-time college students have classes on 2–3 days, often for no more than 12–16 hours total each week. Because the student carries the burden of coming to class and investing in the learning process, attendance in college courses is typically not monitored as closely as in high school, if at all.

If the academic work in college is more difficult in terms of quantity, quality, and the time pressures involved, and students are spending limited time in class, then where and when is the academic work taking place? It takes place outside of class and during your free time. Many students feel prepared for and are excited to accept this increased responsibility for their learning. Along with this responsibility comes greater freedom and flexibility in decision making. Some anticipate that assuming a more active role in their learning will be a straightforward task because they will have much more free time as a result of spending fewer hours in the classroom. Indeed this experience can be liberating for students who wisely choose where to allocate their time and resources. But others fail to anticipate the multitude of nonacademic responsibilities and interests that will compete for this time. In high school these other obligations and distracters often had to wait, but in college the increased free time is there for the taking.

Structure of Courses

In addition to the shortened time frame and reduced meeting times, college courses also have a different structure than those in high school. Part of this structure is evident in college professors' reliance on a syllabus as the primary organizing element of the course. Regardless of how detailed or open ended professors make their syllabus, the course structure it outlines is typically kept intact and serves as a guide throughout the term. You can use the syllabus at the beginning of a term to determine if the course will meet your learning needs and if, given your other commitments, you can sufficiently engage in the course.

College courses have fewer restrictions on student behavior. Although the syllabus may contain guidelines for student conduct, most courses have few rules about behavior in the class. Some professors will establish classroom rules, but they are likely to be more in the spirit of promoting open dialogue than trying to regulate problematic behaviors. Despite there being fewer behavioral rules, most college students will notice that the transition from high school brings more rules for their academic work. In fact, the strictest aspect of most course structures is the schedule according to which the academic work must be completed. Professors vary in their flexibility, but most establish specific deadlines for the material to be covered and assignments to be completed. As a result, some students report feeling there was much more leeway in high school to complete assignments.

Interactions With Others

The academic environment of college differs from that of high school in terms of the interactions you have with your peers and professors. Student populations are typically more diverse in college. One result of this is the increased emphasis placed on openness to and tolerance of diverse points of view, particularly within the classroom. Another implication of a diverse student population is students having personal schedules and priorities that do not necessarily align with their peers. As a result, relationships with fellow students can be less likely to form and harder to sustain than in high school. Relationships with peers in college are more likely to form when you are frequently present on campus and the campus environment is conducive to student interactions outside of class (Kulm & Cramer, 2006; Lundberg, 2004).

Interactions with college professors are quite different than those with high school teachers. With the decreased time spent in the classroom, professors are typically less available. You may also sometimes experience your professors as being less personable that your high school teachers because your interactions are often exclusively focused on academic issues. However, professors do form strong mentoring relationships with outstanding students who are interested in working with them on their research or teaching. These students often get to know their professors much better than they ever did their high school teachers.

Thinking About One's Transition Problems

The scope of the changes that occur in the academic environment when transitioning to college contributes to some degree of academic difficulty for many students. For instance, most students discover at some point that a particular subject or academic task does not come as easy as it once did. Box 2.2 presents several scenarios in which students are encountering common problems in adjusting to the academic environment of college.

Many students encounter difficulties when making the college transition. Although each experience is unique, students tend to interpret their difficulties in patterned ways. These explanatory styles are based on your beliefs about the causes for positive and negative events in your life (Rotter, 1966). In one type of explanatory style, students perceive their academic difficulties as having a direct relationship to their abilities and actions. This response, called an internal locus of control, leads them to believe they have influence over their academic performance and are responsible for both good and bad outcomes. In the second type of explanatory style, known as an external locus of control, students perceive their academic difficulties as having little to no relationship to their abilities and actions. Instead, they believe their academic performance is largely influenced by chance or the will of others.

It is important to be aware of how you typically explain your academic experiences, both positive and negative, because adopting an internal or external locus of control has consequences. For example, college students with an internal locus of control tend to achieve at a higher level academically (Coleman, 1971) and adjust better in the transition to college (Ogden & Trice, 1986). Students with an external locus of control

> **Box 2.2** Examples of Common Academic Problems in Adjusting to College
>
> - Throughout high school and even her first semester of college, Elaina had always earned excellent grades. However the first paper assignment in her history course this term was just returned, and she earned a "D." Elaina is shocked that her grade is so low. She has never received anything below a "B" on a paper before in her life. She is feeling a bit overwhelmed by the experience and is concerned what this means for her overall grade in the course.
> - Alex studied extensively for his final exam in economics. He felt as though he put more time and effort into preparing for this exam than he did for the entire class up until this point. Yet when he sat down to take the exam, he found question after question that he had no idea how to answer. For a moment he wondered if he had been given the wrong exam. Alex completed as many items as he could, then left the classroom feeling disoriented and confused.
> - Sana returned home from work late on a Saturday evening and sat and stared at the mound of schoolwork on her desk. She had two papers due the coming week in critical courses and a quiz in another. On top of that, she was behind in her reading in every course. She had always been skilled at managing her time and completing her academic work. Now she felt that she had dug a hole she might not be able to climb out of.

tend to experience higher levels of stress (Gadzella, 1994) and higher rates of substance use (Segal, 1974). In addition to these correlates, a major problem with both explanatory styles is that the student can become resigned to their academic difficulties. Those with an internal locus of control may become convinced that they lack the ability to succeed. Those with an external locus of control may become convinced that forces outside of themselves will always thwart their success. Students in both situations might accept that they are unable to achieve and subsequently reduce their efforts or quit school altogether. Research suggests that rather than one explanatory style being favorable over the other, students who are flexible in their approach to coping fare better than those who are unable to adapt based on the particulars of the challenge at hand (Gan, Shang, & Zhang, 2007). Regardless of whether the academic difficulties actually stem from personal shortcomings or external factors, there are effective academic strategies that can increase all students' academic success.

Academic Strategies

Academic success in college is largely based on your ability to learn new information and master new skills. Research in cognitive psychology and related disciplines has taught us much about how humans learn. Three elements appear to be particularly important: (1) information must be actively processed, (2) information must be reduced to meaningful and manageable units, and (3) information must be rehearsed and reviewed repeatedly over time. Strategies that facilitate one or more of these processes in your academic efforts will enhance your learning. This section explores six areas in which specific strategies can bolster academic success.

Manage Time Wisely

Time management involves being selective when choosing activities in order to maximize accomplishments within a limited amount of time. The concept receives tremendous attention in business and educational settings as a desirable skill, but it has not been shown to have a consistent impact on grades (Claessens, van Eerde, & Rutte, 2007). This finding may stem from the fact that time management has a more indirect effect on academic performance. In other words, although effective time management may not always translate into academic success, poor time management seems likely to interfere with positive academic results. Effective time management creates the opportunity to engage in other beneficial strategies. For example, setting personal goals appears to play an important role in working efficiently. Students who set such goals work in a more structured manner and are less distracted (Strickland & Galimba, 2001). Some students incorporate this strategy by creating "to do lists" for their academic work that are personal in nature rather than simply listing the tasks that have been assigned.

Students procrastinate on tasks that they perceive to be unpleasant, imposed on them, or requiring skills that they lack (Milgram, Sroloff, & Rosenbaum, 1988). But because these perceptions are based in the framework used to think about the task, they can be altered. When you find yourself procrastinating on an important academic task, examine your thinking about the assignment and attempt to change any negative, maladaptive perceptions. Engaging in the work ahead of deadline will help support a positive outlook on the benefits of the task.

Students who segment large academic tasks into smaller units often perform better on these tasks. Wagner, Schober, and Spiel (2008) discovered that students who worked in series of 30-minute intervals on a variety of tasks had the best academic performance as a result of their efforts. You could incorporate this strategy by resisting the tendency to complete large amounts of academic work in one sitting. Spacing out the tasks in smaller units will be a more efficient use of the time and will likely enhance learning.

Reading Course Material for Comprehension

The amount of material students are assigned to read in their courses dramatically increases in college. Some feel overwhelmed by the shear volume of material they must consume to keep pace. Reading effectively requires processing new information, developing understanding, and retaining this new knowledge. Reading in this manner may be the most important academic skill you master.

Students often believe that when a professor assigns readings that the task is to simply read the corresponding pages. But reading is actually a path to the true goal

Box 2.3   Techniques for Boosting Reading Comprehension

- Examine major topics/concepts to be covered prior to starting reading.
- Generate a list of questions about the topics/concepts that you want answered.
- Think about the topics/concepts before, during, and after reading.
- Skip material that you know is unimportant to comprehending the topics/concepts.
- When you complete a passage, think about the meaning of it and its implications.
- Link the topics/concepts and their meaning to knowledge you already possess.
- As you read, skip forwards and backwards as necessary in order to link key topics/concepts.
- When you finish reading, quiz yourself about the major topics/concepts.
- Have a positive self-concept as a reader – be confident in your ability and encourage yourself.

of comprehending the information and concepts contained in those pages. Consider whether you have ever heard fellow students complain about a low exam grade by saying, "I actually read the chapters this time!" These students are struggling with comprehension of the material, which cannot occur through passively reading words on the page. It requires engaging the information in order to process ideas in an active and deliberate manner.

Numerous reading strategies have been designed to help students comprehend the material. But adopting a specific strategy is unlikely to be uniformly helpful to all students. Instead, you should model the reading tactics of effective readers: (a) read the material thoroughly, (b) actively think about or process the material, and (c) examine this processing and whether it is successful in promoting learning (Yang, 2006). These steps ensure an active construction of meaning from the text. Several strategies that can facilitate these steps are listed in Box 2.3.

Being Engaged in the Classroom

Compared to high school students, college students spend far less time in the classroom. The way you make use of this limited time can significantly impact your academic performance. Professors view classroom time as precious and often use it to expose students to vital information rather than giving general overviews or summaries. This might involve lectures on new material, further explanations and extensions of previously covered material, or activities to enhance understanding of the material. Consequently, improving your ability to learn within this setting should be a priority.

Research indicates there is a modest correlation between class attendance and grades (e.g., Brocato, 1989; van Blerkom, 1992). Of course this correlation does not resolve whether attendance is causing the grade (e.g., students who attend more learn more), the grade is causing the attendance (e.g., students who are learning more attend more), or grades and attendance are being influenced by a third factor (e.g., students attend more and learn more when they are interested in the material). But being present in class certainly provides exposure to course information and the opportunity for you to engage the material. Engaging in class can be uncomfortable for some students and anxiety provoking for others. It is often difficult to answer a professor's question or ask one of your own when none of your classmates are doing so. However, given the importance of this interaction for your learning, encourage yourself to be bold and resist the temptation to passively occupy your seat. Speak up, ask for clarification, and volunteer. You may be surprised at how many of your peers follow your lead.

There is a sizable body of research showing that taking and reviewing notes in class is related to improved performance (e.g., Kiewra et al., 1991). Note taking is a difficult skill that requires multiple cognitive tasks such as holding information in memory, deciphering its meaning, and transcribing it quickly. Research suggests that two components of this process are the most important to taking good lecture notes. Students who are able to copy or transcribe efficiently construct better notes and perform better on assessments (Peverly et al., 2007). Students who add additional information to the notes they transcribe are better able to apply the concepts (Stefanou, Hoffman, & Vielee, 2008). Although some sources for academic strategies recommend that you not write everything down in your notes, enhancing your transcription skills does appear to be an important step. You should then work to add additional information to your notes that captures your understanding of the concepts.

Performing Well on Assignments

Academic performance in college is synonymous with grades. A course grade reflects the degree to which the student has met the learning objectives. Assignments within a course are designed both to facilitate learning and to assess learning. For example, taking an exam both prompts you to study the material more and provides an indication of how successful you have been. As a result, the surest way to succeed is to learn the material. But as you well know, understanding the material is only one part of doing well on an assignment. You must have a host of other skills that allow you to demonstrate your learning.

College course assignments often require you to write. These assignments take many forms, but there are several strategies that are helpful in all writing endeavors. First, start early. Good writing requires time. Assignments completed at the last minute appear that way – hurried, disorganized, incoherent, and error filled. Second, work in stages. Most assignments have several components and often these can be worked on independently until tied together in the later stages. Third, compose a draft and revise it repeatedly. Students are frequently surprised at the errors they committed in a paper after it is graded. This is a clear sign of either not having a draft or failing to revise. If you have difficulty revising your writing, many professors will allow you to ask others for assistance in detecting clarity, organization, grammar, and spelling problems.

College courses use exams to assess student learning. Several strategies for completing exams can have a positive effect on performance. First, always look over the exam before starting in order to develop a plan for working through the items. Second, plan your response to short-answer and essay items before writing. Students are often surprised that they failed to include a key concept in their response or answer one part of the question. Lastly, despite what many of you have been taught, there are numerous research studies that suggest when students change their answers on a multiple-choice item, on average they improve their score (for a review, see Benjamin, Cavell, & Shallenberger, 1984). This is particularly true if you change answers because you have new information that is guiding your decision.

Any discussion of test-taking strategies would be remiss not to mention test-wiseness, or the ability to use features of a test to improve one's score. For example, because the items on exams often pertain to overlapping concepts, some students who struggle with a particular item will glean information from other items to help them determine the answer. Although test-wise strategies vary and their utility on any given test is never certain, students who are taught these strategies tend to perform better (for a review, see Rogers & Yang, 1996). When this occurs, it indicates the presence of two serious problems. First, the grades on such an exam do not solely reflect student learning. Second, students who are not test-wise are at a disadvantage. Consequently, solutions to test-wiseness involve either making exams less susceptible to test-wise strategies or educating all students to be test-wise. Students who have not been exposed to these strategies may be well served to learn them in order not to be at a disadvantage in comparison to peers on exams that are susceptible to test-wise strategies. A sampling of common test-wise strategies are listed in Box 2.4.

Box 2.4   Sample Test-Wise Strategies

- If only right answers are scored (i.e., there is no guessing penalty), always guess for every item.
- If it is allowed, ask your professor for clarification when needed.
- Mark items you are unsure about and return to them once you have completed the other items.
- Use content from other test items to identify correct answers.
- Answer items as the test constructor intended (i.e., keep the author of the test in mind).
- Read all instructions and items carefully, being alert for key words (e.g., except, not, all, but).
- Check your work to be sure the answer indicated is the one you intended.
- For items where partial credit is offered, provide as much information as you know.
- Recognize patterns/tendencies on a professor's test (e.g., "none of the above" is never correct).
- Eliminate options you know are incorrect by physically removing them from consideration.

Studying Effectively

Students often consider studying to be the most important factor determining their academic performance. Unfortunately many students, even those who performed well in high school, never learned effective study strategies. Developing a strong approach to studying that becomes a stable routine is key to your sustained academic success. Students who study in a thoughtful and reflective manner perform better. This type of studying is facilitated by creating a study plan based on the demands of each course. Study plans provide you with a clear sense of what is required and help you manage the allocation of your resources to meet these demands (Biggs, 1985). The plan will work best if it is consistent with the type of material you are learning and the ways in which your learning will be evaluated (Zimmerman, Bandura, & Martinez-Pons, 1992).

Virtually every college student has had the experience of cramming the night before an exam or while sitting in class before a quiz. The research literature on memory provides a clear verdict on the effectiveness of this strategy (Glenberg, 1977; Melton, 1970). The most effective way to learn information is to space studying out over time. Spaced practice or rehearsal is the exact opposite of cramming. It involves studying small segments of the material in a repeated, systematic way. This spacing of the learning process increases comprehension and recall of information, which is required to perform well on exams. Many students also believe that the longer they study the better their grades will be. Yet a systematic investigation into this issue found little to no direct correlation between hours spent studying and grades earned (Schuman, Walsh, Olson, & Etheridge, 1985). Subsequent research has found that there is a significant relationship between investment in studying and grades, but investment is not synonymous with the amount of time spent studying. Rather than counting the hours spent studying, you would be better served by adopting a methodical, disciplined approach in which you are committed to academic effort over other competing activities (Rau & Durand, 2000).

Caring for Yourself

Few college students consider taking care of their health and well-being to be an important component of their academic success. But just as time management makes reading for comprehension possible, and attendance makes engaging in class possible, taking care of yourself will allow you to function at your best. There is an array of things you can do to ensure self-care, and of course there are many things you can do that have a deleterious effect on your health and well-being. Two factors that are known to impact academic performance, and which you have considerable control over, are sleep and stress.

Over 70% of college students experience some type of sleep disturbance (Buboltz, Brown, & Soper, 2001). These students experience problems with concentration, negative emotions, and low mood. As a result, their academic performance is affected (Angus, Heslegrave, & Myles, 1985; Taub & Berger, 1973). Perhaps most alarming is research indicating that students who are sleeping less are not aware of the decline in their functioning (Pilcher & Walters, 1997). These students are unlikely to be aware of their decreased performance in a way that motivates them to alter their behavior. This research indicates that you should make your sleep routine a priority. In addition, if you conclude that your poor sleep habits are not impacting your academic performance, recognize that your lack of sleep could be affecting your ability to accurately make such judgments.

College students typically identify grades as the biggest contributing factor to their stress level (Furr, Westefeld, McConnell, & Jenkins, 2001), and stress has been shown to have a negative impact on academic performance (Felsten & Wilcox, 1992). Research has revealed that stress also has a substantial negative effect on the body's immune responses (for a review, see Segerstrom & Miller, 2004), and illnesses can significantly hinder students' academic performance. It is important to note that much of the research defines stress as a perception that one's resources are inadequate to deal with demands (Lazarus & Folkman, 1984). The positive news in this is that perceptions of stress can be modified. Numerous techniques for coping with stress exist (e.g., progressive muscles relaxation, exercise, breathing, etc.), and you will be well served to explore these and determine which strategies work best for you.

Campus Resources

All students, regardless of whether they are experiencing academic difficulties, benefit from being aware of strategies that can improve their academic performance. In addition, most institutions have resources available to students that will support their academic performance. Some students choose whether or not to make use of these resources, but a large portion of students are often not even aware that they exist. This section of the chapter provides a brief overview of six resources that are commonly available to college students.

Academic Advising

Institutions differ in the role that academic advising plays in the lives of its students. Some require students to attend advising each semester prior to registering for courses. Others have no requirements that students ever attend advising. However, all institutions offer academic advising to their students because they believe it to be a valuable resource. Academic advising provides an opportunity for you to meet with an advisor, often a professor in your major department, who has expertise in guiding students in academic matters. Advisors can assist you in selecting courses that will best fit your needs and interests. They can also provide suggestions and guidance for you regarding your academic performance. Lastly, advisement may be a time when you also consider future career plans. Getting the most out of academic advising requires that you come prepared by bringing specific questions about your academic progress to help structure the meeting.

Writing Centers

Many institutions have writing centers or labs on campus. These centers assist students with all types of writing that are a part of their academic work. Typically these centers are located within English departments and may be staffed by professors or graduate students. You can seek help for either a specific writing assignment or repeated difficulties you are having with your writing. In either case, you must provide your work to the writing center staff for their review. Students who find the writing center experience helpful often return throughout their education for help with various assignments.

Tutoring

Tutoring services are commonly offered in a variety of areas on college campuses. Some students have access to certain tutoring as a result of their status (e.g., athletes, international students). Others can access tutoring through academic departments if they are a major in that department or enrolled in certain courses (e.g., the math department may provide tutoring to all students enrolled in certain courses). These types of tutoring services are typically free to students who meet the eligibility requirements. Of course, additional tutoring is also available in a variety of other formats for a fee.

Disability Support Services

Services provided through disability support programs assist students who have disabilities that impact their academic performance. These programs work with students to ensure that they have the resources necessary to allow them to perform at their best. Students typically seek these services for physical/medical, learning, and psychological disabilities by registering with the disability support program. This usually requires providing documentation of their disability. Registered students can then benefit from a variety of services including educational programs, tutoring, and accommodations for completing their academic work (e.g., extended time on exams).

Career Development Services

Career development programs are designed to provide students with the education and assistance they need to identify and achieve their career goals. These programs provide extensive resources to help you learn about career fields and jobs that may be of interest to you. They also maintain educational resources for learning about your interests, skills, and abilities. These programs provide direct assistance to students who are seeking to gain experience and those who are striving to meet a career goal. For example, some career development programs coordinate opportunities for internship experiences. Others provide services such as résumé and interview preparation. Increasingly these centers are assisting students with using technology to conduct job searches and submit application materials.

Counseling

Institutions with sizable student populations often provide some type of counseling services for their students. The nature and extent of this service varies, but most counseling centers are able to assist you with vocational, academic, and personal matters that are causing problems in your life. Students sometimes assume that were they to seek counseling services they would need to contact a mental health provider in the community. But campus counseling centers often provide certain types of services at no costs to students. If the center is not the best setting to address your situation, they will assist you in getting connected with a professional who can provide the services you need.

Conclusion

We began this chapter by asking you to consider how you decided to attend college and what the experience was initially like. In focusing on the adjustment to college, potential problems were identified and strategies were highlighted for ensuring academic success. The chapter concluded by considering resources available to you to help you succeed. It is important to remember that college students are diverse with varied backgrounds, abilities, and interests. Not all experiences, problems, strategies, or resources will be a good fit for everyone. But being aware of these issues, and knowing how to take action in response to them, will give you a significant advantage in pursuing your educational and career goals.

Suggested Exercises

1. Keep a time log for a week, noting every activity you engaged in and the amount of time you spent on it. Think of this like a register for a bank account where you record each transaction. At the end of the week, calculate the percentage of time you spent engaged in each activity. Compare major categories of activities to see where your time was used. You may want to use this data to create a budget in order to gain better control over where you are spending your time.

2. Using the campus resources section of this chapter, identify and become familiar with each of these resources at your institution. They may be listed on your institution's website, often under the title of "student services" or "academic services." Many of these resources maintain their own websites that provide information about their services.

3. Attend an academic advising meeting with a professor in your major department in addition to that which may be normally required of you. Rather than focusing on course selection or career issues, use this time to talk in detail about your academic performance. Be honest about your strengths and weaknesses. Let this advisor know that you are interested in their honest feedback.

4. Pick one course that you will take next semester and plan an academic makeover for yourself. In the course you select, experiment with some of the academic strategies described in this chapter to alter your typical approach to reading, studying, completing assignments, and engaging in class. Monitor your progress early to be sure that the changes are not adversely affecting your performance. Take notice of what does and does not work for you, and consider which of your new strategies you could incorporate into your other courses.

Suggested Readings

Gardner, J. N., Jewler, A. J., & Barefott, B. O. (2007). *Step by step to college and career success*. Belmont, CA: Wadsworth Publishing.

Feaver, P., Wasiolek, S., & Crossman, A. (2008). *Getting the best out of college: A professor, a dean, and a student tell you how to maximize your experience*. Berkeley, CA: Ten Speed Press.

Newport, C. (2005). *How to win at college: Surprising secrets for success from the country's top students*. New York: Broadway.

References

Angus, R. G., Heslegrave, R. J., & Myles, W. S. (1985) Effects of prolonged sleep deprivation with and without chronic physical exercise, on mood and performance. *Psychophysiology, 22*, 276–282.

Appleby, D. C. (2005, March). *How do college freshmen view the academic differences between high school and college?* Paper presented at the annual meeting of the Midwest Institute for Students and Teachers of Psychology, Glen Ellyn, IL.

Benjamin, L. T., Cavell, T. A., & Shallenberger, W. R. (1984). Staying with initial answers on objective tests: Is it a myth? *Teaching of Psychology, 11*, 133–141.

Biggs, J. B. (1985). The role of metalearning in study processes. *British Journal of Educational Psychology, 55*, 185–212.

Brocato, J. (1989). How much does coming to class matter? Some evidence of class attendance and grade performance. *Educational Research Quarterly, 13*(3), 2–6.

Buboltz, W. C., Jr., Brown, F., & Soper, B. (2001). Sleep habits and patterns of college students: A preliminary study. *Journal of American College Health, 50*, 131–135.

Claessens, B. J. C., van Eerde, W., & Rutte, C. G. (2007). A review of the time management literature. *Personnel Review, 36*, 255–276.

Coleman, J. S. (1971). Equal schools or equal students? In D. A. Gordon (Ed.), *Problems in political economy: An urban perspective* (pp.190–193). Lexington, MA: Heath.

Fastest growing occupations usually requiring a bachelor's degree or more education, projected 1998–2008. (2000). *Occupational Outlook Quarterly, 44*(3), 36.

Felsten, G., & Wilcox, K. (1992). Influences of stress and situation-specific mastery beliefs and satisfaction with social support on well-being and academic performance. *Psychological Reports, 70*, 219–303.

Furr, S. R., Westefeld, J. S., McConnell, G. N., & Jenkins, J. M. (2001). Suicide and depression among college students: A decade later. *Professional Psychology: Research and Practice, 32*, 97–100.

Gadzella, B. M. (1994). Locus of control differences among stress groups. *Perceptual and Motor Skills, 79*, 1619–1624.

Gan, Y., Shang, J., & Zhang, Y. (2007). Coping flexibility and locus of control as predictors of burnout among Chinese college students. *Social Behavior and Personality, 35*, 1087–1098.

Glenberg, A. M. (1977). Influences of retrieval processes on the spacing effect in free recall. *Journal of Experimental Psychology: Human Learning and Memory, 3*, 282–294.

Highest paying occupations usually requiring at least a bachelor's degree. (2001). *Occupational Outlook Quarterly, 45*(3), 40.

Kiewra, K. A., DuBois, N. F., Christian, D., McShane, A., Meyerhoffer, M., & Roskelley, D. (1991). Note-taking functions and techniques. *Journal of Educational Psychology, 83*, 240–245.

Kulm, T. L., & Cramer, S. (2006). The relationship of student employment to student role, family relationships, social interactions and persistence. *College Student Journal, 40*, 927–938.

Lazarus R. S., & Folkman S. (1984). *Stress, appraisal, and coping*. New York: Springer.

Lundberg, C. A. (2004). Working and learning: The role of involvement for employed students. *NASPA Journal, 41*, 201–215.

Melton, A. W. (1970). The situation with respect to the spacing of repetitions and memory. *Journal of Verbal Learning and Verbal Behavior, 9*, 596–606.

Milgram, N. A., Sroloff, B., & Rosenbaum, M. (1988). The procrastination of everyday life. *Journal of Research in Personality, 22,* 197–212.

Ogden, E. P., & Trice, A. D. (1986). The predictive validity of the Academic Locus of Control scale for college students: Freshman outcomes. *Journal of Social Behavior and Personality, 1,* 649–652.

Peverly, S. T., Ramaswamy, V., Brown, C., Sumowski, J. Alidoost, M., & Garner, J. (2007). What predicts skill in lecture note taking? *Journal of Educational Psychology, 99,* 167–180.

Pilcher, J. J., & Walters, A. S. (1997). How sleep deprivation affects psychological variables related to college students' cognitive performance. *Journal of American College Health, 46,* 121–126.

Rau, W., & Durand, A. (2000). The academic ethic and college grades: Does hard work help students to "make the grade"? *Sociology of Education, 73,* 19–38.

Rogers, W. T., & Yang, P. (1996). Test-wiseness: Its nature and application. *European Journal of Psychological Assessment, 12,* 247–259.

Rotter, J. B. (1966). Generalized expectancies for internal versus external control of reinforcement. *Psychological Monographs, 80*(1), 1–28.

Schuman, H., Walsh, E., Olson, C., & Etheridge, B. (1985). Effort and reward: The assumption that college grades are affected by quantity of study. *Social Forces, 63,* 945–966.

Segal, B. (1974). Locus of control and drug and alcohol use in college students. *Journal of Alcohol and Drug Education, 19*(3), 1–5.

Segerstrom, S. C., & Miller, G. E. (2004). Psychological stress and the human immune system: A meta-analytic study of 30 years of inquiry. *Psychological Bulletin, 130,* 601–630.

Snyder, T. D., Dillow, S. A., and Hoffman, C. M. (2008). *Digest of education statistics: 2007* (NCES 2008-022). Washington, DC: National Center for Education Statistics, Institute of Education Sciences, U.S. Department of Education. Retrieved from http://nces.ed.gov/pubsearch/pubsinfo.asp?pubid= 2008022

Snyder, T. D., & Hoffman, C. M. (1991). *Digest of education statistics: 1990* (NCES 1991-660). Washington, DC: National Center for Education Statistics, Office of Educational Research and Improvement, U.S. Department of Education. Retrieved from http://nces.ed.gov/pubsearch/pubsinfo.asp?pubid=91660

Stefanou, C., Hoffman, L., & Vielee, N. (2008). Note-taking in the college classroom as evidence of generative learning. *Learning Environments Research, 11,* 1–17.

Strickland, O. J., & Galimba, M. (2001). Managing time: The effects of personal goal setting on resource allocation strategy and task performance. *Journal of Psychology: Interdisciplinary and Applied, 135,* 357–367.

Taub, J. M., & Berger, R. J. (1973). Performance and mood following variations in the length and timing of sleep. *Psychophysiology, 10,* 559–570.

van Blerkom, M. L. (1992). Class attendance in undergraduate courses. *Journal of Psychology: Interdisciplinary and Applied, 126,* 487–494.

Wagner, P., Schober, B., & Spiel, C. (2008). Time investment and time management: An analysis of time students spend working at home for school. *Educational Research and Evaluation, 14,* 139–153.

Wirt, J., Choy, S., Rooney, P., Provasnik, S., Sen, A., & Tobin, R. (2004). The condition of education 2004 (NCES 2004-077). Washington, DC: National Center for Education Statistics, Institute of Education Sciences, U.S. Department of Education. Retrieved from http://nces.ed.gov/pubsearch/pubsinfo.asp?pubid=2004077

Yang, Y. (2006). Reading strategies or comprehension monitoring strategies? *Reading Psychology, 27,* 313–343.

Zimmerman, B. J., Bandura, A., & Martinez-Pons, M. (1992). Self-motivation for academic attainment: The role of self-efficacy beliefs and personal goal setting. *American Educational Research Journal, 31,* 845–862.

3

Succeeding in the Psychology Major
Adjustments, Common Difficulties, and Strategies

Introduction

What will be the most challenging aspect of your academic work as a psychology major? Perhaps you have completed enough psychology courses to have developed a clear answer to this question. On the other hand, if you have had limited experience in the major, you may feel unsure of how to even generate ideas about what challenges might lay ahead. Regardless of your progress towards completing your degree, being prepared to address challenges when they arise will go a long way towards ensuring your success as a psychology major.

Your fellow students have likely played an important role in shaping your impression of what the academic experience as a psychology major will be like. In fact, many students utilize the input and advice of their peers as their primary source of information about their major. Often conversations among classmates focus on the topics of courses, assignments, and professors. Box 3.1 presents several examples of such information as might be stated by a psychology major. This kind of information can be incredibly useful when it offers accurate insight. But students sometimes share such information in ways that dramatize and exaggerate reality. In addition, what one student views as an obstacle or difficulty may be seen by another student as a key component of their learning experience. Note how the validity and utility of the examples in Box 3.1, as well as their accuracy for any one student, cannot be determined without additional information.

Rather than relying on the advice of peers or trial and error, this chapter provides information that will enhance your chance for academic success in the psychology major. In a previous chapter we provided an overview of common difficulties all students encounter in college, but there are additional challenges that occur for students within the psychology discipline. These challenges often surprise students who initially perceive psychology as being based in common sense or intuition. Students who gravitate to psychology believing it to be a relatively easy route to a bachelor's degree are also often

Box 3.1   Examples of Advice Shared Among Fellow
Psychology Majors

- "You only need to study your notes to make an A in that course."
- "Dr. Ling is the best professor – you'll learn so much in her classes."
- "You can't count that course towards your degree requirements, so taking it is a waste of time."
- "You should wait to take that course until your junior year so that you have more experience."
- "Papers in that course are impossible. They have to be at least 40 pages long."
- "You should definitely join Psi Chi because grad schools weight it heavily."
- "You learn nothing in Professor Hamilton's courses – avoid her at all cost."
- "Be sure to get internship or research experience – it's critical to getting into graduate school."
- "Dr. Torres only lets students conduct research with him if they have a perfect 4.0 GPA."

caught off guard by the academic rigor of the major. Understanding these challenges and how to overcome them is an essential step in your progression as a psychology major. To assist you in this process, the first section of this chapter examines the nature of academic work within psychology. The second section identifies common difficulties that students experience in completing this academic work and examines ways to prepare for addressing these challenges. The final section describes general strategies for succeeding in the psychology major, with emphasis given to utilizing available resources. You may find that you are already aware of some of this information, but remember that effectively implementing this knowledge into your academic work is the goal. Be sure to read the chapter carefully, regardless of your academic success and degree progress to date.

The Nature of Academic Work in the Psychology Major

Each academic discipline is unique in terms of the work required of its students. Once students select a major and begin taking courses, they must adjust to the specific structure, content, and skills emphasized in that particular discipline. Some students select their major in part because they believe the academic work within that discipline is a good fit for their abilities. But even these students will need to modify their academic work to be in line with the unique demands and expectations of their chosen area of study.

Adjusting to the demands and expectations for academic work within the psychology major can lead to difficulties. But remember that it is these challenges, and your ability to successfully overcome them, that make your academic work worthy of a degree in the field. Students respond to these challenges in various ways. Some leave psychology for other majors and seek a degree path that offers less resistance. Others pursue psychology while trying to avoid these difficulties by selecting courses and professors that will minimize the academic demands placed on them. Many others put forth the effort required to adjust successfully to the academic demands, and in doing so, acquire the knowledge and skills that are the foundation of the psychology degree. It is our hope that you will aspire to be among this latter group. In helping you meet this goal, this section of the chapter is designed to prepare you for potential difficulties by making you aware of the nature of academic work in psychology. Such preparation will allow you to respond to academic difficulties by working to overcome these challenges rather than letting them dictate your academic efforts.

What Is Psychology?

Remember that psychology is the scientific study of human and nonhuman animal behavior and mental processes. The field also focuses on the implications and utilization of knowledge discovered through scientific study. As a result, psychologists both generate new research and apply research findings to real world situations. Undergraduate degree programs in psychology cover the broad scope of the field by teaching students: (a) how psychological science is conducted, (b) what knowledge psychological science has yielded to date, and (c) how such knowledge can be applied towards conducting additional research and addressing behavioral and functional problems.

In pursuing its focus on behavior and mental processes, psychology as a field strives to adhere to rigorous ethical standards. These ethics permeate the research and applied work of psychologists, and as a result they play an important role in the education of students within the field. Published by American Psychological Association (APA; 2002), the current ethics code seeks to accomplish several goals: (a) create and maintain integrity in the profession, (b) create and maintain public trust in the profession, (c) guide the practice of psychologists, and (d) establish enforceable standards that are to be followed by psychologists (Fisher, 2003). The enforceable standards in the ethics code cover the diverse range of psychologists' professional behavior. Given the importance of the code to the identity of psychology as a discipline, it is readily available through the APA's website (http://www.apa.org/ethics).

What Students Expect to Learn

Research has indicated that students' expectations for their education in psychology are often incongruent with what psychology degree programs emphasize. McGovern and Hawks (1986) asked undergraduate students and faculty within a psychology program to rate the importance of 19 expectations for what a psychology major should learn. The faculty and students agreed on the relative importance of many of the expectations. For example, learning about career options, lifespan development, and scientific principles of behavior were all viewed as important, while learning about animal laboratory work and psychology of women were all viewed as not as important. The greatest disagreement between student and faculty views involved the two expectations students rated as the most important: gaining applied experience and learning how to help others. Out of the 19 expectations considered, the faculty rated these expectations as the 14th and 16th most important, respectively. Nearly 20 years later, Gaither and Butler (2005) asked a similar question of undergraduate psychology majors regarding the expectations for learning. As with previous research, students expected to learn the science of psychology and skills relevant to research activities, but they also expected to acquire applied skills that are used to address behavioral and functional problems in human populations (e.g., therapy and counseling techniques, interpretation of psychological tests). The research suggests that despite considerable overlap between psychology majors' expectations for their learning and the nature of undergraduate psychology programs, differences in expectations for gaining applied experience and skills are pronounced. Interestingly, student expectations for these learning goals have persisted over time despite the fact that faculty in psychology programs do not see these goals as a core part of the undergraduate psychology degree.

The Nature of the Academic Work

An appreciation for the nature of academic work within the psychology major is best achieved by examining the specific areas that the degree program emphasizes and values. Psychologists have given considerable attention to this topic in recent years. One key component of this work has been the development of guidelines for the undergraduate major by the APA (2007). The guidelines were briefly described in the first chapter, but a more detailed description is presented in Box 3.2. Although undergraduate programs in psychology are free to determine their own learning objectives, the APA guidelines provide an excellent summary of the areas psychology majors can expect will be emphasized in their academic work.

The specific requirements for a psychology degree are selected based on the learning objectives of the individual program. The academic work within the major will possess certain characteristics that reflect these objectives. Four such characteristics are prominent within most undergraduate psychology programs. First, the academic work emphasizes a broad base of knowledge. Undergraduate programs provide students with a breadth of knowledge and skills across the numerous subfields rather than a specific expertise in any one. Second, given the breadth of knowledge and skills taught, the academic work is rigorous. The amount of content students must master is substantial, and successfully learning it requires consuming large portions of information in relatively short periods of time. Third, learning is often demonstrated through writing. In fact, many undergraduate psychology programs can be described as writing intensive. Students write frequently and do so in ways that promote their mastery of content and ability to synthesize disparate pieces of information. Given the prominence of writing within the major, the academic work also emphasizes the development of writing skills. Fourth, knowledge is acquired in an active manner that involves consistent use of critical thinking skills. Academic tasks frequently require students not only to master information but also to analyze and synthesize it. As a result, students are asked not only to learn specific content but also to carefully evaluate the validity of this information.

Box 3.2 APA Guidelines for the Undergraduate Psychology Major

1. *Knowledge Base of Psychology* – Demonstrate familiarity with the major concepts, theoretical perspectives, empirical findings, and historical trends in psychology.
2. *Research Methods in Psychology* – Understand and apply basic research methods in psychology, including research design, data analysis, and interpretation.
3. *Critical Thinking Skills in Psychology* – Respect and use critical and creative thinking, skeptical inquiry, and, when possible, the scientific approach to solve problems related to behavior and mental processes.
4. *Application of Psychology* – Understand and apply psychological principles to personal, social, and organizational issues.
5. *Values in Psychology* – Value empirical evidence, tolerate ambiguity, act ethically, and reflect other values that are the underpinnings of psychology as a science.
6. *Information and Technological Literacy* – Demonstrate information competence and the ability to use computers and other technology for many purposes.
7. *Communication Skills* – Communicate effectively in a variety of formats.
8. *Sociocultural and International Awareness* – Recognize, understand, and respect the complexity of sociocultural and international diversity.
9. *Personal Development* – Develop insight into their own and others' behavior and mental processes and apply effective strategies for self-management and self-improvement.
10. *Career Planning and Development* – Pursue realistic ideas about how to implement their psychological knowledge, skills, and values in occupational pursuits in a variety of settings that meet personal goals and societal needs.

Common Challenges for Psychology Majors

Adjusting to the specific nature of academic work within psychology can be difficult. Reconciling your expectations with the actual learning objectives of the degree program is an important first step. It is also helpful to develop an awareness of some of the common challenges that psychology majors encounter. Whether these particular problems will occur for you during your pursuit of the degree is not certain, but being knowledgeable about these trouble spots and prepared to address them if and when they arise will offer good insurance against academic difficulties.

Understanding the Scientific Basis of the Field

Many students experience difficulties in understanding the scientific basis of psychology. Some struggle with this concept because they continue to view the discipline solely as a practice-oriented or applied field, often claiming that scientific knowledge and skills are irrelevant to their interests in mental health careers. These same students are frequently frustrated at the lack of applied skills being taught in their courses. Other students struggle in a more direct manner with aspects of academic work that relate to the scientific basis of the field, such as understanding concepts in research methodology, experimental design, and statistical analyses. Many of these struggles occur among students who fail to see the relevance of the research process to their learning and future careers. Still others have difficulty with these aspects of their academic work because they lack proficiency with the math and writing skills that would allow them to approach new concepts and ideas with confidence.

Your success in adjusting to academic coursework that emphasizes the scientific basis of the field can be greatly facilitated by taking several steps. First, examine your expectations for the psychology major and compare them to the information shared in this chapter about the nature of academic work in the discipline. Understand that the focus of the field is the scientific study of behavior and mental processes and consider what types of learning objectives, courses, and academic work would be supportive of this focus. Second, recognize that the research and applied areas of the field are intertwined. Arbitrarily separating the two is misguided, and carrying out applied endeavors devoid of grounding in scientific research is unlikely to occur in the discipline of psychology. In fact, if you find that you are only interested in conducting research with no consideration of its implications, or that you are only interested in conducting applied work with no consideration of the research basis, then you should strongly consider pursuing a different major. Otherwise, you may face a long road of questioning the utility of the knowledge and skills you will acquire in your academic work in psychology.

Learning Independently

Students may find the degree of independent learning that must take place in the psychology major challenging. In addition to the large amount of information that must be consumed, the academic work requires students to read sources of information and master difficult concepts. They must be able to grapple with complex ideas, language, methodologies, and analyses. Of course psychology majors are not expected to engage in these learning activities without the guidance and assistance of their professors. However, they must be able to tolerate the ambiguity and uncertainty that comes with this degree of independent learning. Perhaps the greatest consequence for students who struggle with this aspect of the academic work is falling behind. This typically occurs when students procrastinate on academic work that they know will be demanding. Unfortunately, students who fall behind because they view the academic work as too difficult are then faced with the task of completing larger portions of this same work in order to recover.

Incorporating several strategies into your approach to academic work in the psychology major will improve your chances of success in adjusting to the type of learning that is required. First, examine your expectations for the level of independent learning you will need to do in your coursework. Work to combat any expectation you have for passive learning in which you merely attend lectures and casually read the assigned materials. Instead, ready yourself to be an active, engaged consumer of information, both within and outside of class. Second, ask for help when you need it. Although struggling with difficult concepts and ideas is an important part of independent learning in the major, recognize that there are limits to how much of a struggle this should be. Be willing to seek out the assistance of your professors and peers as part of your active learning. However, be sure that when you look for assistance that you have already put forth a concerted effort. Using others' help when you do not yet have a foundation for understanding the material is unlikely to contribute to your learning. Third, make it a top priority to stay up to date with your academic work. This is of course far easier said than done, but dedicating yourself to staying current with course readings and assignments will go a long way towards sustaining your motivation for independent learning, thereby bolstering your performance. When you do fall behind, commit yourself to recovering as soon as possible. For additional tips for managing the workload, refer to the section on academic strategies in the Succeeding in College chapter.

Writing and APA Style

Much has been written about the poor state of students' writing abilities. Research from the National Center for Education Statistics (Snyder, Dillow, & Hoffman, 2008) indicates that only 24% of high school seniors in the United States are proficient writers. Additional research has indicated that college officials believe poor writing is a widespread problem among students (National Commission on Writing, 2006). These observations have contributed to calls for changes in how writing is taught. Psychology students are not immune to these difficulties. In fact, research suggests that psychology students acknowledge that they typically lack the skills necessary to write proficiently in their academic coursework (McGovern & Hogshead, 1990). Many have come to college with inadequate writing skills, while others struggle to adjust to the specific writing expectations of their psychology courses.

Your success in adjusting to the writing demands of academic work in psychology can be enhanced by following several steps. First, strive to understand the purpose of writing in the overall learning objectives for psychology majors. Two of the 10 APA learning objectives pertain directly to writing skills, and several others are related to student writing. Writing is a key skill because both the research and applied endeavors in the field depend heavily on psychologists' ability to communicate effectively with each other and the individuals they interact with. As a result, undergraduate programs in psychology strive to help students become strong writers who appreciate the role of good writing in their academic and professional lives.

A second step to ensuring success in writing is to adopt an organized approach. Often students are intimidated by the scope of a writing assignment. The task of producing a substantial piece of writing that integrates outside sources of information

Box 3.3 Steps for Organizing Literature Review Papers

1. Select a general topic area consistent with your assignment.
2. Read information about this topic area.
3. Revise and narrow your topic.
4. Identify and locate potential sources for your paper.
5. Read these sources for understanding key ideas, taking notes in your own words.
6. Organize your thoughts on the topic and your notes from the sources.
7. Outline the paper, adding as much detail as possible.
8. Pull additional information from sources as needed, finding additional sources if necessary.
9. Compose a draft of the paper.
10. Revise the draft in a repeated fashion.

in a clear, coherent manner can overwhelm them to the point that they avoid tackling the project. As a result of not investing sufficient time and circumventing key steps in the process, some students consistently perform poorly on writing assignments. The most important strategy for countering this pitfall is to create a plan for completing the assignment and following it. Box 3.3 provides a sample guideline for writing literature review papers in an organized fashion.

A third step in adjusting to the writing demands of academic work in psychology is to understand the purpose and function of APA style. Within a few minutes you can probably find several fellow psychology majors who will assert that writing papers in APA style is the bane of their existence. But such frustration is largely born out of negative previous experience with using APA style and a lack of appreciation for its real purpose. APA style is merely an editorial style, or a set of rules and guidelines for preparing written text. The guidelines for this particular style are published in the *Publication Manual of the American Psychological Association* (APA, 2010). Other editorial styles exists (e.g., MLA from the Modern Language Association), and chances are you have been exposed to one or more of them prior to having to learn APA style. This can create some of the same difficulties as trying to learn a new language, but keep in mind why the different styles are needed and why learning APA style is important. Having everyone adhere to the same rules for formatting, organization, expression, and citations facilitates communication and understanding within the discipline. As a student of psychology, it is key that you learn this "language" because you will need to both read and produce writing that adheres to this editorial style.

Conducting Literature Searches

One aspect of the writing process that many students find challenging is searching the existing psychological literature for sources of information. Writing good papers in large part depends upon your ability to identify and locate excellent sources of information. Students who struggle to do this will consequently perform poorly on writing assignments. The difficulties students experience in conducting literature searches often takes one of several forms. In the beginning of their college careers, many students are unfamiliar with how to go about locating sources. Once they learn this process, most will then struggle to sort through the vast number of sources that are available. Even students who have learned how to focus their searches have difficulty deciding what sources are relevant to their paper.

As seen in Box 3.3, several steps precede the point at which you begin to identify and locate potential sources of information for your paper. Completing these steps is essential if your literature search is to be a success. Incorporating several other strategies into your approach will improve your chances of success in conducting literature searches. First, become familiar with the tools to use when attempting to locate sources. The best tools available are online databases. Thousands of these databases exist, and most are organized by the content and types of sources they contain. Entries in these databases contain information about the authors, title of the work, its source, and often a brief summary of the information contained within. There are three such databases that are particularly helpful to psychology students, and each is briefly described in Box 3.4. The libraries of most colleges and universities provide students with access to these and other databases for scholarly sources. In addition, many of these libraries set up the databases in such a way to facilitate your ability to acquire the actual source while searching. It may be immediately available in electronic form, or there may be links provided to help you locate the source at your intuition or request it from other institutions.

Like all software, there is a learning curve associated with becoming proficient at using these databases to find what you need. As a result, practice over time will

Box 3.4 Helpful Databases for Literature Searches in Psychology

- *PsycINFO*: Contains citations for and summaries of journal articles, books, book chapters, dissertations, and technical reports from the field of psychology as well as from other disciplines when relevant to psychological topics. The scope of the database is broad, including sources dating to 1887 and numerous international journals.
- *PsycARTICLES*: Contains full-text articles, as well as citations and summaries, from 42 journals published by the APA. Currently the scope of the database is limited to recent articles, but the APA plans to expand this over time.
- *Psychology and Behavioral Sciences Collection*: Contains full-text articles, as well as citations and summaries, from over 400 journals. The scope of the database goes beyond the field of psychology to include sources from psychiatry and anthropology, as well as sources pertaining to the topic of research methods.

greatly enhance your skill and the likelihood that you will come to see these databases as valuable tools. As is the case with other online search engines, databases
of scholarly works are driven by the type of search terms you enter. Search terms
are often key words that pertain to your topic, and databases can be searched for
all instances where these terms appear in any part of the source. However, such
searches frequently return tens of thousands of sources, which means the vast
majority of these will be irrelevant to your paper and not useful. As a result, search
terms can be focused more narrowly by combining multiple terms and/or searching
for more specific information such as an author's name, part of the title, the name
of the source, or the date of publication. The key to executing good and productive
searches is your willingness to experiment with your search terms and build upon
your searches.

A third step in conducting good literature searches involves understanding how
to use the results of your searches. Even well constructed searches often identify a
hundred or more sources that have relevance to your paper topic. Navigating these
results can be overwhelming, but with practice students can learn to do this quite
well. Results of searches are best examined in chronological order, starting with the
most recently published (most databases automatically return results in this order).
Start by reading the titles of sources and identifying those that seem relevant to your
topic. Then examine the abstracts of these articles and again determine which are
most relevant. Scan the text of those articles whose abstracts seem most promising,
and identify the articles that provide the most useful information. Those identified
articles will then need to be read carefully as you work to identify important concepts
and ideas you wish to incorporate into your writing. Keep in mind that once you
identify an article as a good fit for your topic, the sources used within this article may
also prove to be helpful for you paper.

Strategies for Success

Although success in the psychology major is in large part determined by your ability
to adjust to the nature of the academic work and deal with the challenges that arise,
there are several broader steps you can take to support your progression towards
earning the degree. This final section of the chapter describes three general strategies
for succeeding in the major.

Planning Courses and Degree Progression

One of the most helpful strategies you can undertake to ensure your success in and
progression through the psychology major is to plan carefully how you will go about
completing your degree requirements. Carefully planning the courses you will take
has several advantages. It will provide you with a clear and accurate perception of
exactly what you must do in order to graduate. Having this plan will also help keep
you on track towards earning your degree. In addition, making the plan will assist
you in selecting courses that will prepare you for the next step in your career.

The best way to go about planning your courses and degree progression is to first obtain the exact requirements for earning the psychology degree at your institution. These are typically accessible in the undergraduate catalog for your institution as well as through departmental materials. Many psychology departments even provide students with a checklist of the degree requirements. The second step involves planning your entire college coursework, beginning with your first semester of college and going all the way through to the semester in which you will graduate. Your plan should focus on satisfying the degree requirements while adhering to all restrictions, such as prerequisites. You should also plan courses that meet your interests and prepare you for your plans after graduation. But remember that the plan will only be useful if it is realistic. Take into account both your previous academic history and other commitments that will compete for your time. For example, if you have struggled to complete successfully four or five courses per semester due to academic difficulties, family obligations, or work demands, then your planned coursework should accurately reflect what you are capable of completing in a term. Lastly, keep the plan and update it at the end of each semester. Do not be alarmed when you need to deviate from it due to a course not being offered or schedule conflicts. In fact, having the plan will greatly facilitate your ability to deal with such changes in ways that do not delay earning your degree.

Planning Relevant Experiences

After earning their degree, or in the late stages of their college careers, students majoring in psychology frequently indicate that they wish they had gained experience outside of the classroom that would have been relevant to their employment or graduate school pursuits. This typically occurs as students confront the fact that the career paths they are about to pursue require this type of experience or give priority to individuals who have it. The three types of these experiences commonly available to students include internships and practica, research assistantships, and teaching assistantships. Box 3.5 provides a description of common activities within each of these experiences.

In addition to opening doors in your career pursuits, gaining experience outside of the classroom provides several benefits. It frequently provides students with a new perspective on their career aspirations. Some students feel that these experiences solidify their goals while others walk away having changed their minds about their career path. In addition, students who gain these types of experiences develop knowledge and skills that typically cannot be acquired through traditional coursework. Often these are among the skills that most appeal to employers and graduate schools. Finally, these experiences have a tendency to contribute to students developing a more mature perspective on their academic and career goals. This resonates with employers and graduate schools that seek individuals with clear understandings of themselves and their goals.

Students in most psychology programs are informed of the benefits of gaining experience outside the classroom by their professors and advisors. Yet once students become engaged in their academic work, few of them seek it out and commit time to

Box 3.5 Common Elements of Experience Outside
              the Classroom

- Intern/Practicum Student:
  - Provide general assistance in the operations of the organization.
  - Interact with clients/patients of the organization.
  - Write reports summarizing organizational activities and/or gathered data.
  - Observe the work of professionals employed by the organization.
- Teaching Assistant:
  - Administer/monitor exams.
  - Produce course materials (e.g., handouts, lectures, review sheets, quizzes, exams).
  - Conduct study or review sessions.
  - Grade course assignments and record grades.
  - Assist the professor with class meetings.
- Research Assistant:
  - Collect, score, code, enter, and analyze data.
  - Conduct literature searches and obtain source materials relevant to research studies.
  - Contribute to the development and design of new research studies.
  - Prepare materials for and participate in the presentation/publication of research results.
  - Maintain lab space and equipment.
  - Complete administrative tasks (e.g., make calls, process mail, schedule appointments).

it. This is in part understandable because academic work likely has more immediate consequences (e.g., grades). But the consequences of not obtaining these experiences can be even more significant in terms of their impact on your career. In addition, gaining experiences outside of the classroom can be a difficult and intimidating process for students because these opportunities must be actively sought out and pursued. This stands in stark contrast to the passive nature of selecting and registering for courses.

There are several things to keep in mind if you are seriously considering seeking experience outside of the classroom. First, recognize that there are limited opportunities to gain this experience and that you may be competing with peers for these positions. As such, your academic abilities, previous experience, and motivation will weigh heavily in determining whether or not you are selected. Second, understand that although these positions are occasionally advertised, students more often learn about them by actively seeking them out. Talk to peers who are involved in these activities and faculty members who work with research and teaching assistants to get a feel for what opportunities are available. Talk with organizations that offer internships or that you are interested in working with about the possibility for positions in the future.

Utilizing Available Resources

Psychology majors sometimes struggle needlessly to overcome challenges in their academic work. There are several valuable resources readily available in almost every psychology department that can be of assistance. This section highlights four such resources in an effort to encourage you to take greater advantage of them.

Perhaps the greatest resources students have at their disposal are the professors of their courses. These faculty members are certainly knowledgeable about the course material and assignments, but they also possess expertise on broader issues relevant to student success such as study skills, institutional resources, and degree requirements. These professors' varied teaching styles and approaches to courses can also be used to your advantage. Although striving to take courses from professors that you enjoy and learn from is one component of this, you should also be taking courses from professors who can help you address weaknesses in your academic skills. For example, if writing, statistics, and/or public speaking are areas of weakness for you, talk to peers about which professors do an excellent job of teaching and guiding students in these areas. Resist the temptation to take courses from professors who do not emphasize these skills.

Besides the professors of your current courses, you should also view the other faculty members in your department as potential resources. Some of the faculty may have backgrounds in subfields that match your interests, or perhaps they attended graduate school at an institution that is of interest to you. In these cases, the faculty member can provide excellent information that you can use to guide your goal formation and decision making. Faculty members also may offer teaching and research assistantships that would allow you to gain the outside of class experience that employers and graduate schools value. Given the important role a faculty member in your department might play in your academic and career progression, it is vital that you keep your interactions with all faculty professional and focused.

Another important resource available to psychology majors is the various activities, programs, and organizations sponsored by psychology departments. Many academic departments regularly invite guest speakers to present on their research or other topics of interests. These events are typically open to anyone interested in attending. Departments also sponsor student groups such as Psi Chi, the national honor society in psychology, or Active Minds, a mental health awareness and advocacy group. These organizations provide students with opportunities to work with their peers on various projects related to the discipline while also gaining valuable experience in leadership and group work. Departments often also host research symposiums or conferences that feature student research projects. These events provide great opportunities for students engaged in research to showcase their work and for students considering such activities to learn about the opportunities that exist.

Lastly, the psychology department office likely provides several important resources that are helpful to students. The administrative staff are usually knowledgeable about the major, degree requirements, institutional policies and regulations, and resources available to students. The staff may also be your access point if you need to arrange a meeting with a faculty member, advisor, or the department chair. The office typically has printed materials and forms relevant to the major. Information is also frequently posted concerning graduate programs, internships, assistantships, and job opportunities. Many departmental offices maintain a small library of books that are useful for majors, including common textbooks, study guides, and career and graduates school preparation guides. Keep in mind that most departments maintain websites that provide some of this information in an online format, including faculty biographies and contact information, syllabi from courses, and announcements about events as well as opportunities for outside experiences.

Conclusion

The psychology major can be a challenging path to earning your bachelor's degree. Academic difficulties and obstacles will certainly arise at points along the way. Preparing to overcome these begins with developing an awareness of the issues involved. Understand the nature of the academic work in psychology and how this unique perspective and way of thinking will influence what you will be asked to learn as a student. Recognize that there are some common challenges that students encounter and that there are helpful strategies in minimizing the impact of these on your performance. Finally, learn that there are valuable resources at your disposal to help ensure your success in completing the major. Taking these steps will go a long way towards ensuring that psychology moves from simply being your major to being your degree.

Suggested Exercises

1. Familiarize yourself with the psychology faculty at your institution. Begin by studying their biographies, which are often available on the departmental website. If faculty have their own websites or resources for learning more about their professional work, read this information as well. Begin to identify which faculty members share your interests in terms of careers, research, and professional activities. Strive to get to know these faculty over time by taking courses with them, seeking them out as advisors, and initiating conversations about their work.

2. Practice conducting a literature search and writing APA style citations by taking the following steps:
   a. Select a topic of interest to you (e.g., language development, sleep disorders, treatment of autism, memory problems) and choose two relevant terms to use in conducting a search using PsycINFO. For example, if your topic was language development, you might conduct a search

using the terms "language development" and "infants." Save the first 10 results.
   b. Conduct a second search by altering the search terms. Using the above example, you might change "language development" to "language acquisition," or you might change "infants" to "infancy." Examine the first 10 results and compare them to the results you saved from the first step. Pay attention to the types of sources you find with each search and determine which are more relevant to your topic.
   c. Refine your search terms further in order to generate results that are in line with your topic. Then choose five sources from the results. Select a mixture of articles, books, and book chapters. Write an APA-style reference entry for each of these sources using the APA *Publication Manual*. Ask an experienced peer, writing consultant, or professor to look at your references and give you feedback.

Suggested Readings

Landrum, R. E. (2002). Maximizing undergraduate opportunities: The value of research and other experiences. *Eye on Psi Chi, 6*(2), 15–18.

Landrum, R. E., & Davis, S. F. (2007). *The psychology major: Career options and strategies for success* (3rd ed.). Upper Saddle River, NJ: Prentice Hall.

Silvia, P. J., Delaney, P. F., & Marcovitch, S. (2009). *What psychology majors could (and should) be doing: An informal guide to research experience and professional skills.* Washington, DC: American Psychological Association.

References

American Psychological Association. (2002). Ethical principles of psychologists and code of conduct. *American Psychologist, 57,* 1060–1073.

American Psychological Association. (2007). *APA guidelines for the undergraduate psychology major.* Washington, DC: Author. Retrieved from http://www.apa.org/ed/resources.html

American Psychological Association. (2010). *Publication manual of the American Psychological Association* (6th ed.). Washington, DC: Author.

Fisher, C. B. (2003). *Decoding the ethics code: A practical guide for psychologists.* Thousand Oaks, CA: Sage Publications.

Gaither, G. A., & Butler, D. L. (2005). Skill development in the psychology major: What do undergraduate students expect? *College Student Journal, 39,* 540–552.

McGovern, T. V., & Hawks, B. K. (1986). The varieties of undergraduate experience. *Teaching of Psychology, 13,* 174–181.

McGovern, T. V., & Hogshead, D. L. (1990). Learning about writing, thinking about teaching. *Teaching of Psychology, 17,* 5–10.

National Commission on Writing. (2006). *Writing: The view from campus.* National Commission on Writing for America's Families, Schools and Colleges.

Snyder, T. D., Dillow, S. A., and Hoffman, C. M. (2008). *Digest of education statistics: 2007* (NCES 2008-022). Washington, DC: National Center for Education Statistics, Institute of Education Sciences, U.S. Department of Education. Retrieved from http://nces.ed.gov/pubsearch/pubsinfo.asp?pubid =2008022

Resources

APA Education Directorate – Pre-College and Undergraduate Resources
http://www.apa.org/ed/precollege/index.aspx
Psi Chi
http://www.psichi.org
Active Minds
http://www.activemindsoncampus.org

4

Assessing and Developing Career Goals

Introduction

"What do you want to be when you grow up?" You likely remember being asked and providing an answer to this question as a child. Perhaps as an adult you have even found yourself posing the question to children. We find children's answers amusing given that they are more likely to offer plans for being a superhero or princess than a regional manager. But our amusement reveals as much about our own thinking about careers as it does the child's. Children's career aspirations often clash with our sensibilities about how the world works, particularly in terms of the pressures that create a need to work and constrain our choice of careers.

As adults, our society emphasizes careers as a defining element of who we are. Getting to know another person routinely involves sharing information about each others' occupations. Knowing the answer helps us feel as though we have a clearer sense of who the person is. But adults often do not answer questions about their careers as freely as they did as children. The question posed to children recognizes an inherent flexibility and open-ended quality to the child's career development. Children respond by thinking about what it is that they would like to do, considering "jobs" they are familiar with, and then selecting one that seems like a good idea. In contrast, the question we pose to adults about their career seeks information about their present status. It is no surprise then that adults respond by describing their current occupation, the organization they work for, and the nature of their work. Our assumption in these exchanges is that adults' careers are already determined and to some degree stable.

How does the transition occur from a child with wide open career possibilities to an adult with an established career? Most adults began with educational goals in mind (e.g., "I have to finish high school," or "I want to get a college degree"). While completing their education, or sometimes shortly thereafter, they consider their career goals. Once they take on a particular career, many later consider their life goals, often in response to feeling that their career is not helping them achieve these goals (e.g.,

"I wish I had more financial security," or "If only I had more free time to spend with my family"). This pattern of goal setting is common. Many individuals realize later in life that their education is restricting their pursuit of career goals, and their career is restricting their pursuit of life goals. Real world circumstances lead many to pursue an education before carefully considering their career options. These same forces cause some to pursue a career before carefully considering their life goals. But because the order in which adults consider and develop these goals can have significant consequences, we would like to encourage you to approach your goals differently.

Career goals occupy a position of prominence throughout this text and are emphasized in this chapter. In fact, the chapter begins with a discussion of the nature and value of career goals. However, we also want to stress that career goals have little meaning or value in isolation from education and life goals. As a result, our approach to actual goal setting in this chapter asks you to consider your life goals first, career goals second, and educational goals third. For each area, you will be invited to complete a brief self-assessment exercise and then to respond to specific questions about your goals. We believe that the order in which these three areas are explored is key. Assessing your life interests and abilities facilitates forming life goals. Your life goals will then inform the assessment of your career interests and abilities, and in turn the formation of career goals. And finally, your career goals will inform the assessment of your educational interests and abilities, as well as the development of educational goals. You may have already established some educational and career goals without thinking in depth about life goals – this is fine. The approach we are suggesting is not strictly linear. We strongly encourage you to revisit goals in any of these areas as you have new experiences and your perspective changes. Begin to think about the development of these goals as an ongoing, lifelong process that can support both your career success and your overall well-being.

The Nature and Value of Career Goal Setting

Career Development Theories

Psychologists, along with researchers in several other fields, have been interested in the topic of career development for some time because it involves aspects of human development, functioning, and overall well-being. Their work has led to the creation of multiple theories on the process of career development. These theories have been used to create methods of assessing career interests and techniques for guiding individuals in developing and pursuing career goals. Each theory views the process of career development differently by emphasizing diverse factors that influence an individual's selection of a career.

Career development theories can be placed into several categories. Trait or factor theories (e.g., Parsons, 1909) emphasize the role that an individual's personal characteristics play in their career choices. Individuals are thought to possess unique combinations of traits (e.g., abilities, values, personality, achievements), and careers are thought to require a unique set of factors for an individual to be successful.

The match or mismatch between the two is believed to play a critical role in career development. Type theories (e.g., Holland, 1959) suggest that individuals adopt a few overall dispositions or tendencies that make them drawn to careers that satisfy their unique needs. Individuals thus seek out occupations that allow them to express their skills in order to derive satisfaction. Developmental theories (e.g., Super, 1963) stress that career preferences develop and mature over time and are therefore subject to change. As individuals' self-concepts change with experience, their preference for and satisfaction with different types of careers also evolve.

Regardless of which theory best matches your personal thinking about career development, each approach recognizes that career goals are not selected in an arbitrary manner. Instead, these goals are dependent upon many aspects of the individual and their unique set of experiences. Keep in mind that your personality, life circumstances, and current developmental stage might all play a role in shaping your career goals.

Approaches to Career Goal Setting

Despite the rich theoretical diversity on the subject of career development, and the fact that these theories stress that careers are multi-determined, information presented to the general public about this topic is often overly focused on the career itself. Many of the books, websites, and questionnaires available on career goal setting focus exclusively on helping you identify a handful of careers that are supposedly the best fit for you. You might be wondering, "Isn't that the purpose of developing career goals?" The answer is, in part, yes. Identifying careers that fit some aspects of you as a person is a worthy outcome. But those of you who have tried using these resources likely have had a more mixed reaction. Individuals often report that the process only confirms the career ideas they already had. Others report that the results are so at odds with their career ideas that they have no intention of further exploring the suggested careers. Still others might learn about career options they had not previously considered, and they then must explore these further. In all of these situations, individuals who engage in a process that generates career options typically do not walk away from the experience with clear, well-developed career goals. As an alternative, an approach placing the selection of specific careers within a broader framework that establishes a variety of interrelated goals is more meaningful and provides the individual with greater control over the process.

Setting Career Goals as an Active Process

Assuming greater control over your career goals begins with forming them in as active a manner as possible. Too often individuals find themselves in particular careers as a result of circumstances rather than purposeful planning and choice. This has numerous potential consequences. First, individuals can feel locked into a career when they lack the necessary skills to transition elsewhere or when they cannot afford to give up their current position to pursue additional goals. Second, individuals can dislike their careers when they feel that their jobs are forced upon them out of necessity and provide little to no satisfaction. If there are consequences to not actively developing career goals, why do individuals fail to do so? Many take on careers out of financial necessity then find that this situation constrains their goal setting. Others find the active development of career goals to be an overwhelming endeavor. Many believe they do not have sufficient information about themselves and the job market to make such an important decision. They fear they will choose the wrong career path and come to regret the decision later.

Concerns over making an error in developing your career goals can be reduced if you begin to view the development of goals as an ongoing, evolving process. This approach is particularly important if you want to weather the sometimes dramatic changes that can occur in the job market. Table 4.1 presents data on several careers that have changed substantially over the past decade in terms of the percentage of the workforce engaged in those types of activities. Numerous factors can bring about such changes. For example, developments in computer technology and data storage have contributed to a greater need for database managers as organizations gather more information about their clients, products, and operations. Increased availability of information, particularly through the internet, has driven organizations to increasingly call upon the services of public relations and publicity specialists. Yet some of these same developments in technology have contributed to declines in the demand for typists and travel agents. Societal changes can also play a role in shifts in career fields. As individuals have become increasingly comfortable with the idea of investing personal wealth and striving to manage their own retirement income, the demand for financial managers and planners has risen. Shifts in the demographics of a population can also impact career fields, evidenced by

Table 4.1　Change in Percentage of Workforce Employed in Careers Between 1997 and 2007

Specific Careers	Change in Percentage of Workforce
Public Relations Specialists and Publicity Writers	+114%
Financial Managers	+91%
Interior Designers	+59%
Home Health Aides	+51%
Child Care Workers	+42%
Data Base Administrators	+23%
Sales Agents, Advertising	+12%
Typists, Including Word Processing	−70%
Sewing Machine Operators, Garment	−53%
Travel Agents	−36%
Switchboard Operators	−32%
Computer Programmers	−31%
Flight Attendants	−15%
Machinists	−14%

Note. Change in percentage calculated using data from "May 2007 National Occupational Employment and Wage Estimates," by United States Department of Labor, Bureau of Labor Statistics, 2008, retrieved from http://www.bls.gov/oes/current/oes_nat.htm, and "1997 Occupational Employment and Wage Estimates," by United States Department of Labor, Bureau of Labor Statistics, 1997, retrieved from http://www.bls.gov/oes/oes_dl.htm.

the increasing need for home health care workers as large segments of the population begin to reach ages that require greater health care needs.

Changes in the demand for certain careers are sometimes gradual and easily forecasted. But other shifts are dramatic and unforeseen, such as those in response to economic downturns. This has led some to argue that individuals entering the workforce should anticipate changing careers, not simply jobs, multiple times in their working life (Bolles, 2007). This requires being prepared to change career goals as forces dictate without knowing exactly how and when these changes will occur. Individuals whose career goals are derived solely from their career aspirations are most at risk of being unable to shift with the changing occupational environment. In contrast, those who develop career goals through a careful self-assessment in which career goals are rooted in a larger understanding of self and interrelated goals will have less difficulty modifying their plans as needed.

The Value of Career Goals

In addition to providing grounding in the face of shifting and uncertain forces in the career environment, having well-developed career goals provides other, less obvious benefits. For example, adolescents who have clear goals related to their abilities and future careers have better school attendance and fewer disciplinary issues (Oyserman, Terry, & Bybee, 2002). They also possess higher levels of self-esteem, even when self-esteem is rated by an outside observer (Chiu, 1990). College students who have developed specific career goals are more likely to act in ways that support their persistence in their education (Hull-Blanks et al., 2005). Among employees, those who set career and work goals experience better adjustment to their current employment situations (Kubota, 1982).

Establishing specific career goals may serve not only to help achieve those goals but also to foster one's overall health and well-being. For example, employees' satisfaction with their careers is correlated with both having obtainable goals and being committed to those goals (Roberson, 1990). Lee, Bobko, Earley, and Locke (1991) discovered that employees who form clear goals and have support for them have more positive attitudes about their work. In addition, they found that employees who were dissatisfied with their work were more likely to experience stress, conflict, and failure related to their career goals. The relationship between career goals and job satisfaction is important because a clear relationship exists between job satisfaction and physical and mental health (e.g., Cass, Siu, Faragher, & Cooper, 2003; Faragher, Cass, & Cooper, 2005).

Assessing Self and Developing Life Goals

Life goals are aspirations you have for yourself across your lifespan. They can be things you want to do before the end of your life or things that you want to make an integral part of your life throughout. Examples include experiences you want to have, things you want to accomplish, the type of person you want to be, and the nature of relationships you want to have. If these goals sound fairly global, that is by design. General goals can be channeled into a variety of specific activities as situations and resources allow. Importantly, individuals who form life goals report higher levels of subjective well-being (Headey, 2008). Expressing life goals in written or verbal form has also been correlated with physical health and well-being (Harrist, Carlozzi, McGovern, & Harrist, 2007; King, 2001).

Formulating life goals may seem like a daunting task, especially when you are trying to decide on your major or what courses you should take next semester. The task should feel less overwhelming if you keep in mind that life goals often change, and they can become more specific over time. Keep in mind that generating life goals, even if they are fairly general at this time, will promote the formation of meaningful career goals.

Developing meaningful life goals is dependent upon having sound knowledge about oneself. Therefore, the first step should be a careful assessment of your various life interests and preferences. Many forms of self-assessment can lead to this end result. Examples include self-reflection, journaling, meditation, psychotherapy, and counseling. Certainly these methods cannot be duplicated within this chapter, but one component that they all share in common, taking stock of one's life priorities, can be explored. Box 4.1 presents several common components of individuals' lives

---

Box 4.1 Self-Assessment of Life Interests and Preferences

Instructions: Read the following list carefully and decide how important each element is in your life. Assign each element a ranking using the numbers 1 to 16, with "1" indicating the most important element in your life and "16" indicating the least important.

Appearance / image	_____
Autonomy / choice / control	_____
Contribute to others / better society	_____
Joy / fulfillment	_____
Faith / spirituality	_____
Family	_____
Meaningful, sustained relationships	_____
Minimization of pain, disappointment, loss	_____
Money / financial status	_____
Power / influence	_____
Interests and hobbies	_____
Recognition / admiration	_____
Security	_____
Self-awareness / self-understanding	_____
Structure / predictability / stability	_____
Success / accomplishing things	_____

and asks you to rank them in order of their importance to you. This task is not intended to serve as a comprehensive self-assessment of life interests and preferences. Instead, it is designed to stimulate your thinking about these issues in a way that will assist in formulating life goals. The life components listed are general in nature and likely mean different things to different people. This allows you to think and respond to them in ways that best capture your unique approach to life. As with all of the assessment and goal setting tasks presented in this chapter, you should not feel constrained by the specific elements provided. Feel free to add you own components in order to best capture important areas of your life that are not represented.

There are also many ways to go about formulating life goals. We believe that reflecting on your personal interests, preferences, ideas, aspirations, etc., then considering how these translate into specific goals, is an excellent place to start. Box 4.2 provides several questions, grouped into six domains, which are designed to stimulate your thinking about specific life goals. This list is not exhaustive because it is important not to feel overwhelmed when beginning this process. Remember to use your prioritized interests and preferences from Box 4.1 to guide your goal formation. Feel free to revise or add

Box 4.2 Questions to Stimulate the Formation of Life Goals

Structure
- How much control will you have over your daily life?
- How much predictability will there be in your daily life?

Learning
- What types of knowledge will you gain?
- To what degree and in what ways will you engage the world and information about it?

Leisure
- What types of hobbies and activities will you do in your free time?
- What contributions or services will you provide to others?

Relationships
- What role will personal relationships (friendship and romantic) play in your life?
- What pattern of communication will you engage in with significant others?

Status
- What financial status will you obtain?
- What will be your physical and mental health status?

Environment
- What will be you living situation/home environment?
- What types of communities will you associate with and/or create?

questions as you see fit, but respond honestly and thoughtfully to the items. You may want to keep a record of your ideas for reference before moving on to the next section.

It is important to keep in mind that variations in your life goals may or may not guide your decision about whether to major in psychology. Because the discipline is broad and includes many different subfields, individuals with widely differing life interests and preferences still find that pursuing an education in psychology meshes with their life goals. However, having a clearer sense of your life goals will help inform your thinking about careers, which in turn will help shape decisions you make about your education.

Assessing Self and Developing Career Goals

Once you have begun to clarify some of your life goals, it will be easier to recognize the tremendous impact they can have on your ideas about future careers. For example, an individual who develops life goals that give priority to family involvement and having a high level of stability in their daily life is unlikely to be satisfied in a career that requires extensive travel. This is not to say that career goals can never impact life goals. In fact, when some career opportunities present themselves, a reevaluation of life goals may be necessary. But even in these situations, you will be in a better position to make decisions about your career if you already understand how such shifts will affect your life goals.

Early in their lives, many individuals focus on obtaining their career goals. This emphasis is often feasible because younger individuals are more willing to delay life goals for the pursuit of their career path. But when career and life goals come to be at odds, the result is often some level of dissatisfaction in the career. The best possible remedy for any such conflict is to ensure that your career goals are not only in line with your life goals but also that they actually support one another. For example, if one of your life goals is to obtain a particular financial status, then have a congruent career goal. The greater the synchrony between one's life and career goals, the more likely one's career experiences will be rewarding and fulfilling.

Allow the life goals you began developing in the previous section to serve as a foundation for now considering your career goals. As was the case with setting life goals, it is best to begin by assessing oneself in several important areas. Most individuals strive to pursue careers that they find intrinsically interesting, and most employers hire individuals who have the skills needed for a position. Therefore, working to identify and prioritize your career-relevant abilities will provide a good starting point for beginning to develop career goals. Box 4.3 presents a list of abilities and asks you to select and rank those that best fit you. The abilities are divided into categories that reflect the focus of these skills. You may find that your abilities are primarily within one category or that that they branch across all three. Again, this task in isolation falls short of providing a thorough self-assessment of your career abilities and interests, but it should help stimulate your thinking about the topic in a way that will enhance your formulation of career goals. As with the previous exercises, feel free to add additional abilities to best capture your unique experiences.

Box 4.3   Self-Assessment of Career Related Abilities

Instructions: Read the following list carefully and decide which of the career abilities best describe you. Select and rank your top 10 abilities using the numbers 1 to 10.

Working With Information		*Working With People*		*Working With Things*	
Analyzing	____	Advising	____	Adjusting	____
Calculating	____	Assisting	____	Assembling	____
Classifying	____	Caring	____	Calibrating	____
Comparing	____	Conducting	____	Carrying	____
Compiling	____	Confronting	____	Composing	____
Connecting	____	Consulting	____	Constructing	____
Coordinating	____	Coordinating	____	Controlling	____
Creating	____	Counseling	____	Creating	____
Designing	____	Demonstrating	____	Designing	____
Developing	____	Enforcing	____	Disassembling	____
Diagnosing	____	Entertaining	____	Driving	____
Editing	____	Evaluating	____	Emptying	____
Examining	____	Influencing	____	Guarding	____
Experimenting	____	Initiating	____	Guiding	____
Expressing	____	Leading	____	Handling	____
Forecasting	____	Listening	____	Illustrating	____
Gathering	____	Mentoring	____	Installing	____
Inspecting	____	Motivating	____	Loading	____
Interpreting	____	Negotiating	____	Maintaining	____
Observing	____	Organizing	____	Manipulating	____
Organizing	____	Persuading	____	Monitoring	____
Perceiving	____	Providing	____	Moving	____
Planning	____	Representing	____	Performing	____
Presenting	____	Serving	____	Preparing	____
Reading	____	Sharing	____	Refining	____
Reporting	____	Speaking	____	Regulating	____
Researching	____	Supervising	____	Remodeling	____
Scheduling	____	Teaching	____	Repairing	____
Synthesizing	____	Training	____	Selling	____
Translating	____	Treating	____	Tending	____

Use your identified abilities from Box 4.3 as a starting point for beginning to formulate several career goals. Box 4.4 provides several questions that address key areas of career goals. The questions are grouped into the same six domains used earlier to organize the life goals questions. Again, the list is far from exhaustive, so revise or add questions as you see fit. Be sure to record your ideas for reference as you continue to work towards developing specific goals.

Box 4.4 Questions to Stimulate the Formation of Career Goals

Structure
- How much autonomy and independence will you have in your work life?
- Will you be led/supervised/managed or will you lead/supervise/manage others?

Learning
- What types of skills will you need to acquire through ongoing training?
- In what ways will your work challenge you?

Time
- What will your daily schedule or working hours be like?
- How will your work impact your free time?

Relationships
- What type of people will you work with/around/for?
- What role will relationships with coworkers play in your life?

Status
- What type of earnings and benefits will you receive?
- In what ways will your work provide opportunities for you to advance?

Environment
- What will your work setting/environment be like?
- How will your work impact your physical location (e.g., residence, commute, travel)?

Variations in your career goals will influence your decision about whether to major in psychology, and if so, what occupation to pursue. But by formulating career goals that are broader than simply identifying a desired occupation, you do not limit yourself to one particular educational path. In addition, the varied areas within the psychology field, as well as the related occupations at the bachelor's and graduate level, are capable of satisfying a wide range of career goals. Rather than dictate your educational goals, your career goals should inform your thinking and decision making as you make choices about your education and training.

Assessing Self and Developing Educational Goals

So far you have been working through tasks designed to help clarify your life and career goals. When this process begins to develop momentum, you may find yourself breathing a sigh of relief. Perhaps for the first time in your life you may begin to feel that you have a sense of direction and purpose in terms of your future career path. However, there is one final step to consider, that of assessing and developing your educational goals.

Because many careers require a minimum level of education, your ability to secure a particular career will be heavily influenced by your educational choices and accomplishments. At times these requirements only specify a particular degree or general area of training. For example, an entry-level management position may require a bachelor's degree with a major in business, human services, or a social science. But other careers can have more specific requirements. For example, positions as a clinical psychologist require a doctorate in clinical psychology from an accredited program along with coursework and training in specific areas of practice. As a result, your developing career goals and interests may play a critical role in shaping your educational goals.

If you are already in college, you may be wondering, "What is the purpose in developing educational goals now?" Certainly you have already started your pursuit of certain educational goals, like graduating from college. But chances are your career interests and goals are still being formulated. As these goals become clearer, aspects of your education will need to change accordingly. In other words, the time that remains in your pursuit of a college degree is vital, and the goals you set now will help shape the outcome of these experiences. Also, many of you need to begin preparing for education beyond a bachelor's degree, regardless of whether this entails graduate or professional school immediately after college or at a later point in your career.

Although your career plans will have a substantial influence on your educational interests and goals, it is vital that you not allow them to be the sole determining factor. Students sometimes state that because they want a particular career that requires a certain level of education, then they must now seek that education. This sounds logical, but the student who forms an educational goal in this manner is setting themselves up to fail. Students who enter college, graduate, and professional programs with this mindset are often not academically or mentally prepared to take on such a goal. Even if they possess the academic skills to succeed, viewing their education solely as "a means to an end" does not bode well for their sustaining the high levels of motivation and perseverance that these levels of education require.

Allow the life and career goals you began developing in the previous sections to serve as a foundation for now considering your educational goals. As with setting these previous goals, it is best to take some time before developing educational goals to assess your educational interests and abilities. One major factor to consider is your academic skills. Students can make full use of the academic skills they have by putting themselves in educational situations that maximize these resources. At other times the lack of particular academic skills can significantly affect the goals one develops and the pursuit of them. As a result, evaluating your academic skills can be a key element of conducting an assessment of your educational interests and abilities. Box 4.5 presents a list of skills that are critical to academic success at all levels. The task presented is for you to identify which of these skills are among your greatest academic strengths and weaknesses. As with the previous self-assessment tasks, identifying strengths and weaknesses is but one part of a thorough self-assessment of educational interests and preferences, but it should stimulate your thinking about issues relevant to formulating educational goals.

Box 4.5   Self-Assessment of Academic Strengths and Weaknesses

Instructions: Read the following list carefully. Identify which academic skills are strengths and which are weaknesses for you by marking them with an "S" for strength or a "W" for weakness. Then rank your three greatest strengths and your three greatest weaknesses from among those you identified, using the numbers 1 to 3.

Academic Skill	Strength or Weakness	Ranking
Accepting and using feedback	S	
Completing exams or quizzes	S	1
Concentrating or focusing	S	
Following directions	S	2
Giving presentations	W	
Listening in class or being attentive	S	3
Managing time or workload	W	
Organizing self and materials	S	
Participating in class	S	
Planning or prioritizing	W	
Preparing for exams or quizzes	S	
Reading and studying course materials	S	
Relating effectively to peers	W	2
Relating effectively to instructors	W	1
Staying motivated	S	
Taking notes in class	S	
Using technology to gather information	S	
Working in groups or teams	W	3
Writing or preparing written assignments	S	

Any self-assessment of one's academic abilities only partially captures the various factors that might shape your eventual educational pursuits. Yet, you can use your identified strengths and weaknesses as a starting point for beginning to formulate your educational goals. Box 4.6 provides several questions that address key areas of educational goals. The questions are grouped into the same six domains used earlier to organize the life and career goals questions. Again, the list is far from exhaustive, so revise or add questions as you see fit. Be sure to record your ideas for future reference.

Of the three areas of goals considered in this chapter, certainly your educational goals are the most likely to impact directly your decision of whether to major in psychology. But keep in mind that students pursuing a bachelor's degree in psychology can have vastly different educational experiences. The school you attend, courses

Box 4.6 Questions to Stimulate the Formation of Educational Goals

Structure
- How much autonomy and independence will you have in your educational life?
- How will your learning and progress be evaluated?

Learning
- What type of learning environment will you seek out (e.g., resources, class size, hands-on)?
- How academically rigorous will your education be?

Time
- How many years will you dedicate to pursuing your education and training?
- How much time during a week will you dedicate to pursuing your education and training?

Relationships
- What will your interactions with faculty/instructors be like?
- What role will relationships with coworkers play in your life?

Status
- What type of financial investment will you make in your education?
- What will be the reputation of the institution you attend?

Environment
- What will your institution's setting/environment be like?
- In what geographic location will you pursue your education?

you take, activities you engage in, and effort you exert will combine to produce your overall educational experience. Deciding on your major is only the beginning of this process, and thankfully you have much control over how these other elements of your education come together to support your career and life goals.

Conclusion

Our goal in this chapter was to help you begin to think about the value of viewing life, career, and educational goals as interdependent. In addition, we gave you several suggestions and methods for beginning to think about your interests in each of these areas and how these inform the development of clear goals. For the most part, the other chapters of this book place emphasis solely on the area of career goals. However, we hope that as you continue reading about the various subfields of psychology, and the steps you can take to prepare for your career, that you keep this chapter in mind.

Having a clearer sense of your life, career, and educational goals will enhance both your understanding of the information to come and the usefulness of it in helping you identify psychology-related careers that may be in your future.

Suggested Exercises

1. Familiarize yourself with the career services provided to students at your institution. Many colleges and universities have a career services center or office that provides helpful career-related information and assistance to students, typically free of charge. Develop an understanding of what types of resources they provide, and if possible, arrange a meeting with a career counselor to discuss your progress in developing career goals.

2. Complete several additional self-assessment tasks to supplement those provided in the chapter. Use these additional tasks to gather more information about your life, career, and/or educational interests and abilities as you work to further develop your goals. Many self-assessment tasks are available online either for free or for a small fee, but be cautious about how you interpret any feedback. Rather than view the results as definitive information about you or your career goals, view it as yet another piece of potentially helpful information to use in formulating goals for yourself. Several websites offer overviews of the numerous online self-assessment tools available, including:
   - Quintessential Careers, at http://www.quintcareers.com/online_assessment_review.html
   - The Riley Guide, at http://www.rileyguide.com/assess.html

3. Attend a career fair. Career fairs are typically organized by colleges and universities to provide students with opportunities to interact with area businesses and organizations. Fairs are often advertised by your institution's career services center or through the offices that coordinate student activities. If your institution has no information about career fairs, contact the career services centers of neighboring institutions to inquire about any upcoming fairs they are familiar with. Many students believe that if they are not currently seeking a job, that they have nothing to gain from attending a career fair. But by attending you will learn about a variety of opportunities in your area that you may not have even known existed.

Suggested Readings

Curran, S. J., & Greenwald, S. (2006). *Smart moves for liberal arts grads: Finding a path to your perfect career*. Berkeley, CA: Ten Speed Press.

Pollak, L. (2007). *Getting from college to career: 90 things to do before you join the real world*. New York: HarperCollins.

References

Bolles, R. N. (2007). *What color is your parachute? 2008: A practical manual for job-hunters and career-changers*. Berkeley, CA: Ten Speed Press.

Cass, M. H., Siu, O. L., Faragher, E. B., & Cooper, C. L. (2003). A meta-analysis of the relationship between job satisfaction and employee health in Hong Kong. *Stress and Health: Journal of the International Society for the Investigation of Stress, 19*, 79–95.

Chiu, L. (1990). The relationship of career goal and self-esteem among adolescents. *Adolescence, 25*, 593–597.

Faragher, E. B., Cass, M., & Cooper, C. L. (2005). The relationship between job satisfaction and health: A meta-analysis. *Occupational and Environmental Medicine, 62*, 105–112.

Harrist, S., Carlozzi, B. L., McGovern, A. R., & Harrist, A. W. (2007). Benefits of expressive writing and expressive talking about life goals. *Journal of Research in Personality, 41*, 923–930.

Headey, B. (2008). Life goals matter to happiness: A revision of set-point theory. *Social Indicators Research, 86*, 213–231.

Holland, J. L. (1959). A theory of vocational choice. *Journal of Counseling Psychology, 6*, 35–45.

Hull-Blanks, E., Kurpius, S. E. R., Befort, C., Sollenberger, S., Nicpon, M. F., & Huser, L. (2005). Career goals and retention-related factors among college freshmen. *Journal of Career Development, 32*, 16–30.

King, L. A. (2001). The health benefits of writing about life goals. *Personality and Social Psychology Bulletin, 27*, 798–807.

Kubota, Y. (1982). An empirical study on the effect of career goal setting. *Japanese Journal of Experimental Social Psychology, 21*, 149–157.

Lee, C., Bobko, P., Earley, P. C., & Locke, E. A. (1991). An empirical analysis of a goal setting questionnaire. *Journal of Organizational Behavior, 12*, 467–482.

Oyserman, D., Terry, K., & Bybee, D. (2002). A possible selves intervention to enhance school involvement. *Journal of Adolescence, 25*, 313–326.

Parsons, F. (1909). *Choosing a vocation.* Boston: Houghton Mifflin.

Roberson, L. (1990). Prediction of job satisfaction from characteristics of personal work goals. *Journal of Organizational Behavior, 11*, 29–41.

Super, D. E. (1963). Vocational development in adolescence and early adulthood: Tasks and behaviors. In D. E. Super, R. Starishevsky, N. Martin, & J. P. Jordan (Eds.), *Career development: Self-concept theory essays in vocational development* (pp. 79–95). New York: College Entrance Examination Board.

5

Using Your Bachelor's Degree
Preparing for the Job Market

Introduction

This chapter details a variety of issues related to preparation for employment upon graduation with a bachelor's degree. Topics covered include:

- work settings of recent graduates;
- what employers want from applicants for entry-level positions and ways to develop these attributes while in school (e.g., suggested coursework and experiences);
- finding entry-level positions;
- preparing job application materials (e.g., cover letters and résumés);
- preparing for and completing job interviews and considering offers.

Before we jump into the topics, we would like to highlight a few points to keep in mind. As noted earlier in the book and as a reminder, the bachelor's degree in psychology can be seen from two distinct perspectives (a preprofessional degree and a liberal arts degree). The preprofessional degree mirrors the natural sciences in that to become a physician, dentist, surgeon, etc., you first earn your bachelor's degree in one of the sciences and then continue your education in medical/dental school. The corollary with psychology is that to become a psychologist you first earn your bachelor's degree in psychology then continue your education in graduate school. In this way, the student is using the bachelor's degree as a stepping stone (i.e., a preprofessional degree). From the second perspective, the liberal arts degree provides the student with a well-rounded education in the humanities, fine arts, natural sciences, and social sciences. A liberal arts education provides the student the opportunity to gain general knowledge and critical thinking and communication skills that can be applied to a wide array of circumstances (i.e., job settings and opportunities). With this in mind, the vantage point of this chapter is using the bachelor's degree in psychology as a liberal arts degree, which is, using your bachelor's degree as a foundation for entering the job market immediately upon graduation.

Second, for those of you wishing to pursue graduate training immediately upon completion of the bachelor's degree, don't discount the information in this chapter. Many, if not most, of the suggestions and pointers offered in this chapter are equally valid for those who want to pursue graduate training upon completion of the bachelor's degree and those who decide to continue their education at a later time.

Last, although this chapter addresses preparation for the job market with a bachelor's degree, keep in mind that these are general pointers, suggestions, and insights. For those wanting to enter the job market immediately upon graduation (which is the case for most students), do not forego the second half of this book mistakenly believing that working within the subfields of psychology is only open to those with graduate training and degrees. This belief is far from the truth. Many people work in the specialized subfields of psychology as support staff, technical assistants, etc. As a result, each of the subfield chapters includes an entire section on positions available to those with a bachelor's degree. Check them out!

Work Settings of Recent Graduates

What can you do with a bachelor's degree in psychology? The better question may be "What *can't* you do with a bachelor's degree in psychology?" Granted that this may be overstating it, but the truth is that a liberal arts degree in psychology puts you in a great situation for entry-level positions. Your degree program provides you with the opportunity to gain a well-rounded education in the humanities, fine arts, natural sciences, and social sciences. A liberal arts education provides the student the opportunity to gain general knowledge and critical thinking and communication skills that can be applied to a wide array of circumstances (i.e., job settings and opportunities). The opportunities provided by most psychology programs are due in no small part to guidance provided by the American Psychological Association (APA, 2007) via their Task Force on Psychology Major Competencies. The Task Force developed (and regularly revises) a "set of optimal expectations for performance at the completion" (p. v) of the bachelor's degree. The set includes 10 goals that most undergraduate psychology programs address and attempt to achieve via the curriculum offered to the psychology major. Some of the skills noted in the 10 goals are critical thinking, research methods, technological literacy, communication, international awareness, and personal development.

The opportunities provided by departments attempting to achieve the goals developed by APA (2007), placed the 88,134 students obtaining her/his bachelor's degree in psychology in 2004–2005 (U.S. Department of Education, National Center for Education Statistics, 2007) in excellent shape for pursuing a variety of career paths upon graduation. Box 5.1 provides a sampling of the wide variety of entry-level positions possible with a bachelor's degree in psychology. We hope the box inspires some career ideas that you may not have considered. For additional ideas take a look at Appleby's (2006) listing which is available at http://www.teachpsych.org/otrp/resources/appleby06.pdf. Remember that these are just *examples* of possible positions. It is not meant to limit your ideas or neglect other great entry-level career choices for those with a bachelor's degree in psychology. We also encourage you to review the

Box 5.1 A Sample of Various Entry-Level Positions Possible With a Psychology Degree

Activity Leader

Admissions Evaluator

Advertising Assistant

Assistant Account Executive

Community and Social Service Worker

Case Worker

Community Relations Representative

Copywriter

Corporate Merchandising

Corrections Officer

Correctional Caseworker

Cottage Parent

Probation Officer

Professional Employment Recruiter

Program Developer

Youth Corrections Officer

Crisis Intervention Counselor

Customer Service Representative

Customs/Immigration Officer

Employment Agency Counselor

Food and Beverage Assistant Manager

Health Club Assistant Manager

Human Resources Personnel

Hospice Coordinator

Hotel Event Management

Public Opinion Surveyor

Public Relations Assistant

Recreation Specialist

Sales Representative

Social Service Professional Staff

Wage/Benefits Analyst

International Student Advisor

Job Developer

Junior Market Analyst

Labor Relations Specialist

Market Research Analyst

Media Buyer

Media Planner

Mental Health Coordinator

Personnel Assistant

Personnel Interviewer

Statistician Assistant

Technical Writer/Communicator

Television/Media Research

Note. Information comes from *Psychology-related career titles* (n.d.), retrieved from www.uncwil.edu/stuaff/career/Majors/psychology.html.

positions in light of the information provided in the chapter on assessing and developing your career goals.

According to the National Science Foundation's (NSF) 2006 National Survey of Recent College Graduates, representation of recent recipients of bachelor's degrees in psychology significantly varied among the three main employment sectors (Proudfoot, 2008). Thirty percent of recent psychology graduates were employed in educational institutions. In its definition of educational institutions, NSF includes "elementary and secondary schools, 2-year and 4-year colleges and universities, medical schools, university-affiliated research organizations, and all other educational institutions." Nine percent of recent psychology graduates worked in the government sector. NSF "includes local, state, and federal government, military, and commissioned corps" in its definition of the government sector. By far, the largest employment sector of recent recipients of bachelor's degrees in psychology is business/private industry at 61%. This number includes both nonprofit organizations and those individuals who are self-employed. Additionally, NSF defines this sector as private industry and business which "includes all private for-profit and private not-for-profit companies, businesses, and organizations, except those reported as educational institutions." Importantly, this same NSF survey found the median salary for recent recipients of bachelor's degrees in psychology was $30,000 in 2006, meaning half made more and half made less than this amount.

What Employers Want from Applicants for Entry-level Positions (How to Develop What Employers Want)

Although the types of employment and settings are varied, research strongly suggests that employers seek out particular skills and attributes in applicants. In their annual publication (*Job Outlook*), the National Association of Colleges and Employers (NACE; 2007) reports the top candidate qualities/skills rated by employers. However, knowing what skills are valued and knowing how to develop them are different. As a result, beside each of the top five qualities reported by NACE, we list possible strategies in developing these skills, keeping in mind that the skills developed and the methods used to develop them fit nicely on a résumé. Résumés are discussed later in this chapter.

Communication Skills (Verbal and Written)

With a mean rating of 4.6 out of a possible 5, this skill set tops the list reported by NACE (2007). Two of the most common ways to develop communication skills are writing term papers and reports and making oral presentations. Frequent opportunities exist to build and refine verbal and written skills in your program. As is the case with most upper-level coursework and your research-oriented courses (e.g., Experimental Psychology), term papers and literature reviews are common place. If you are not a good writer or simply want to improve your writing skills, certainly take advantage of the resources at your university (e.g., writing centers).

Strong Work Ethic

This quality tied with communication skills for first place (NACE, 2007). In many ways, this quality must be developed (i.e., demonstrated) over time. For example, class attendance and participation demonstrate a commitment to the educational process. This quality is also demonstrated through punctuality and time consciousness. Arriving on time to class, completing assignments when due, etc. illustrate to those around you (e.g., the faculty who will be your future references) that you take your education seriously. The strength of your work ethic is also demonstrated by the quantity and quality of your work product. Do you do the minimum? Is it obvious that you are taking the course because it is "required"? Enrolling and excelling in some of the optional coursework may demonstrate a strong work ethic too. Optional courses like practica and advanced research courses should be considered.

Teamwork Skills (Works Well With Others)

Teamwork skills came in third with a mean of 4.5 out of a possible 5 (NACE, 2007). Teamwork skills can be developed inside a particular course and outside of coursework. Inside the classroom, group projects and activities can be utilized. Although not a favorite aspect for many students, employers' desire for this skill and professors' beliefs in the value of collaboration, support the use of group assignments. Teamwork skills can be developed outside of traditional coursework too. For example, involvement in a service project as a member of your psychology club or honor society is an opportunity to develop this skill and demonstrate your aptitude in this area. In terms of coursework, courses in the areas of social psychology and industrial-organizational psychology often incorporate group activities, given the nature of the subfields.

Initiative

Initiative ranked fourth and achieved a mean of 4.4 (NACE, 2007). Students show initiative when they seek out opportunities to get more experience and practice. Students who have initiative often go above and beyond the requirements of a particular course assignment. As a result, opportunities to demonstrate initiative abound in the under-graduate curriculum. Students who do the minimum in order to finish quickly give clearly negative information to their professors (i.e., their future references). Also, students who are not self-motivated lack initiative. Those students who need significant amounts of guidance (i.e., "hand holding") lack initiative typically. Taking advantage of extracurricular activities like leadership opportunities in the department clubs and organizations can demonstrate your initiative.

Interpersonal Skills (Relates Well to Others)

Interpersonal skills ranked fifth (NACE, 2007). A common question that is asked of references is how well a person relates to others, both peers and those in authority. Is the student open to criticism and feedback? Is he/she argumentative, always trying to get that missed point back on the exam? Does the student get along well with classmates? We have all had that person in class who dominates the discussion or asks/answers all of the questions. Encouraging peers to offer their perspective and listening closely to those peers who may disagree with you demonstrates your skill in this area. Additionally, professors can not comment on your behavior if you do not engage in class discussion, avoid department activities (e.g., club activities and fundraisers), etc. Equally important, although professors generally love to interact with students (one of the great things about our jobs), professors certainly do not want to remember you for being the one that *required* tons of attention. In addition to learning about interpersonal skills in courses like Social Psychology, Family Psychology, and Group Psychology, working with a professor one-on-one on a research project or departmental project (e.g., a psychology club fundraiser) will provide the professor with an opportunity to observe your interactions with others (and them too!).

Rounding out NACE's (2007) top 10 skills are problem-solving skills (4.4), analytical skills (4.3), flexibility/adaptability (4.2), computer skills (4.1), and technical skills (4.1). Although employers were not asked by NACE to rate the importance of grades (i.e., Grade Point Average; GPA), 62.3% of the employers responding to the survey indicated that they screen applicants based on GPA. This strongly suggests that the more tangible attributes of a potential employee are not overlooked or forgotten.

Collegegrad.com (2008) presents a different but similar perspective on what employers want from new college graduates. The results of the survey produced eight criteria. The criteria with accompanying percentage of employers ranking it as "most important" are:

1. The student's major (42%)
2. The student's interviewing skills (25%)
3. The student's internships/experience (16%)
4. Other miscellaneous qualifications (10%)
5. The student's computer skills (3%)
6. The student's personal appearance (2%)
7. The student's GPA (1%)
8. The college the student graduated from (1%)

As can be seen from the criteria, 16% indicated that internships/experience is the "most important" criteria in evaluating new college graduates. In other words, experience counts! Summer jobs, part-time jobs, structured volunteer experiences, field practica, and internships/externships all provide opportunities to gain experience. Complementing the finding by Collegegrad.com is a 2005 NACE survey that found that employers rate relevant work experience, internship experience, any work experience, and co-op experience as "very important."

But what about psychology majors in particular? Appleby (2000) developed a list of job skills that employers who interview psychology majors value. The job skills categories along with examples within each category are presented in Box 5.2. In sum, and comparing them to other research findings, the skills valued in psychology majors were not much different than those noted earlier for liberal arts majors in general and all majors.

Based on these types of data, Lloyd, Kennedy, and Dewey (1997) developed suggestions of coursework that may bolster some of these skills employers seek. The skills they identified along with suggested psychology coursework are listed here.

- *Knowing How to Learn.* For this skill set, Lloyd and her colleagues suggest coursework in Introductory Psychology, Psychology of Adjustment, and Cognitive Psychology.
- *Competence in Reading, Writing, and Computational Skills.* Lloyd et al. suggest courses like Psychological Statistics, Research Methods, Experimental Psychology (especially those with a lab portion), and History and Systems.
- *Communication Skills.* For this set of skills, the authors again suggest Research Methods and Experimental Psychology.

Box 5.2 Job Skills That Employers Who Interview Psychology Majors Value

1. *Social Skills*
   - Deals effectively with a wide variety of people
   - Displays appropriate interpersonal skills
   - Handles conflict successfully
   - Works productively as a member of a team

2. *Personal Skills*
   - Shows initiative and persistence
   - Exhibits effective time management
   - Holds high ethical standards and expects the same of others
   - Remains open-minded during controversies

3. *Communication Skills*
   - Listens carefully and accurately
   - Speaks articulately and persuasively
   - Writes clearly and precisely

4. *Information Gathering/Processing Skills*
   - Plans and carries out projects successfully
   - Thinks logically and creatively
   - Gathers and organizes information from multiple sources

5. *Numerical/Computer/Psychometric Skills*
   - Displays computer literacy
   - Performs and interprets descriptive and inferential statistics

Note. Information comes from Appleby (2000).

- *Self-Management Skills.* Lloyd and her colleagues provide a host of possible psychology courses to develop these skills. Their suggestions include Psychology of Adjustment, Health Psychology, Field Practica, Directed Research, Behavior Modification, and Lifespan Development.
- *Adaptability.* Research Methods, Experimental Psychology, and Behavior Modification are suggested as possible avenues for development of this quality.
- *Group Interactional Skills.* For this set of skills, the authors suggest courses in the area of race and ethnic relations, Industrial-Organizational Psychology, Social Psychology, Psychology of Adjustment, and Motivation and Emotion.
- *Influence Skills.* Applied Psychology, Industrial-Organizational Psychology, Social Psychology, and Behavior Modification are suggested as possible ways to develop this set of skills.

In their article, Lloyd and her colleagues (1997) apparently recognize that the majority of students entering the job market enter the business/private industry sector and that many students pursue employment in the human services sector as well. As a result, these authors provided suggestions for coursework to take for those interested in pursuing careers in these areas. In addition to suggested coursework in the business and economics disciplines, Lloyd et al. suggested courses like the Psychology of Women, Psychological Statistics, Industrial-Organizational Psychology, Applied Psychology, Social Psychology, and Field Practica for those students interested in the business sector. For those interested in the human services area, they suggested Child Psychology, Lifespan Development, Behavior Modification, Abnormal Psychology, Tests and Measurement, Field Practica, Substance Abuse, Psychology of Women, Theories of Personality, and Health Psychology.

Obviously, we realize that students can not take all of the suggested courses. There just isn't enough time! Regardless, knowing what potential employers want in applicants and knowing the associated coursework that may provide opportunities to develop those skills puts you in a better place when selecting your coursework. Fortunately, regardless of which data are reviewed or highlighted, the typical curriculum associated with a bachelor's degree in psychology provides the opportunity to develop each of these qualities, putting you in a good place for entry-level positions upon graduation. Again though, the challenge for the student is to choose coursework wisely, keeping in mind his or her ultimate career goal.

Finding Entry-Level Positions

Now that you know what employers want, where do you find these entry-level positions? Before you start looking for positions, revisit your self-assessment completed in the Assessing and Developing Career Goals chapter. Be guided by your values, that is, how you really are and not just how you think you "should" be. With this understanding in mind, begin your search.

Recruiting Methods

Although it may go without saying, there are effective methods and ineffective methods for searching for jobs. The same is true for the employers looking to fill entry-level positions. As a result, knowing what employers have found effective can shed light on what may be effective for the new college graduate. NACE (2007) surveyed employers to find out what are the most and least effective recruiting methods. The top five most effective methods for employers were on-campus visits, students who had internships through their organization, employee referrals, co-op program through their organization, and career or job fairs. The five least effective methods for employers were recruitment advertising through printed materials, internet banners, newspaper advertising on campus and in local newspapers, virtual career and job fairs, and video interviewing. As is the case for most of us, we need to make the most of our limited time and busy schedules. As a result, knowing where employers find the most success in recruiting new employees will prove useful in deciding where to spend your time!

Resources

Finding actual job openings can be difficult. This difficulty is due in no small part to the problem that only 10–15% of current job openings are posted in the traditional manner (i.e., newspaper advertisements; DeGalan & Lambert, 2001). As a result, the majority of job openings may go unnoticed. In hopes of decreasing the problem of the "hidden job market," Box 5.3 lists a variety of resources and resource ideas, both traditional and nontraditional, to assist you in the job search.

As can be seen from the resources listed in Box 5.3, jobs and opportunities will not likely come looking for you. Instead, you will have to go looking for them. This process along with letting people know you are looking for a position and establishing connections in the field that you want to pursue as a career are all considered networking. Networking will serve you well in your endeavor to find that perfect job. In fact, networking is invaluable.

Box 5.3   Job Search Resources and Where to Find Job Openings

General Job Websites
- www.monster.com
- www.collegegrad.com

Government Employment Websites
- www.usajobs.gov
- www.governmentjobs.com
- www.usa.gov/Citizen/Topics/Work_for_the_Government.shtml

Diversity-related Employment Websites and Resources
- Published by a university in the United Kingdom (Cardiff University Careers Service, 2006), this publication provides some pointers on how to identify disability and diversity-friendly employers. www.cf.ac.uk/carsv/resources/How_to_Identify_Disability_and_Diversity_Friendly_Employers_Booklet.pdf
- Lesbian, Gay, Bisexual, and Transgender-friendly – www.gayjob.biz
- American Foundation for the Blind – www.afb.org/Community.asp?Type= Employment
- General diversity-related online resources:
  - diversityinc.com
  - career.berkeley.edu/Disab/EmpRes.stm

Local papers – Many post their classifieds online too

University resources
- Career centers and libraries – Most universities have these resources
- Your professors

Community resources
- Employment agencies
- Temporary employment agencies

Preparing Job Application Materials: Job Applications, Résumés, and Cover Letters

The two most important pieces of a job application are the résumé and cover letter. Both are always carefully and thoughtfully prepared. They are both always typed.

Résumés

There are two basic types of résumé, functional and chronological. The core part of the functional résumé is organized by skill type (e.g., sales experience, leadership experience, writing experience, and interpersonal experience). Box 5.4 provides an example of a functional résumé. The core part of the chronological résumé is organized by dates of activities (e.g., July 2009–July 2010; July 2010–present). Box 5.5 provides an example of a chronological résumé.

Regardless of the type of résumé, all résumés have the basic elements in common. First, all résumés should be one page long, no more. It should be printed on good quality white/off white paper, not pink, powder blue, beige, purple, etc. (The same paper should be used for the cover letter too.) The résumé should be individually tailored to the position (not generic). When individuals mass mail generic résumés and cover letters, it strongly indicates that care and attention to detail are not strong attributes of the applicant. Generic résumés and cover letters stand out from the crowd and not in a good way. In constructing the résumé and cover letter, action verbs should be used, display techniques should be consistent (e.g., Times New Roman size 12 font throughout), and abbreviations should be avoided. Some of the common headings within a résumé are as follows.

Name and contact information.   As seen in the examples, this information is typically centered at the top of the résumé. Be prepared and willing to be contacted at all of these. In other words, if you do not want to be contacted at your current place of employment, do not include that phone number/address. Additionally, only provide professional e-mail addresses and phone voicemail messages. For example, a professional e-mail address would be one with your name in it like RSmith@abcxyz.com, not FunnyBunny21@abcxyz.com. Also, a professional voice message on your voicemail does not include the latest pop song as an introduction. If you have a professional web page you may want to include it too. Some universities encourage or require students to develop a web page to display their writing samples, résumés, etc. On this point, you may want to do a web search of yourself (e.g., Google, Facebook, Myspace) to see what employers can find out about you. They will do this too!

Career objective.   This single sentence or phrase is typically located immediately after the contact information and summarizes your career goal(s).

Educational background.   This heading typically includes the degrees you have earned as well as those you are expecting (e.g., BS expected May 2016). Along with the location

Box 5.4 Example Functional Résumé

Joyce E. Brawley
1000 Chastain Rd.
Kennesaw, GA 30144
(770) 555-5555
JoyceEBrawley@emailnow.com

Career Objective

To obtain an entry-level position in the human resources area that utilizes my strong interpersonal and research skills

Education

Your University, Atlanta, GA; Bachelor of Science in Psychology, May 2013
Minors: Statistics and Human Services; GPA: 3.6/4.0; Graduated Cum Laude

Relevant Skills

- Technical Skills

Extensive experience with SPSS Statistical Package and Microsoft Office (Word, Excel, PowerPoint, Publisher, and Access); Familiar with Dreamweaver web design software

- Writing Skills

Coauthored paper presented at regional psychology conference. Extensive experience with American Psychological Association writing style, including writing empirically-based papers. Helped develop, pilot, and analyze an employee satisfaction survey while on internship

- Organizational Leadership

Secretary for two years and President for one year of my university's Psychology Club. Headed the annual fundraiser two consecutive years in which over $10,000 was raised for battered women and abused children. Treasurer for 1 year for the Psi Chi chapter.

Employment

Your University, Atlanta, GA, 2010–2013 (Psychology computer lab assistant)
Summer Employment, Inc., Bates, GA, 2009 (File clerk)
Sunday Eatery, Clivetown, GA, 2007–2008 (Hostess and wait staff)
Signatory Stores of Liza, Simpsonville, GA 2004–2007 (Retail staff)

Honors and Professional Society Memberships

Outstanding Undergraduate Psychology Major Graduate Award – 2010–2011
Psi Chi Honors Society – 2011-present
American Psychological Association (student affiliate) – 2012-present
Society for Human Resource Management (student member) – 2012-present

Availability

Immediate

Box 5.5   Example Chronological Résumé

Joyce E. Brawley
1000 Chastain Rd.
Kennesaw, GA 30144
(770) 555-5555
JoyceEBrawley@emailnow.com

Career Objective

To obtain an entry-level position in the human resources area that utilizes my strong interpersonal and research skills

Education

May 2013   Bachelor of Science in Psychology; Minors: Statistics and Human Services
Your University, Atlanta, GA; GPA: 3.6/4.0; Graduated Cum Laude

Relevant Experience

August 2010 – May 2013   Your University, Atlanta, GA
Psychology Computer Lab Assistant
- Assisted students and faculty with American Psychological Association writing style, including writing empirically-based papers
- Routinely used SPSS and Microsoft Office (Word, Excel, PowerPoint, Publisher, and Access)
- Occasionally used Dreamweaver web design software

August 2012 – May 2012   Your University, Atlanta, GA
Human Resources Intern
- Assisted in the development, piloting, and statistical analysis of an employee satisfaction survey
- Presented results to director of human resources
- Coauthored paper based on findings and presented it at a regional psychology conference
- Routinely interacted with administration, faculty, and employees in a professional role

August 2009 – May 2013   Psychology Club
Active Member
- President from 2012–2013, Secretary from 2010–2012
- Headed annual fundraiser 2 consecutive years in which over $10,000 was raised for charity

Honors and Professional Society Memberships

Outstanding Undergraduate Psychology Major Graduate Award – 2010–2011
Psi Chi Honors Society – 2011–present (Served as treasurer from 2012–2013)
Society for Human Resource Management (student member) – 2012–present
American Psychological Association (student affiliate) – 2012–present

of the university where you obtained your degree(s), you will also want to include your major, your grade point average, and any graduation honors (e.g., cum laude and summa cum laude).

Relevant experience.   Due to space limitations, only relevant experience is noted/described. This section also varies based on the amount of your experience and the positions you seek. For example, you may include your multiple retail experiences for a management trainee position at a local store but not include it when applying to work at a daycare center. In that situation you may highlight your volunteer experience with kids at the local community center.

Relevant skills.   This section focuses on the specific skills you will bring to bear on the position. These skills may include your computer knowledge, writing skills, statistical knowledge (including software packages like SPSS), and foreign languages.

References.   Depending on available space, you may provide a list of references and accompanying contact information for them. Sometimes, résumés only include an indication of references being available upon request. If included, always ask permission of someone before listing him/her as a reference and give them notice of when and where you are sending your application/résumé.

Additional headings.   Additional headings may include relevant extracurricular activities, military experience, honors societies, volunteer experiences, professional affiliations/memberships, and selected achievements. Obviously, not all headings will be used in each of your résumés. Instead, they will vary depending on the type of position and the skills you are trying to highlight. Regardless of the headings used, the information found in your résumé should be accurate. Even small inaccuracies can prove fatal for a job prospect.

Cover Letters

A cover letter always accompanies a résumé. An example of a cover letter is provided in Box 5.6. Cover letters consist of three main sections/paragraphs and are most often one page or less in length. The first section identifies why you are writing, what job you are applying for, and where you found the job. The second section (middle paragraph) relates your background to the position. At this point you reference the match between your skills, experiences, and goals and the organization's needs. Information on most organizations (e.g., their mission, history, business plan/goals) can be found online. Be specific and tailor the letter to the position. General, nonspecific, "boilerplate" letters reflect poorly on you and your interest in the company and position. The last paragraph/section should reiterate your interest in the company and position. At that point, you should state what you will do next (e.g., call, e-mail to check on receipt of application, where the process stands, etc.) and invite the reader to contact you.

Box 5.6 Example Cover Letter

Joyce E. Brawley
1000 Chastain Rd.
Kennesaw, GA 30144
(770) 555-5555
JoyceEBrawley@emailnow.com

June 27, 2013

Beverly Longstreet
State Human Resources Inc. of California
135-B Tango Place Rd. SW
Madera, CA 93636

Dear Ms. Longstreet

Please let this letter and the attached résumé serve as my application for the human resource associate position at your company. I learned of this opening from an advertisement on your company's website.

Based on the information provided in the advertisement and information on your organization's website, it appears that there is an excellent fit between your needs and my background and career goals. According to the position description, you are seeking an individual with a bachelor's degree in psychology who has strong interpersonal skills, organizational experience, and background in customer satisfaction survey development. As can be seen in the attached résumé, I graduated cum laude with my BS in Psychology last month. During my education I had the opportunity to intern in the university's human resources department. During that internship I helped develop, pilot, and analyze the results from an employee satisfaction survey. Based on the results, my supervisor and I developed a set of recommendations for the administration that would hopefully improve employee retention. I presented the findings to the director of human resources as well as at a regional conference. The skills developed through this internship match nicely with the background you desire.

My strong skills in working with others individually and in teams along with my desire to relocate to your area correspond well with the available position. I would appreciate the opportunity to speak with you regarding the position. Please feel free to contact me at 770-555-5555 or email me at the above address. I will touch base with you next week to make sure you received the application. I look forward to hearing from you in the near future.

Sincerely,

[Signature]

Joyce E. Brawley

Enclosure

Keep Track of Where You Send Your Applications!

Given that most job seekers will send out lots of applications, it can be difficult to keep track of the specifics of positions. A good way to address potential memory glitches and keep your applications straight is to use a spreadsheet (e.g., using Microsoft Excel). In a spreadsheet, indicate the following for each application sent:

- Contact person at the organization
- Address of the organization – Sometimes you may apply at more than one branch or location
- Date the application was sent
- Response – Did they receive the application? Did they offer an interview?
- Job type – Retail sales, managerial, human resources, etc.
- Salary (if known)
- Date decision to be made (if known)

Preparing for and Completing Job Interviews and Considering Offers

Preparing for the Interview

Before the interview, refresh your memory about why you applied for the position at the company. First, review the information on the position (e.g., the job advertisement). Second, review the information available on the company/program. Third, review your résumé and your application. Remember, each of your résumés and cover letters will be different, emphasizing only those skills and attributes pertinent to that particular position. Fourth, do a mock interview with your college's career center advisor/counselor. Most universities provide some form of coaching and preparation for interviews. (Note: Most of these services are also available to graduates even years after they have graduated.) Fifth, practice in front of the mirror and role-play with friends who will provide *critical* feedback. Although it is nice to get positive feedback (especially the day of the interview), the days/weeks leading up to the interview should be focused on areas in need of improvement. Some practice interview questions are provided in Box 5.7. Another way to get feedback on your interviewing style is to videotape yourself as you will appear on the interview day and practice answering questions. Being videotaped can create some anxiety which might match the anxiety experienced on the interview day, allowing you the opportunity to find ways to manage the anxiety (e.g., deep breathing and practicing answers to common questions).

Although it is sad to say, appearance counts. As a result, in the days and weeks leading up to an interview, you will want to choose an outfit that fits the professional situation for which you are applying. Some pointers on appearance can be found at the University of North Carolina – Wilmington's Career Center website at www.uncw.edu/stuaff/career/dressforsuccess.htm. In general, you will want to dress conservatively, wearing a dark suit, tie for men, neat hair, minimal jewelry, and minimal

Box 5.7 Practice Interview Questions

- Tell me what you know about our organization and the position.
- Where do you see yourself in 5/10 years?
- What background experience do you have?
- What is your greatest strength?
- What is your greatest weakness?
- What do you think you will bring to the organization?
- Tell me about a time when you had a conflict at work. How did you resolve it?*
- Tell me about an ethical dilemma you have encountered in the past. How did you address it?*
- We are interviewing quite a few people, why should we hire you?
- Tell me about yourself.
- What do you like to do in your spare time?
- Is there anything else you would like us to know about you?
- How has your background and education prepared you for the job you are seeking with us?

* These behavioral-type interview questions are common. As a result, you may want to spend some additional time preparing for this type of question.

make-up/cologne. In terms of your outfit, you will want to wear it prior to the interview so that you can ensure a comfortable fit.

The Day of the Interview

On the day of the interview, you should arrive early but not too early. You will want to allow plenty of time for traffic and parking problems. If you arrive too early for the interview (i.e., more than 15 minutes), take the time to review a copy of your application and the information you have on the organization and the person who will be interviewing you (if available). In terms of what to take with you to the interview, it is generally recommended that an interviewee have a notepad and pen, a copy of his/her application, several copies of an updated résumé (in case the person you are meeting with has not reviewed it), and a copy of your questions. Box 5.8 provides some ideas for questions you might ask.

It is a given that you will be asked a variety of questions about your application and interest in the position and organization. Fortunately, your preparation through role-playing with friends and in front of the mirror has helped with this aspect of the interview. Additionally, there are generally typical questions that are asked by the interviewer that revolve around your strengths, skills, weaknesses, salary requirements, and career goals. However, you will also be expected to ask questions. Instead of having to think on your feet, having your questions prepared in advance can relieve some stress. Referring to your notes for this part and taking notes on answers to the

Box 5.8 Possible Questions to Ask a Potential Employer

- What is the financial outlook of the organization?
- Where do you see the organization in 5/10 years?
- What is the biggest challenge facing the organization?
- Where in the hiring process are you?
- When do you think a hiring decision will be made?
- What do you like most about the organization?
- How many applicants are you interviewing?
- How would you describe the work atmosphere?

Box 5.9 Some Additional Interview Pointers

- Demonstrate knowledge of the company/organization and the position.
- Be prepared to discuss your career plans.
- Show enthusiasm for the position (but not too much).
- Avoid evasiveness. Be direct with your answers when possible.
- Give eye contact, but do not stare.
- Be prepared to discuss your skills and experience, including limitations/weaknesses.
- Don't smell (i.e., too much perfume/cologne).
- Talk but not too much; engage in the conversation, but don't dominate it.
- Focus on the interview.
- Exude confidence, not arrogance.
- Eliminate street slang.
- Be honest, starting with your application and résumé.

Note. Some of the pointers come from Landrum and Davis (2007) and Martin (2007).

questions is a good idea. It is difficult to remember what someone said hours, days, or weeks later given the stress of the interview day. Box 5.9 provides a list of some additional pointers for the interview.

After the Interview

After the interview is complete, send a thank-you note. Since most interviewees do not send one, it will set you apart in a good way. Depending on the situation, a note card or even an e-mail will be sufficient. Calling the interviewer to deliver a thank you is not best. Unless you have genuine questions (e.g., you received another job offer and want to see where they are in their hiring process), it is best not to call.

Considering Job Offers

Be prepared for getting a job offer. In order to be prepared, you will want to have a minimum salary in mind. A good way to determine this amount is by developing a budget of your monthly expenses and multiplying these expenses by 12 to determine the yearly expenses. Once this number is calculated, multiply it by 1.35 to determine the approximate salary needed before taxes. Knowing this number can make the negotiation of salary easier. Also, keep in mind that the salary offered is rarely the highest amount the employer can afford. Employers assume the potential employee will negotiate, and as a result, they will hold back some of the salary to allow for this negotiation. Additional pieces to consider when offered a job are:

- Will you be able to pay your bills?
- What is the work environment like? Friendly/collegial?
- What opportunities exist for raises and advancement?
- Will the company help with relocation expenses?
- What are the benefits? Do they include parking, health insurance, dental insurance, life insurance, and retirement?
- How is vacation and sick time accrued?
- What type of office space and equipment are provided?
- Is there administrative support?
- Are there professional development opportunities?
- Are the hours flexible or set?
- If the job involves a client load or caseload, what is it?
- What is the cost of living in the community where you will be living and working? (This varies greatly. We recommend using one of the cost-of-living calculators online to approximate the difference between where you currently live and where the new job is located.)

Suggested Exercises

1. Using O*Net (online.onetcenter.org), investigate three careers that interest you.
   a. What is the average salary for that position in your state?
   b. What are the typical work activities?
2. Based on your investigation in Suggested Exercise 1, choose the career that most interests you and do an informational interview of someone in that field. The following link will provide assistance with structuring the interview (Crosby, 2002: www.bls.gov/opub/ooq/2002/summer/art03.pdf)
3. Utilizing one of the internet resources listed in this chapter, find a current job opening that requires a bachelor's degree in psychology.

   a. What is the position?
   b. Where is it located?
   c. What are the application procedures?
   d. What is the salary?
4. Using the information in this chapter develop two résumés.
   a. Base your first résumé on your current experiences, background, and training.
   b. Base your second résumé on what you hope to accomplish by the time you graduate.
5. Using the information from this chapter, write a cover letter for a position in the field that you want to pursue.

References

America's Career Resource Network. (n.d.). Retrieved from http://www.acrnetwork.org/about.htm

American Psychological Association. (2007). *APA guidelines for the undergraduate psychology major.* Washington, DC: Author. Retrieved from http://www.apa.org/ed/psymajor_guideline.pdf

Appleby, D. (2000, Spring). Job skills valued by employers who interview psychology majors. *Eye on Psi Chi, 4*(3), 17. Retrieved from http://www.psichi.org/pubs/articles/article_80.asp

Appleby, D. C. (2006). *Occupations of interest to psychology majors from the dictionary of occupational titles.* APA Division 2–Society for the Teaching of Psychology's Office of Teaching Resources in Psychology. Retrieved from http://www.teachpsych.org/otrp/resources/appleby06.pdf

Cardiff University Careers Service. (2006). *A careers service guide to . . . How to identify disability and diversity friendly employers.* Retrieved from http://www.cf.ac.uk/carsv/resources/How_to_Identify_Disability_and_Diversity_Friendly_Employers_Booklet.pdf

CareerOneStop. (n.d.). Retrieved from http://www.careeronestop.org/

CareerZone. (n.d.). Retrieved from http://www.nycareerzone.org/

Collegegrad.com. (2008). *Survey results detail what top entry level employers want most.* Retrieved from http://www.collegegrad.com/press/whatemployerswant.shtml

Crosby, O. (1999, Summer). Résumés, applications, and cover letters. *Occupational Outlook Quarterly, 43*(2), 3–14. Retrieved from www.bls.gov/opub/ooq/1999/summer/art01.pdf

Crosby, O. (2000, Summer). Employment interviewing: Seizing the opportunity and the job. *Occupational Outlook Quarterly, 44*(2), 14–21. Retrieved from http://www.bls.gov/opub/ooq/2000/summer/art02.pdf

Crosby, O. (2002, Summer). Informational interviewing: Get the inside scoop on careers. *Occupational Outlook Quarterly, 46*(2), 32–37. Retrieved from http://www.bls.gov/opub/ooq/2002/summer/art03.pdf

DeGalan, J., & Lambert, S. (2001). *Great jobs for psychology majors* (2nd ed.). Chicago: VGM Career Books.

Gehlhaus, D. (2007–2008, Winter). What can I do with my liberal arts degree? *Occupational Outlook Quarterly, 51*(4), 3–11. Retrieved from http://www.bls.gov/opub/ooq/2007/winter/art01.pdf

Jones, E. (2006, Summer). Internships: Previewing a profession. *Occupational Outlook Quarterly, 50*(2), 16–18. Retrieved from http://www.bls.gov/opub/ooq/2006/summer/art02.pdf

Landrum, R. E., & Davis, S. F. (2007). *The psychology major: Career options and strategies for success* (3rd ed.). Upper Saddle River, NJ: Pearson/Prentice Hall.

Lantz, C. (2008). *Psychology student employability guide: From university to career.* York, United Kingdom: The Higher Education Academy Psychology Network. Retrieved from http://www.psychology.heacademy.ac.uk/docs/pdf/p20080915_Employability_Guide.pdf

Lloyd, M. A., Kennedy, J. H., & Dewey, R.A. (1997, August 28). *Suggested courses to develop skills that prospective employers want.* Retrieved from http://www.psywww.com/careers/suggest.htm

Martin, C. (2007). *Interviewers' pet peeves.* Retrieved from http://career-advice.monster.com/interview-preparation/Interviewers-Pet-Peeves/home.aspx

National Association of Colleges and Employers. (2005). *Job outlook 2006.* Bethlehem, PA: Author. Retrieved from http://www.naceweb.org/pubs/JobOutlook/joboutlook2006/JO6.pdf

National Association of Colleges and Employers. (2007). *Job outlook 2008: November 2007.* Bethlehem, PA: Author. Retrieved from http://www.naceweb.org/pubs/JobOutlook/2008/JO8.pdf

Proudfoot, S. (2008, February). *Infobrief: An overview of science, engineering, and health graduates: 2006.* Washington, DC: National Science Foundation Directorate for Social, Behavioral, and Economic Sciences. Retrieved from http://www.nsf.gov/statistics/infbrief/nsf08304/nsf08304.pdf

Psychology-related career titles. (n.d.) Retrieved from http://www.uncwil.edu/stuaff/career/Majors/psychology.html

University of North Carolina Wilmington Career Center (n.d.). *Dress for success.* Retrieved from http://www.uncw.edu/stuaff/career/dressforsuccess.htm

U.S. Department of Education, National Center for Education Statistics. (2007). *Bachelor's, master's, and doctor's degrees conferred by degree-granting institu-* *tions, by sex of student, and field of study: 2005–06.* Retrieved from http://nces.ed.gov/programs/digest/ d07/tables/dt07_265.asp?referrer=list

Resources

- Many universities have career web pages. These sites are often more trustworthy than the general internet findings. Here are two examples:
  a. careerctr.kennesaw.edu/
  b. www.uncw.edu/stuaff/career/
- Résumé resources on the web – Be careful of online and paid services! We discourage online and paid résumé services because they often use templates instead of tailoring a person's information to specific jobs. In contrast, we recommend your university career center. Most university career centers will help you with résumé writing. Some helpful resources available online are:
  a. Crosby's (1999) "Resumes, Applications, and Cover Letters" (www.bls.gov/opub/ooq/ 1999/summer/art01.pdf)
  b. jobstar.org
  c. www.rileyguide.com
  d. www.eresumes.com
- General job search and preparation resources:
  a. http://resources.monster.com/
  b. www.quintcareers.com
  c. www.jobweb.com
  d. www.collegegrad.com
- Psi Chi – The National Honor Society in Psychology has dozens of brief articles on career preparation. Go to this link and browse *Eye on Psi Chi* articles related to "career preparation" on the drop-down menu: www.psichi.org/pubs/search.asp.
- O*Net Resource – online.onetcenter.org. Provides a wide variety of information on occupations.
- CareerOneStop – www.careeronestop.org. "A U.S. Department of Labor-sponsored website that offers career resources and workforce information to job seekers, students, businesses, and workforce professionals to foster talent development in a global economy."
- CareerZone – www.nycareerzone.org. "The CareerZone website brings together multiple sources of career and labor market information to make career exploration and planning for the future a little easier."
- America's Career Resource Network – www.acrnetwork.org. "ACRN is focused on helping students and adults make the best possible decisions about education, training and career development. ACRN helps learners identify their skills and interests, and plan an education and training pathway that makes the most of their natural abilities and leads directly to fulfilling work."
- Occupational Outlook Quarterly – http://www.bls.gov/opub/ooq/. Bureau of Labor Statistics' quarterly publication of occupation-related information. Topics include:
  a. What can I do with my liberal arts degree? (Gehlhaus, 2007–2008) www.bls.gov/opub/ ooq/2007/winter/art01.pdf
  b. Internships: Previewing a profession (Jones, 2006) www.bls.gov/opub/ooq/2006/summer/ art02.pdf

c. Employment interviewing: Seizing the opportunity and the job (Crosby, 2000) www.bls.gov/opub/ooq/2000/summer/art02.pdf

- Lantz, C. (2008). *Psychology student employability guide: From university to career.* York, United Kingdom: The Higher Education Academy Psychology Network. Link: http://www.psychology.heacademy.ac.uk/docs/pdf/p20080915_Employability_Guide.pdf

Topics covered include:
a. Assessing your interests
b. Creating a résumé
c. Networking
d. Interviewing

6

The Preprofessional Degree
Preparing for Graduate School

Introduction

As noted earlier, the undergraduate degree can be viewed from two perspectives. The first perspective views the bachelor's degree in psychology as a liberal arts degree. As such, the student pursuing this path has the primary goal of entering the job market upon graduation. The second perspective views the bachelor's degree in psychology as a preprofessional degree. This is similar to pre-dental, pre-medicine, and pre-law. As such, the student taking the preprofessional view of her/his bachelor's degree in psychology has the primary goal of gaining admission to graduate school either immediately upon graduation or at some point in the future. Although these perspectives have significant similarities (e.g., the same curriculum to complete the bachelor's degree), preparation issues significantly differ. This chapter addresses those differences with the hope that students will make the most of their undergraduate experience, preparing them for the competition involved in application to graduate school and success upon admission to the graduate program. Topics addressed in this chapter include deciding to go to graduate school, choosing the best courses, making good grades, gaining research experience, gaining field/work experience, establishing a mentoring relationship, getting involved in professional organizations, getting involved on-campus, and getting involved in the community.

Is Graduate School Right for You?

Before getting into specific graduate school preparatory issues, we would first like to look at graduate school from a broader perspective. As discussed in the chapter that focuses on applying to graduate school, the application process is no easy task and neither is graduate school itself. In fact, the *10-year* doctoral completion rate is only 65.1% for psychology (Council of Graduate Schools PhD Completion Project,

2008). Given the difficulty, why should someone want to go to graduate school? The most obvious reason is that most of the specialized skills associated with psychology are gained *only* at the graduate level (e.g., program evaluation, employer/employee consultation, psychotherapy, psychological testing, and advanced research skills). The undergraduate degree in psychology provides the solid foundation for the acquisition of these skills at the graduate level. The second part of this book spends considerable time reviewing the graduate-level skills learned in the specific subfields of psychology. In short, there are a number of skills learned in graduate school that makes the process not only worthwhile but also very enjoyable. Salazar and Frincke (2005) note 15 skills developed and improved during graduate training, regardless of the subfield studied. These skills include understanding group dynamics, objective thinking, ability to argue and defend different viewpoints, computer skills, and the scientific method. Box 6.1 provides a list of all 15 skills.

Another, often overlooked reason to complete graduate training is employment status and prospects. A survey of recent doctorate recipients reported an unemployment rate of 3.1% (Wicherski & Kohout, 2007). Furthermore, 77.1% of those surveyed indicated that the employment position they currently held was their first choice. In terms of how long it took to find employment, 41.4% found their current position prior to completing their graduate program, and 32% found their position within 3 months. Only 7.8% took more than six months to find their current position. Last but definitely not least, respondents to the survey indicated an overall positive level of satisfaction with their current position.

Box 6.1 Skills Developed and Improved During Graduate School

Ability to function in various roles/environments
Teaching skills (inside and outside the classroom)
Interviewing skills
Public speaking skills
Computer skills
Ability to argue and defend different viewpoints
Scientific method skills
Research methods, data analysis, and statistic skills
Ability to integrate information from multiple sources
Ability to evaluate information/data critically
Ability to understand group dynamics
Ability to appreciate and work with differing viewpoints
Ability to accept criticism and rejection
Objective thinking skills
Ability to tolerate and work with ambiguity

Note. Information comes from Salazar and Frincke (2005).

Even given these very positive attributes, how do you know if graduate school is right for you? Over the years, authors have attempted to provide some guidance to students trying to answer this question (e.g., Fretz & Stang, 1988; Keith-Spiegel, 1991; and Kuther, 2006). Regardless of the reference used, all urge students who are considering graduate study to be honest with themselves. For example, it takes a great deal of self-motivation and organizational skills to succeed in graduate school. Because these are generally viewed as positive attributes, students may tend to indicate possessing these qualities when in reality they do not. An inaccurate self-assessment would be a mistake as it sets you up for failure. Box 6.2 provides some personal qualities and behaviors to evaluate when making your decision. We provide them with the hope that you will pursue the path that is the best fit for you.

Box 6.2 Twenty Personal Qualities and Behaviors Consistent With Graduate Training

How accurately do the following qualities and behaviors describe you?

1. Comfortable living below the poverty line
   - Although many programs offer tuition remission and stipends, rarely is the stipend enough to prevent borrowing money.
2. Enjoys writing
   - Most courses require extensive writing assignments. Interestingly, graduate school professors often give a *maximum* length to term papers as opposed to minimum lengths for undergraduates.
3. Enjoys doing research
   - Depending on the type of program, the majority of your time outside of your regular coursework will be spent doing research for your professors, working on your own research (e.g., your master's thesis or doctoral dissertation), and helping colleagues with their research.
4. Good with statistics
   - Most programs require at least a couple of advanced statistics courses. Some require one each semester. Regardless, students will be required to use and understand statistics in their own research on a regular basis.
5. Enjoys reading psychology books and journals
   - Background reading consumes significant amounts of time. This reading includes not only course reading but also reading related to your research. This reading includes large amounts of original empirical research too. Luckily, it is typically in an area you enjoy!
6. Can delay gratification (short term and long term)
   - Graduate students often make difficult decisions, putting off personal preferences for necessities that serve the ultimate goal. For example, it is not uncommon for graduate students to:

    a.   Study instead of going to a party or watching television

    b.   Eat at home instead of at restaurants

    c.   Have roommates instead of living alone

7.   Enjoys studying for hours at a time (e.g., 6–8 hours per session, multiple times per week)

- Although graduate students certainly have fun too, a significant part of their time is spent studying. When not in class or in their lab (i.e., doing research, collecting data, analyzing data), they are often studying. Unlike many of the courses you will have in your bachelor's program, graduate school is a building process in which you are required to retain information not only for the test but also for the duration of the program and your career.

8.   Can easily concentrate

- Successful graduate students are able to focus their attention on a particular course, project, situation, etc., even though other forces may be impinging on them (e.g., a noisy roommate, neighbor, television).

9.   Organized

- Graduate school requires the ability to get and stay organized. This is especially important given the large quantity of material to be learned and increased time commitments.

10.   Gets above average/excellent grades

- Most graduate programs do not allow any Cs. In fact, the expectation is "A" work in all courses. Bs, although sufficient in most programs, suggest that you may be struggling.

11.   Desires graduate training not because of status (e.g., "being called Doctor")

- The novelty of being called "Doctor" soon wears off. More times than not, when someone calls you "doctor," they need/want something from you.

12.   Desires graduate training not because of an imagined high salary

- Although salary is significantly greater with a graduate degree, few areas of psychology command top salaries. Industrial-Organizational Psychology is an exception.

13.   Strong desire to learn

- Without a strong desire to learn, it is very easy to get sidetracked from your ultimate goal of a graduate education.

14.   Has strong interpersonal skills

- Graduate students routinely interact with a variety of individuals. Interpersonal skills are very important in dealing with fellow graduate students, professors, department staff, and your own students (for those who are teaching assistants).

15.   Can receive and respond effectively to critical feedback

- As a graduate student, you will receive vast quantities of critical feedback. With the feedback comes the expectation that you will remedy any weakness immediately.

16. Enjoys school and the school environment (i.e., class, library, labs)
   • Graduate students spend the majority of their time in the academic environment. There are few escapes beyond holidays with family. Oftentimes your social activities and even your roommates are program-related.
17. Driven to accomplish
   • Graduate students are expected to be self-starters. Very little hand-holding is provided. In fact, the more supervision required for some activities, the more negatively you will be viewed by the professors. There is an expectation that you will seek out the answers to questions on your own, not relying on your professors for all the answers.
18. Devoted to the discipline
   • Graduate students in psychology develop a clear and strong identity within the discipline. Although some of the response may be self-protective since they have invested a lot of themselves in the graduate school venture, it is uncommon to find a graduate student that is not clear in his or her commitment to the discipline.
19. Does not mind (enjoys) giving presentations
   • Graduate students routinely give presentations. These include presentations in their own graduate courses, teaching undergraduate courses, and presenting research at conferences.
20. Can tolerate ambiguity
   • As you are learning in your undergraduate program, psychology is not a clear-cut science. Ambiguity is a cornerstone to the discipline. Graduate students must tolerate and in some cases embrace this aspect. For some subfields of psychology (e.g., clinical psychology), decisions that affect people's lives must be made even in the face of uncertainty.

Course Selection

The American Psychological Association (APA) annually publishes an excellent resource for students investigating different graduate school programs, *Graduate Study in Psychology* (GSP; see APA, 2010). Historically, GSP included information on courses required/recommended by specific graduate programs. In fact, Smith (1985) and Lawson (1995) summarized the information found in GSP. Remarkably, their findings were similar. Mentioned in more detail in the Careers in Forensic Psychology chapter, Helms and Mayhew (2006) found similar findings when investigating forensic psychology programs. Although GSP no longer provides this information, it is arguable given the overlap in these studies that these same courses would be a solid foundation for a student preparing for graduate school today. Box 6.3 presents an alphabetical listing of all courses rated as required/recommended/optional in these three studies. Regardless of the program type (i.e., experimental, clinical, or forensic), the research foundation courses (i.e., Research Methods, Experimental Psychology, and Statistics)

Box 6.3 Alphabetical Listing of Required/ Recommended/Optional Coursework for Graduate School Applicants

Abnormal Psychology
Child Development
Cognitive Psychology
Developmental Psychology
Experimental Psychology
History and Systems
Introduction to Forensic Psychology
Learning
Perception
Personality Psychology
Physiological Psychology
Principles of Psychological Testing
Research Methods
Social Psychology
Statistics

Note. These courses were listed by at least one of the studies (Helms & Mayhew, 2006; Lawson, 1995; Smith, 1985).

dominate graduate programs' preferences, once again underscoring the scientific basis of psychology. In addition, clinical and counseling psychology programs tend to prefer foundational courses in Abnormal Psychology, Personality Psychology, Developmental Psychology, Principles of Psychological Testing, and Learning. Along with the research foundation courses, the experimental psychology graduate programs (e.g., developmental psychology and social psychology) tend to prefer courses in Learning, Social Psychology, Abnormal Psychology, Personality Psychology, Developmental Psychology, and Physiological Psychology.

In addition to choosing your psychology coursework wisely, you should also choose your non-psychology coursework wisely. We discourage taking "fluff" courses (e.g., sailing, golf). If you must do so, wait until your very last semester so that they do not appear on your transcripts submitted with your graduate school applications. Graduate faculty who review applications tend to view these courses as a waste of valuable time, time that could have been spent doing research or minoring in a related area. For example, electives in the math and natural sciences areas are strongly encouraged. In fact, we recommend filling at least a portion of your electives with several courses in statistics. Most math departments offer upper-level courses in statistics. Obviously if you want to pursue a graduate degree in animal behavior, physiological psychology, or neuroscience, we recommend biology and chemistry coursework too.

Timing of your coursework is also important. Discussed in the next chapter, some graduate programs require applicants to take the Psychology Subject Test (a standardized test developed by Educational Testing Service). As the name indicates, this test covers all areas of psychology. Students usually take it during the Fall semester of their senior year, immediately prior to applying to graduate school programs for admission the following Fall semester. As a result, students are strongly encouraged not to postpone taking the "harder" psychology courses (e.g., Cognitive Psychology, Sensation and Perception, Physiological Psychology) until their senior year. Doing so will put you at a significant disadvantage when taking this test. Even if the graduate programs you want to attend do not require it, graduate faculty will want to see excellent grades in these upper-level courses on your transcript. This means that you will need to complete at least some of them in time so that they show up on your transcript. Moreover, we encourage seeking opportunities to accentuate your courses through additional work. For example, many universities have an honors program or college that allows students to explore required (and additional) coursework in more depth. Exceeding the required minimum in your coursework demonstrates your commitment to education.

An additional timing issue is starting your major coursework early. We recommend beginning your coursework for the Psychology major in your first semester of college by taking General Psychology (or Introduction to Psychology). Lower-level coursework is often required prior to taking any of the upper-level coursework. Additionally, you will want to take your research foundation coursework (e.g., Research Methods, Experimental Psychology, and Statistics) as early as possible. This is important because faculty will generally not allow you to work with them on research projects until you have successfully completed the research foundation coursework. Discussed in a later section of this chapter, research experience is almost always a top ranked criteria when evaluating graduate school applicants (e.g., Lawson, 1995).

Students also have concerns about withdrawing from courses. Although the preference is for students to have no withdrawals on their transcript, students should have no more than one or two withdrawals at most. The reason for this preference is that withdrawals indicate one of two possible personal attributes of the student. First, it may indicate that the student took on more responsibility than he/she could handle. Not knowing your limits is not a good attribute. Second, a withdrawal may indicate that the student could not do the work. Given the significant increase in difficulty of graduate work, not being able to successfully complete an *undergraduate* course is not a good sign for later success in graduate school. In short, withdrawals only signal and draw attention to potential negative attributes.

Grades and Grade Point Average

A student's grades and grade point average (GPA) are very important pieces of the graduate school application. As a result, it is imperative to begin your undergraduate career strong and stay strong. In other words, it is difficult to raise a low GPA. The next question students almost always ask is "What is a *good enough* GPA?" Although it varies by program, recent research indicates that the average *minimum* required overall GPA of applicants in 2003–2004 was 3.11 for doctoral programs and 2.92 for masters' programs (Norcross, Kohout, & Wicherski, 2005). The associated *minimum* required Psychology GPA was 3.17 for doctoral programs and 3.05 for master's programs. However, the minimum required is significantly different than what is actually accepted. In fact for these same years (2003–2004), the study found that the *actual* overall GPA was 3.54 for applicants accepted to doctoral programs and 3.37 for applicants accepted to masters' programs. For some programs (e.g., clinical psychology PhD programs), the *actual* over-all GPAs can be close to 4.0. Knowing this information, students will often mistakenly opt to take "fluff" courses to raise their GPAs. As noted in the previous section, this is unwise. The reason it is unwise is that graduate school faculty expect (and verify) that the GPA a student has is based on an adequate, if not rigorous, curriculum/coursework sequence. Also, keep in mind that calculation of your GPA when applying to graduate school includes all coursework at all universities attended. This includes the summer course you took at the local community college. Your GPA also includes the grade you received in the course you "retook" for a higher grade plus the grade in the original course. It also includes your first semester of college before you transferred to your current college. In short, it includes *everything*. The GPA that graduate schools want you to report is all inclusive. Earlier chapters in this book provide some concrete strategies for improving the likelihood of success in college and in the psychology major.

Research Experience

In addition to objective criteria (e.g., GPA), nonobjective criteria (e.g., letters of recom-mendation, personal statements, and interviews) are also used to evaluate applicants to graduate programs. Research experience is one of these nonobjective criteria. In fact, experience helping professors with their research projects and experience collaborating with a professor on your own research idea are excellent preparation for graduate school. Box 6.4 provides a list of some of the benefits of engaging in research.

Box 6.4   The Benefits of Research Experience

- Acquire knowledge and skills outside of the classroom (hands-on experience)
- Work individually with a faculty member
- Contribute to the scientific literature/advance science (including possible authorship credit)
- Exposure to research techniques
- Practice written and oral communication skills by preparing articles for submission to journals and conferences and presenting at conferences
- Establish a mentoring relationship

Note. Information comes from Landrum (2002).

Appropriately enough, the importance of research experience is verified by research studies. Smith (1985), Lawson (1995), and Norcross et al. (2005) reviewed the importance of having this experience when applying to graduate school. All three studies relied on analysis of data provided in the GSP. Regardless of the years reviewed or whether reviewing masters or doctoral programs, research experience was rated very highly.

Two additional studies surveyed graduate school faculty. Keith-Spiegel, Tabachnick, and Spiegel (1994) surveyed 123 graduate faculty members regarding the importance of a host of nonobjective criteria. Research experience resulting in authorship credit in a peer-reviewed publication received the highest overall rating (i.e., a 4.45 out of a possible 5). In a more recent survey of faculty involved in selecting students for graduate study in forensic psychology, research activity received a mean of 2.94 out of a possible 3 in importance (Helms & Mayhew, 2006). In fact, its mean clearly placed it as the most important nonobjective criteria in the study, ahead of letters of recommendation and personal statements. In summary, it appears that regardless of the research methodology used, research experience enjoys a place at the top in terms of its evaluative importance for graduate school applicants. It is important to highlight the fact that this finding remains consistent over time.

So how do you get involved in research? First you will want to begin early. Because relationships with faculty take time to develop and research takes time to complete, your first year of college is not too early to begin. Ask your professors what kind of research is being done and if you can help. Some advanced students may need some help with their research studies too. Offer to collect and enter data for a professor. Offer to gather background literature for his or her study. These initial activities will demonstrate your commitment to research and increase the likelihood that a faculty member will include you in his or her later projects as well as work with you on developing your own project. Also, you will want to branch out and work with multiple faculty members too. As discussed in the next chapter, you will need at least three letters of recommendation to accompany your applications to graduate school. As a result, you will want to make sure that at least two of the three faculty members who write letters for you will be able to address your research experience first-hand.

An additional point needs to be kept in mind. Students often start gaining research experience too late (e.g., their last year). As a result, they do not have time to advance through the process of assisting a professor to developing/completing their own study. Because research studies take time to complete, beginning a study during your last year will likely not result in a completed project before it is time to send out graduate school applications. (Most applications are due in late November and December for admission the following Fall semester.) Also, Kaiser, Kaiser, Richardson, and Fox (2007) found that not all research experiences are valued equally by graduate programs. The results of their survey clearly indicated that four types of research experiences outranked the others. These top experiences, in order of importance, were:

1. research experience that resulted in a refereed/peer-reviewed publication,
2. publishing a senior thesis,
3. first author of a refereed/peer-reviewed publication, and
4. giving a paper presentation at a regional conference.

As can be seen from these results, bringing the research project to fruition and disseminating the results are very important. Given that seeing an article accepted and actually published can take a year or more after submission and that deadlines for some conference submissions can be six months in advance, getting started early is imperative. Fortunately, you know this now which puts you ahead of many of your competitors.

Internships, Field Practica, and Work Experience

Internships, field practica, and work experience can be valuable points of reference not only for the student but also the graduate faculty reviewing the student's application. Graduate faculty members routinely hear from perspective students that they are really interested in this particular area of psychology, whatever *this* area is. When students are asked *how* they know they are interested in this area, the graduate faculty member often receives a blank stare or an equally unsophisticated response of "I just know." As you already know, intuition does not hold much value in this field. On the other hand, a student that can support his or her interest in a particular field with first-hand experience of working with a particular population (e.g., children) or in a particular setting (e.g., a correctional environment) places herself or himself above the pack of other applicants or interviewees. Walter (2007) provides the following six benefits in pursuing this type of experience:

1. Clarifies a student's interests and goals
2. Develop skills
3. Provides networking opportunities
4. Enhances graduate school applications
5. Allows application of what has been learned
6. Increases awareness of your own strengths and weaknesses.

Opportunities to gain experience are typically available to those students who are genuinely interested. Oftentimes, departments have field practicum courses, and university career services centers and faculty have connections in the community to jumpstart an experience. Opportunities vary from being an undergraduate teaching assistant for those with the goal of entering academe to being a behavioral technician at a program for children with developmental disabilities for those interested in being a clinical psychologist. Even in universities that do not have these types of opportunities, community settings often have volunteer programs (e.g., psychiatric hospitals). Regardless, you will want an experience that provides ample supervision and structure. Unstructured and unsupervised activities typically do not carry much weight on applications. Additionally, given time and financial demands, some students have found paying jobs in related settings that prove useful to their eventual career goals. For those that take time off before going to graduate school, working in a field that is directly related to the graduate program you wish to pursue is very important. Last but not least, a supervisor of your field-related work is a possible source for another letter of recommendation too.

Mentoring

A mentor is a person who is able to provide ongoing direction to a novice seeking to enter the same field. In academe, a mentor is a professor who guides the student through his or her education, always keeping in mind the student's career goals. The guidance provided by a mentor is based not only on experience but also on what the research has shown to be helpful when pursuing certain goals (e.g., encouraging research experience). In searching for a mentor and beginning a mentoring relationship, a student should keep in mind three characteristics: interpersonal skills, personal attributes, and professional competencies (Appleby, 1999). Box 6.5 lists the four components of each characteristic.

Although comfort with the mentor should come first, the student will do well to choose a mentor in a field similar to the one he or she wants to pursue. For example, although a clinical psychologist could provide some excellent general perspectives on preparing for graduate school in social psychology, a better resource and potential mentor would be a social psychologist. In this example, the social psychologist would likely be more familiar with the available training programs and have connections to graduate faculty in the social psychology area. In looking at Box 6.5, you might be thinking that deciphering who might be a good mentor is impossible or at least too

---

Box 6.5   Characteristics and Components of an Effective Mentor

Interpersonal Skills
   Caring and Encouraging
   Promoting and Sponsoring
   Supporting and Protecting
   Challenging and Demanding
Personal Attributes
   Mature and Wise
   Friendly and Optimistic
   Admired and Respected
   Trustworthy and Dependable
Professional Competencies
   Qualified and Competent
   Experienced and Seasoned
   Knowledgeable and Informative
   Professionally Involved and Active

Note. Information comes from Appleby (1999).

complicated and time consuming to be useful. However, a couple of tools can help you measure a potential mentor in advance.

1. Base part of your decision on having had the mentor as a professor.
2. Gravitate to the more challenging and demanding professors.
3. Seek out the professors who generally work with students.
4. Focus on those professors who produce (i.e., professors who have students regularly presenting at conferences and being accepted into graduate schools).

These four pointers should make the process significantly easier for you.

Getting Involved in Professional Organizations

Membership in a professional organization provides many and varied opportunities for the undergraduate student. Unfortunately, Koch (2006) notes that many students join professional organizations simply to list them on their vita or résumé. However, students interested in really getting involved in their respective field are encouraged to join and get active. In fact, most professional organizations provide student memberships at significantly reduced cost.

One of the benefits of joining a professional organization as a student member includes eligibility to apply for travel awards and research grants specifically for students. For example, the RiSE-UP Award from the Association for Psychological Science (APS) aims "to cultivate scholarly research in psychological fields related to socially and economically under-represented populations, as well as to acknowledge outstanding research conducted by student members" (www.psychologicalscience.org/apssc/riseup). Submissions for this award are reviewed by student members. As a result, even though you may not submit a grant/award proposal you could volunteer to review other students' proposals. Experience providing feedback to colleagues/peers, especially in regard to research, is an excellent skill to highlight on a graduate school application. APS's Student Caucus may have a representative already on your campus. To find out, refer to the web link listed in Box 6.6. If your campus does not have a representative, this is another opportunity for you to become involved!

Benefits of belonging to a professional association also include the opportunity to network with other students and professors at other universities. Most student memberships also include the organization's publications. For example, student affiliates of the APA receive the association's main journal, the *American Psychologist*, as well as their monthly magazine, *Monitor on Psychology*. These publications give you the opportunity to stay abreast of some of the current happenings in the field.

Because it may be more difficult to get involved in the larger national associations (e.g., APA), the APA divisions, the regional psychological associations, and the

Box 6.6   Professional Organizations

National Organizations
- American Psychological Association – www.apa.org/students
- Association for Psychological Science (APS) – www.psychologicalscience.org
- Association for Psychological Science – Student Caucus – www.psychologicalscience.org/apssc

Regional Associations
- Eastern Psychological Association – www.easternpsychological.org
- Midwestern Psychological Association – www.midwesternpsych.org
- New England Psychological Association – www.nepa-info.org
- Rocky Mountain Psychological Association – www.rockymountainpsych.org
- Southeastern Psychological Association – www.sepaonline.com
- Southwestern Psychological Association – www.swpsych.org
- Western Psychological Association – www.westernpsych.org

APA Divisions
- The APA has 54 divisions devoted to specific interest areas (e.g., Psychotherapy, Addictions, and Developmental Psychology).
- A list of all divisions along with links to their respective websites can be found at: www.apa.org/about/division.html

Diversity-Related Organizations
- Asian American Psychological Association – www.aapaonline.org
- Association of Black Psychologists – www.abpsi.org
- Society for the Psychological Study of Lesbian, Gay, and Bisexual Issues – www.apadivision44.org
- Society for the Psychological Study of Men and Masculinity – www.apa.org/divisions/div51
- Society for the Psychology of Women – www.apa.org/divisions/div35
- Society for the Study of Ethnic Minority Issues – www.apa.org/divisions/div45

State/Territory/Provincial Psychological Associations
- A list of all state/territory and provincial psychological associations with links to their respective websites can be found at: www.apa.org/practice/refer.html

International Psychological Associations
- A list of international psychological associations with their respective websites and contact information can be found at: www.apa.org/international/natlorgs.html

state/territory/provincial psychological associations may provide an opportunity for involvement. Box 6.6 provides links to some resources to get you started. Granted this type of activity is not as highly valued as research experience. However, being actively involved in a professional organization clearly demonstrates your current and long-term commitment to the field. This commitment is especially visible when your activity level in the organization is high and has occurred for an extended period of time (i.e., more than a year).

Getting Involved on Campus

Similar to professional organizations, getting involved on campus by being active in psychology-oriented clubs and honor societies demonstrates commitment to the field. This commitment and involvement will be noticed by the faculty members in your department, including those who will be writing letters of recommendation for you. The two most common student organizations are a psychology club and Psi Chi – The National Honor Society in Psychology. For those students at junior and community colleges, Psi Beta – The National Honor Society in Psychology for Community and Junior Colleges is sometimes available. Although most psychology clubs do not have requirements for membership, the honor societies do. These requirements include completion of a certain number of psychology courses and a minimum 3.0 GPA on a 4.0 scale. If you do not have Psi Chi or Psi Beta at your university or college, consider starting a chapter. The first author (Helms) was a founding member of the Psi Chi chapter at his undergraduate university. Involvement in one of these organizations is typically more accessible and readily identifiable in comparison to external professional organizations. However, the same principle applies; simply being a member is not enough. The student must be active. Fortunately, opportunities to serve in student organizations that are related to psychology are usually available. Some of the opportunities include being an officer (e.g., president, treasurer) and participating in fundraising activities (e.g., raising money for a local charity via a bake sale).

Community Service and Extracurricular Activities

Although potentially beneficial educationally, most graduate programs do not rate community service and extracurricular activities very high when evaluating graduate school applicants. In fact, these activities are generally last in the rankings (Norcross et al., 2005). This does not mean that these activities are not given any value. Regardless, given time and resource limitations, students are encouraged to focus their efforts on research experiences first and the other activities noted in this chapter prior to devoting time to activities in this realm (e.g., fraternity or sorority involvement).

Box 6.7 Timeframe of Suggested Activities for Preparing for Graduate School

First Year
- In addition to focusing on your university's general education coursework, complete lower-level psychology coursework.
- Begin taking the required math and science coursework along with statistics coursework.
- Begin attending department activities (e.g., join and participate in the psychology club).
- Get involved with research by asking professors if you can help them with their research.
- Identify a potential mentor by observing his or her activities inside and outside the department.
- Attend a local/state/regional psychology conference.

Second Year
- Complete the research foundation coursework (e.g., Research Methods and Experimental Psychology).
- Join Psi Chi and become involved in its activities.
- Join a professional association and become involved.
- Increase your research activity.
- Discuss with a faculty member the possibility of developing your own research idea.
- Attend another local/state/regional psychology conference.

Third Year
- Take the majority of your upper-level psychology coursework in preparation for the Graduate Record Exam Psychology Subject Test.
- Hold an office in Psi Chi or the Psychology Club.
- Become involved with RiSE-UP in APS or similar research-oriented activity.
- Complete first research study with a professor and present it at a conference.
- Work with your professor to submit manuscript to a peer-reviewed journal.
- Begin work with another professor on research.

Fourth Year
- Continue research activities with at least two professors.
- Present another study at a conference.
- Work with your professor to submit the new research to a peer-reviewed journal.
- Complete a field practicum, teaching assistantship, internship, etc.
- Maintain level of activity in the organizations.

Note. Specific information on the application process and timeframe is provided in the Applying to Graduate School chapter.

Suggested Exercises

1. Using your department's web page, investigate two psychology faculty members who may be potential mentors to you.
   a. In what area of psychology is his/her degree?
   b. What research does he/she do?
   c. Has she/he published any articles? (If so, find a recent one and read it.)
   d. Does she/he ever work with students? If so, how can you tell?
   e. Does his/her research interest you?
   f. Contact the professor you are most interested in working with and ask if he/she needs any help on a project.
2. Obtain a copy of your university's student handbook that includes descriptions of the courses offered throughout the university. (Typically, a listing can also be found online too.) Based on your ultimate educational and career goals, plan out the remainder of your undergraduate education. Be sure to include courses in the areas recommended in this chapter (e.g., upper-level statistics courses).
3. Use Box 6.2 "Twenty Personal Qualities and Behaviors Consistent with Graduate Training" for this exercise. Rate each of the personal qualities on a scale from 1 (Not at all Like Me) to 5 (Absolutely Like Me). Sum your ratings. Answer the following questions.
   a. Does the number surprise you?
   b. Which qualities are most like you?
   c. Which are least like you?
   d. Which do you think will be the most difficult for you?

Suggested Readings

American Psychological Association. (2007). *Getting in: A step-by-step plan for gaining admission to graduate school in psychology* (2nd ed.). Washington, DC: Author.

Buskist, W., & Burke, C. (2007). *Preparing for graduate study in psychology: 101 questions and answers* (2nd ed.). Malden, MA: Blackwell.

Keith-Spiegel, P., & Wiederman, M. W. (2000). *The complete guide to graduate school admission: Psychology, counseling, and related professions* (2nd ed.). Mahwah, NJ: Lawrence Erlbaum Associates Publishers.

References

American Psychological Association. (2010). *Graduate study in psychology: 2010*. Washington, DC: Author.

Appleby, D. (1999, Spring). Choosing a mentor. *Eye on Psi Chi, 3*(3), 38–39.

Association for Psychological Science. (2008). *RiSE-UP research award*. Retrieved from http://www.psychologicalscience.org/apssc/awards/riseup.cfm

Council of Graduate Schools PhD Completion Project. (2008). *Program completion and attrition data*. Retrieved from http://www.phdcompletion.org/quantitative/program.asp

Fretz, B. R., & Stang, D. J. (1988). *Preparing for graduate study in psychology: Not for seniors only!* Washington, DC: American Psychological Association.

Helms, J. L., & Mayhew, L. L. (2006). *Undergraduate preparation for graduate training in forensic psychology*. APA Division 2–Society for the Teaching of Psychology's Office of Teaching Resources in Psychology. Retrieved from http://teachpsych.org/otrp/resources/helms06.pdf

Kaiser, J. C., Kaiser, A. J., Richardson, A. J., & Fox, E. J. (2007, Winter). Perceptions of graduate admission directors: Undergraduate student research experiences: Are all research experiences rated equally? *Eye on Psi Chi, 11*(2), 22–24.

Keith-Spiegel, P. (1991). *The complete guide to graduate school admission: Psychology and related fields.* Hillsdale, NJ: Erlbaum.

Keith-Spiegel, P., Tabachnick, B. G., & Spiegel, G. B. (1994). When demand exceeds supply: Second-order criteria used by graduate school selection committees. *Teaching of Psychology, 21,* 79–81.

Koch, C. (2006, Fall). Student memberships lead to greater opportunities in psychology. *Eye on Psi Chi, 11*(1), 27–28.

Kuther, T. L. (2006). *The psychology major's handbook* (2nd ed.). Belmont, CA: Thomson/ Wadsworth.

Landrum, R. E. (2002, Winter). Maximizing under-graduate opportunities: The value of research and other experiences. *Eye on Psi Chi, 6*(2), 15–18.

Lawson, T. J. (1995). Gaining admission into gradu-ate programs in psychology: An update. *Teaching of Psychology, 22,* 225–227.

Norcross, J. C., Kohout, J. L., & Wicherski, M. (2005). Graduate study in psychology: 1971 to 2004. *American Psychologist, 60,* 959–975.

Salazar, M., & Frincke, J. (2005, April). *Yesterday, today, and tomorrow; Careers in psychology: 2005, What students need to know.* Paper presented at the annual convention of the Western Psychological Association, Portland, OR.

Smith, R. A. (1985). Advising beginning psychology majors for graduate school. *Teaching of Psychology, 12,* 194–198.

Walter, T. J. (2007, Spring). The undergraduate psychology internship: Benefits, selection, and making the most of your experience. *Eye on Psi Chi, 11*(3), 24–26.

Wicherski, M., & Kohout, J. (2007). *2005 doctorate employment survey.* Washington, DC: American Psychological Association's Center for Psychology Workforce Analysis and Research. Retrieved from http://research.apa.org/des05.html

Resources

- APA Science Directorate: Lists resources to help undergraduate students find research experiences and internships. http://www.apa.org/science/undergradopps.html
- Psi Beta – The National Honor Society in Psychology for Community and Junior Colleges: www.psibeta.org
- Psi Chi – The National Honor Society in Psychology: www.psichi.org
  - *Eye on Psi Chi* Magazine (www.psichi.org/pubs/eye/home.asp): Regularly provides career-related resources; searchable database

7

The Preprofessional Degree
Applying to Graduate School

Introduction

In the last chapter, we began the discussion of how you can prepare during your undergraduate years for graduate training in psychology. We continue that discussion in this chapter by taking the process to the next level. This chapter examines the procedures and expectations typically involved in successfully applying to graduate school. Topics include preparing for entrance exams (i.e., the Graduate Record Exam and Psychology Subject Test), selecting appropriate graduate programs, preparing vitae and statements of intent, preparing application materials, interviewing, and making decisions about the program's fit with your goals and interests.

The Subfields of Psychology

Before diving into the application process, it is important for you to begin narrowing your interest areas. To help you accomplish this task we have listed here some of the main subfield areas of psychology. Although each of these areas is covered in more detail in the second part of the book, a brief description is provided here to give you some ideas as you begin exploring various graduate programs. However, the list is by no means complete. In fact, the book *Graduate Study in Psychology* (GSP) by the American Psychological Association (APA; 2010) lists over 100 areas of study in its index. For now, we will focus on these.

Experimental Psychology

Experimental psychology is the scientific study of psychological phenomenon. The two major organizations devoted to experimental psychology are the Association for

Psychological Science (APS; http://www.psychologicalscience.org/) and APA Division 3 – Experimental Psychology (http://www.apa.org/divisions/div3/).

Developmental Psychology

Developmental psychology is the scientific study of "age-related changes that occur as a person progresses from conception to death" (Weiten, 2008, p. 306). Three of the major organizations devoted to developmental psychology are APA Division 7 – Developmental Psychology (http://ecp.fiu.edu/APA/div7/), the Society for Research in Child Development (http://www.srcd.org/), and APA Division 20 – Adult Development and Aging (http://apadiv20.phhp.ufl.edu/).

Social Psychology

Social psychology is the scientific study of the "influences that people have upon the beliefs and behaviors of others" (Aronson, 2004, p. 5). The major organization devoted to this subfield is APA Division 8 – Society for Personality and Social Psychology (http://www.spsp.org/).

Cognitive Psychology

Cognitive psychology is the scientific study of how people think. It includes contributions from the diverse areas of memory, language processing, and decision making. Two of the major organizations devoted to cognitive psychology are the Cognitive Neuroscience Society (http://www.cogneurosociety.org/) and the Cognitive Science Society (http://cognitivesciencesociety.org/).

Physiological Psychology

Physiological psychology (also known as biological psychology and behavioral neuroscience) is the scientific study of the biology of behavior. To learn more about this subfield visit APA's Division 6 – Behavioral Neuroscience and Comparative Psychology (http://www.apa.org/divisions/div6/).

Industrial and Organizational Psychology

Industrial and organizational (I/O) psychology is the scientific study of people in work/business organizations. I/O psychology is both a research and applied field of study. The major organization devoted to this subfield is APA's Division 14 – Society for Industrial and Organizational Psychology (http://www.siop.org/).

Clinical Psychology

Clinical psychology integrates theory, science, and practice in an effort to "understand, predict, and alleviate maladjustment, disability, and discomfort" and to "promote human adaptation, adjustment, and personal development" (Society of Clinical Psychology, n.d.; http://www.apa.org/divisions/div12/aboutcp.html). The major organization devoted to clinical psychology is APA's Division 12 – Society of Clinical Psychology (http://www.apa.org/divisions/div12/).

Counseling Psychology

Counseling psychology integrates theory, science, and practice in an effort to promote "personal, educational, vocational, and group adjustment in a variety of settings" (Society of Counseling Psychology, n.d.; http://www.div17.org/about.html). In addition to information provided later in the text, more information about counseling psychology may be found at APA's Division 17 – Society of Counseling Psychology (http://www.div17.org/).

School Psychology

School psychology is "concerned with the science and practice of psychology with children, youth, families; learners of all ages; and the schooling process" (APA, 2008; http://www.apa.org/crsppp/schpsych.html). The two major organizations devoted to school psychology are APA Division 16 – School Psychology (http://www.indiana.edu/~div16/index.html) and the National Association of School Psychologists (http://www.nasponline.org/).

Educational Psychology

Educational psychology is the subfield of psychology devoted to improving "curriculum design, achievement testing, teacher training, and other aspects of the educational process" (Weiten, 2008, p. 18). APA's Division 15 – Educational Psychology is the major organization devoted to this subfield (http://www.apa.org/divisions/div15/).

Exercise and Sport Psychology

Exercise and sport psychology is "the scientific study of the psychological factors that are associated with participation and performance in sport, exercise, and other types of physical activity" (APA Division 47, 2008; http://www.apa47.org/studInfo.php). Two of the major organizations devoted to exercise and sport psychology are APA's Division 47 Exercise and Sport Psychology (www.apa47.org) and the Association for Applied Sport Psychology (http://www.appliedsportpsych.org/).

Health Psychology

Health psychology is an interdisciplinary field devoted to promoting, improving, and maintaining healthy functioning as well as preventing and treating illness. Two of the major organizations devoted to this area of study are APA's Division 38 – Health Psychology (http://www.health-psych.org/) and the Society of Behavioral Medicine (http://www.sbm.org/).

Neuropsychology

Experimental neuropsychology develops and clinical neuropsychology applies knowledge of brain-behavior relationships to human problems. APA's Division 40 – Clinical Neuropsychology (http://www.div40.org/) and the British Psychological Society – Division of Neuropsychology (http://www.bps.org.uk/don/) are devoted to this area of study.

Forensic Psychology

Bartol and Bartol (1999) define forensic psychology as:

> both (a) the research endeavor that examines aspects of human behavior directly related to the legal process . . . and (b) the professional practice of psychology within, or in consultation with, a legal system that encompasses both criminal and civil law and the numerous areas where they interact. (p. 3)

The main organization devoted to this area is APA Division 41 – American Psychology-Law Society (http://www.ap-ls.org/).

Deciding on the Type of Graduate Education

The four levels of graduate education are certificate, masters, specialist, and doctoral. We describe each of these levels as well as the types of degrees within each level where applicable. We will begin at the graduate certificate level and move up to the highest level of education available in the social sciences, the doctorate.

Graduate Certificates

Graduate certificates are offered in a variety of areas (e.g., geropsychology, conflict resolution, psychopharmacology). The certificate programs are generally a year long. These programs allow individuals to gain additional education in a specified area. Certificate programs often do not provide specific skills training. Rather, they provide additional coursework in a circumscribed area and typically at the beginning graduate level. When specific skills training is a part of the program, students usually must already possess a graduate degree prior to enrollment. This requirement helps ensure a base level of knowledge and expertise. Regardless, graduate certificates are not graduate degrees. However, they may give you additional background in an area that will make you more attractive than someone with a bachelor's degree or someone without the additional coursework.

Master's Degrees

Master's degrees are offered in all areas of psychology. These programs are typically two years long, although applied programs (e.g., clinical psychology and counseling psychology) may take additional time due to practicum requirements. Two types of master's degrees are available. These are the Master of Arts (MA) and the Master of Science (MS) degrees. Although historically the MS degree required significantly more research experience than an MA degree, these lines are blurrier now. However, be cautious of programs that do not help students build a strong research foundation (e.g., requiring a thesis). Not all master's degree programs require a thesis (an independent research project that the student develops, carries out, and defends). However, if you plan on continuing your education at the doctoral level either immediately upon graduation or at a later time, you will want to choose a master's program that requires a thesis.

Master's degree programs are also designated as terminal or nonterminal. Terminal master's degree programs are not a part of a doctoral program and as such prepare the individual to enter the job market upon graduation. This does not mean that individuals in a terminal master's degree program can not continue their education at the doctoral level. In fact, terminal master's degree programs are sometimes excellent *proving grounds* for students. Because terminal master's programs have lower entrance requirements than doctoral programs (Norcross, Kohout, & Wicherski, 2005), students who may not have the best GPAs or enough research experience may opt to apply to master's programs to gain or improve their standing. Keep in mind, though, that the average GPA of incoming students in terminal master's degree programs was 3.37 (Norcross et al., 2005). Box 7.1 lists some reasons given by Norcross, Sayette, and Mayne (2008) to obtain a master's degree first instead of proceeding immediately to a doctoral program.

Nonterminal master's degree programs are part of a doctoral program and as such students will continue with their studies until they earn their doctorate (at the same university, in the same program). For nonterminal master's degree programs, these students enter a doctoral graduate program and earn their master's degree along the way. This is very common in the field of psychology.

Box 7.1   Reasons to Pursue a Master's Degree First*

Low grade point average (GPA)
Weak/low Graduate Record Exam (GRE) scores
Limited research experience
Limited clinical experience
Uncertain about career goal
Missed deadlines for doctoral programs
Weak letters of recommendation
Limited background in psychology

*Norcross, Sayette, & Mayne (2008).

Specialist Degrees

The specialist degree can be either a specialist in psychology (PsyS) or a specialist in education (EdS). The EdS degree is significantly more common and dominates this level. In general, the specialist degree is an expanded master's degree program. This typically 3-year-long program is found almost exclusively in the school psychology domain. In a nutshell, the 3-year degree comprises two years of practica and coursework, one year of full-time internship in a school environment, and a project. The project is generally an expanded form of a thesis research study. Detailed information on the field of school psychology (including necessary education and training) may be found in the second part of the book.

Doctoral Degrees

There are three types of doctoral degrees in psychology: the doctor of philosophy (PhD), doctor of psychology (PsyD), and doctor of education (EdD) degrees. Although the EdD is offered in some counseling psychology and developmental psychology programs (7 programs), the PhD (999 programs) and PsyD (96 programs) degrees are the most common doctoral degree programs in psychology (APA Center for Psychology Workforce Analysis and Research, 2007). As a result, this section will focus on the PhD and PsyD degrees. Regardless of the type, the doctoral degree is the highest degree available in psychology. Although postdoctoral training and programs are common (especially in the applied areas), the doctoral degree is the final step possible in the formal education process.

Non-health service provider subfields of psychology.   For the non-health service provider subfields of psychology (e.g., experimental psychology and social psychology), doctoral programs lead to the PhD degree and tend to last approximately 4 or 5 years. The majority of the time in the respective program is spent in one of two activities, coursework and research. Given the empirical basis of psychology, coursework tends to center on the respective research findings in the area of study and expanding research methodology skills including advanced statistics coursework. Outside of coursework, much time is devoted to research activities, your own and your major professor's research. The term *major professor* refers to the professor who accepted you into the program or with whom you have established a mentoring relationship. As such, the major professor directs much of your work, including course selection and your dissertation. The dissertation is the large research study that you complete prior to graduating with your doctorate. Although approved and supervised to some extent by your major professor, the development of the ideas behind your dissertation and bringing the study to fruition are your responsibility. Additionally and once completed, you must defend your dissertation in front of a committee comprised of your major professor and other faculty members. A successful defense is the final hurdle to obtaining your doctorate in most programs.

Health service provider subfields of psychology.   Different training models exist for the health service provider subfields of psychology (i.e., clinical psychology, counseling psychology, and school psychology). Although covered in more detail later in the Careers in Clinical Psychology and Counseling Psychology chapter, this information bears mentioning here due to its importance. There are three general training models for professional clinical psychology programs. These models have been adopted to greater and lesser degrees by the other two applied health service provider subfields within psychology (counseling psychology and school psychology). The three models are the Boulder Model, the Vail Model, and the Academy of Psychological Clinical Science (APCS) Model.

In 1949, the Conference on Training in Clinical Psychology was held in Boulder, Colorado (Matthews & Anton, 2008). Named after the host city, the Boulder Model for training clinical psychologists was developed in which students would be well trained in both clinical research skills and application skills. The incorporation of these two definitive aspects of the field is also referred to as the scientist-practitioner model.

In 1973, the National Conference on Levels and Patterns of Professional Training in Psychology met and endorsed the practitioner-scholar model (Matthews & Anton, 2008). Often referred to as the Vail Model (so named after the conference's host city), this model proposed that training in clinical application skills could dominate the doctoral training, placing significantly less emphasis on research skills and production. The Vail Model is analogous to the practitioner models of medicine (MD), dentistry (DMD), and veterinary medicine (DVM). Programs adopting this model would focus on training students to be consumers of research more than producers of research. By the time the conference met, the first program utilizing this model had already begun at the University of Illinois in 1968. Although the University of Illinois program is no longer around, several other early programs still train students today (e.g., Widener University since 1970, Baylor University since 1971, and Rutgers University since 1973). Interestingly, many still view the PsyD degree which sprung from this model as being "new" even given a 40+ year history. Today, there are 96 PsyD programs, including over 50 that are APA-accredited (APA Center for Psychology Workforce Analysis and Research, 2007). We will discuss accreditation later in the chapter.

As alluded to in the previous paragraph, to reduce confusion, Peterson (1976) argued that programs training practitioners be designated by the PsyD degree and those programs training scientists/researchers be designated with the PhD degree. This differentiation was not sufficient for some in the clinical psychology subfield and resulted in the development of the Academy of Psychological Clinical Science (APCS; n.d.). The dissatisfaction resulted from what some saw as a departure from the scientific basis of clinical psychology. Sometimes referred to as the "Super Boulder Model," programs subscribing to the model commit heavily to the clinical research enterprise in training graduate students. A current listing of these programs may be found at the APCS website (http://psych.arizona.edu/apcs/members.php).

As you are thinking about this information please keep in mind that with the possible exception of the APCS model, strict adherence to these models by individual programs is rare. Each program ends up putting its own unique stamp on its training. Basically, clinical psychology programs vary in their balance of the two themes (practice and research training). In fact, it may be additionally or even more informative for you to ask the programs in which you are interested what percentage of the training is devoted to practice (e.g., learning and practicing psychotherapy and psychological assessment) and what percentage is devoted to research endeavors (e.g., statistics coursework, research laboratory work, data collection and analysis, research publication/ presentation). The answer will likely provide you with important information as you select programs to pursue.

Finding Available Graduate Programs

One of the early steps to selecting a graduate program is to review what programs are available. Several resources can help you in your quest. These include:

- *Graduate Study in Psychology* (GSP; APA, 2010) – Produced annually, this publication provides a listing of graduate programs in psychology. For each program it includes such information as accreditation status, application information, financial assistance available, and placement of students upon graduation. GSP also provides an index that lists programs by subfield and by geographic location.
- Academy of Psychological Clinical Science (http://psych.arizona.edu/apcs/ members.php) – This website provides a listing of programs that adhere to the APCS Model. Links to the member programs are provided when available.
- APA Division Websites – The appendix provides a listing of APA's divisions along with their respective web links. Many of these divisions provide lists of programs in the respective area.
- *Insider's Guide to Graduate Programs in Clinical and Counseling Psychology* (Norcross et al., 2008) – Provides reports on clinical and counseling psychology programs. The reports include information on research areas, clinical opportunities, theoretical orientation of faculty, statistics of recent applicants, and average length of time to complete program. A unique feature of the guide is a Likert-type scale that rates programs on a continuum from practice-oriented to equal emphasis to research-oriented.
- The Subfields of Psychology Chapters – When available, the chapters in this text covering careers in the respective subfields provide information on where to find programs. Also, some of the chapters provide program rankings when the research is available (e.g., Careers in Forensic Psychology).

Evaluating the Graduate Programs You Find

As you can see from reviewing any of the resources noted in the previous section, there are a wide variety of graduate programs available in psychology. In fact, APA's Center for Psychology Workforce Analysis and Research (2007) notes that 1,102 programs conferred doctoral degrees in psychology in the 2005–2006 school year. As a result, evaluating the myriad of programs that pique your interest may be difficult and cumbersome. To help with the evaluative process, we suggest the creation of an Excel or SPSS file in which you can organize the program information important to you. Box 7.2 provides

Box 7.2 Potential Program Variables to Review

- School Reputation
- Geographic Location
- Type of Program (PhD, PsyD, EdD)
- Field of Study (e.g., developmental psychology, social psychology)
- Balance Between Research and Practice (mainly for applied psychology programs)
- Any Required Undergraduate Coursework
- Diversity Representation in Faculty and Students
- Number of Applications
- Number of Offers
- Number of Incoming Students
- Mean/Median GRE Verbal
- Mean/Median GRE Quantitative
- Mean/Median GRE Analytical Writing
- Mean/Median Psychology Subject Test
- Mean/Median GPA
- Mean/Median Psychology GPA
- Mean/Median Last Two Years GPA
- Number of Program Faculty
- Theoretical Orientation (for clinical/counseling programs)
- Program Tracks
- Percentage of Students Receiving Full Tuition Waiver
- Percentage of Students Receiving Assistantship Only
- Percentage of Students Receiving both Full Tuition and Assistantship
- Annual Cost of the Program (considering tuition waivers/assistantships)
- Research Areas Available
- Faculty Members Name You Are Interested in Working With
- Grant Activity
- Personal Interview Required/Optional
- Teaching Experience Available (since many will end up in academe)
- Percentage of Students Applying for Internship Accepted to APA Accredited Site (Clinical/Counseling/School Psychology only)
- Percentage of Students Licensed (applied programs only)
- Mean/Median Time to Completion of Program
- Placement of Students Upon Graduation (e.g., academe, research institutes, practice)
- Attrition rate
- Accreditation (regional and APA)

a list of possible variables to consider. Once you have your worksheet ready, begin filling in the blanks. Although the variables are easily filled, evaluating the meaning of some of the variables may be more difficult. As a result, we provide some pointers to help in your evaluation of the personal meaning of the information.

Application and Acceptance Rates

The number of applications to a program and the program's acceptance rate are easily understandable variables. The evaluative information they provide can be invaluable. In fact, acceptance rates are significantly different based on program type. For example, research-oriented programs (e.g., experimental psychology) have fewer applications and higher acceptance rates (although still rigorous) while practice-oriented PhD programs have larger numbers of applications and lower acceptance rates. Additionally, freestanding PsyD programs (i.e., those that are not affiliated with a university, although they may use "university" in their name) accept approximately 50% of their applicants, university-based PsyD programs accept approximately 41% of their applicants, Boulder-Model clinical PhD programs accept approximately 10% of their applicants, and APCS Model clinical PhD programs accept approximately 6% of their applicants (Norcross et al., 2008). Looking at the information in a different way, the higher the acceptance rate the higher the likelihood you will get into the program. From another perspective, the higher the acceptance rate, the higher the likelihood that people who are not qualified will get into the program. The reason this last piece is so important is that being accepted into and even graduating from a program is not the end of the story. You will also need to find a job, and for those in the clinical, counseling, or school psychology fields, you will also need to get licensed. Although this is covered in another chapter, suffice it to say that students from PsyD programs with higher acceptance rates have significantly lower scores on the tests necessary for licensure compared to PhD graduates (Kupfesmid & Fiola, 1991; Maher, 1999). In fact, the correlation between the mean score on the Examination for Professional Practice in Psychology (EPPP; the national licensing exam) and a program's acceptance rate is −0.64 (Templer & Arikawa, 2004).

This information does not mean that you should not apply to PsyD programs. Remember, the first author (Helms) has a PsyD degree. Rather, it means that the higher the acceptance rate, the lower the quality/rigor of the program generally, resulting in graduates not prepared for the rigors of the licensure process or the professional practice of psychology. These concerns are so real that one of the original proponents of the Vail Model strongly encouraged a merciless evaluation of existing programs with implicit hope that weak, ineffectual, and poor programs be eliminated (Peterson, 2003). Given the time, energy, and financial resources expended by students for their educations, we eagerly welcome this prospect.

Grade Point Average (GPA)

Recent research indicates that the average *minimum* required overall GPA of applicants in 2003–2004 was 3.11 for doctoral programs and 2.92 for master's programs (Norcross et al., 2005). The associated *minimum* required Psychology GPA was 3.17 for doctoral programs and 3.05 for master's programs. However, the minimum required is *significantly* different than what is actually accepted. In fact for these same years (2003–2004), the study found that the *actual* overall GPA was 3.54 for applicants accepted to doctoral programs and 3.37 for applicants accepted to master's programs. For some programs (e.g., clinical psychology PhD programs), the *actual* overall GPAs can be close to 4.0. In summary, you will want to look at the statistics of students admitted to the program in recent years. If your GPA is substantially lower than the mean or median listed (i.e., more than 0.2 points lower), you probably will not be a viable candidate. Additionally, our experience tells us that students often inaccurately believe that *desire* to go to graduate school will somehow make up for GPA or GRE inadequacies. Succinctly put, this is not the case.

Graduate Record Exam and the Psychology Subject Test

Although it leaves a bad taste in most students' mouths, standardized admissions tests are an important part of the application to graduate school. The importance is predicated on its ability to compare students from a wide variety of educational experiences/universities. You know as well as we do that a 3.8 GPA at one school does not mean the same thing as a 3.8 at another school. In fact, students with the same GPAs at the same school may differ. Think about a peer you may know that only takes the "easy" professors and the "easy" electives. Now you are getting a sense about why it is important to have a measure that is consistent across individuals and across situations. The General Test (sometimes referred to as simply the GRE) and the Psychology Subject Test of the Graduate Record Exam (GRE) are the two examinations most often required by graduate programs.

The General Test of the Graduate Record Exam (GRE) is a computer-based exam developed and marketed by the Educational Testing Service (ETS; 2008). The General Test consists of three components: Quantitative Reasoning, Verbal Reasoning, and Analytical Writing. Both the Quantitative and the Verbal Reasoning components have a score range from 200 to 800 and are scored in 10-point increments. The Analytical Writing component, introduced in 2002, has a score range from 0 to 6 and is scored in half-point increments.

According to ETS (2008), the Verbal Reasoning component of the General Test is intended to measure examinees' abilities to "analyze and evaluate written material and synthesize information obtained from it; analyze relationships among component parts of sentences; [and] recognize relationships between words and concepts" (www.gre.org). In terms of the Quantitative Reasoning component, ETS says that it is intended to measure examinees' abilities to "understand basic concepts of arithmetic, algebra, geometry, and data analysis; reason quantitatively; [and] solve problems in a quantitative setting" (www.gre.org). The Analytical Writing component measures examinees' abilities to "articulate complex ideas clearly and effectively; examine claims and accompanying evidence; support ideas with relevant reasons and examples; sustain a well-focused, coherent discussion; [and] control the elements of standard written English" (www.gre.org).

In terms of graduate school, 74% of doctoral and 57% of masters programs in psychology require the General Test (Norcross et al., 2005). Although the minimum required combined Quantitative Reasoning and Verbal Reasoning score averaged 1066 for doctoral programs and 952 for master's programs, 1183 was the *actual* mean General Test score for incoming doctoral students. For incoming master's students, 1055 was the *actual* mean General Test score (Norcross et al., 2005). Keep in mind that this includes both applied psychology and experimental psychology programs. That is, the mean General Test scores for clinical psychology programs tend to be significantly higher than mean scores for experimental psychology programs. This leads to an important point. The minimum requirement is *rarely* enough to attain an admission offer. In fact and as you can see, the minimum required score is over 120 points *below* the actual score of admitted doctoral students.

For the Analytical Writing component, Briihl and Wasieleski (2004) reported that only 35% of psychology graduate programs utilized the score in their admission decisions. However, this may change in coming years as familiarity with this relatively new component increases. In other words, you will still want to study and do your best on it!

The Psychology Subject Test of the GRE is currently a paper and pencil test given three times a year (ETS, 2008). Although the specific dates change annually, the testing months are typically April, October, and November. Students often choose the October administration because it allows enough time to submit scores to graduate programs as well as enough time into the Fall semester to learn some of the advanced coursework covered by the exam that they may be currently taking. For actual test dates, visit www.gre.org.

The Psychology Subject Test has three content areas that cover all areas of psychology with varying degrees of emphasis (ETS, 2008). It consists of approximately 205–215 questions with five answer options. When scored, the test produces two subscores (i.e., experimental and social) that range from 20 to 99 and a total score that ranges from 200 to 990. According to ETS (2006), the three content areas with respective topics and percentage of questions on the test are:

- Experimental Subscore Area
  - Accounts for approximately 40% of the questions
  - Covers Learning, Language, Memory, Thinking, Sensation and Perception, and Physiological Psychology
- Social Subscore Area
  - Accounts for approximately 43% of the questions
  - Covers Clinical and Abnormal Psychology, Lifespan Development, Personality, and Social Psychology
- Other Areas
  - Accounts for approximately 17% of the questions
  - Covers general areas (e.g., history and Industrial-Organizational Psychology) and Measurement and Methodology.

Norcross et al. (2005) reported that 29% of doctoral and 13% of master's psychology programs require the Psychology Subject Test. Mean minimum required scores were 552 for doctoral programs and 495 for master's programs. *Actual* mean scores of incoming graduate students were 633 for doctoral programs and 577 for master's programs. This 80+ point discrepancy is yet another reason to ignore the minimums and focus on the averages of recent incoming students.

In terms of associated costs for the tests, the General Test currently costs $140, and the Psychology Subject Test costs $130. However, the costs do not stop here. An official report of your scores must be sent to the graduate programs. These cost $20 per report. These costs are certainly disincentives to take the tests more than once. However, many students do retake the test in hopes of obtaining a higher score. According to ETS (2008), scores typically increase about 20 points on the General Test. Of course, your score may also go down. Keep in mind that generally speaking, an additional 20 points on your score will not typically make a difference in your viability for a program. Students mistakenly hope that scoring those additional 20 points will help them reach the minimum required or the average of incoming students last year. We have already covered the issue with the required minimum (i.e., ignore those scores). Curiously, students sometimes miss the fact that an average score for incoming students means that scores were generally surrounding that score with some falling above and some falling below. Schools reporting median scores can be easier to evaluate in that half of the incoming students score better and half score worse than that score. However, whether it is the mean or median, scores likely tightly bunch around those scores (i.e., have very small standard deviations). In other words, it is highly unlikely that 20 points will make a difference. As a result, we recommend against retaking the test unless something traumatic happened during the testing (e.g., you passed out or had a heart attack). Remember too that all scores for the past five years are reported to the programs. This means that the schools will see every attempt you make and may wonder why you took the test more than once.

In terms of preparing for the General Test, there are hundreds of books, online resources, and programs that can help in your preparation. However, we do give the warning that some of the strategies available are costly and unproven. As a result, buyers beware! Regardless, some of the basic tried and true strategies include taking as many practice tests as possible (and under test-like conditions), memorization of words that have been on the test in the past, improving writing skills for the Analytical Writing component, and studying basic algebra and geometry skills.

In terms of the Psychology Subject Test, you have been preparing your entire under-graduate education. However, you will need to prepare much more. One mistake students make is that they wait until their last semester or final year to take the "harder" psychology coursework (e.g., physiological psychology). As a result, much of the information on the test will be completely unfamiliar. Our suggestion is to take as much of the core psychology coursework prior to your senior year and save your electives for the senior year. Additionally, studying your text books and taking as many practice Psychology Subject Tests as possible will likely prove useful.

Students also ask about how much time they should spend preparing for the tests. In general we recommend concerted weekly effort for six months. For the first month or so, you may only devote a few hours every other day for the test. This amount will increase to everyday as the test approaches. You will want to note that we mean intense studying during these times and not simply light reviews of the components.

Stipends Versus Loans Versus Eventual Salary

Most good programs provide financial assistance to their graduate students. Financial assistance can come in the form of:

- Tuition waivers: No tuition is charged by the university. Sometimes registration and other fees still apply but are minimal.
- Research assistantships: You will work in a faculty member's research lab in exchange for a stipend (i.e., a certain amount of money that can help defray living expenses).
- Teaching assistantships: You will teach undergraduate courses in exchange for a stipend. Under supervision, you may teach a variety of courses from Research Methods to Introduction to Psychology.
- Scholarships: Due to your undergraduate record and GRE scores (relative to other incoming students) you may receive additional financial awards.

Unfortunately, not all programs offer these types of assistance. In fact, some programs report providing financial assistance, but when you read the fine print, all they provide is access to student loans or an extremely small percentage of students are awarded stipends or assistantships (e.g., only one or two students get stipends or tuition waivers). In reviewing the variables on programs, percentage of students receiving tuition waivers, assistantships, and both will give you insight into a program's financial commitment to students. In general, good programs will not admit students that they are unable to support at least partially.

In terms of the data, Wicherski and Kohout (2005) reported that 68% of the 2003 doctorates had debt related to their education when they graduated. However, the differences in debt level are striking (and disturbing to some) when viewed through the lens of program type: 74% of those in the practice-oriented subfields (e.g., clinical psychology) and 54% of those in the research-oriented subfields (e.g., social psychology) reported some level of debt. For those in the practice-oriented subfields, the median level of debt was $67,500. For those in the research-oriented subfields, the median level of debt was $22,000. That is a huge difference! Wicherski and Kohout also looked at degree type. For those receiving their PsyD degree, the median debt level was $90,000. Their research shows that this is a $37,000 increase in the median debt level for this group in only 6 years. For those receiving their PhD in clinical psychology, the median debt level was $50,000. This was an increase of $14,000 from their survey 2 years earlier.

The piece we encourage you to take away from this variable is in relation to eventual salary. Loans must be repaid, and at this level of debt, a substantial chunk of your salary will go directly to your loans for many years (decades) after graduation. It is also important to compare debt level to expected salary. In the same survey noted earlier, Wicherski and Kohout (2005) note that the median starting salary for those new doctorates was $52,556. Out of context, this amount seems quite substantial. For those graduating with substantial debt potentially due in part to nonsupportive programs (e.g., programs not offering tuition waivers), this amount diminishes rapidly.

Unfortunately, our experience is that students are often blinded by their desire to attend graduate school – at any cost. This experience is further complicated by programs that prey on this desire.

Research

This variable refers to both the amount of research required and the type of research occurring in the program. The type of research is rather straightforward. What topics are the faculty members pursuing? This information is often readily available via the faculty member's web page or via a literature search for his or her publications. A program's web page may also have a link to the respective faculty member's vita, a rich source of information. (Developing your own vita is discussed in an upcoming section of this chapter.)

In terms of the amount of required research and reminiscent of the discussion of the various models of training, some programs require heavy amounts of research and others require very little. In reviewing the faculty in the program, some insight into this variable may come from the faculty member's website. For example and if listed, do the faculty co-author papers, posters, and publications with students? If so, how many do they collaborate on each year? Some programs have a website devoted to current graduate students' activities. This resource can provide information too. An additional piece to consider is the outlet for their publications. Are they publishing in the top journals in the field?

Once this information is compiled, you will need to decide how important research productivity and experience are to you. If you plan on pursuing a research-oriented career (e.g., academe), the heavier the research requirements and the more plentiful the opportunities to conduct research in graduate school, the better it will be for you in the long run.

Grant Activity

Closely tied to the research area, grant activity is an important variable to consider. Grant activity refers to the number, monetary amount, type (government or private), and duration of financially sponsored activities of faculty members. Large, multi-year government grants indicate a stable program and associated faculty on the grant. It can signify to you that the program will be able to financially support you in your studies. Depending on the program, the stipend that pays you for your teaching assistantship or research assistantship as well as covers your tuition may come directly from a grant.

Time to Complete Program

Program websites often note the length of their program. As we noted, research-oriented programs are typically 4–5 years long, and practice-oriented programs are 5–6 years long typically. However, the program's curriculum may not match the average length of time it takes its students to complete the program. In truth, the listed curriculum can be aspirational rather than typical. As a result, it will be more informative for you to find out the average length of time for a student to complete the program. This information is available in most resources including GSP (APA, 2010).

Attrition Rate

Not surprisingly, not everyone who starts a graduate program completes the training. This fact is referred to as a program's attrition rate. When programs do a good job of selecting qualified students that fit their program, attrition rates will be extremely low (and even 0%). However, even for programs that do a good job selecting appropriate students, some students may still leave the program. The reasons students leave a program are varied and include such issues as:

- Change of interest – The student decided that the field of study was not for him/her.
- Academic issues – The student was not able to maintain adequate academic standing. For most graduate programs adequate standing is a 3.0 minimum. In reality, most students typically earn all A's.
- Asked to leave – Students may be asked to leave a program. Typical reasons for these "requests" are poor collegiality, personal problems affecting quality of work, and ethical infractions. Being asked to leave is rare but does occur.
- Personal and financial reasons – Life circumstances sometimes conspire to prevent completion of a program.
- All But Dissertation (ABD) – Completion of the large independent research project (i.e., the dissertation) often prevents individuals from completing their program in a timely manner. Although most will eventually complete their dissertations, some will remain in a state of limbo for years until the program terminates their standing. Most programs allow only a limited amount of time to complete your dissertation.

Teaching Experience

Because many individuals completing their doctoral degree will end up with careers in academe, teaching experience will be important. Although some programs ensure that all students have some experience in the classroom, other programs provide the experience only as an option or even not at all. When applying for academic positions upon graduation, it will be impressive to include substantial teaching experience, especially if you were the instructor of record and not only an assistant.

Placement of Students in Internships

For those of you interested in the applied subfields of school psychology, counseling psychology, and clinical psychology, a year-long predoctoral internship will conclude your doctoral training. The application process is extremely competitive, and not all applicants are matched to positions. In fact, there are not enough sites for everyone that applies. The Association of Psychology Postdoctoral and Internship Centers (APPIC) administers the matching process for internship. Information on APPIC is available on their website at www.appic.org. Of the 3,492 applicants participating in the 2008 internship match process, 2,749 applicants were successfully matched. In other words, a little over 21% of the applicants did not get matched. In terms of evaluating programs, good programs typically hover around 100% of their students getting internships. To more finely evaluate programs, it is also enlightening to see how many of their students got their first or second choice of internship site. Additionally, it is important to note that large freestanding PsyD programs match at significantly lower rates than smaller university-affiliated PhD programs (APPIC, 2006). Remember, you can not finish your program until you complete the internship. Since the match takes place only once a year, without an internship match, you will be spending another year waiting around for the next match. All of this information is readily available on most programs' websites and via the APPIC website.

Placement of Students after Graduation

Graduate programs are proud of their students' accomplishments. This includes where their students go on internship and postdoctoral training and where they are employed. As a result, most programs provide this information readily. For your evaluation purposes, if most of a program's students end up in clinical environments and you want to pursue an academic career, this information may sway your decision to apply. The opposite may also be true of a program. If you want to practice and the school prepares students for careers in academe, it may not be a good match for you.

Licensure of Students after Graduation

For students applying to clinical, counseling, and school psychology doctoral programs, licensure of students upon graduation and completion of postdoctoral training is a key issue. Knowing what percentage of students in the program become licensed *and* how quickly is critical. In general, all students in applied programs should become licensed as psychologists upon completion of the appropriate requirements. The additional factor that is equally important to evaluate is the number of times it takes for a program's students to pass the required exams. What percentage of students passes the licensure exams on the first try? What is the average score of students on the national exam (i.e., the EPPP)? Most states institute a passing score of 70% on the EPPP. Obviously, programs whose students routinely take more than one attempt and whose EPPP average hovers around 70% or lower are programs to avoid. We can not imagine a worse feeling than completing all of the educational requirements for licensure (doctorate and postdoctorate) and not being able to pass the licensure exams due to poor training. Important to reiterate from earlier, EPPP scores are significantly lower for PsyD programs than traditional PhD clinical programs (Templer & Arikawa, 2004). As a result, you will need to be even more diligent when evaluating PsyD programs in this regard.

APA Accreditation

Closely tied to the previous section on licensure, APA accreditation of graduate programs in clinical, counseling, and school psychology is extremely important. In fact, you will be unable to get licensed in many states/jurisdictions if you do not graduate from an APA-accredited program. In terms of evaluating a graduate program in one of these subfields of psychology, APA accreditation is a starting point. It is an indication that the program meets *minimum* standards. In other words, knowing a program is accredited is the starting point and not the ending point. Additional pieces to evaluate are how long the program has been accredited and when the next site visit is. This information is found in every December issue of the *American Psychologist*, the monthly journal published by the APA.

Geographical Location

Although geographical location may be important to you (e.g., staying close to family), this is not something that is considered by graduate programs. In fact, you will be competing for your place in graduate school with people from all over the country (and world sometimes). Also, geographical locations that are less desirable may provide you with a better chance of admission since others may not apply in as large numbers and when they apply may not accept an offer of admission. We encourage you to keep this in mind as you apply – broadly.

In summary, as you are evaluating programs that interest you, be sure to assess your own qualifications. How well do you match their criteria? *Desire* to pursue graduate education will not overcome poor or mediocre qualifications. The additional piece to consider is if graduate school is right for you. Can you pursue your desired career without graduate training? Other parts of the book can help with this piece.

Selecting Programs to Pursue

Keeping the above characteristics in mind, review 40 to 50 programs from one of the resources noted earlier. The review should include familiarizing yourself with all of the variables noted in Box 7.2 for each program and all of the information available on the programs' websites. Once your review is complete and for the 20–25 that "float" to the top for you, e-mail to see if the professors you are interested in working with at the school are taking students for the coming year. (Because this information is sometimes on the program's website, be sure to check there first.) Contacting professors should be done at the beginning of the Fall semester of your senior year. *Be careful!* Your e-mail should be extremely thoughtful and professional. In fact, we recommend having your undergraduate mentor or one of the faculty members who will be writing a letter of recommendation for you read it prior to sending it. Some schools do not have a mentor model but rather admit a group of students who decide within the first year or so of the program with whom they would like to work. Touching base with those professors with whom you are interested in working is still not a bad idea.

When it is time, which is typically November or December for doctoral programs and sometimes a little later for master's programs, we strongly recommend applying to 10–15 programs. Based on the information you have collected on the 20–25 programs that "floated" to the top (given the professors will be taking students for the upcoming year), we recommend the following breakdown for the 10–15 to which you will apply:

- Half of your applications should be to programs where you *exceed* the statistics of their recent admissions (i.e., last 2 years).
- A quarter of your applications should be to programs where you *meet* the statistics of their recent admissions (i.e., last 2 years).
- A quarter of your applications should be to programs where you are *slightly below* the statistics of their recent admissions (i.e., last 2 years).

This strategy will hopefully cover your bases by providing coverage of *dream* programs and *back-up* programs.

Preparing Vitae – An Essential Part of Your Application Packet

Although vitae are similar to résumés, there are important differences. Unlike résumés, vitae provide the "complete" story. Unlike résumés which should not be more than one page, vitae can be 20, 30, or more pages for professionals who have been in the field for a while. For the student applying to graduate school, his or her vita will likely be 4 pages. To clarify, these 4 pages assume one-inch margins on all sides, single-spaced line spacing, and Times New Roman 12 font. The four pages should be devoted to accomplishments and pertinent information and not fluff! With the exception of the "Career Objective" heading which is almost never used in vitae, the potential headings noted in our discussion of résumés will generally fit for vitae too. However, you will also want to include additional information/headings regarding your research experiences and psychology and psychology-related coursework. In terms of research experiences, this section includes such information as papers and poster presentations given at conferences, publications, and any research assistance you provided to others (e.g., data entry or administering research protocols for a faculty member). All of your presentations and publications should be in correct APA format.

In terms of listing coursework, the psychology coursework you should list is evident (i.e., all psychology courses). The psychology-related coursework you list will depend on your interest area. If you are pursuing an industrial-organizational psychology graduate program, your coursework in business and advanced statistics would be listed. If you are pursuing clinical psychology graduate programs, your coursework in advanced statistics would be listed. Box 7.3 provides an example vita. We encourage you to seek lots of feedback on the layout of your vita and the information you include. Additional examples of vitae may be found online. Your professor may even let you take a look at his or her vita!

Box 7.3   Example Vita

Laura Jasmine Ashley
100-B Chastain Rd. Apt. #123
Kennesaw, GA 30144
(555) 555-5555
LauraJasmineAshley@emailnow.com

Education

May 2012 (anticipated)   **Bachelor of Science in Psychology**
Kennesaw State University
Kennesaw, GA
Current GPA: 3.82
Current Psychology GPA: 4.0
Last 2 Years GPA: 4.0

Publication

Ashley, L. J., & Smith, L. P. (2011). LGBT student attitudes in introductory psychology courses. *Undergraduate Studies in Sex Research*, *15*, 316–328.

Conference Presentations

Ashley, L. J., & Helms, J. L. (2010, April). *Differences between students and the community: Attitudes toward sexual orientation minorities.* Paper presented at the annual Georgia Undergraduate Research in Psychology conference, Kennesaw, GA.

Ashley, L. J., & Smith, L. P. (2011, May). *Student gender attitudes: The inside is worse than the outside.* Poster session presented at the annual Association for Psychological Science conference, Ann Arbor, RI.

Other Research Experiences

Careen, Z. L. (2009, March). *Gender inequity in psychology programs.* Poster session presented at the Gender Studies in Psychology annual conference, Jacksonville, FL. (Assisted Dr. Careen with survey administration and data entry)

Careen, Z. L. (in progress). *Rankings of developmental psychology programs.* Unpublished research, Kennesaw State University, Kennesaw GA. (Assisted Dr. Careen with data entry and coordinated all students involved in the project)

Fall 2009 – Spring 2010   **Lab Member**, Animal Behavior Lab
Kennesaw State University
Faculty Mentor: Dr. Dorothy Williamson

Research projects: Influence of environmental factors on the procreation of rats including relative birth weight of offspring

Responsibilities: Coordinated data collections by first-year psychology students, maintained rat colony, data analyses, managed and developed online survey databases, recruited participants, submitted IRB proposals

Clinical Experience

Fall 2009 – present   **Behavior Therapist**
Atlanta, GA
Supervisor: Dr. Lillian V. Veins
Description: Part-time position working with children who are diagnosed with pervasive developmental disorders (e.g., Asperger's and Autism)
Responsibilities: Duties include administering behavioral protocols developed by the psychologists on staff

Teaching Experience

Fall 2010   **Undergraduate Teaching Assistant**
Life-span Developmental Psychology
Supervisor: Dr. Dorothy Williamson
Responsibilities: Developed materials for class, web site construction, provided evaluative feedback on student work, answered student questions, and tutored students

Research Application and Writing Skills

SPSS
SAS
Microsoft Office Products (Excel, PowerPoint, MSWord)
APA Format

Honors and Awards

Fall 2010   **Outstanding Undergraduate Teaching Assistant Award**
Department of Psychology, Kennesaw State University

April 2010   **First Place for Paper Presentation: Georgia Undergraduate**

Research in Psychology (GURP) Conference

Fall 2008 – Spring 2011   **President's List and Dean's List (every semester)**

University Involvement and Leadership Experience

Fall 2008 – present	**Psychology Club** President (Fall 2010 to present) *Coordinated the 2008 and 2009 annual charity benefit which raised over $5,000 each year*
Fall 2009 – present	**Psi Chi** Treasurer (Fall 2009 through Spring 2010)

Professional Affiliations

2009 – present	**American Psychological Association** *(Student Affiliate)*
2009 – present	**Association for Psychological Science** *(Student Affiliate)*
2009 – present	**Association for Psychological Science Student Caucus** APS Student Caucus Campus Representative Program, Kennesaw State University Campus Representative (2009–present) APS Student Caucus, Research on Socially and Economically Underrepresented Populations (RiSE-UP) Committee member (2009–present) RiSE-UP Lesbian, Gay, Bisexual, Transgender, and Queer Individuals subcommittee member (2010–present) RiSE-UP Women's Issues subcommittee member (2010–present)

Coursework

Psychology Coursework*	**Related Coursework**
General Psychology	Elementary Statistics
Careers in Psychology	Advanced Statistical Analysis
Research Methods in Psychology with Lab	Human Communications
Experimental Psychology with Lab	Biology I and II
Life-Span Developmental Psychology	Anatomy and Physiology I and II
Abnormal Psychology	Contemporary Health Issues
Social Psychology	Deviance and Social Control
Theories of Personality	Sociology of Mental Illness
Learning and Conditioning	Family Health and Human Sexuality
Perception	Social Organization
Physiological Psychology	Juvenile Delinquency
Psychopharmacology	Honors Directed Study
Introduction to Counseling Psychology	Honors Colloquium I and II
Field Practicum in Psychology	Honors Senior Capstone Experience
Senior Seminar in Psychology	

* Psychology GPA: 4.0

Current Research and Interest Areas
Gender Issues in Psychology and Law
Sexual Orientation Minorities
Gender Issues in Health Psychology

Hobbies

Playing the piano, hiking, bicycling, and cooking

References

Dr. Zelda L. Careen
Assistant Professor
Department of Psychology
Kennesaw State University
Kennesaw, GA
(555) 555-5555
zeldalsmith@kennesaw.edu

Dr. Jameson L. Helms
Associate Professor
Department of Psychology
Kennesaw State University
Kennesaw, GA
(555) 555-5555
drjameson@kennesaw.edu

Dr. Dorothy Williamson
Professor
Department of Psychology
Kennesaw State University
Kennesaw, GA
(555) 555-5555
drdorothy@kennesaw.edu

Statements of Intent and Admissions Essays

With mean ratings of 2.63 and 2.81 out of a possible 3 for master's programs and doctoral programs, respectively, the importance of the statement of intent to admissions committees cannot be overestimated (Norcross et al., 2005). The statement of intent is also called the statement of purpose and personal statement. Regardless of the wording used, the statement is an indication of:

- your academic background and how it has prepared you for graduate study in this specific field (e.g., research experience);

- why you want to attend graduate school in general;
- why you want to attend that *specific* graduate program (e.g., the match between the program and your research/practice interest areas);
- which faculty you are interested in working with in terms of research; and
- your ultimate goal upon graduation (i.e., career goals).

In fact, these points can form an outline for your statement in terms of information to cover. Although there will be similarities among the letters to the different programs, each statement should be specific to the program of interest. Nothing speaks more negatively than a canned, nonspecific, generic letter. The thinking on the recipient's end will be, "If he or she couldn't take enough time to personalize the information for our program, then he or she must not be that interested."

On second thought, although it is still extremely negative, there is something even worse than a generic letter. A statement that is not grammatically accurate is probably the "kiss of death" for your application. Given that you have "all the time in the world" to construct this statement including getting lots of feedback from your faculty and peers, even one minor error may be perceived as a lack of attention to detail and sloppiness (not good attributes for a potential graduate student). As a result, always remember that this statement (as well as all of your application materials) is a writing sample. In this vein, statements should be Times New Roman 12 font with 1-inch margins and double-spaced (unless single-spaced is allowed). If single-spacing is allowed, take advantage of it! But remember, no fluff is allowed. In truth, programs often specify a maximum length (e.g., 2–3 pages, double-spaced) so there is little room for "fluff." If no length is specified, 3–4 pages should be the goal. In terms of length, use the maximum length indicated as the general required length (without exceeding it). Appleby and Appleby (2007) provide some additional "kisses of death" for your personal statement in Box 7.4.

Box 7.4 Four Kisses of Death for Your Personal Statement*

- *"Avoid references to your mental health."* – This may raise concern about your ability to function as a graduate student.
- *"Avoid excessively altruistic statements."* – A strong need to help others may be seen as a stronger desire than to perform research and other required foundational activities.
- *"Avoid providing excessively self-revealing information."* – This may suggest a problem with appropriate and healthy interpersonal boundaries.
- *"Avoid inappropriate humor, attempts to appear cute or clever, and references to God or religious issues when these issues are unrelated to the program to which you are applying."* – This may be interpreted as both an indication of inappropriate boundaries and a lack of awareness of the seriousness of the process.

* Appleby and Appleby, 2007, p. 21.

In addition to requiring a personal statement, many programs also require answers to other essay questions. These essays tend to require short answers (e.g., one page or less) and focus on certain aspects of the program or your qualifications (e.g., "Which area of research interests you most and why?). The same level of seriousness, care, and preparation should be given to these answers as was given to your personal statement.

On a final but related note, both Appleby and Appleby (2007) and Bottoms and Nysse (1999) strongly urge students not to misinterpret the "personal" nature of the required statements and essays. In this situation, *personal* should not in any way be construed as meaning private. In fact, it should instead be defined as your *professional* statement of purpose. In other words, it is inappropriate to discuss personal issues like mental health, your philosophy of life, or religion. This type of information will doom your application to the reject pile. For more information on statements of intent and example essays, we encourage you to access the web resources noted at the end of the chapter.

Letters of Recommendation

Applications to graduate school require letters of recommendation from individuals who know you well in relation to your professional and academic life. Most programs require three letters of recommendations. These letters should be from professors who know you well and have worked with you personally (e.g., on research projects or on Psychology Club activities). All letter writers would preferably be psychologists (i.e., your professors). At least two of them absolutely need to be psychologists. We would recommend that at least two of the three be professors with whom you have collaborated on research. Having individuals that do not know you well (e.g., a professor that you have only worked with in a class or two) write letters suggests to the admissions committee that you were not actively involved in your education. Furthermore, if your interaction with a professor consists only of coursework (i.e., you took a class or two with the professor), the information provided in such a letter can readily be found on your transcript in the form of your grades. In other words, you want to have letters from professors who have taught you in coursework and who have worked with you outside of class on significant projects.

A question we often get from students is about letters from non-psychology professors or psychologists outside of academe (i.e., practicing applied psychologists in the community). Non-psychology professors and psychologists outside of academe are often unfamiliar with what is valued in the graduate school application process due to no experience or dated experience. As a result, their letters may be more (unintentionally) harmful than helpful. The question that admissions committees may ask is why did you not have your psychology professors write letters, with the implication that you did not have good relationships with them or were not involved. This impression is certainly not something you want to convey!

In terms of logistics relevant to letters of recommendation, you will want to allow your recommenders at least 4 to 6 weeks to write the letters (excluding weekends, holidays, and school breaks). In this vein, you will want to give faculty deadlines that are relative to when you will send the application and not when the application deadline occurs. Faculty may misinterpret the application deadline as their due date, making your application late and often not considered further in the process as a result.

Graduate programs want your recommenders to comment on such attributes as creativity, leadership, ability to accept criticism, ability to work independently, research skills, writing ability, etc. As a result, most recommenders will want you to waive your right to read the letter. Faculty may feel freer in their evaluations of these attributes, and the letter may carry more weight as a result. In fact, some faculty will not write letters when students do not waive their rights to read their letters. In other words, we recommend waiving your right to read the letter. The truth is that you should trust your writers or ask someone else. Your recommenders should be genuinely excited to write that strong positive letter of recommendation for you. Hesitation in writing a letter should indicate a less than strong letter may be on the horizon. If this is your feeling, we encourage you to seek another recommender since mediocre letters and strong positive letters with even a small negative can put your application in the "reject" pile. Box 7.5 lists materials to include in a packet to each of your letter writers. We encourage you to be cognizant of these tips. Recommenders do not like disorganization, a characteristic they will be commenting on in the letter. Including the information in a binder with dividers separating the different programs is an excellent idea. It communicates organizational skills and respect and understanding of the cumbersome process of letter writing.

Box 7.5   Materials Included in a Packet for the Faculty Providing You With Letters of Recommendation

- A short cover letter indicating the contents of the packet and the agreed upon date that you will return to pick up the letters.
- A checklist of all programs with information on due dates, type of program, any special information (e.g., "This is my top choice because of the research they do on heart disease.").
- A copy of your vita.
- A chronological list highlighting the courses and significant activities/ interactions you had with the letter writer.
- A copy of your personal statement (the generic one that is nonspecific to a program is sufficient).
- An unofficial copy of your transcript.
- An unofficial copy of your GRE and Psychology Subject Test scores.
- Any required recommendation forms.
- Web addresses/links (along with passwords) to recommendation forms that must be filled out online.
- A preaddressed envelope for the recommendation form and letter (stamped if the faculty member has to mail it himself or herself) for each program as appropriate.

The Graduate School Application Packet

As noted later in Mayhew's "Ten Tips From a Successful Applicant," proper and professional preparation of your application packet is extremely important. Some important points on the packet include:

- Send materials all at once. If possible, send everything together (including letters of recommendation and official transcripts). This will decrease the likelihood of materials getting lost.
- Send your packet at least two weeks before the deadline. This will ensure that it arrives on time. Plus, if it does not arrive for some reason, you have time to submit another packet before the deadline. Not meeting the deadline is an extremely negative sign. In fact, your materials are not likely to be reviewed at all, but we are sure your application fee will be processed.
- Submit all of your materials in a nice neutral folder that has your name and contact information neatly typed on the front. This provides not only a professional presentation but also a mechanism to keep all of your materials together.

We encourage you to review Mayhew's *Tips* for additional pointers. Box 7.6 provides a checklist of contents to include in your packet. We strongly encourage you to use this as a guide. In summary, your application packet must be impressive enough that they want to invite you for an interview or make you an offer.

Box 7.6 Checklist for Preparing the Application Packet for Mailing – Making the Right Impression

— Cover letter:
- Indicating that this is your application to their graduate school
- Indicating to which program you are applying (since most departments have multiple programs) Note: Even if a department has more than one program in which you are interested, you should only apply to one program. Applying to more than one makes you look indecisive.
- Indicating the contents of your application
- Requesting that they mail the enclosed postcard when your application is complete

— Vita

— Copy of your GRE General Test and Psychology Subject Test Scores (Original is sent by ETS)

— Official copy of your transcripts in a sealed envelope (and signed/stamped over the seal) – If the program requires transcripts to be sent by the school, include a photocopy of your transcripts in the packet.

— Writing samples – maximum of two – Possible examples include:
  • Copy of a publication you authored or co-authored
  • Copy of your senior thesis
  • Copy of a research article you authored and submitted for publication
  • Copy of a poster you presented
  • Copy of a research article you presented at a conference
— Copies of publications and conference presentation handouts
— Personal statement (Remember: Times New Roman 12 font; Proofread)
— Application forms
— Additional essays required by the program
— Self-addressed stamped postcard for them to mail when your application is complete
— Letters of recommendation in sealed envelopes (signed over seal), unless required to send them separately

Interviewing

Most graduate programs in the applied psychology subfields (i.e., clinical, counseling, school, and industrial-organizational) require an interview. In fact, 93% of clinical psychology and counseling psychology programs require some type of interview prior to an offer of admission (Oliver, Norcross, Sayette, Griffin, & Mayne, 2005). Research-oriented subfields (e.g., social, developmental, experimental) generally do not require interviews. Interviews can take place on the phone, in person, or both. In terms of clinical and counseling psychology programs, Oliver et al. indicate that 27% require an in-person interview, 62% prefer an in-person interview, 4% require a telephone interview, and 7% do not require an interview. Because interviews are costly (airfare, hotel, car rentals, food), you will want to keep this in your mind as you make your budget for the interview season. Some programs acknowledge this expense and assist with housing (e.g., current students volunteer to let applicants sleep on their couches). Although you may request a telephone interview if you are unable to travel for an interview, you will want to understand that this puts you at a disadvantage relative to others who interview in-person. As a result, we strongly encourage attending an in-person interview when invited.

Suggestions Specific to In-Person Interviews

Before beginning these suggestions and to eliminate redundancy, we encourage you to review information about attire (e.g., wearing a business suit) and preparation (e.g., doing a mock interview and reviewing program materials and your application) provided earlier in the book. That information applies here too. Keeping these sugges-tions in mind, you can focus yourself during the course of the interview day (or days) on that information most important to you (i.e., Is this program right for me?). During the course of the interview day(s), you will likely meet with faculty and students in both formal and informal settings. Regardless of the setting, you are being evaluated continually, including by the current students. As a result, you will want to be aware of your behavior in all of these settings (e.g., limiting alcohol use at a dinner or social event).

Some applicants are blessed with multiple interview offers. However, multiple interview offers have their own downside. Because interviews are generally conducted on Fridays in later January, February, and early March, overlap may occur in interview dates. Although some programs provide alternative interview dates for students with scheduling conflicts, others do not. As a result, you may be in the position of needing to rank the two or three programs with conflicting interview dates and request phone interviews with the ones coming in second and third. Regardless of the stress, count yourself lucky to have such a situation arise!

Suggestions Specific to Telephone Interviews

For telephone interviews, you will still want to prepare, including ensuring a distraction-free environment for the interview. For the interview, you will want to make sure you are dressed as you would be in an in-person interview (helps remind you of the importance of the call) and have your materials (e.g., application, program information, biographies of those who are calling if known) laid out in front of you (to reduce paper shuffling while on the phone). Norcross et al. (2008) suggests preparing a telephone card (i.e., a single sheet of paper that notes specifics of the program). These specifics should include:

- name of the university and program
- faculty research interests
- faculty you would like to work with and why
- questions you have for the program (see Box 7.7 for possibilities)
- why you are interested in the program

Having this information readily available on each program to which you applied is not a bad idea. This will help you in case a program calls you without warning and wants to talk with you at that moment.

For both phone and in-person interviews, you will want to convey a sense of enthusiasm about the program. This excitement can be displayed via your knowledge of the program and the program's faculty members (including their research programs and publications). Enthusiasm is communicated not only by your answers to their questions but also the questions that you ask. Box 7.7 provides some examples of potential questions you may be asked and that you might ask as well. In general, your preparation for the interview should include a list of questions for the individuals you will meet, including the current students. Furthermore, engaging your interviewer in a discussion of his or her research interests and how those interests match your interests is an excellent goal for the interaction.

Box 7.7   Potential Questions for Graduate School Interviews

Questions by you:
- What percentage of your students publishes before they graduate?
- Is there any formal training for teaching?
- How are most students funded?
- What are your current research studies?
- In what research projects are your students currently involved?
- What courses do your students assist with teaching this semester?
- What is the first-attempt pass rate for your students on the licensure exams? (Applied Programs Only)
- Where do your students find employment?
- What is the typical class size?
- How often do you meet with your graduate students?
- What are the student-professor relationships like (i.e., collegiality)?
- At which conferences do students regularly present?
- Is financial support available for travel to conferences?
- Are summer stipends available?
- What community placements are available for practica?
- What is the biggest strength of the program?
- If you could change something about the program, what would that be and why?

Questions for you:
- Why are you interested in our program?
- What made you decide on this subfield of psychology?
- What do you know of my (the interviewer's) research program?
- What research studies are you interested in conducting?
- What is your theoretical orientation? (For Applied Programs Only)
- What research background do you have?
- What applied experiences do you have? (For Applied Programs Only)
- What do you plan on doing upon receiving your graduate degree?
- What do you see as your biggest strength/weakness?
- What do you like to do for fun/to relax?
- What questions do you have for us?

Thank You Notes

Once all interviews with a particular program are complete (whether the interview was in person or via telephone), we encourage you to send a thank you note to those involved in your interview. Send the note immediately as programs tend to make decisions about offers relatively soon after the interview days conclude. Both thank you note cards and e-mails are generally acceptable in the academic environment. The note should indicate your continuing, genuine interest in the program and your enjoyment of the interview day(s). Sending a thank you note is, generally, the last contact you will have with a program before decisions and offers are made by the program. As a result, you will want to ensure that the note is professional.

Making Your Decision

In our experience, admission offers are made relatively soon after interviews are complete. As a result, offers typically begin to be made in late February and continue until April 1. All offers (along with financial assistance accompanying an offer) must be made by April 1. Although you may accept an offer before April 15, you are allowed until April 15 to make your decision. After April 15, positions not filled/accepted may be offered to others. Given the stress associated with a decision of this magnitude, we encourage you to rank order the offers you receive. Some of the variables you may want to consider in your ranking include many of the attributes that helped you narrow your original list. (See Box 7.2.) We also encourage you to talk with family, your undergraduate mentor, and your letter writers. These individuals continue to be invested in your success and want the right fit for you and your career goals.

Once you have arrived at your decision, make it! When you notify the graduate program of your acceptance (in writing or via e-mail), you will then want to notify the other programs that are continuing to consider you. Releasing your other offers allows those programs to offer your spot to someone on their "wait list." By releasing your spot, you will make someone very happy! Last but not least, thank your letter writers and let them know your decision.

Plan B: What if I Don't Get in?

As is obvious from the percentage of acceptances for programs noted earlier, not everyone that applies to graduate school will get an offer to attend. As a result and even if you followed every suggestion given by us and others, success is not guaranteed (although our experience suggests that the likelihood is increased). As a result, you will want to develop an alternative plan. Our main suggestion for a "Plan B" is to consider applying to master's programs instead of doctoral programs if you do not have a master's degree or if you did not apply to them already. Beyond the possibility of simply having "bad luck," the likelihood is that there are reasons that a student did not get an offer. These reasons can include:

- applying to only high-ranked programs;
- not applying widely enough (geographically or otherwise);
- low GPA/GRE relative to the mean/median of a program's recent acceptances;
- no research experience.

In thinking about your alternative plan, we encourage you to sit with a trusted faculty member who you believe will provide unadulterated critical feedback and suggestions. Give yourself a breather before you do this though. April 16 may be too soon for some. However, in terms of the suggestion of applying to master's programs, some master's programs have late deadlines. As a result, you may consider applying immediately.

Box 7.8 Timeline for Applying to Graduate School

Junior Year

Fall and Spring Semesters	Take advanced psychology courses (e.g., physiological psychology, psychological testing, cognition, perception). These will help prepare you for the Psychology Subject Test.
Spring Semester	Study for the GRE General Test and Psychology Subject Test.
Summer Semester	Take the GRE General Test.
	For the programs in which you are interested (the initial 40–50 programs), review professors' publications as well as the other variables listed in Box 7.2.

Senior Year

August	Narrow down your list of programs to the top ones (approximately 20–25). Review each remaining program in more detail.
	Order and inspect a copy of your transcript to ensure that it is error-free.
	Develop your vita and an initial personal statement that can provide you with a starting point.
September	Contact professors at the graduate programs to see if they are taking students for the following year.
	Finalize your list of schools to which you will apply (approximately 10–15).
	Develop a file for each program in order to keep all information together.
	Fine tune your vita and personal statement. Get *lots* of feedback!
	Deliver packets of information to the faculty who will be writing your letters of recommendation.

October	Take the Psychology Subject Test.
	Order official transcripts.
	Have GRE scores sent to programs.
Early November	Retrieve letters of recommendation.
Mid November–December	Finalize your applications and make a copy of each for the program's respective file.
	Mail your applications.
	Verify that applications were received.
January–Mid March	Wait.
	Interview.
	Wait some more. (Don't forget your current coursework! It can preoccupy you as you wait!)
	Develop some back-up plans in case you receive no offers.
April 1	Deadline for offers from graduate schools
April 15	Submit your decision to the graduate schools on (or preferably before) this date.
Post-April 15	E-mail your letter writers regarding your decision, thanking them for their letters and assistance.

Ten Tips From a Successful Applicant

Laura L. Mayhew
University of South Florida

Kudos to you for considering graduate school! The admission requirements and application process can seem daunting, but don't let that deter you from pursuing your goals. With forethought, organization, and taking advantage of any and all resources available to you, you can be fully prepared, and the application process can go smoothly . . . and hopefully lead to an admission offer! Here are some suggestions to help you with your preparations.

1. Consider your options . . . and really consider a multitude of them.
   Although you may have very specific ideas regarding what you want to do in your career

and what programs you want to pursue, allow some flexibility. For example, if you are pursuing a research-oriented degree, don't immediately dismiss a program because a professor's line of research doesn't perfectly match with your interests. Graduate school is a training period, and you can always tailor your research (or practice, teaching, etc.) more specifically to your liking when you complete your graduate studies.

2. Be a superstar student, and study your tush off for the GRE to earn high scores.

   Like it or not, GPA and GRE scores are always considered in graduate admissions. Although minimum and average GPAs vary among programs, you need to do well in your undergraduate coursework for admission to (and success in) most graduate programs. Start now! You can't build a stellar GPA in one semester. Similarly, GRE score requirements vary by program, but you want to do as best as you can. And, in order to do your best you need to study, study, STUDY, and practice, practice, PRACTICE. In addition to studying the specific test areas (e.g., learning GRE-quality words, reviewing math concepts, practicing analytical writing), take as many practice tests that you can get your hands on.

3. Professor who??? Get to know you professors.

   In order to get strong positive recommendation letters it helps if your professors actually know who you are! Take and excel in multiple classes with the same professors, put in extra face time with them outside of class (e.g., drop in during office hours to discuss coursework and graduate school), and get involved with professors' projects. Besides increasing the possibility of getting stellar recommendations you might actually learn a thing or two (a lot of these folks tend to be pretty smart).

4. Research! Research! Research!

   Although the importance of research experience varies among programs, it is essential for many PhD programs, and it probably won't hurt your chances with programs that emphasize other experiences. Apply for research assistantships in professors' laboratories, or, if there aren't structured labs, ask your professors what upcoming projects they have and inquire how you can contribute. Also consider approaching a professor about a directed study or completing a senior thesis . . . and always look for opportunities to present (or even better, publish) your research.

5. In a similar vein . . . Get experience!

   Practical or clinical experience is important to some programs. Participate in practicum opportunities if your department offers them. Entry-level employment and structured volunteer experience in your field (including research-based positions) can be impressive to admissions committees. In addition, get involved with your department's psychology club and Psi Chi. Become a student affiliate of professional organizations in the field. The Association for Psychological Science Student Caucus (APSSC) is a great international organization in which to get involved. Unlike some other professional organizations, the APSSC offers many opportunities for undergraduates. These types of experiences are great for professional activities you could encounter in your career and look great on your vita to boot!

6. Apply to a *lot* of schools with varying degrees of entrance/requirement difficulties. Again, flexibility is important. There are many people who want to go to graduate school in the same area that *you* are interested. In other words, competition is stiff, and admission is never guaranteed. To increase your chances for admission don't limit yourself to only top-tier programs. Find out where you stand (i.e., your attributes vs. the programs' statistics), and apply to a variety of programs where

you meet and exceed the typical student's credentials plus some of those dreamy programs where you might not be quite up to par.

7. Contact professors at the schools you are considering before applying.

Find out whether or not the professors plan to take students (if it is a mentor-based program) for the upcoming year. This information is often posted on programs' websites, but the contact can benefit you by putting your name "out there." A professor might give you just a bit of extra consideration when your application packet arrives because of the prior contact with you. An e-mail also serves as an opportunity to show genuine interest in the professor's work. Who doesn't like to hear accolades about their work? Similarly, you may try to get in touch with students in a program with questions you may have. Students' opinions of applicants can sometimes influence acceptances, and they can give you a perspective you'll likely want to hear . . . After all, your goal is to be in their position next year, right?

8. Be sure your application materials are organized and professional . . . and seek the opinion of multiple professors to ensure the quality.

Your application is the graduate program's first impression of you, so make sure it looks professional! Ask multiple professors to review and help you tweak your personal statement and vita. They will know what admissions committees value. Place all required application materials in a folder, and include photocopies of materials that may have been sent separately (e.g., transcripts, GRE scores). You also want to make sure your application was received, but don't call. Instead, include a self-addressed stamped postcard with the name of the university on it for staff to send to you upon receipt of your application.

9. Prepare for interviews.

Many programs require interviews prior to an admission's offer. An interview is your chance to impress the faculty. Prepare stellar answers to common interview questions. Also, prepare questions that you want to ask them! Having your own questions is important because it shows that you are really interested. Read up on the faculty's publications, and be prepared to discuss your possible contributions to their research program. Prepare questions to ask students because you will likely be spending time with them (and being interviewed by them) at dinners or in other less formal situations. Remember to ask about anything that would be relevant to you considering spending several years at this place (unless, of course, you are concerned about the bar/club scene! Save that for later, not the interview!!)

10. If at first you don't succeed, try, try again.

You will *have* to be persistent as a graduate student. So, if you don't get accepted the first time you apply, consider it an opportunity to build up your persistence skills! Get more experience, seek guidance, work on your application materials, and go for it again in the next round!

I hope you find these tips useful in your pursuit of even higher higher education. Good luck!

Note: Laura L. Mayhew earned her bachelor's degree in psychology from Kennesaw State University. Due to her academic accomplishments, Laura received the University System of Georgia Board of Regents' Academic Recognition Scholar Award (2005–2006). She is a member of APSSC and the American Psychological Association of Graduate Students. Currently, Laura is a graduate student in the PhD program in Clinical Psychology at the University of South Florida, her first/top choice. Her research is predominantly in the health psychology area.

Suggested Exercises

1. Using one of the resources noted in the chapter, identify two programs in your area of interest. Develop an Excel or SPSS file based on the variables listed in Box 7.2 and fill in the spreadsheet for each of the programs.
2. Using the sample vita and other resources identified in this chapter as a guide, create the vita that you would like to have when you apply for graduate school. (Once completed, let it serve as a guide for your undergraduate activities!)
3. Using one of the programs you identified in the first exercise, develop a mock application. (Applications can often be downloaded. If not, choose a similar program that does have a downloadable application.) As part of the application, develop a cover letter and statement of intent specific to that program.

Suggested Readings

American Psychological Association. (2007). *Getting in: A step-by-step plan for gaining admission to graduate school in psychology*. Washington, DC: Author.

American Psychological Association. (2010). *Graduate study in psychology*. Washington, DC: Author.

Buskist, W., & Burke, C. (2007). *Preparing for graduate study in psychology: 101 questions and answers* (2nd ed.). Malden, MA: Blackwell.

Keith-Spiegel, P., & Wiederman, M. W. (2000). *The complete guide to graduate school admission: Psychology, counseling, and related professions* (2nd ed.). Mahwah, NJ: Lawrence Erlbaum.

Norcross, J. C., Sayette, M. A., & Mayne, T. J. (2008). *Insider's guide to graduate programs in clinical and counseling psychology: 2008/2009 Edition*. New York: Guilford.

References

Academy of Psychological Clinical Science. (n.d.). *Mission and specific goals*. Retrieved from http://psych.arizona.edu/apcs/mission.php

American Psychological Association. (2008). *Archival description of school psychology*. Retrieved from http://www.apa.org/crsppp/schpsych.html

American Psychological Association. (2010). *Graduate study in psychology*. Washington, DC: Author.

American Psychological Association Center for Psychology Workforce Analysis and Research. (2007). *Doctorates awarded in 2005–06: Subfield by degree type*. Retrieved from http://research.apa.org/doctoraled11.html

American Psychological Association – Division 47 – Exercise and Sport Psychology. (2008). *What is exercise and sport psychology?* Retrieved from http://www.apa47.org/studInfo.php

Appleby, D. C., & Appleby, K. M. (2007, Spring). How to avoid the kisses of death in the graduate school application process. *Eye on Psi Chi, 11*(3), 20–21.

Aronson, E. (2004). *The social animal* (9th ed.). New York: Worth.

Association of Psychology Postdoctoral and Internship Centers. (2006). *APPIC match 2000–2006: Match rates by doctoral program*. Retrieved from http://www.appic.org/downloads/APPIC_Match_2000-06_by_Univ.pdf

Association of Psychology Postdoctoral and Internship Centers. (2008). *2008 APPIC match statistics*. Retrieved from http://www.appic.org/match/5_2_2_1_10_match_about_statistics_general_2008.html

Bartol, C. R., & Bartol, A. M. (1999). History of forensic psychology. In A. K. Hess & I. B. Weiner (Eds.), *Handbook of forensic psychology* (2nd ed., pp. 3–23). New York: John Wiley & Sons.

Bottoms, B. L., & Nysse, K. L. (1999, Fall). Applying to graduate school: Writing a compelling personal statement. *Eye on Psi Chi, 4*(1), 20–22.

Briihl, D. S., & Wasieleski, D. T. (2004). A survey of master's-level psychology programs: Admissions criteria and program policies. *Teaching of Psychology*, 31, 252–256.

Educational Testing Service. (2006). *The GRE Psychology Test*. Retrieved from www.gre.org

Educational Testing Service. (2008). *Graduate Record Exam*. Retrieved from www.gre.org

Kupfersmid, J., & Fiola, M. (1991). Comparison of EPPP scores among graduates of varying psychology programs. *American Psychologist*, 46, 534–535.

Maher, B. A. (1999). Changing trends in doctoral training programs in psychology: A comparative analysis of research-oriented versus professional-applied programs. *Psychological Sciences*, 10, 475–481.

Matthews, J. R., & Anton, B. S. (2008). *Introduction to clinical psychology*. New York: Oxford University Press.

Norcross, J. C., Kohout, J. L., & Wicherski, M. (2005). Graduate study in Psychology: 1971 to 2004. *American Psychologist*, 60, 959–975.

Norcross, J. C., Sayette, M. A., & Mayne, T. J. (2008). *Insider's guide to graduate programs in clinical and counseling psychology: 2008/2009 Edition*. New York: Guilford.

Oliver, J. M., Norcross, J. C., Sayette, M. A., Griffin, K., & Mayne, T. J. (2005, March). *Doctoral study in clinical, counseling, and combined psychology: Admission requirements and student characteristics*. Poster presented at the 76th annual meeting of the Eastern Psychological Association, Boston, MA.

Peterson, D. R. (1976). Need for the doctor of psychology degree in professional psychology. *American Psychologist*, 31, 792–798.

Peterson, D. R. (2003). Unintended consequences: Ventures and misadventures in the education of professional psychologists. *American Psychologist*, 58, 791–800.

Society of Clinical Psychology. (n.d.). *What is clinical psychology?* Retrieved from http://www.apa.org/divisions/div12/aboutcp.html

Society of Counseling Psychology. (n.d.). *About Division 17*. Retrieved from http://www.div17.org/about.html

Templer, D. I., & Arikawa, H. (2004). Concerns about professional schools. *American Psychologist*, 59, 646–647.

Weiten, W. (2008). *Psychology: Themes and variations* (7th ed., Briefer version). Belmont, CA: Thomson.

Wicherski, M, & Kohout, J. (2005). *2003 doctorate employment survey*. Retrieved from http://research.apa.org/des03.html

Resources

Program Rankings

(Please note that these rankings tend to change quickly. They are provided only as a beginning point, not as an ending point!)

* PhDs.org
    Description: "Search and rank 23,517 programs at 2,356 universities based on *your* priorities. Data come from the National Science Foundation, the National Research Council, and the National Center for Education Statistics."
    Link: http://graduate-school.phds.org/
* National Academy of Sciences' Research-Doctorate Programs in the United States: Continuity and Change
    Description: ". . . examines 3,634 programs in 41 fields at 274 institutions. The report contains data on a large number of variables for the individual programs and an analysis of various aspects of the 41 fields across different dimensions."
    Link: http://books.nap.edu/html/researchdoc/researchdoc_tables.html
* The Gourman Report
    Description: Ranking of U.S. Psychology PhD programs by area
    Link: http://www.socialpsychology.org/ggradoth.htm

Statement of Purpose Resources

- Accepted.com
  Description: Provides examples and dos and don'ts for writing your statement of purpose for graduate school
  Link: http://www.accepted.com/grad/personalstatement.aspx
- Massachusetts Institute of Technology – Career Services
  Description: Provides pointers on graduate school admission essays and statements as well as examples (although mainly in the engineering field)
  Link: http://web.mit.edu/career/www/workshops/gradschool/statement.html
- University of California – Berkley – Career Center
  Description: Provides pointers on graduate school admission essays and statements
  Link: http://career.berkeley.edu/Grad/GradStatement.stm

Vita Preparation

- Landrum, R. E. (2005, Winter). The curriculum vita: A student's guide to preparation. *Eye on Psi Chi*, *9*(2), 28–29, 42.
  Link: http://www.psichi.org/pubs/articles/article_475.asp

General Resources

- PsycCareers – APA's Online Career Center
  Description: APA website devoted to career issues in psychology, including curriculum vitae development and interviewing tips
  Link: http://psyccareers.apa.org/
- Psi Chi – The National Honor Society in Psychology
  Description: Publishes *Eye on Psi Chi*, a magazine with topical and timely articles on such issues as preparing for graduate school, getting research experience, and preparing for entrance exams. Website includes a searchable database of topics from past issues.
  Link: http://www.psichi.org/
- About.com – Graduate School (by Tara Kuther)
  Description – Information on topics like letters of recommendation, admissions essays, and preparing for the GRE
  Link: http://gradschool.about.com/
- Social Psychology Network – Online Psychology Career Center
  Description – Information on topics like preparing a vita (including examples) and letters of recommendation; also provides useful links to additional resources like program rankings.
  Link: http://www.socialpsychology.org/

Part II

The Subfields of Psychology

8

Careers in Research
Experimental, Developmental, Social, Cognitive, and Biopsychology

Introduction

The scientific process forms the core of psychology. Because all psychologists are trained in how to design research, gather data, and analyze results, research-based careers occur in every subfield of the discipline. Given the involvement of so many psychologists in research, it is impossible to capture all the variations within and among these careers in a single chapter. However, an overview of five subfields that are explicitly oriented towards conducting research can provide you with a sense of what these types of careers entail.

Before turning to various research careers in the field, let us first consider a key question. What is research? Research involves gaining knowledge about the world around us in a specific way. Although we gain knowledge daily by reasoning about situations, accepting the view of authority figures, or experiencing things first-hand, each of these methods of understanding are prone to error and bias. In contrast, research uses methods and techniques specifically designed to ensure the objectivity of the knowledge gained. Psychologists use these methods and techniques to answer questions about behavior. Even though these questions stem from their own curiosity, psychologists allow the data they gather to answer the question rather than relying on intuition, logic, authority, or personal experience.

Research is a creative endeavor full of excitement and possibilities. Despite this, undergraduate psychology majors do not typically rank the research-oriented subfields high among their future career goals (Gallucci, 1997). This lack of interest appears to be in place even before students select psychology as their major. For example, new majors indicate that they do not expect research and statistics to be a priority in their psychology courses (McGovern & Hawks, 1986). Apparently many students choose the psychology major while still unfamiliar with what the field entails. In fact, many students have a misconception that the field involves only applied work in mental health (Webb & Speer, 1985). Yet out of the doctoral degrees granted in psychology in the

United States between 1996 and 2005, approximately 25% were in the five research intensive subfields considered in this chapter (National Science Foundation, 2006). Students' lack of understanding about the role of research in the field likely stems from limited contact with psychologists who are doing this work. As a result, few students can conceptualize what a research-oriented career in psychology would be like. Changing this perception begins with being better informed.

Defining the Subfields

Experimental Psychology

Experimental psychologists' expertise is in conducting psychological research. It is true that conducting research is emphasized in all areas of psychology. Training in research methodology, experimentation, and statistics will be a core part of your education as an undergraduate and as a graduate student in the field. But, experimental psychologists choose to pursue a subfield that places the ability to design and conduct psychological research at the forefront of their training. In order to give you a better sense of the kinds of research these psychologists might conduct, Box 8.1 lists several research questions that experimental psychologists have sought to answer in recent years.

Because their research skills and expertise are general enough to be applied to a variety of topics, experimental psychologists are not tied to conducting research in any one area. However, most do choose a specialty or concentration for their career while in school. Graduate programs in experimental psychology, and the faculty who guide them, often have a particular research focus. Students attending these programs develop knowledge in these areas while becoming experts in general research methods. This can be a confusing point for undergraduate students since their professors who are trained as experimental psychologists may or may not identify themselves as such. For example, one professor may identify herself as an experimental psychologist while another states he is a cognitive psychologist. Yet both could conduct research on essentially the same topic.

Box 8.1 Questions Addressed by the Research of Experimental Psychologists

- How do certain characteristics of a task affect one's success in completing it?
- What visual features facilitate the detection of emotions in facial expressions?
- What factors would lead an eyewitness to falsely identify an innocent suspect?
- How do people make decisions when presented with information that contradicts their beliefs?
- What practice or rehearsal schedules should be followed in order to maximize learning?
- What characteristics of a stimulus contribute to the conditioning of fear?

Reading the research literature is a good way to gain additional understanding of careers in research within psychology. For each of the subfields discussed in this chapter, we will summarize elements of a recent research article to further demonstrate the rich diversity of topics investigated in the field. For example, Smith, Redford, Haas, Coutinho, and Couchman (2008) recently compared the ways that humans and rhesus monkeys judge objects to be the same or different. While viewing pairs of geometric figures with varying degrees of difference in their shape, the humans and monkeys labeled each pair as "same" or "different." Humans applied the label of "different" to pairs that varied to any degree, including those with only slight differences. However, monkeys were far more likely to label pairs with slight discrepancies as being the "same." The authors concluded that humans have a qualitative or all-or-nothing approach to judging same and different. In contrast, they argued that monkeys have a quantitative understanding of the concepts that takes into account the degree of discrepancy. The results of the study shed light on both species' cognitive and perceptual functioning, which could improve our understanding of a host of behaviors that require judgments of sameness and difference.

Developmental Psychology

Developmental psychologists' expertise is in the scientific study of human development. Emotional, cognitive, and physical development are all areas of potential focus. In their research, developmental psychologists keep two broad themes in mind. First, they view development as occurring across the lifespan. Important changes take place at all ages, not just in childhood and adolescence. Second, they view development from a global perspective. Change always occurs within a specific context, and what happens developmentally in one culture might not occur in the same way within a different culture. To better understand the types of research developmental psychologists might conduct, Box 8.2 provides several examples of research questions that have received attention in recent years.

Box 8.2 Questions Addressed by the Research of Developmental Psychologists

- How does direct experience with a task affect a child's ability to complete it in the future?
- What factors contribute to young children's ability to think about and visually recognize themselves?
- How do the events of normal aging affect life satisfaction?
- What types of experiences can hinder the normal progression of language development?
- How does the quality of the relationship between a child and parent affect the child's relationships as an adult?
- What role do characteristics of the environmental play in adolescents' responses to stress?

Studying human development is a complex task. Change at any point in a person's development is dependent upon a host of factors such as genetics, physiology, nutrition, education, personality, culture, and environment. Developmental psychologists must understand something about each of these sources of influence. Their particular research interests might only concentrate on a select few, but they are likely to collaborate with professionals who possess expertise on the others. Although most developmental psychologists continue to be focused on research in their careers, increasing numbers of them are also pursuing applied endeavors. These psychologists often conduct research on interventions designed to address a developmental issue. For example, they may design a program to address language delays in preschoolers and then assess its effectiveness in various settings.

As one example of research within the developmental psychology subfield, consider a recent study by Tardif et al. (2008). The authors investigated the idea that infants all over the world first acquire and use nouns when learning to speak. They recruited the caregivers of children between the ages of 8 and 16 months from English, Mandarin, and Cantonese speaking households. The caregivers reported the words the child was speaking. Analysis of these lists revealed strong similarities. Words for daddy, mommy, bye, uh-oh, woof, and hi were among the top 20 most common words in all three languages. In addition, the authors found strong similarities in the types of words that were spoken. Yet rather than find a universal bias for using object naming nouns, the authors discovered that the consistency across cultures was for words pertaining to people. The results highlight the combined role that genetics and culture play in human development.

Social Psychology

Social psychologists' expertise is in understanding human behavior as it occurs within social contexts. Their research focuses on how humans' thoughts, actions, and feelings are influenced by various aspects of the social environment. They also investigate how humans relate to one another in these environments. Social psychologists interested in individual behavior examine both the characteristics of an individual that influence his/her social interactions and how these characteristics in turn influence the social group. Other social psychologists focus more exclusively on group behavior. Their interests often address how group characteristics and actions affect members and how group behavior and decision making can differ from that of an individual. Box 8.3 provides several examples of research questions that have received attention in recent years by social psychologists.

Social psychology has much in common with other subfields including clinical, counseling, cognitive, and personality psychology. In fact, psychologists in each of these areas investigate topics related to behavior in social contexts such as aggression, stereotypes, interpersonal relationships, and attributions. The research of social psychologists can similarly have direct applications at the societal level. For example, knowledge in social psychology might be used to develop a school-based program to reduce prejudice and stereotyping. Or knowledge about how consumers make individual judgments might be used to help increase a population's use of mass transportation.

Box 8.3   Questions Addressed by the Research of
Social Psychologists

- What factors contribute to whether an individual finds someone else to be attractive?
- How much influence do others' expressed perceptions of an event have on an individual's perception of the same event?
- Why are stereotypes so resistant to change?
- What aspects of a salesperson's behavior influences the customer's decisions the most?
- Does exposure to interpersonal violence foster subsequent aggressive behavior?
- Why do some individuals confess to a crime they did not commit?

To provide an example of the kind of research that is possible within social psychology, consider a recent study by Eberhardt, Goff, Purdie, and Davies (2004). The authors investigated whether humans link social categories (e.g., class, gender, age) with general concepts (e.g., leader, good, unhappy) in such a way that the perception of one can be influenced by the presence of the other. Participants first completed a task in which they had to quickly locate a picture on a screen. The picture appeared as a blurred composite of many faces. However, it also contained an image of a white face, black face, or line drawing. This image was displayed so briefly that the participants did not consciously detect it. Participants then viewed images of various objects that were degraded in quality. As these images became increasingly clear, they identified them as quickly as possible. Several of the objects were crime relevant, such as a gun, while others were crime irrelevant, such as a book. There was no difference between the participants in terms of how quickly they identified the crime irrelevant objects. However, participants who had been subliminally exposed a black face identified crime-relevant objects quicker than those who viewed a white face or the line drawing. Participants exposed a white face identified the crime-relevant objects slower than those exposed to the line drawing. The results suggested that stereotyped associations between the social category of "race" and the general concept of "criminal activity" can have a marked impact on visual perception, regardless of the participant's racial attitudes. The Eberhardt et al. study also serves as an excellent example of how the research-oriented subfields in psychology often overlap in focus, in this case combining the elements of attitudes, perception, and cognitive processing as they pertain to a social phenomenon.

Cognitive Psychology

The expertise of cognitive psychologists consists of understanding how human and non-human animals acquire and use knowledge. Because knowledge acquisition and

Box 8.4 Questions Addressed by the Research of Cognitive Psychologists

- What factors contribute to distortions in memory?
- How do features of one's language shape the ability to think about certain concepts?
- What elements of multimedia-based instruction facilitate learning?
- What types of information are most often relied on to solve problems?
- What role does imagining a piece of information play in transferring it into memory?
- What factors contribute most to the comprehension of read text?

use involves a host of diverse skills and abilities, cognitive psychologists can be found investigating a wide range of topics. Yet most of these pertain to the processes that allow information to either be taken in, processed, stored, retrieved, or expressed. Each of these processes can function at varying levels of effectiveness. As a result, some cognitive psychologists strive to understand how these processes can be facilitated while others focus on how they are hindered. To help you conceptualize the types of research cognitive psychologists might conduct, Box 8.4 provides several examples of questions that researchers have focused on in recent years.

Given cognitive psychologists' interests in topics such as attention, information processing, perception, memory, reasoning, language, and communication, the overlap between this subfield and other disciplines has grown in recent years. It is quite common to find cognitive psychologists collaborating with colleagues in education, cognitive science, medicine, linguistics, and computer science. In addition, many cognitive psychologists investigate topics that have an applied focus. For example, research on factors that facilitate or hinder learning and memory can be used to improve human performance. Components of educational and occupational training programs borrow heavily from the cognitive psychology research literature.

To better demonstrate the vast potential in cognitive psychological research, consider a recent investigation conducted by Kuefner, Cassia, Picozzi, and Bricolo (2008). The authors investigated whether the same cognitive processes that contribute to the "other race effect" also contribute to an "other age effect." The "other race effect" occurs when individuals have greater difficulty discriminating faces that are not of their own race. The authors initially found that adults were better at recognizing adult faces compared to faces of newborns and children. They then recruited adult participants with varying degrees of experience with children. Participants viewed a target face and had to pick which of two other faces matched the target. The results indicated that participants with limited experience with children were quicker and more accurate when matching adult faces compared to child faces. The adults with extensive experience with children were able to match adult and child faces equally well. The authors concluded that while an "other age effect" does appear to exist, the strategies used in recognizing faces can be adjusted with experience.

Biopsychology

Biopsychologists' expertise is in exploring the links between behavior and biology. These links can be investigated from a variety of perspectives. As a result, this specialty area includes and/or overlaps with the work of physiological psychologists, behavioral neuroscientists, and cognitive and clinical neuropsychologists. What distinguishes biopsychologists from other psychologists studying similar topics are the methods used in their research. They apply biological principles in studying the links between biological functioning and behavior. Consequently, they spend time investigating such topics as neuroanatomy, neural communication, pharmacology, endocrine functioning, and genetics. In order to give you a better sense of the kinds of research biopsychologists might conduct, Box 8.5 lists a few research questions that these psychologists have sought to answer in recent years.

Biopsychologists are interested in establishing how biological systems affect behavior and how behaviors affect biological systems. Emphasis is given to understanding how these interactions normally occur and how they occur when there are interfering factors at work. For example, some biopsychologists investigate the impact of disease processes, such as Parkinson's or schizophrenia, on the body. Others examine the influence that substances, such as medications or environmental toxins, have on biological and behavioral processes.

As an example of the types of research that are possible within the biopsychology subfield, consider a recent study by Kleykamp, Jennings, Sams, Weaver, and Eissenberg (2008). The authors investigated the effectiveness of nicotine patches in helping individuals stop smoking. Participants in the study smoked at least 15 cigarettes per day and had smoked for at least two years. They completed four trials on separate days, during which they received nicotine patches with varying dosage levels. For each trial, the participant had refrained from smoking for the 8 hours prior. During the trial they completed computerized assessment measures and provided blood samples in order

---

Box 8.5   Questions Addressed by the Research of Biopsychologists

- How can sensitivity to pain be altered?
- What neurotransmitters are involved in the various forms of mental illness?
- What role do hormone levels play in mood?
- How do certain genetic conditions affect motor control?
- What are the short- and long-term effects of stress on the body?
- How do sleep patterns and the effects of sleep deprivation change with age?

to measure nicotine levels. Several hours into each trial, participants were allowed to smoke as they wished. The results indicated that the use of a nicotine patch reduced some of the symptoms that regular smokers experience when they do not smoke. The patches also diminished some of the effects of smoking, such as heart rate increase, and lowered the intensity and frequency of smoking. The authors found no differences for these effects between male and female participants. In conclusion, the authors noted that although nicotine administration appears to be a useful aid in efforts to stop smoking, the presence of nicotine in the system alone is not sufficient to eliminate all of the symptoms that occur with smoking abstinence. This suggests that the symptoms smokers experience when they do not smoke are only partly based on nicotine withdrawal. Other non-nicotine factors (e.g., the action of smoking, the smell of a lit cigarette) may also play a role in withdrawal symptoms.

The Work

Because the psychologists who pursue careers in research come from diverse subfields and have diverse interests, it is impossible to briefly describe the nature of this work in all of its possible forms. Instead we will describe some of the characteristics and issues that are common across all research-oriented careers in the field. In doing so, we hope to provide a clearer sense of the activities, settings, salaries, and employment issues that are part of the professional lives of psychologists who pursue careers in research.

Core Activities

Most experimental, developmental, social, cognitive, and biopsychologists seek out their careers because they are interested in learning more about a specific topic through conducting research. As a result, most expect to spend the bulk of their professional lives engaging in the scientific process. But these careers frequently involve the closely related activities of administration and teaching and supervision.

Research.   Research is a process of discovery. Researchers begin with a question about a particular topic then gradually gather more and more evidence to help answer that question. Importantly, the evidence that is discovered is eventually shared with colleagues in the field who allow this new knowledge to guide and inform the types of questions they are asking in their own research. Over time, this process yields an increasingly sophisticated knowledge base that informs additional research. Eventually this research may begin to impact our daily lives in a direct manner. Psychologists who pursue careers in research do so because they enjoy this endeavor.

   The research conducted by psychologists can be classified as either basic or applied in nature. The goal of basic research is to advance our understanding of some topic. For example, a developmental psychologist might seek to understand the age at which children can classify or categorize certain types of objects. Or a cognitive psychologist might explore how characteristics of presented information affect memory for that information. The knowledge that basic research generates answers questions about how something works. This knowledge typically sparks additional research. In contrast, the goal of applied research is to use existing knowledge for a specific purpose, typically solving a real-world problem. To extend the previous examples, consider that the developmental psychologist who gains knowledge about children's object categorization later conducts research on the effects of teaching children these strategies. The cognitive psychologist who gains an understanding of how the features of presented material affect memory later investigates whether varying the layout of textbooks improves learning. Although some psychologists conduct both basic and applied research, most spend their careers pursuing one or the other.

Teaching and supervision.　Psychologists who pursue research careers are involved in generating new knowledge. Because this research is often conducted in academic settings, many of them also teach and supervise students who are pursuing a psychology degree. Typically these psychologists teach courses within their area of expertise. At the undergraduate level they teach courses that provide a general overview of their subfield. At the graduate level they teach courses specific to their particular interests. For example, a cognitive psychologist might teach an undergraduate course titled "Introduction to Cognitive Psychology" and graduate courses titled "Pattern Recognition and Analysis" and "Neurolinguistics." Many of these psychologists also supervise undergraduate and graduate students' research. They use their expertise in the subfields and in conducting research to guide student learning. In turn, these students assist psychologists in their research. These mutually beneficial relationships play an important role in the research careers of psychologists and the training of future psychologists.

Administration.　Some research careers in psychology include less direct involvement in the research process. Psychologists with expertise in a specific area can be responsible for overseeing research conducted by other professionals. Often this type of activity occurs within an agency that provides grant funding for research. Before such funds are given, the proposed research projects must be carefully evaluated. The projects are then subject to reviews while the research is being conducted and after the project is complete. Many companies that conduct research also depend upon administrators to oversee this work. These types of administrative roles are best filled by individuals who possess expertise in the research process and the skills necessary to work with diverse groups of people. Research-oriented psychologists often fit this description well.

Settings

Experimental, developmental, social, cognitive, and biopsychologists must carry out their careers in settings that can support their research, including the physical facilities and the money necessary to complete projects successfully. Colleges and universities are some of the most common settings providing this support, as evidenced by the fact that approximately 50% of all recent graduates in the research subfields of psychology are employed full-time in academic settings (American Psychological

Association [APA], 2005a). The largest portion of these is employed in settings where their responsibilities may consist of teaching, research, service, and administration. Although most of these individuals work in psychology departments, others are employed in related departments such as cognitive science, biology, education, and statistics. These occupations involve numerous challenges and rewards that are unique to this setting. Additional information on them is provided in the Careers in Academe chapter.

Approximately 26% of recent graduates in the research-oriented subfields of psychology are employed full-time in private sector and government positions (APA, 2005a). These positions can include responsibilities as a researcher or administrator depending on the specific setting and nature of the work. Many psychologists are hired into these positions because their expertise, either in a particular subject or with a particular methodology, will be of benefit to the organization as it pursues areas of research. Some of these psychologists function as analysts or database managers by overseeing the collection and analysis of large data sets to answer questions related to a company's goals. Others may function in the role of consultants that guide the development and design of new research. Still others in government positions might conduct research or help craft policies and initiatives related to their area of expertise.

Salaries

The salaries earned by experimental, developmental, cognitive, social, and biopsychologists vary widely based on the type of career they pursue and the setting in which they work. According to the U.S. Department of Labor (2007), 80% of psychologists not in the clinical, counseling, or industrial/organizational subfields earned an estimated annual salary between $36,200 and $128,630, with a median income of $79,570. Much of the variation within these estimates stems from the discrepancy that often exists between academic or government positions and those in the private sector. Typically the private sector positions command a higher salary. However, advanced positions in academic and government settings can include salaries that rival those of the private sector positions.

Employment Issues

Finding employment in a research-oriented career in psychology is heavily dependent upon the funding available to the institutions that offer such positions. It might also depend upon a particular institution's current financial status. For example, universities that are well funded either by the state or through private endowments may hire many faculty members in the same year that neighboring universities are struggling to keep the positions they currently have. Similar disparities among government agencies can occur based on trends in the research fields as well as changes in the funding allocated. Private sector positions depend heavily on current economic conditions and the degree to which a company is willing to fund research positions at a given time. The message here is that in research careers, employment opportunities and the security of the positions are dependent upon the funding sources supporting the research.

It is also important to keep in mind that in all types of settings, research careers will carry expectations for productivity. Companies may expect that a certain number of projects be completed by a deadline. Academic positions may be dependent upon the researcher securing sufficient funding through grants and producing a certain number of publications in a period of time. Although productivity expectations are a reality of most careers, they can be particularly challenging in research positions given that the research process is by definition unpredictable.

Training and Preparation

Earning a Degree

The primary goal of graduate programs in experimental, developmental, social, cognitive, and biopsychology is to make each student an independent researcher. Despite studying different topics and populations, using varying methodologies, and pursuing diverse career paths, all of these future psychologists strive to leave graduate school with the knowledge and skills to conduct their own research.

Doctoral programs.   Doctoral programs in these subfields of psychology within the United States vary in availability. The largest number are in the cognitive, developmental, and social areas, with each offering approximately 100 doctoral-level programs in the subfield and related areas (APA, 2005b). The fewest number are available in the more general subfield of experimental psychology, though about 30 such programs exist. Each program within a given subfield will vary in terms of the topics emphasized, the faculty's expertise, and the training offered. Each of these factors combines to affect the nature of the careers that graduates of these programs pursue. One variation that is often of immediate concern to undergraduates trying to select a program is the amount of funding provided to graduate students. Typically graduate programs in the research subfields provide substantial financial support to students, often in the form of tuition waivers, stipends, and assistantships. These programs do so because the research intensive nature of the training supports the research of the faculty, who can in turn secure grant funding to support the program. Thus these programs seek to pay students for the work they contribute to the program. In addition, these funding sources are one way that programs attract and recruit the best students. For a more detailed overview of these issues, refer to the Applying to Graduate School chapter.

Master's programs.   Although often fewer in number than doctoral programs, master's level programs exist in experimental, developmental, social, cognitive, and biopsychology. The largest number is in experimental psychology (APA, 2005b). Graduates of master's level programs in the research-oriented subfields typically either seek employment that utilizes their training or pursue a doctoral degree. Many of these programs strive to train students with one of these two outcomes in mind. Programs that offer a terminal master's degree train students who intend to seek employment following graduation. Programs that offer a non-terminal master's degree train students who intend to seek additional education at the doctoral level. Although some programs identify themselves accordingly, others are less clear. Inquiring about what recent graduates of the program are currently doing will often provide the best indication of what the training will best prepare you to do. However, keep in mind two important things about master's level programs in experimental, developmental, social, cognitive, and biopsychology. First, a master's degree in one of these areas does not make you a psychologist. Instead, your career options will be in research-oriented positions that will tap your quantitative, statistical, and writing skills. Second, although completing a master's degree may make your application more attractive to a doctoral program, most do not grant course credit for a prior master's degree. Instead, they will expect you to complete the bulk of the training they require in their doctoral program.

Postdoctoral training. Postdoctoral training is a common element in experimental, developmental, social, cognitive, and biopsychologists' education. Recent data indicated that over half of all new graduates of doctoral programs in these subfields immediately pursue postdoctoral training (APA, 2005a). Postdoctoral training serves as an important period of time in which these new psychologists hone their skills and begin developing their own research programs. In addition, many employers prefer to hire individuals who have research experience beyond their graduate school training.

Preparing for Graduate Training as an Undergraduate

If the subfields of experimental, developmental, social, cognitive, and biopsychology are of interest to you for your future career, there are several things you can do as an undergraduate student to prepare. Most important among them is focusing on developing your knowledge through coursework and your skills through research experience.

Coursework. To prepare for graduate study in a research-oriented subfield of psychology, you must first and foremost be highly successful in your required courses that cover the topics of statistics, research methods, and experimental design. The concepts and skills addressed in these courses are the basis of careers in research. Therefore you should not only excel in but also enjoy these courses. In addition, most psychology departments offer upper-level courses in the areas of cognitive, developmental, social, and biopsychology. Outside of psychology, students interested in these career areas should strongly consider taking courses in the natural sciences, particularly biology and chemistry. These courses provide additional training in the scientific process and knowledge that relates to scientific inquiries in psychology. Finally, additional coursework in statistics can be of great benefit.

Activities. Hands-on research experience is invaluable for any student considering graduate training in a research-oriented subfield of psychology. You will develop a feel for what a research career would be like and will have the opportunity to decide if this type of work is the best fit for you. Such experience often provides students with a clearer sense of their specific interests in the field. Graduate programs that train students in the research-oriented subfields of psychology tend to believe that having research experience prior to graduate school is a must. They understand that such experience leads students to be more informed in their selection of a subfield. In addition, having a strong record of research experience speaks volumes about a student's potential as a graduate student.

Working in Research Related Areas With a Bachelor's Degree

As discussed in previous chapters, the bachelor's degree in psychology can be thought of as either a liberal arts or preprofessional degree. If you are interested in a research-oriented career in psychology, you should view your undergraduate education as preparation for pursuing the doctoral degree. Although students with sufficient research training and proficiency can secure employment in a research-oriented career with a bachelor's or master's degree, the level of autonomy and control they will have over the research they conduct will be limited. The authority to design and oversee research, as well as to seek grant funding, typically resides only with doctoral level professionals. However, some psychology students choose to pursue research-oriented careers with less education because they find the work inherently rewarding and/or they view such additional experience as an important step in their career path.

Research Assistant or Lab Technician

Employment as a research assistant or lab technician involves responsibility for aspects of ongoing research projects. These positions are often available with institutions or companies that have active, ongoing research programs that require numerous employees to manage and operate. Often there are tiers of researchers with varying responsibilities that are consistent with their training and expertise. At the bachelor's level, research assistants often are responsible for the day-to-day maintenance and upkeep of laboratory space and equipment. In addition, many have data entry and database management duties. If they have relevant experience, research assistants might be involved in data collection through conducting interviews, administering questionnaires, taking measurements, or obtaining specimens. According to the U.S. Department of Labor (2007), the median salary estimate was $35,870 for research assistants in the social sciences and $38,130 for technicians in the life, physical, and social sciences.

Analysts

Bachelors' level positions that are focused on data analysis are also available with some institutions and companies. Students with strong quantitative, statistical, and computer skills would be eligible for such positions. The job duties often entail working with research or analyst teams to examine data in order to answer questions that are essential to the successful functioning of the organization. According to the U.S. Department of Labor (2007), the median salary estimate was $60,300 for market research analysts and $63,440 for budget analysts.

Advertising and Sales

Many bachelor's level positions sought by psychology majors are in for-profit settings. For example, those with specific interests in the social psychology subfield might seek positions in the areas of advertising or sales. These areas allow for applications of social psychological principles towards the goals of predicting and influencing consumers' behavior. With a bachelor's degree, these positions are likely to be in the areas of account representatives, managers, and direct sales. According to the U.S. Department of Labor (2007), the median salary estimate was $42,820 for advertising sales agents, $34,460 for retail sales managers, and $40,600 for real estate sales agents.

Teacher

Psychology majors who are drawn to the developmental subfield area but who are seeking to find employment with a bachelor's degree might want to consider teaching. Teaching positions provide an opportunity to engage with students at various points in their development and have an impact on their learning. In addition, teachers often play a substantial role in their students' growth in many other areas, including social and emotional development. Although undergraduate psychology programs do not equip students with the background and skills necessary to earn a teaching certification, many school districts allow individuals to begin teaching while they work to complete their certification. According to the U.S. Department of Labor (2007), the median salary estimate was $47,900 for middle school teachers and $49,420 for secondary school teachers.

Testing the Waters

Marie Balaban, PhD
Eastern Oregon University

As you consider a research-related career, your undergraduate training should include learning to read research and learning to do research.

Getting Your Feet Wet: Reading Research

Textbook authors synthesize information from a wealth of sources to explain controversies or distill conclusions. For example, are the pros and cons of reaching puberty early or late, with respect to peers, different for girls than for boys? You read the textbook authors' interpretation of the research findings, but some results seem contradictory. Psychology majors should develop skills in finding, understanding, and evaluating original sources. You might grow skeptical about a conclusion after examining a study's methods or you might be convinced after reading a carefully controlled study.

Primary research typically refers to published journal articles that report the work's background, methods, results, and discussion. Wading through primary sources can be challenging and may require reading the paper more than once. Authors use jargon intended for experts in the field, and advanced statistical analyses can be confusing. Look at the tables or figures to find key results and at the first part of the discussion to find the authors' description of their findings.

Reading one article often leads to related sources. Reading research is like navigating a mystery: what has been done, why, and what questions are propagated as you explore further? If you enjoy this process, then perhaps a research career is right for you!

A more general reason to read primary research sources is to build your confidence for using these kinds of sources in future circumstances. Perhaps you will want to look up current information on a treatment in sports medicine or research on family relationships for adopted children. Knowing how to look beyond the popular information will be a valuable asset.

Diving In: Doing Research

Most psychology majors quickly discover that hands-on research experience is important on a practical level for graduate school and career preparation. At a deeper level, the process of discovery can be exciting. Seek out research opportunities and start early (perhaps sophomore year). Ask faculty if they need a research assistant. Find out whether your program offers opportunities for individual student research projects. Do you have a question to explore? The topic that you investigate does not have to be the topic you eventually pursue in graduate school or a career. One former student of

mine completed an excellent, detailed project on parsing language in adults, and then earned a PhD in child clinical psychology. During your undergraduate years, you might work with more than one faculty member or you might stay in one research lab.

Participating in research gives you the chance to find out whether you like delving into a research question. You may find that, like the rest of us, you will make mistakes and learn from them. Another former student of mine unwittingly photocopied only one side of a two-sided temperament questionnaire, and used it throughout a study; the results could not be scored or used. That was a harsh lesson to face! Being a research assistant also gives you a "home" within your psychology department and connections – with professors, postdoctoral fellows, graduate students, or other undergraduates. The ripple effect from these connections can be long-lasting if you pursue a research career.

You might present your research at a student conference, co-author a presentation at a professional conference, or co-author a publication. You will also gain expertise in some of the following skills: using library databases, understanding research ethics and informed consent procedures, using software for collecting data, using spreadsheets, making graphs, using and interpreting statistical programs, designing posters for presentations. All of these accomplishments are good practical qualifications for graduate school or careers. Moreover, perhaps your research findings will make a splash by providing insight that advances the field of psychology as well as the next wave of textbooks.

Note. Dr. Marie Balaban is a developmental psychologist and a professor of psychology at Eastern Oregon University. She has authored over 25 peer reviewed journal articles on the topics of infant sensation, perception, and cognition, as well as psychophysiological measurement. Dr. Balaban teaches courses on development, cognition, sensation and perception, emotion, and statistics.

Professional Spotlight

Cynthia L. Pickett, PhD

Education:
- Bachelor of Arts (BA) in Psychology from Stanford University (1994)
- Master of Arts (MA) in Social Psychology from Ohio State University (1996)
- Doctor of Philosophy (PhD) in Social Psychology from Ohio State University (1999)

Position:
Associate Professor of Psychology at the University of California, Davis

Description of Position:
My time is split between conducting research and teaching. I maintain an active program of research involving several graduate students and undergraduate research assistants on topics such as social identity, the self, social cognition, and intergroup relations. I teach undergraduate and graduate courses on these topics as well.

Most Significant Professional Accomplishment:
I was named by the Association for Psychological Science as a "Rising Star" in psychology.

Favorite Publication:
Pickett, C. L., Bonner, B. L., & Coleman, J. M. (2002). Motivated self-stereotyping: Heightened assimilation and differentiation needs result in increased levels of positive and negative self-stereotyping. *Journal of Personality and Social Psychology, 82,* 543–562.

Areas of Research:
I investigate self, social identity, social cognition, and intergroup relations.

Professional Memberships:
- Association for Psychological Science
- Society of Experimental Social Psychology
- Society for Personality and Social Psychology
- Social Psychology Network

Most Rewarding Aspect of Your Career:
I love the scientific process of developing and testing hypotheses, and it is great that in academia one can choose the questions that one pursues. I also find teaching to be a fun and rewarding experience. I enjoy exposing students to new theories and ideas and trying to get them as excited about the material as I am.

Words of Advice to the Student Who Is Interested in Your Subfield:
If possible, try to get involved in research at your undergraduate institution. It will give you a new appreciation for how social psychologists study social behavior and test their theoretical models.

Suggested Exercises

1. Think for a moment about some aspect of human behavior that has piqued your curiosity in recent days. Perhaps you observed an aggressive driver or children playing a game. Formulate a question about some aspect of what you observed. Now look to the research literature and see what is known about the question you formulated. Based on what you find in your search, revise your question. Observing behavior, generating questions, and examining the literature are all part of the scientific process that occurs in psychological research, and they are great ways of fostering your research ideas.

2. Identify the faculty members in your psychology department whose backgrounds are in experimental, developmental, social, cognitive, or biopsychology. Select one whose research area interests you and ask them to provide you a reference for a research article that is important in their subfield. Read the article and develop one or two questions about it. Consider posing these questions to the faculty member, either in person during their office hours or by email. Inquiries and conversations such as these are important in helping you determine what areas of research you find compelling.

3. Investigate opportunities for gaining research experience. Some departments of psychology post openings for research assistant positions in a faculty member's lab. In other departments these positions can only be learned about by having conversations with faculty members about opportunities to assist them. Keep in mind that even research experience outside of your area of interest can be valuable in helping you decide if a research career in psychology is right for you. If opportunities within your department are limited, consider contacting faculty members at neighboring institutions to ask about volunteering in their research labs.

Suggested Readings by Topic Area

Experimental Psychology

Healy, A. F., & Proctor, R. W. (Eds.) (2004). *Comprehensive handbook of psychology: Vol. 4, Experimental psychology.* New York: John Wiley & Sons.

Mandler, G. (2007). *A history of modern experimental psychology: From James and Wundt to cognitive science.* Cambridge, MA: MIT Press.

Developmental Psychology

Lerner, R. M., Easterbrooks, M. A., & Mistry, J. (Eds.) (2004). *Comprehensive handbook of psychology: Vol. 6, Developmental psychology.* New York: John Wiley & Sons.

Liben, L. S. (Ed.). (2008). *Current directions in developmental psychology* (2nd ed.). Boston: Allyn & Bacon.

Social Psychology

Millon, T., & Lerner, M. J. (Eds). (2004). *Comprehensive handbook of psychology: Vol. 5, Personality and social psychology.* New York: John Wiley & Sons.

Ruscher, J., & Hammer, E. Y. (Eds.). (2004). *Current directions in social psychology.* Upper Saddle River, NJ: Prentice Hall.

Cognitive Psychology

Levitin, D. J. (Ed). (2002). *Foundations of cognitive psychology: Core readings.* Cambridge, MA: MIT Press.

Spellman, B. A., & Willingham, D. T. (Eds.) (2005). *Current directions in cognitive science.* Upper Saddle River, NJ: Prentice Hall.

Biopsychology

DeVries, A. C., & Nelson, R. J. (2007). *Current directions in biopsychology.* Englewood Cliffs, NJ: Prentice Hall.

Gallagher, M., & Nelson, R. J. (2004). *Comprehensive handbook of psychology: Vol. 3, Biological psychology.* New York: John Wiley & Sons.

References

American Psychological Association. (2005a). *2005 doctorate employment survey*. Washington, DC: Author.

American Psychological Association. (2005b). *Graduate study in psychology 2005*. Washington, DC: Author.

Eberhardt, J. L., Goff, P. A., Purdie, V. J., & Davies, P. G. (2004). Seeing black: Race, crime, and visual processing. *Journal of Personality and Social Psychology, 87*, 876–893.

Gallucci, N. T. (1997). An evaluation of the characteristics of undergraduate psychology majors. *Psychological Reports, 81*, 879–889.

Kleykamp, B. A., Jennings, J. M., Sams, C., Weaver, M. F., & Eissenberg, T. (2008). The influence of transdermal nicotine on tobacco/nicotine abstinence and the effects of a concurrently administered cigarette in women and men. *Experimental and Clinical Psychopharmacology, 16*, 99–112.

Kuefner, D., Cassia, V. M., Picozzi, M., & Bricolo, E. (2008). Do all kids look alike? Evidence for an other-age effect in adults. *Journal of Experimental Psychology: Human Perception and Performance, 34*, 811–817.

McGovern, T. V., & Hawks, B. K. (1986). The varieties of undergraduate experience. *Teaching of Psychology, 13*, 174–181.

National Science Foundation. (2006). *Science and engineering doctorate awards: 2005* (NSF 07-305). Retrieved from http://www.nsf.gov/statistics/nsf07305/

Smith, J. D., Redford, J. S., Haas, S. M., Coutinho, M. V. C., & Couchman, J. J. (2008). The comparative psychology of same-different judgments by humans (Homo sapiens) and monkeys (Macaca mulatta). *Journal of Experimental Psychology: Animal Behavior Processes, 34*, 361–374.

Tardif, T., Fletcher, P., Liang, W., Zhang, Z., Kaciroti, N., & Marchman, V. A. (2008). Baby's first 10 words. *Developmental Psychology, 44*, 929–938.

U.S. Department of Labor. (2007). *May 2007 national occupational employment and wage estimates*. Retrieved from http://www.bls.gov/oes/current/oes_nat.htm

Webb, A. R., & Speer, J. R. (1985). The public image of psychologist. *American Psychologist, 40*, 1063–1064.

Resources by Topic Area

Experimental Psychology

Society of Experimental Psychology – Division 3 of the APA
    http://www.apa.org/divisions/div3
Association for Psychological Science
    http://www.psychologicalscience.org

Developmental Psychology

Developmental Psychology – Division 7 of the APA
    http://ecp.fiu.edu/APA/div7
Adult Development and Aging – Division 20 of the APA
    http://apadiv20.phhp.ufl.edu

Social Psychology

Society for Personality and Social Psychology – Division 8 of APA
  http://www.spsp.org
Society of Experimental Social Psychology
  http://www.sesp.org

Cognitive Psychology

Cognitive Science Society
  http://cognitivesciencesociety.org/index.html

Biopsychology

Behavioral Neuroscience and Comparative Psychology – Division 6 of APA
  http://www.apa.org/divisions/div6

9

Careers in Industrial and Organizational Psychology

Introduction

As humans, we spend a large portion of our lives engaged in work. Our personality, skills, motivations, knowledge base, attitudes, and employment history are among the many factors that influence our functioning as employees and shape our work experiences. These experiences are also affected by the characteristics of the work itself. Relationships with coworkers, the nature of the tasks, interactions with superiors, compensation, and environmental conditions all impact the work experience. Industrial and organizational psychologists, hereafter referred to as I/O psychologists, spend their careers investigating this important part of human existence. Their focus is the well-being of the employee and the organizations that employ them.

Many undergraduate students are interested in the subfield of I/O psychology. Data shows that 4.8% of all PhDs granted in psychology in the United States are in the I/O subfield (American Psychological Association [APA], 2008). Part of the draw for students is the diversity of topics explored. Box 9.1 provides a brief list of some of the many issues that I/O psychologists seek to address in their work. Another attractive component for students is the combination of scientific and applied endeavors in the subfield. I/O psychologists address the issues described in Box 9.1 by conducting scientific research and applying these findings to real-world situations in the workplace. This emphasis has led some to describe I/O psychology as the subfield that seeks to maximize human capitol.

Defining the Subfield

The industrial and organizational elements in the name of this subfield reflect more about its history than its current practice. In the past I/O psychologists often focused on either the industrial or the organizational aspects of issues involved in the

Box 9.1 Common Topics Addressed by I/O Psychologists

- Facilitating major changes to the organization, structure, or mission of a company.
- Selecting the most effective and efficient methods for recruiting and hiring new employees.
- Creating a work environment that ensures employee productivity and satisfaction.
- Gathering, evaluating, and responding to customer satisfaction data.
- Determining which candidates for a position or promotion are the most qualified.
- Reducing employee stress, turnover, absenteeism, burnout, and low productivity.
- Building collaborative and cooperative work teams.
- Evaluating or appraising employees' work.
- Eliminating incidents of harassment, discrimination, and conflict.
- Increasing employee motivation, dedication, and commitment.

intersection between psychology and business. But this divide has all but disappeared as present day I/O psychologists increasingly focus on both sets of issues. Many have come to see the previous divide as somewhat artificial. In fact, I/O psychologists outside of the United States often refer to themselves as work, occupational, or organizational psychologists, and there is some momentum in the United States to consider renaming the subfield (Landy, 2008). However, in order to understand the work of I/O psychologists, it is still useful to understand how the industrial and organization components of their work can differ. Keep in mind that many I/O psychologists engage in both industrial and organizational related activities.

Industrial Psychology

Industrial psychology concentrates on the individual employee and his or her behavior. As a result, the activities involved in this area are often referred to as personnel psychology. The emphasis of industrial psychology is on structuring the individuals who engage in work. In doing so, I/O psychologists help companies select and place employees, evaluate them as they work, and train them to improve their performance.

Selection and placement.   Companies of all shapes and sizes struggle to know who to place into a vacant position. This dilemma occurs for new hires from the outside and for promotions from within. Many companies develop their own methods for accomplishing this task. However, these can vary widely, and their effectiveness is often unknown. For example, some companies leave the hiring and promoting decisions in the hands of executives or administrators. Although these individuals may have a good grasp for the operations of the company and have experience in making such decisions, they might be biased in how they evaluate candidates. Despite their best intentions, they might simply not have the knowledge or skills to select the candidates who will perform the best in the position. In contrast, other companies use more elaborate systems of applications, interviews, and tests. But having data on and consistency across applicants is still no guarantee that the ones who rise to the top in this process will perform the best in the position.

I/O psychologists assist in hiring and promotion situations by bringing their expertise to bear on the selection process. First, they obtain a thorough understanding of the position that needs to be filled. Second, they devise and implement methods of obtaining information about candidates in order to determine how well they fit the position requirements. This might include recruiting tools, screening measures, applications, interviews, and assessments. The assessment component varies depending on the nature of the position, but common areas of focus include cognitive abilities, work-related knowledge and skills, physical abilities, personality, honesty/integrity, and interpersonal skills. Importantly, I/O psychologists use assessment techniques that are reliable, valid, and effective. This is critical given that the assessment process can be costly, especially for companies who normally use less scientific methods. However, the payoff for these companies can be substantial if the I/O psychologist is able to help them save resources, make the hiring process fair, and increase the rates of successful hires.

Performance evaluation and appraisal.   Once employees are hired, there is a need to periodically gauge the effectiveness of their work. Information about employees' performances influences how the company perceives them. An appraisal might lead the company to alter an employee's compensation package, require additional training, or adjust the degree of supervision provided. Information about performance also ultimately plays a role in the company's decision to retain, terminate, or promote an employee. I/O psychologists devise and implement methods for obtaining this type of information through performance evaluations. They begin by establishing the criteria that the company deems important for its employees. I/O psychologists then implement systems for evaluating and tracking employee performance over time.

Training and education.   Once employees are working in their positions and their performances are being evaluated, often there is a need to provide training and education to assist them in acquiring new knowledge and skills. This is necessary if employees have areas of weakness, but it also becomes vital when they are asked to take on new tasks or responsibilities outside their expertise. I/O psychologists help companies assess employees' needs for training and education, often as a part of ongoing performance evaluations. They also assist with the development and implementation of training programs by establishing and/or leading courses and workshops. Some I/O psychologists focus solely on training executive-level employees, often referred to as executive coaching, in order to expand their administrative and managerial skills. Much of the emphasis in traditional training and education programs is placed on improving the productivity and effectiveness of the employee in their current position. However, I/O psychologists are increasingly assisting companies with training employees for the possibility of future promotions. Termed succession planning, this process assists companies in dealing with vacancies at the executive and management levels by having an established network of potential candidates trained and screened for these positions.

Organizational Psychology

Organizational psychology concentrates on the workplace, or the behavior of the company as a whole. The focus is on how characteristics of the organization affect productivity and the well-being of the company. I/O psychologists who do this work help companies evaluate and organize themselves by examining such issues as their inherent structure, leadership, environment, worker satisfaction, and organizational change.

Organizational structure.   Whether it is carefully planned or simply emerges as a byproduct of their decision making, all companies have inherent structure. I/O psychologists assist companies in evaluating their structure and implementing changes designed to improve productivity. For example, a company's management structure will dictate how information is communicated, problems are addressed, and decisions are made. Or the structure of work teams will determine how responsibility for problems and successes are shared. I/O psychologists can also assist companies in dealing with structures that may be somewhat outside of the business itself such as relationships with labor unions or community organizations. Although not entirely internal to the company, these relationships can play a major role in productivity and the ability of the company to accomplish its goals.

Leadership.   Throughout most of the time that I/O psychology has existed as a subfield, much research and applied efforts have focused on the issue of leadership. As a result of this knowledge base, I/O psychologists can assist companies with understanding the types of leadership styles that are the most effective in different situations. They help institute and run leadership training in which managers and supervisors are exposed to leadership theories and guided in implementing them into their work. In some situations, I/O psychologists might assist a company with restructuring their leadership by altering such things as the types of responsibilities held and the chain of command.

Environment.   The overall climate of the workplace can have a substantial effect on the productivity of individual employees and the company as a whole. I/O psychologists often assess organizational climates and facilitate changes to address problems. Among the common areas of focus are the degree of emphasis on health and safety, the reduction and management of stress, and the improvement of channels of communication. Improving an organizational environment also means attending to the worker's sense of community and their commitment to the company. I/O psychologists can help address some of the threats to a cohesive and productive climate such as harassment, discrimination, and unethical conduct.

Job satisfaction and commitment.   Two of the biggest threats to productivity for companies occur when workers are dissatisfied with their jobs and are uncommitted to the organization. Employee dissatisfaction and lack of commitment can fuel problems such as absenteeism, turnover, and customer dissatisfaction. I/O psychologists work to help companies boost employee satisfaction and commitment by evaluating and altering the factors that contribute to these conditions. In particular, they work to help structure employee's pay and benefits in ways that promote a sense of fairness and justice. Environmental or climate changes can also go a long way to improving employee's satisfaction with their job. For example, incentive programs that reward employees for their productivity through the allocation of additional compensation, prizes, vacation time, or perks within the company, can help create satisfied and committed employees.

Organizational change and development. Given the ever-changing marketplace and situational demands that arise, companies periodically adjust their practices, structures, and positions. Often these adjustments must be made in response to conditions or factors that are thrust upon the organization. I/O psychologists can be of great help to companies undergoing such changes. In particular, organizations that are going through mergers, acquisitions, relocations, downsizing, and expansion must successfully weather these changes to stay in business. These events can lead to dramatic changes in the structure, leadership, and environment of a company. Just as I/O psychologists assist stable companies with these issues, they can assist companies in flux by creating strategic plans for adjustments and monitoring their success.

Legal and Policy Issues

Because there can be a host of legal issues involved in the hiring, firing, promotion, and evaluation processes, issues of policy in the workplace are a common concern for I/O psychologists. Problems in these areas often arise with respect to an individual employee, but creating policies that prevent such problems takes place at the organizational level. As such, the area of legal and policy issues is another example of how I/O psychologists' work can no longer be easily divided into industrial or organizational topics. These psychologists assist companies in dealing with policy issues when they arise in specific situations and preparing for them to occur in the future. They often train management to carry out their business while adhering to the law. They also help companies craft internal policies and guidelines to reduce the occurrence of these problems. Finally, other I/O psychologists assist companies once a problem has already occurred by guiding their actions to address it and/or assisting with legal cases where the company's actions are being challenged.

The Work

Core Activities

I/O psychology is a broad subfield encompassing issues ranging from hiring a single employee to guiding an organization through massive restructuring. The psychologists

Box 9.2   Recent Openings in the I/O Psychology Subfield

Position: Project Manager
Setting: Applied Psychological Techniques (APT) Inc.
Responsibilities: Manage and execute consulting projects across a range of client industries. Design and implement organizational interventions, train clients, provide advice on HR matters, interpret statistical analyses, deliver presentations, and participate in litigation support.
Position: Assistant Professor
Setting: Auburn University
Responsibilities: Maintain an active research program publishing in I/O areas, teach undergraduate and graduate courses in area of specialization, and support the outreach efforts of the I/O graduate program.
Position: Associate Director, Global Talent Management
Setting: Bristol-Myers Squibb
Responsibilities: Direct global performance management, design a new online performance management system, oversee integrated workforce analytics, consult with sales division to ensure integration with talent management processes.

who engage in this work typically approach these issues either as a consultant, an administrator, or a researcher. In order to provide a glimpse of the diversity of these careers, Box 9.2 provides a few examples of recent positions advertised for I/O psychologists. The careers that I/O psychologists select shape the types of activities in which they engage.

Consultation.   Consulting refers to the act of providing one's expertise to an individual or organization, typically in exchange for compensation. Individuals from a wide variety of professions engage in consulting. Although psychologists from all subfields serve as consultants, it is I/O psychologists that most often conduct their professional careers in this role. Consultants in I/O psychology provide their clients with assistance on personnel and organizational issues. Some are retained as consultants for extended periods of time, during which time they may advise a company on any relevant issues that arise. Others are retained only to help the company deal with a specific issue, such as hiring for a particular job or helping guide the organization through a transition in leadership. Because consultants are sought after and paid for their expertise, they often travel to where there is demand for their services. In addition, there is an expectation that once these services are provided, the relationship will end. Of course, companies that have successful experiences with I/O psychologists as consultants routinely hire them again for other issues that arise in the future.

Administration.   Some I/O psychologists choose to work within organizations in administrative positions rather than from the outside as consultants. The descriptions of these positions vary and can include such titles as director, vice president, or manager of such areas as human resources, development, employee relations, or training. These psychologists are typically seen as the experts in an organization on the worker, workplace, and productivity issues. The nature of I/O psychologists' training means that these positions will typically involve other administrative responsibilities as well. So in addition to assisting the company with assessing and implementing important changes, the I/O psychologist who works within the organization often is responsible for a team of employees who help carry out these changes and evaluate them over time.

Research.   Because I/O psychology is a subfield that emphasizes both science and applied practice, many I/O psychologists chose to focus their careers on conducting research. These psychologists are experts in research methods, experimental design, and statistical analyses of data related to the intersection of psychology and business. Because many of them conduct their research in organizational settings, they are often experts at confidentiality and ethical issues involved in collecting data in the workplace. Their research concentrates on personnel and organizational issues that impact productivity such as selection techniques, training programs, environmental factors, and leadership models. This research is essential to creating new techniques for applying psychological principles to the workplace and for evaluating the effectiveness of existing techniques. The dissemination of this information through publications keeps I/O psychologists informed. Box 9.3 provides a sampling of journals that publish I/O psychology research.

Settings

Given the diversity of their work, I/O psychologists carry out these activities in a variety of settings. According to a recent survey (Khanna & Medsker, 2007), the largest portion of I/O psychologists, approximately 42%, are employed in academic settings. Their responsibilities often include teaching, research, service, and administration,

Box 9.3   Journals That Publish I/O Psychology Research

- Journal of Applied Psychology
- Personnel Psychology
- Academy of Management Journal
- Academy of Management Review
- Organizational Behavior and Human Decision Processes
- Journal of Occupational and Organizational Psychology

though some may be hired only to teach or conduct research. Although many of these I/O psychologists are employed in departments of psychology, a large number hold positions in schools of business, management, or engineering. Many I/O psychologists are employed in private-sector consulting organizations through which they provide consulting services to companies and individuals. These consulting organizations vary widely in their design. A small number of I/O psychologists (6%) are self-employed in their own private consulting practices, but a larger portion (21%) work for regional, national, and multinational consulting firms (Khanna & Medsker, 2007). Approximately 25% of I/O psychologists are employed in organizations and businesses (Khanna & Medsker). These psychologists provide their expertise on personnel and workplace issues from within the company rather than as an outside consultant. As a result, they are often responsible for the design, implementation, and evaluation of a host of initiatives and processes related to employee selection, placement, and evaluation, and organizational training, structure, and environment.

Salaries

The salaries earned by I/O psychologists depend largely on the type of work they perform and the setting in which it is conducted. According to the U.S. Department of Labor (2007), 80% of I/O psychologists earned an estimated annual salary between $38,910 and $136,840, with the median income for these psychologists being $80,820. These figures place I/O psychologists among the highest wage earners of all the subfields in psychology. Although this fact may contribute to students' interest in I/O psychology, it is important to consider the advantages and disadvantages of the factors that contribute to these wages. I/O psychologists as a group often command a higher salary because a large portion of them work as consultants in either consulting firms or private practices. As is the case with all professionals who work in such practices, the income potential typically exceeds that of careers in business, academic, or government settings. But consultation work involves parallel risks given that one's income can be heavily influenced by market forces such as competition and the demand for one's services. I/O psychologists who work in organizations and businesses, as well as those who hold academic positions in schools of business, also tend to receive a higher salary. Otherwise, these organizations and institutions risk losing these professionals to lucrative consulting practices. In addition, when the expertise and services that I/O psychologists provide to their businesses and institutions have a direct impact on their productivity and profits, these savings typically translate into higher salaries.

Employment Issues

Given the nature of their work, I/O psychologists' careers can be dramatically impacted by numerous societal and economic factors. Although virtually all individuals' careers are dependent upon their performance in their positions, I/O psychologists in consulting and business settings are directly engaged in activities designed to improve productivity and efficiency. Their work is intended to have a direct impact on a company's bottom line. Because profitability is a primary interest of businesses, companies that hire I/O psychologists expect to see a return on this investment. Without it, not only might the I/O psychologist's current position be at stake, but their professional reputation and ability to secure future positions could also be in jeopardy.

Shifts in the characteristics of employees and the market require I/O psychologists to adjust their techniques. For example, increased globalization in the business market has meant that I/O psychologists must be prepared to assist companies with issues that arise from having an international presence. Consider the difficulties involved in structuring a company's leadership, communication, environment, selection processes, and evaluation procedures when its workforce becomes multinational. Even companies whose operations remain within the United States need assistance as their workforce ages and becomes increasingly diverse.

The technological advances of the last few decades have led to rapid changes in the nature of work and the ways that most companies conduct business. These advances have contributed to the extinction of some positions and the creation of others that did not exist only a few short years ago. In addition, workers who continue to engage in the same type of work now do so in different ways, including working from home. These changes have impacted the types of issues I/O psychologists assist companies with and the ways in which they do so. For example, the activities of employee selection and evaluation have become increasingly automated. Some I/O psychology consulting firms exclusively provide companies with systems for managing their personnel and human resources issues.

Training and Preparation

Degree Options and Licensure

Careers in most subfields of psychology require a doctoral degree. For the subfields that involve applied work with clients and patients (e.g., clinical psychology, neuropsychology), these psychologists must obtain a professional license from the state within which they practice. Without it, they cannot refer to themselves as psychologists or engage in the practice of psychology while working with the public (for a more detailed discussion of licensure as a psychologist, see the Careers in Clinical Psychology and Counseling Psychology chapter). As a result, I/O psychologists who intend to refer to themselves as psychologists and engage in the practice of psychology when working with clients must be licensed in most states. However, there are two scenarios in which an individual might engage in a career that is related to I/O psychology yet not seek licensure. First, some individuals with doctorates in I/O psychology opt not to be licensed if the work they engage in does not constitute the practice of psychology (e.g., academic careers, human resources positions). Second, some individuals obtain master's degrees in I/O psychology or related areas and as a result are not eligible for licensure as a psychologist. The individuals in both of these scenarios are able to conduct applied work in business settings, often using concepts and methods that are relevant to I/O psychology. This is allowable only if they do not refer to themselves as psychologists, do not engage in practices unique to psychology (e.g., psychological testing), and do not engage in practices that could pose a threat of harm to the public (Sackett, Thomas, Borman, & Champion, 1995). Given this situation, master's degrees in I/O psychology and related disciplines have become an increasingly popular option for individuals seeking careers in this area.

Some leaders in the I/O psychology subfield strongly support the requirement of licensure for I/O psychologists given the limitations on the practice of unlicensed individuals and the confusion that can occur about their expertise (e.g., clients must understand that those without a license are consultants, not psychologists). In fact, the Association of State and Provincial Psychology Boards (ASPPB), along with the National Register, characterize I/O psychology as a practice area, encourage licensure, and designate graduate programs that meet established training standards (ASPPB, 2001; ASPPB/National Register Designation Committee, 2008). Although there are competing perspectives on the importance of licensure for this subfield, our perspective is that it is typically best to adhere to the higher standard that designated programs tend to adopt.

Far more than making you eligible for licensure, the type of degree you earn reflects the nature and extent of your training. Therefore, the degree will have a direct impact on the types of jobs you are qualified to seek. Currently, the majority of I/O psychologists have doctoral degrees. With this level of education and training they can work in virtually any area of I/O psychology. Because this degree has been the standard in the field for some time, master's level programs were for years ignored by mainstream I/O psychology (Trahan & McAllister, 2002). But demand for master's level training options, both from potential students and employers of graduates, continued to grow. As a result, the number of programs available expanded. This situation caused the Society for Industrial and Organizational Psychology (SIOP; 1994) to create guidelines for master's level programs. Guidelines had existed for some time for doctoral programs (SIOP, 1999), so these were adapted for the master's level. Table 9.1 presents an overview and comparison of these guidelines. Keep in mind that master's programs not only emphasize fewer guidelines than doctoral programs, but they also provide less depth of coverage of those guidelines that overlap with doctoral programs. Research has found that for the most part the master's level programs in I/O psychology are meeting these guidelines (Trahan & McAllister, 2002).

Variations in Graduate Programs

Graduate programs that offer degrees in I/O psychology and related fields identify themselves with a variety of titles. Box 9.4 provides a list of some of the more common program names. Although there is a degree of similarity across the education and training provided by these programs, do not overlook the meaning behind these titles. Typically these names reflect the basic focus or orientation of the program, and it is this focus that will serve as the foundation for your future career. Once

Table 9.1   Summary of Guidelines for Doctoral and Master's Programs in I/O Psychology

Guidelines	Doctoral	Master's
General Knowledge and Skills:		
• Consulting and Business Skills	x	
• Ethical, Legal, and Professional Contexts of I/O Psychology	x	x
• Fields of Psychology	x	x
• History and Systems of Psychology	x	x
• Research Methods	x	x
• Statistical Methods/Data Analysis	x	x
Content Areas:		
• Attitude Theory, Measurement, and Change	x	x
• Career Development	x	
• Consumer Behavior	x	
• Criterion Theory and Development	x	x
• Health and Stress in Organizations	x	
• Human Performance/Human Factors	x	
• Individual Assessment	x	
• Individual Differences	x	x
• Job Evaluation and Compensation	x	
• Job/Task Analysis and Classification	x	x
• Judgment and Decision Making	x	
• Leadership and Management	x	
• Organization Development	x	x
• Organization Theory	x	x
• Performance Appraisal and Feedback	x	x
• Personnel Recruitment, Selection, and Placement	x	x
• Small Group Theory and Team Processes	x	x
• Training: Theory, Program Design, and Evaluation	x	x
• Work Motivation	x	x

Box 9.4   Common Titles of Graduate Programs in I/O Related Areas

- Applied Psychology (with a concentration in I/O psychology)
- Human Resources (and Management)
- I/O Psychology
- I/O Psychology and Human Resources Management
- Organizational Behavior (and Evaluation, Development, Analysis, Management)
- Organizational Psychology
- Social and Organizational Psychology

you complete one of these training programs, remember that you should only identify yourself according to your training and licensure status. For example, if you earn a doctoral degree from a graduate program in I/O psychology and hold a license as a psychologist, you should describe your education and training as being in I/O psychology and should identify yourself as a psychologist. If you hold a degree (doctoral or master's) from a graduate program in organizational behavior and do not hold a license as a psychologist, you should describe your education and training as being in organizational behavior and should not identify yourself as a psychologist.

Earning the Degree

As with most graduate degrees, doctoral and master's degrees in I/O psychology and related areas involve multiple components of training. Formal coursework serves as a foundation of these programs, ensuring students possess essential knowledge in areas such as research methods, statistical analysis, and ethics. As a result, coursework is often heaviest for students at the start of their graduate training. As they advance, graduate students take on greater amounts of independent study. They also begin to engage in supervised experiences that are designed to promote learning through active engagement and skill acquisition. Depending on the nature of the graduate program and its learning objectives, supervised experiences can focus on training and skill building in either research or applied endeavors. Many graduate programs in the I/O psychology subfield also place emphasis on students gaining on-the-job training through internship and apprenticeship experiences. Often students work for a semester or two in a research, business, or consultation setting. These experiences allow them to observe professionals engaged in the work and begin to apply their developing skills.

Preparing for Graduate Training as an Undergraduate

As an undergraduate student considering the possibility of pursuing graduate training in I/O psychology or a related area, it is important to keep in mind that there are things you can and should be doing to prepare. In particular, the coursework and activities you engage in now can affect graduate programs' interest in you in the future.

Coursework. Given the variations we have discussed within programs in the I/O psychology subfield, it is difficult to establish absolute recommendations for undergraduate coursework that will best prepare you for graduate level training. However, there are core courses in most undergraduate psychology curriculums that are judged to be vital for students aspiring to enter I/O psychology graduate programs. These courses, as well as relevant course areas outside of psychology, are listed in Box 9.5. Notice that although courses in research, leadership, and organizational issues are important,

Box 9.5 Recommended Undergraduate Coursework for I/O Psychology

Courses Within Psychology
Research Methods
Experimental Psychology
Industrial/Organizational Psychology
Psychological Testing
Career Development
Motivation and Leadership
Group Dynamics
Ethics
Cross-Cultural Psychology
Learning and Behavior
Social Psychology

Course Areas Outside of Psychology
Statistics
Business/Management
Human Resources
Computer Science

students also benefit from a solid background in behavior, diversity, social psychology, and business.

Activities.   Training at both the master's and doctoral levels in I/O psychology involves a strong emphasis on research methods and statistical analysis. As a result, these programs are particularly interested in students who not only have the necessary coursework in these areas but also have experience conducting research. For undergraduate students, this experience is best gained by working closely with a faculty member either to assist them with their research or to conduct independent research. Because many schools do not have I/O graduate programs and I/O faculty are not as commonly found in undergraduate psychology departments, faculty who conduct research in I/O psychology often are not readily accessible to undergraduate students. As a result, you should consider working with a non-I/O psychology faculty member if you find their research interesting and relevant. Often faculty who focus on social, cognitive, and clinical psychology topics are engaged in projects that overlap with I/O psychology. Another option is to consider seeking research experience outside of your own department. Often faculty in business programs or in neighboring graduate psychology departments are engaged in I/O psychology related research and might be willing to allow you to assist.

In addition to research training and experience, some graduate programs in I/O psychology value students having had experience in business settings. Internship experiences, whether through formal programs in your department or informally created through your own initiative, can be helpful in securing such experience. Consulting firms that engage in I/O psychology and related practices may provide such positions. Finally, employment in human resources or closely related areas can also serve as a valuable experience in preparation for graduate school.

Working in Areas Related to I/O Psychology With a Bachelor's Degree

As discussed in earlier chapters, the bachelor's degree in psychology can be thought of as a liberal arts degree or a preprofessional degree. As such, it neither automatically qualifies you to enter a particular career field nor provides you with a defined set of skills that employers easily recognize and value. Instead, your ability to secure employment in an area related to I/O psychology with only a bachelor's degree will in large part depend upon you gaining relevant experience as an undergraduate, identifying positions for which you qualify, and effectively conveying your knowledge and skills to potential employers. There are a number of career and employment opportunities that tap aspects of I/O psychology. Many of these bachelor's level careers allow for working directly with businesses to address employee and organizational issues. The most common options include management and human resources positions.

Management

Leadership positions within organizations often provide a rewarding career with considerable opportunity for advancement. Students who are interested in I/O psychology because of its emphasis on structuring the individual worker and organization might find that management positions provide opportunities to have an impact in these areas. The responsibilities of a given management position will of course vary based on the nature of the organization and the job description, but involvement in employee selection, evaluation, and training, as well as input into organizational structure and environment, is common. According to the U.S. Department of Labor (2007), the median salary estimate was $84,440 for all types of managers.

Human Resources

Human resource professionals are responsible for a wide array of tasks within businesses and organizations. Traditionally human resource departments managed the technical details of recruiting, hiring, promoting, firing, and compensating employees. This included completing necessary paperwork and maintaining up-to-date information about each employee. In recent years the responsibility of human resource professionals has expanded to include greater authority in decision making about personnel matters. In addition, many of these departments are now in charge of employee assessment, training, and evaluation procedures. With the expanding role of human resources within companies and institutions, the types of positions available have also grown. Individuals who work in human resources now hold a variety of titles, including benefits coordinator, personnel administration, and human resources associate. In addition, training and certification programs for human resource positions are now common and play a large role in one's ability to secure certain positions and salaries. According to the U.S. Department of Labor (2007), the median salary estimate was $54,280 for human resources, training, and labor relations specialists.

The Flexibility of the Doctoral Degree in I/O Psychology

Russell E. Johnson, PhD
University of South Florida

I can remember back to when I was a senior undergraduate student and knowing that I wanted to study I/O psychology in graduate school, so the decision to apply to I/O graduate programs was an easy one. What was not easy, however, was figuring out exactly what I wanted to do *after* earning a graduate degree in I/O psychology. Did I want to focus on research and teaching as a professor at a university or college? Did I want to work in the "real world" as an internal or external consultant for a private company or work for a public organization like the government or military? Although I was about to receive a BA in psychology, these were difficult questions to answer without having had any in-depth training in I/O psychology. Fortunately, earning a doctoral degree in I/O psychology prepares students for all of those aforementioned careers, whether it is as a professor, consultant, or human resource manager. Thus, one source of flexibility for people with doctoral degrees in I/O psychology is the various employment opportunities that are available to them.

I/O psychologists are trained according to the scientist/practitioner model, which provides students with the knowledge and skills to conduct research and interpret findings, as well as the knowledge and skills to apply research findings to actual problems that plague companies and employees. For example, as a graduate student, I was exposed to research concerning various employee abilities and dispositions that influence job performance (e.g., cognitive ability, personality). I then had opportunities to apply this knowledge, for example, by developing selection tests that identified the highest performing employees from a pool of job applicants. As it turned out, I particularly enjoyed the research and teaching aspects of my graduate training, so I ventured down the path to become a professor of I/O psychology. However, had it turned out that I did not enjoy lecturing and conducting experiments, it would have been possible for me to transition into a job working as an internal or external consultant instead. This degree of career flexibility provided by graduate training in I/O psychology is a luxury that does not extend to all disciplines.

A second source of flexibility is the wide range of topics available for study by I/O psychologists. Because I/O psychology represents the application of psychological theories and principles to the workplace, any and all topics studied by psychologists are fair game. For example, social psychology research on topics like group influences (e.g., groupthink) and social relations (e.g., prejudice) are applied to the workplace by I/O psychologists. I/O psychologists also make use of cognitive psychology research on topics like learning (e.g., practice effects) and decision-making (e.g., heuristics). As a final example, developmental psychology research informs I/O psychologists about the physical and psychological changes that employees undergo as they age and transition into retirement. Thus, the field of I/O psychology is flexible because it draws from a broad range of perspectives, each of which contributes something unique to understanding work organizations and their employees. If exposure to a variety of topics within psychology and having numerous career options sound appealing to you, then pursuing graduate training in I/O psychology is worth considering!

Note. Dr. Russell Johnson is an industrial/ organizational psychologist and an assistant professor of psychology at the University of South Florida. He has authored over 20 peer reviewed journal articles on such topics as implicit information processing, employee self-identity, and work attitudes and perceptions. Dr. Johnson teaches undergraduate and graduate courses on organizational psychology, motivation, and leadership.

Professional Spotlight

John Chan, PhD

Education:
- Bachelor of Arts (BA) in Psychology from Emory University (1998)
- Master of Arts (MA) in Industrial/Organizational Psychology from the University of Tennessee (2001)
- Doctor of Philosophy (PhD) in Industrial/Organizational Psychology from the University of Tennessee (2003)

Position:
Senior Professional Services Consultant, SuccessFactors

Description of Position:
I implement and consult on talent management systems. These systems help global multinational organizations be more efficient in evaluating, developing, and organizing their people and knowledge base.

Most Significant Professional Accomplishment:
I developed the internal infrastructure for a global organization that otherwise was in danger of collapsing. The company then grew and matured their talent management process on a global basis within a couple of years.

Favorite Publication:
Paddock, J. R., Terranova, S. E., Joseph, A. L., Chan, F. M., Loftus, E. F., Manning, C., et al. (1998). When guided visualization procedures may backfire: "Imagination Inflation" and predicting individual differences in suggestibility. *Applied Cognitive Psychology, 12,* S63–S75.

Areas of Research:
I investigate international comparisons of optimism and its effects on workplace productivity and job burnout.

Professional Memberships:
- American Psychological Association
- Association for Psychological Science
- Society for Industrial Organizational Psychologists

Most Rewarding Aspect of Your Career:
The most rewarding aspect of my career is helping companies realize the importance and value of creating efficient talent management processes and developing their people. In turn, this helps people develop and grow personally and professionally in the workplace, which will be reflected in all aspects of their lives.

Words of Advice to the Student Who Is Interested in Your Subfield:
Find out as much as you can about I/O psychology and all the different directions it can take you. There is a wide variety of positions in this field so get a head start on your career by engaging in internships as early and often as possible. Your early experiences will be priceless in your future career.

Suggested Exercises

1. Select a major business or organization and learn about how it currently operates in areas relevant to I/O psychology. For example, if you select a major retail chain, seek to learn about how it selects employees, evaluates employees' work, trains its leaders, or structures the work environment. Information may be readily available about some of the larger companies because books and articles are often written about their history, transformations, and current business practices. If possible, talk with employees of the company to gain an inside perspective.

2. Locate a job advertisement for a human resources position that you could potentially qualify for as an undergraduate student. Investigate the responsibilities associated with the position, as well as those of the department in which you would work. Consider whether such a position might provide good experience to help you decide if I/O psychology is right for you or prepare for graduate school in the subfield.

3. Identify a consulting firm that offers I/O psychology and/or related services to organizations and learn about the types of services they provide. The majority of these firms maintain a strong Web presence in order to effectively market themselves. Contact consultants within the firm and inquire whether they would be willing to correspond with you about their job and the educational path they took to arrive at their current position.

Suggested Readings by Topic Area

Hedge, J. W., & Borman, W. C. (Eds.). (2008). *The I/O consultant: Advice and insights for building a successful career*. Washington, DC: American Psychological Association.

Kuther, T. L. (2005). *Your career in psychology: Industrial/organizational psychology*. Belmont, CA: Wadsworth.

Lowman, R. L. (Ed.). (2006). *The ethical practice of psychology in organizations* (2nd ed.). Washington, DC: American Psychological Association.

Northouse, P. G. (2006). *Leadership: Theory and practice*. Thousand Oaks, CA: Sage.

References

American Psychological Association. (2008). *2008 graduate study in psychology*. Washington, DC: Author.

Association of State and Provincial Psychology Boards. (2001). *ASPPB model act for licensure of psychologists*. Retrieved from http://www.asppb.org/publications/model/act.aspx

Association of State and Provincial Psychology Boards/National Register Designation Committee. (2008). *Doctoral psychology programs meeting designation criteria, 2008*. Retrieved from http://www.nationalregister.org/designate_intro.html

Khanna, C., & Medsker, G. J. (2007). *2006 income and employment survey results for the Society for Industrial and Organizational Psychology*. Retrieved from http://www.siop.org/bookspubs.aspx

Landy, F. J. (2008). What shall we call ourselves? Food for thought. *The Industrial/Organizational Psychologist, 46*(2), 11–12.

Sackett, P., Thomas, J., Borman, W., & Champion, M. (1995). Proposed revision of SIOP policy on licensure: Call for comments. *The Industrial-Organizational Psychologist, 33*(1), 12–20.

Society for Industrial and Organizational Psychology, Inc. (1994). *Guidelines for education and training at the master's level in industrial/organizational psychology*. Arlington Heights, IL: Author.

Society for Industrial and Organizational Psychology, Inc. (1999). *Guidelines for education and training at the doctoral level in industrial/organizational psychology*. Bowling Green, OH: Author.

Trahan, W. A., & McAllister, H. A. (2002). Master's level training in industrial/organizational psych-ology: Does it meet the SIOP guidelines? *Journal of Business and Psychology, 16*, 457–465.

U.S. Department of Labor. (2007). *May 2007 national occupational employment and wage estimates*. Retrieved from http://www.bls.gov/oes/current/oes_nat.htm

Resources

Society for Industrial and Organizational Psychology – Division 14 of APA
  http://siop.org
Society for Consulting Psychology – Division 13 of APA
  http://www.div13.org
Society of Human Resource Management
  www.shrm.org
National Human Resources Association
  www.humanresources.org

10

Careers in Clinical Psychology and Counseling Psychology

Introduction

Which area in the field of psychology interests you most in terms of a future career? When undergraduate psychology students are asked this question, the majority respond with clinical psychology or counseling psychology (Gallucci, 1997). The popularity of these subfields is heavily influenced by two factors. First, clinical psychology and counseling psychology enjoy far greater exposure than the other subfields. As a result, you are more likely to come in contact and be familiar with clinical and counseling psychologists given the nature of their work. Second, a large portion of psychology students report that their career interests are influenced by a desire to "help people." Although vague, this statement reflects a wish to work directly with others in a treatment context. Once students understand that only a few of the subfields within psychology engage in applied work with individuals seeking mental health treatment, many focus their interests in these areas.

The notion that the entire field of psychology involves applied work in mental health is a common misperception (Webb & Speer, 1985). There are numerous subfields that have no focus on mental health whatsoever. In addition, all areas in the field, including clinical psychology and counseling psychology, engage in scientific research. But this misperception is not entirely without basis. Consider that the popularity of the clinical and counseling psychology subfields among undergraduate students translates into greater numbers of individuals pursuing these careers. According to the National Science Foundation (2006), clinical psychology and counseling psychology are the top subfields in the discipline in terms of the number of doctoral degrees granted. For all doctoral degrees granted in psychology in the US between 1996 and 2005, 37% were in clinical psychology and 14% were in counseling psychology. Given the popularity of these subfields, a thorough exploration of them and the various training and career issues involved should prove informative as you consider your future career options in the field.

Defining the Subfields

Clinical Psychology and Counseling Psychology

Clinical psychology and counseling psychology are applied subfields because the work conducted in these areas has direct applications to human functioning. But being applied in focus is not enough to distinguish these areas from other applied subfields (e.g., health psychology, industrial/organizational psychology). What is unique to clinical psychology and counseling psychology is a focus on improving human functioning by understanding and alleviating psychological dysfunction and distress.

The clinical psychology and counseling psychology subfields emphasize the integration of science, theory, and practice. Clinical or counseling psychologists might spend the bulk of a day conducting research or providing services to patients, but they remain mindful of how all three areas contribute to their understanding. For example, a clinical psychologist conducting a psychological evaluation must be aware of the latest research and theory pertaining to the assessment measures being used and the questions being answered. Likewise, a counseling psychologist researching the prevalence of mental illness among college students must understand the theoretical foundations of the topic and the implications for those who may provide treatment to this population.

Thus far we have discussed the subfields of clinical psychology and counseling psychology as if they are one and the same, but they are not. As a student you may encounter sources of information that will claim that the two subfields are either indistinguishable, or as is more often claimed, that the differences are so small that it is not worth trying to draw a distinction. Unfortunately, for students who are attempting to select a subfield of interest, develop career goals, and contemplate graduate training, such overgeneralizations are not helpful. There are indeed distinct differences in the clinical psychology and counseling psychology subfields, and these differences have implications for the graduate training and professional careers of students who select them.

The Society of Clinical Psychology defines clinical psychology as integrating theory, science, and practice in an effort to "understand, predict, and alleviate maladjustment, disability, and discomfort" and to "promote human adaptation, adjustment, and personal development" (http://www.apa.org/divisions/div12/aboutcp.html). The Society of Counseling Psychology defines counseling psychology as integrating theory, science, and practice in an effort to promote "personal, educational, vocational, and group adjustment in a variety of settings" (http://www.div17.org/about.html). Both definitions encompass the diverse activities of clinical and counseling psychologists, which include researching, teaching, assessing, diagnosing, treating, consulting, and supervising. Thus, clinical and counseling psychologists share an integrative approach and strive to improve human functioning. But, their emphasis in doing so varies. Clinical psychologists tend to concentrate on understanding psychological symptoms, distress, and disorders, with the goal of developing and providing interventions that treat these conditions. Counseling psychologists tend to concentrate on understanding human adjustment with the goal of developing and providing interventions that return patients to their normal functioning and promote growth. Although these distinctions are subtle, they translate into significant differences in terms of the professional practice and training of clinical and counseling psychologists. For the remainder of the chapter, we will largely be discussing these two subfields together given their similarities. However, in areas where important distinctions occur, we will outline these differences.

The Work

Core Activities

Given the breadth of their training, it is difficult to briefly describe the work that clinical and counseling psychologists engage in without omitting large segments of some of these individuals' professional activities. However, the bulk of their activities can be divided into four general categories: practice, research, administration, and teaching and supervision.

Practice. The term practice is typically used in reference to activities that involve providing direct services to patients. This is sometimes referred to as clinical or applied work and can involve a range of activities including treatment, assessment, and consultation. When clinical and counseling psychologists provide treatment services, they usually conduct psychotherapy or counseling sessions with individuals, couples, families, or groups. Psychotherapy and counseling involve the application of psychological and counseling theories to create treatment interventions that reduce patients' distress, improve their capacity to cope, and enhance their well-being. Important differences exist between these interventions in terms of the types of problems that are conducive to each and the interventions typically applied. These differences are summarized in Box 10.1.

Consider how two patients, both experiencing depression, might be best served by seeking either psychotherapy or counseling. Patient A experiences a wide array of depressive symptoms that are intense and long-lasting. The symptoms have been present since adolescence, and while they fluctuate at times in response to life events, often the symptoms appear to occur without any relation to Patient A's current experiences. Patient B experiences only a few depressive symptoms, and they have primarily only

Box 10.1 General Comparisons between Psychotherapy and Counseling

	Psychotherapy	*Counseling*
Severity of Problem	More severe	Less severe
Nature of Problem	Internal to self, broad in scope	External to self, narrow in scope
Length of Treatment	Longer-term	Shorter-term
Focus of Treatment	Cure the problem	Restore functioning and growth

occurred since the death of a close friend a few months earlier. Patient B's symptoms also appear to be in large part influenced by situational factors such as stress at work and reminders of the friend's death. Although both patients in these scenarios would likely benefit from psychotherapy or counseling, the severity and nature of the depressions suggest that Patient A is a better candidate for psychotherapy and Patient B is a better candidate for counseling.

Clinical psychologists are more apt to provide psychotherapy, and counseling psychologists are more apt to provide counseling. However, the types of treatment these psychologists provide are based primarily on their training and the settings in which they practice. The differences between psychotherapy and counseling are generally agreed upon in the field, but consumers of these services, as well as clinical and counseling psychologists themselves, often use the terms more loosely. In addition, a patient might engage in both psychotherapy and counseling at various stages of a treatment.

Assessment is also a core part of clinical and counseling psychologists' practice. Assessment refers to any type of formal evaluation of a patient, typically through the use of standardized tests and interview techniques. Assessments are performed in order to answer specific questions about a patient and his or her functioning. Often these questions pertain to determining a diagnosis, making recommendations for treatment, or generating information about the functioning of symptoms. Although some elements of the practice of clinical and counseling psychology are not unique to these subfields (e.g., some other mental health professionals conduct psychotherapy or counseling), performing psychological assessments has generally been exclusive to the work of clinical and counseling psychologists, with a few exceptions. In fact, the practice and valuing of assessment has been a cornerstone of the clinical and counseling psychology subfields. Assessment tools and approaches vary widely, but most clinical and counseling psychologists are trained at designing assessments, conducting them, interpreting the results, providing feedback, and authoring written reports that integrate the findings. Their proficiency with assessment and the degree to which they use it in their practice varies based on their training and the settings in which they work.

Most clinical and counseling psychologists also engage in consultation as part of their practice. Consultation involves offering opinions and recommendations on the basis of one's expertise. Clinical and counseling psychologists most often provide consultation to fellow mental health professionals regarding the treatment or assessment of a patient. This is a vital part of their work because it allows professionals to combine their expertise in the service of providing the best care. Clinical and counseling psychologists also offer consultation to individuals outside of the mental health field. For example, they may provide expert opinion to attorneys regarding a case that involves mental health issues.

In some instances, clinical and counseling psychologists can prescribe psychotropic medications as part of their professional practice. These psychologists must have specialized training, which typically includes coursework in physiology, biochemistry, and neuroscience, as well as extensive supervised experience and the successful completion of a national certification exam. Currently only two states in the United States, New Mexico and Louisiana, allow psychologists with such training to prescribe.

However, many others have considered similar legislation since the mid 1980s. The movement in large part grew out of a U.S. Department of Defense demonstration project that successfully trained psychologists to safely and effectively prescribe psychotropic medications. Supporters of this move argue that clinical and counseling psychologists, given their expertise, are in an excellent position to integrate psychotropic medications into the overall treatment of a patient's mental illness. Others note that patients often have difficulty accessing psychiatric care, particularly in rural areas and when uninsured. Having some psychologists prescribe might help alleviate this problem. Opponents of the move have argued that even with specialized training, psychologists would lack the necessary knowledge and experience to prescribe safely. Others have cautioned that such a move would further shift mental health treatment to a biological model that relies on medications as the primary mode of treatment rather than psychological or social interventions. The controversy and debate around granting prescriptive authority to select psychologists will continue to develop as additional states consider this type of legislation.

Research.   Compared to practice, the design and conduction of research plays a more varied role in the work of clinical and counseling psychologists. This is in large part due to the fact that psychologists' training in graduate school differs in its emphasis on research methodology and conducting original research. At a minimum, clinical and counseling psychologists should be trained to be highly sophisticated consumers of psychological research. Such training would equip them to be able to locate, read, understand, appraise, and apply new scientific research to their work with patients. On the other end of the spectrum, some clinical and counseling psychologists devote their entire career to conducting research. The majority fall somewhere in between these two end points.

Clinical and counseling psychologists engage in diverse research projects, but there are several common areas of focus given their training and expertise. One involves investigating various treatment and assessment techniques. This might include developing new techniques or evaluating the effectiveness of established ones. Another research area consists of seeking to better understand psychological disorders by investigating their symptoms, prevalence, development, and impact. Still other clinical and counseling psychologists focus their research on issues that are central to the professions, such as the training of future psychologists, supervision, and ethical decision making. For examples of these and other types of research, Box 10.2 lists several journals that publish clinical and counseling psychology research.

Administration.   Clinical and counseling psychologists who are involved in administration typically oversee and manage both the operations of mental health treatment facilities and the staff who provide services within these facilities. Administration responsibilities are more likely to be a part of clinical and counseling psychologists' careers when they are employed in large settings such as outpatient and inpatient clinics. In addition, administrative activities are more often given to individuals who have substantial experience in the field.

Box 10.2   Journals That Publish Clinical and Counseling Psychology Research

- Psychotherapy: Theory, Research, Practice, Training
- Journal of Consulting and Clinical Psychology
- Journal of Counseling Psychology
- Clinical Psychology: Science and Practice
- Journal of Abnormal Psychology
- Psychological Assessment

Teaching and supervision.   Many clinical and counseling psychologists teach and supervise students either in undergraduate institutions, graduate programs, or medical schools. Even those who spend most of their careers providing treatment and assessment services will at times teach a course in order to have variety in their work life, stay in touch with developments in the field, and give back to the profession. Supervision is a special form of teaching. It involves overseeing the work of students and trainees who are learning to provide psychotherapy, counseling, and assessment services. Many clinical and counseling psychologists provide supervision because they understand that this type of mentoring plays a central role in trainees' development into competent psychologists.

Theoretical Orientation

Many factors determine what types of activities clinical and counseling psychologists engage in and the ways in which they conduct their work. One significant source of influence is their theoretical orientation. Theoretical orientation refers to the theory, or combination of theories, that a clinical or counseling psychologist adopts. Psychological theories are often broad and complex in their details, but at their core they offer a framework for understanding human behavior. In other words, these theories are models for how one might think about human behavior, its development, and how it can be modified. Some of the more common theoretical orientations include cognitive-behavioral, psychodynamic, humanistic, existential, relational, self-psychology, family systems, object relational, interpersonal, and solution-focused. Because of their complexity, the various theories complement each other in some areas and conflict in others. As a result, most clinical and counseling psychologists identify best with one or two theories. These ideas guide their understanding of and response to patients' unique experiences and situations.

Despite the substantial role of clinical and counseling psychologists' theoretical orientation in their practice, students interested in these subfields often have limited understanding of how one's particular theoretical orientation comes to be. One significant source of influence comes from the graduate program in which these psychologists are trained. Programs usually have a dominant theoretical orientation that flows from the orientations of the faculty. During training, students tend to gradually adopt the orientation in which they are immersed. Although theoretical orientations are robust and often persist over time, some clinical and counseling psychologists experience shifts in their orientations during their careers.

Settings

Given the diversity of their training, clinical and counseling psychologists seek employment in a variety of settings. The most common among these are private practices, outpatient clinics, inpatient clinics or hospitals, and academic institutions.

Private practice and outpatient clinics.   When students envision working as a clinical or counseling psychologist, many first imagine doing so in a private practice. Approximately 30% of clinical and counseling psychologists work in an independent private practice or outpatient clinic setting immediately after graduation, including group-owned practices and community-based clinics (APA, 2005). Individuals who pursue private practice often do so because of the autonomy that comes with owning one's own business. Most enjoy a great deal of control over their time and income. However, as with owning a business in any field, private practice in psychology comes with complications, which will be discussed later. Outpatient settings are typically clinics that patients visit for mental health services and then leave. Outpatient clinics tend to be significantly larger than private practices. Many clinics have a dozen or more professional staff including clinical and counseling psychologists, psychiatrists, counselors, and social workers. Many outpatient clinics have a particular focus or emphasis in the services they provide (e.g., anxiety disorders, eating disorders). In structuring themselves in this way, these clinics ensure that they maintain a strong patient base and are able to provide services to a large number of patients. Outpatient clinics can be free standing, similar to a large private practice, or affiliated with larger institutions such as hospitals. In addition, many counseling psychologists work in outpatient clinics within universities and colleges, providing services to members of the campus community and at times helping to train future mental health professionals.

Academic.   Approximately 18% of clinical and counseling psychologists are employed full-time in academic institutions immediately after graduation (APA, 2005). The largest portion of these is employed in university or college settings where their responsibilities may consist of teaching, research, service, and administration. Other clinical and counseling psychologists are employed in medical school settings where they participate in the education of physicians, provide treatment to patients, and conduct research. The nature of academic positions in psychology is explored in detail in the Careers in Academe chapter.

Hospital and inpatient.   Approximately 23% of clinical and counseling psychologists are employed full-time in hospital or inpatient settings after graduation (APA, 2005). Inpatient settings are those in which patients seek mental health services that require residing in the treatment facility for a period of time. These settings are often necessary when the particular problem a patient is experiencing is too severe to be treated or assessed in a private practice or outpatient clinic. Some clinical and counseling psychologists prefer to work in these settings because their expertise lies in assessing and treating severe mental illness. Other psychologists are drawn to these settings because they enjoy the fast pace and unpredictability that often accompanies this work. These settings also tend to promote a high degree of collaboration among professionals from different disciplines, often in the form of treatment teams that are responsible for patient care.

Salaries

The salaries earned by clinical and counseling psychologists depend on the type of work they perform and the setting in which it is conducted. According to the U.S. Department of Labor (2007), 80% of clinical and counseling psychologists earned an estimated annual salary between $37,300 and $104,520, with a median income of $62,210. As with all professions, earnings vary according to geographic region as well as rural and urban settings. Recent trends in the mental health fields have had a substantial effect on clinical and counseling psychologists' income. Among these trends, two are noteworthy for their dramatic impact on not only salaries but also professional activities: managed care and master's level mental health professionals.

Massive health care reforms initiated in the United States in the 1970s radically altered the ways in which the health care insurance system allocates resources to patients and reimburses professionals for providing services. Since then, the traditional indemnity insurance plans that reimbursed psychologists for the service they provided have by and large been replaced with managed care plans that only reimburse for contracted services at set rates. Managed care organizations utilize numerous cost control strategies to maximize their profits. These strategies have contributed to greater competition among clinical and counseling psychologists for patients and greater willingness to provide services for reduced fees (Hayes, Barlow, & Nelson-Gray, 1999). In controlling costs, managed care organizations have also sought the services of master's level mental health providers because these professionals are willing to accept lower reimbursement rates corresponding to their education and training levels. As a result, clinical and counseling psychologists who wish to provide services through certain managed care plans have been forced to accept increasingly lower rates as the number of master's level mental health providers has grown. Both of these consequences have only further elevated the competition for patients and membership on managed care panels, meaning psychologists have less ground for negotiating their rates and the types of services they offer.

Surveys of licensed psychologists have found that 80% report that managed care has had a negative impact on their work and careers (Phelps, Eisman, & Kohout, 1998). Additional studies have revealed that psychologists whose caseloads include more managed care cases report that they work longer hours, experience more stress and emotional exhaustion, receive less supervision, and are less satisfied with their incomes (Rupert & Baird, 2004). So why are psychologists working with managed care at all? First, managed care did address substantial problems in the mental health care system related to rampant costs. Many psychotherapy and counseling treatments previously were conducted with little to no oversight or quality control. Second, managed health care allows for larger numbers of individuals to have access to some form of mental health care that they might not otherwise be able to afford. Lastly, being an approved provider for managed care organizations often leads to a more predictable flow of new patients and referrals.

Employment Issues

Clinical and counseling psychologists enjoy flexibility when they are on the job market. Those with the most extensive training have the option of working in almost any environment including inpatient, outpatient, academic, correctional, education, government, business, research, nonprofit, and private practice settings. Those with less extensive training, or training that focused intently in only one or two areas, will have fewer options but will be more attractive to employers seeking specific skills. To demonstrate the range of employment options, Box 10.3 provides summary information from several recent job ads for clinical and counseling psychologists.

Box 10.3   Recent Openings in the Clinical and Counseling Psychology Subfields

Position: Research Psychologist
Setting: Center for Army Leadership
Responsibilities: Conducting research that contributes to improved leader performance and combat readiness. Assessment, research methods, and data collection skills are applied in the development and evaluation of leader training.

Position: Assistant Professor
Setting: Wheaton College
Responsibilities: Teach applied courses in the undergraduate program. Maintain a research and scholarship program. Mentor undergraduate students and collaborate with them on research.

Position: Consulting Psychologist
Setting: California Department of Mental Health
Responsibilities: Evaluate inmates for potential as sexually violent predators using a standardized assessment battery. Testify in court as an expert witness.

Position: Director of Psychological Counseling Services
Setting: College of New Jersey
Responsibilities: Administrate a campus counseling center by guiding the delivery of mental health services to a student population, generating new initiative on campus, managing resources, ensuring accreditation for services and training programs, and establishing networks on and off campus.

Establishing employment through owning a private practice offers a number of benefits including greater control over your time, income, and the nature of your work. But much like owning any other business, private practices have their own set of complications. They can be costly to operate because you as the owner become fully responsible for all overhead, including purchasing facilities and maintaining them. Although some clinical and counseling psychologists do all of their own scheduling, billing, and paperwork, many find this time consuming and hire staff to assist in this work. Any employees of the practice then become the responsibility of the owner. Like all personal businesses, private practices are subject to economic conditions and patients' desires for services. Owners of private practices must manage their resources well and be prepared to both weather changes in the market and respond to them by changing their approach. Because of these issues and potential problems, many clinical and counseling psychologists work together to establish private practices in order to share the costs, time, and risks involved. Still others will work for a private practice, typically paying a percentage of their income, in order to enjoy some of the benefits without having to be responsible for managing the business. All of this being said, private practices have the potential to be one of the more rewarding and lucrative settings in which clinical and counseling psychologists can work.

Related Careers

Before moving forward with a closer examination of how clinical and counseling psychologists are trained for their careers, it is important to note that there are a variety of careers outside of the psychology field that also engage in applied work regarding human behavior. In particular, there are several that are directly involved in mental health issues. Before making decisions about you own career goals, you should understand the similarities and differences of these careers and those in clinical and counseling psychology.

Psychiatrists. Psychiatrists conduct research and/or provide services in the areas of diagnosis and treatment of mental illness. Like all other physicians, they are first trained in medical school and then receive more focused training in their specialty area during residency. Because the core of their training is in medicine, psychiatrists approach the diagnosis and treatment of mental illness using a medical model, meaning they apply treatments to alleviate identified symptoms and diagnosed conditions. Although psychiatrists previously provided psychotherapy as one form of treatment, and some still do, most now use psychotropic medications as their primary method for treating mental illness.

Clinical social workers. Clinical social workers are concerned with the effects of social problems and strive to improve the human condition. Their training typically includes a master's degree in social work with an emphasis on clinical or applied interventions. One source of confusion about the profession of clinical social work stems from the fact that some jobs, particularly within government agencies and nonprofit organizations, may carry a title of social worker. However, individuals who occupy these positions may or may not be required to have the same level of education and training required for clinical social workers. The core of clinical social workers' training is in social theory and its applications within a societal system, particularly with regards to illness and dysfunction. Given the scope of this focus, their professional activities are diverse and include interventions at individual, group, community, and societal levels. These interventions are usually designed either to help individuals access social services (e.g., medical care, housing) or to provide services directly (e.g., counseling). Depending on their training and activities, social workers can be employed in a variety of settings including hospitals, justice systems, government agencies, nonprofit organizations, and private practices.

Counselors and therapists.   Because the terms "counselor" and "therapist" are widely applied to a variety of professions and endeavors, this category is the most diverse within the related careers. Generally speaking, counselors and therapists in the mental health arena provide counseling and therapy services of some type to individuals and groups. The training and occupations of these professionals determine what specific services they provide. Common areas of concentration in the counseling field include school counseling, mental health or professional counseling, and addictions counseling. Common areas of concentration in the therapy field include marriage and family therapy, occupational therapy, and recreational therapy. The training required for these careers varies based on the nature of the work, but typically a master's degree in the field is required.

There are similarities between clinical and counseling psychologists and these related careers, but the differences matter greatly. The distinct training and backgrounds of each of these professionals leads them to think in highly divergent ways about human behavior and how it is best changed. Consumers of mental health services who struggle to distinguish between clinical social workers, counselors, therapists, psychiatrists, and psychologists will fail to appreciate the different approaches these professionals adopt and the unique expertise they offer. As a result, consumers may not seek out the professional that is best suited to understand and provide assistance with their particular problem. Likewise, if you have interest in a mental health related career but fail to investigate or understand these distinctions, you run the risk of selecting a career path based not on desired expertise but on less pertinent factors such as salaries, ease of graduate school acceptance, and time spent in training.

Training and Preparation

Earning the Degree

In order to practice, clinical or counseling psychologists must earn a doctoral degree in psychology. There are two degree options: the doctor of philosophy degree (PhD) and the doctor of psychology degree (PsyD). Because both degrees are at the doctoral level, they have several components in common. Thus, if you are considering training to be a clinical or counseling psychologist, regardless of which degree you pursue, you can expect to have these elements as part of your graduate education.

Earning a doctoral degree in clinical or counseling psychology requires completing relevant coursework. Most doctoral programs in these subfields require students to complete courses in foundational areas such as development, assessment, ethics, research methods, physiology, statistics, and treatment. Coursework is heaviest at the beginning of graduate training, but it soon decreases as more time is invested in gaining applied experience. Applied training is started under the watchful eyes of supervisors. As this training advances, students gradually take on more applied experiences with increasing difficulty and less restrictive supervision. Depending on the emphasis of the particular graduate program, students pursuing a doctoral degree will often assist faculty with their research and ultimately engage in some type of independent research project. Although this project is typically an empirical research study, or dissertation, a few graduate programs allow students to complete literature reviews or case studies to satisfy this requirement. Because these alternatives to the traditional dissertation do not provide for training in conducting empirical research, they are not suited for students who intend to incorporate any level of research activities into their careers.

Doctoral degree options.   The existence of the PhD and PsyD degrees is the result of figural events in the history of the field. The clinical and counseling psychology subfields first emerged at the beginning of the 20th century when groups of psychologists who studied human behavior began to apply this knowledge in order to improve human functioning. These early clinical and counseling psychologists separated from colleagues who resisted any move towards applications of psychological science, yet they remained committed to the scientific basis of their work. After decades of applying psychological theory and research to practice, clinical and counseling psychologists established the first set of training standards in 1949. Known as the Boulder model, these standards emphasized the need to prepare clinical and counseling psychologists for both practice and research careers. To accomplish this goal, training programs were based in university settings that could support research. All students were required to complete a final project that was research based, which resulted in a PhD. The PhD is an academic degree that can be earned in most disciplines. Those who earn a PhD possess not only in-depth knowledge about a particular subject but also expertise in how to gather and generate additional knowledge about the topic. The Boulder model called for training programs to provide as much funding as possible for students and to keep the number of students low in order to maximize mentorship opportunities.

In the 1960s, pressure was mounting to create an alternative training model. This pressure arose because many students were interested in clinical and counseling psychology careers that would focus exclusively on providing treatment and assessment services rather than conducting research, teaching, and supervision. This new model would train psychologists to be skilled consumers of research but would stop short of training them to conduct research. Instead, it would focus more on the development of practice skills. As a result of this pressure, the Vail model was officially recognized in 1973 and the PsyD degree was created to reflect the difference in expertise these psychologists would have. In the years since, the distinctions between the Boulder and Vail model have become less stark. Other models for training have emerged and graduate programs in the clinical and counseling psychology subfields now offer varying degrees of emphasis in applied and research training. Some PsyD programs now offer much less research training than the Vail model ever intended, while others offer much more. Some PhD programs are offering much less applied training than the Boulder model ever intended, while others offer much more. The best measure of the type of training a program offers is a thorough examination of the program's training components and an evaluation of the psychologists they produce.

The PhD and PsyD degrees primarily differ in the nature of the training involved, and additional information about these degree options is contained in the chapter entitled The Preprofessional Degree: Applying to Graduate School. In practice, these differences translate into several other important distinctions, which will be discussed in a later section of this chapter. But one important difference to consider at this point is how the degree is viewed. Just as the first clinical and counseling psychologists were disparaged for their efforts to apply psychological theory and research to working with patients, the PsyD degree model was initially disparaged for its reduced emphasis on research training and skills. Concerns focused on the extent to which this altered training might adversely affect the PsyD holders' efforts to secure employment. Studies investigating this potential bias have in large part found no support for it (Hershey, Kopplin, & Cornell, 1991). However, this is confounded by the fact that holders of the PhD and PsyD degrees tend to seek employment in different types of settings (Gaddy, Charlot-Swilley, Nelson, & Reich, 1995). For example, the vast majority of clinical and counseling psychologists who are employed in academic settings hold the PhD degree. This is likely due to the fact that academic positions typically require some level of research production from faculty, and in general psychologists trained in PsyD programs are unlikely to possess the research experience or interest to pursue these positions.

Master's degrees.   Master's degrees in clinical or counseling psychology are available in some graduate programs. However, since a doctorate is required to practice as a clinical or counseling psychologist, these master's degree programs have been the subject of debate. Individuals who earn these degrees are usually able to engage in limited practice activities as long as they are supervised by a doctoral-level professional. In other states, they may qualify for licensure and independent practice as a professional counselor or mental health counselor, but not as a psychologist.

The lack of a terminal master's degree option in clinical or counseling psychology that would lead to independent practice often puzzles students. Historically there has been pressure for the field to create this option, but many clinical and counseling psychologists have resisted it out of concern that such an option would involve reduced training standards. As a result, clinical and counseling psychologists continue only to be educated at the doctoral level. Partly in response to this, a host of master's degree options have emerged in other fields to meet demand for a master's level entry into mental health careers. Some clinical and counseling psychologists are pleased that the training standards for entering the field were preserved. Others have criticized this move by noting that had a master's option been created, these mental health professionals would have a background in psychology and psychologists would have likely retained control over how these individuals are trained.

Predoctoral internship. In addition to coursework, applied experiences, and an independent project, all students pursuing doctoral degrees in clinical or counseling psychology must complete a predoctoral internship. The predoctoral internship is a year-long experience in which students work full-time providing treatment and assessment services. Because this experience comes after students have completed their graduate education, with the exception of the dissertation or final project, the internship serves as a capstone to the student's applied training. While on internship students have the opportunity to learn new skills and further refine the skills they have already acquired.

Predoctoral internships vary widely in terms of experiences, settings, workload, and compensation. The majority of internship sites are approved by an organization known as the Association of Psychology Postdoctoral and Internship Centers (APPIC). APPIC coordinates the application and selection process that matches students with their most desired internship sites, and vice versa. A major concern about this process in recent years has been the shortage of internship sites compared to the number of students seeking positions. In 2008, 21% of the students seeking an internship site were unmatched (APPIC Board of Directors, 2008). This imbalance appears to be a trend resulting from reduced internship sites and increased numbers of students seeking internship placements. The number of sites is shrinking due to the costs of offering training programs, and the number of students is growing due to the increase of professional schools in psychology and the number of students they train each year (Kaslow & Keilin, 2006). Although professionals in the field are working to address this problem, it is likely to persist for some time and may affect students who are interested in pursuing the doctoral degree in clinical or counseling psychology.

Variations in Graduate Programs

Graduate programs in clinical and counseling psychology vary in two important ways: the emphasis placed on research versus applied experience and the overall quality of the training. The balance between research and applied training is a variable that graduate schools readily disclose. They are invested in having students who will be satisfied with the training experiences they offer, so they are clear in their program descriptions as to what extent students are expected to conduct research versus applied work. Graduate schools are far less clear in describing the quality of their training. This is in part due to the fact that there is little data available that compares the quality of various clinical and counseling psychology programs in a reliable and valid manner. As a result, graduate schools often do not have a clear idea of how the quality of their training compares to other programs. However, several factors that are known to these programs and applicants greatly impact training quality. These include the level of institutional and external funding for the program, the expertise of faculty, the resources provided to students, and the success of students in securing internship placements, licensure, and employment.

There are two basic types of graduate programs in clinical and counseling psychology: university-based and professional school programs. University-based programs are affiliated with and housed in established universities and colleges, often in these institutions' psychology departments. Their training programs are most closely aligned with the traditional scientist-practitioner model that results in the PhD. The professional school programs are housed in institutions established for the purpose of educating and training clinical and/or counseling psychologists. These institutions can either be university affiliated, meaning they have some relationship to an established university or college, or free standing, meaning they operate independently of any university or college. The professional school programs are most closely aligned with the scholar-practitioner model that results in the PsyD, although some university-based programs offer the PsyD as well.

In addition to training philosophy, some of the starkest differences in these two types of programs are related to how they are funded. University-based programs receive funding through the budgets of their home institutions. In addition, the faculty in these programs are typically involved in research that is supported by external sources of funding. These grants support research but also help support the needs of the program. Professional school programs are in a different position. Because many are free standing or only loosely affiliated with a university or college, they typically receive limited or no financial support from other institutions. In addition, the faculty in these programs seldom engage in research that generates grants. It is important that students who are considering graduate school in clinical or counseling psychology understand these differences. Several of these have been discussed in the literature. In particular, Norcross, Castle, Sayette, and Mayne's (2004) study comparing PsyD and PhD programs in clinical psychology yielded many noteworthy findings, several of which are summarized in Table 10.1. Some of these factors will have a real and immediate impact on your chances of being selected for a program and the financial costs of attending. They will have a less immediate impact on the training you receive. They may have a longer-term impact on the skills and abilities you acquire and, as a result, the types of employment you will seek.

The American Psychological Association (APA) is the organization that accredits doctoral programs in clinical psychology and counseling psychology. The APA has established training standards that all accredited programs must follow, including specific requirements for coursework, applied training, and research experience. The purpose of accreditation is to provide some consistency among graduate programs while ensuring that graduates have a certain level of knowledge and expertise required to enter the career field. Graduate programs must apply for APA accreditation and then be reviewed by the APA at great depth. Because programs can change over time, programs must regularly prove that they meet the APA standards or risk their

Table 10.1 Differences in Graduate Programs in Clinical and Counseling Psychology

	University-based Programs	Professional School Programs
Training Model	Scientist-practitioner	Scholar-practitioner
Degrees Offered	PhD, some PsyD	PsyD
Acceptance Rates	14%	41%
Receiving Full Financial Assistance	72%	18%
Students Enrolled Each Year	9	33
Securing Accredited Internships	93%	74%

accreditation status. Programs that are not APA accredited fall into several categories. Some are adequate programs that for some reason have opted not to pursue APA accreditation. Others may be working to ensure that their program meets the standards so that they can apply in the near future. Still, other programs lacking APA accreditation simply cannot meet the standards. Some have attempted and been denied or perhaps had their accreditation suspended or revoked. Others, often because of lack of resources, are unable to offer the types of training experiences the APA requires. Given the meaning of a program's accreditation status, it should come as no surprise that APA-accredited doctoral programs in clinical or counseling psychology are among the most competitive of all graduate programs in terms of admissions.

How important is it to attend a graduate program that has APA accreditation? For students who opt to attend an unaccredited program, there are two consequences to consider. First, the training components that are lacking in these programs may place you at a disadvantage for securing a predoctoral internship, postdoctoral training, and employment, particularly when you are competing against individuals who attended APA accredited programs. Second, some states will not grant a license as a psychologist to an individual who attended a graduate program that lacked APA accreditation. Other states will allow these individuals to take additional coursework or gain additional training experiences in order to satisfy the licensure requirements, but this varies from state to state and changes over time. As a result, attending an unaccredited program may greatly restrict your (and even eliminate many) employment opportunities.

Licensure

To better understand the way professional licensure works, think for a moment about a driver's license. The state in which you live has established rules that require the possession of a valid, current driver's license in order to operate a motor vehicle. Obtaining a driver's license involves proving that you have met these requirements. Most states restrict the age of the driver and their driving ability. After individuals earn a driver's license, their behavior while using the license is also restricted. They must occasionally renew their license and prove their eligibility. They must obey rules and laws that govern their driving behavior, including what types of vehicles they are allowed to drive. Failing to follow these restrictions can result in the loss of the license. Can an individual operate a motor vehicle without a license? Of course they can, but they usually do so in violation of the law and thereby place their ability to earn a license in jeopardy.

All licensure processes work much like a driver's license, and many different professionals must be licensed in order to offer services to the public. This licensure process has three main purposes. First, it protects the public by ensuring that only those professionals who are qualified to provide these services do so. Second, it regulates the practice of a profession. By requiring a license to do something, the state is then able to establish standards for earning the license and can monitor the actions of the professional. Third, requiring a license protects the use of a title. Most states license clinical psychologists and counseling psychologists with the general title of "psychologist" or "licensed psychologist." This is typically done so that different types of applied psychologists (e.g., clinical, neuro, industrial/organizational) can be licensed under the same process. State laws prohibit individuals who do not hold a license as a psychologist from referring to themselves as such. This protects consumers of services from being misled and ensures that all licensed professions are protected from having unqualified individuals market themselves as something they are not.

Because states establish the laws and rules that guide the professional licensure process, the requirements for licensure vary from state to state. This can produce problems for psychologists who obtain licensure in one state and then relocate to a state with stricter licensing requirements. Although there have been efforts in the field to improve cooperation among states in recognizing each others' licenses, a process known as reciprocity, progress in this area has remained slow. Despite the differences between state's licensing requirements, there are some fairly common components to the licensure process for clinical and counseling psychologists. Licensure as a psychologist always requires a doctoral degree in one of the applied areas of psychology. In addition, all states require some amount of postdoctoral training experience where one's work is supervised by a licensed psychologist. The states differ widely in the hours that are required. Some require only 1,000 hours and allow hours accumulated during the predoctoral internship to count towards this requirement. On the other end of the spectrum, some states require 4,000 hours of postdoctoral experience, all of which must be accumulated after the degree is earned. All states require satisfactory completion of the national licensing exam, or the Examination for Professional Practice of Psychology (EPPP). Again, states vary in what they determine is a passing score with the range being 70–80% correct. Many states have additional requirements that are not as consistent. For example, some have state level exams that address their specific laws and rules. These exams are typically either in a written or oral form and focus on state laws and ethical practice. Extensive information about the licensure process for psychologists, as well as the requirements for each state, can be accessed through the Association of State and Provincial Psychology Boards' website (http://www.asppb.org).

Professional licensure is a critical issue in the related mental health careers of professional counseling, clinical social work, and marriage and family therapy. The licensure process is similar in structure to that for clinical or counseling psychologists. Each state establishes its own requirements, and the degree of uniformity on a national level varies by profession. However, the components of specified education, training, supervision, and exam performance are present in most cases.

A license to practice psychology, as well as other mental health professions, must be maintained. Typically this involves renewal, and most states currently require licenses to be renewed every two years. In addition to paperwork and fees, renewal often involves documenting or attesting that one has completed any requirements that are in place for renewal. The most common requirement is continuing education requirements. States establish a minimum amount of additional training and education that psychologists must complete in order to renew their licenses. Most states also specify certain types of training that must be obtained (e.g., ethics, diversity) and the ways in which it can be acquired (e.g., workshops, self-study, conferences).

Another key component of maintaining one's license is ensuring that the license is not revoked as a result of failure to adhere to the rules and guidelines that regulate the practice of the profession. The most common reasons that states revoke a psychologist's license are for violations of professional ethics. Many states have adopted all or parts of the APA Ethical Principles of Psychologists and Code of Conduct into their state law or regulations, meaning that any violation is subject to both ethical and legal consequences. Still, other licenses are not maintained because psychologists fail to renew them or to complete the required continuing education. In addition, many states have established rules that allow for the revocation of professional licenses for behavior that is seen to be incongruent with the professional practice, such as felony convictions, crimes of moral turpitude, and defaulting on student loans or child support payments.

Preparing for Graduate Training as an Undergraduate

Because many of the issues discussed thus far take place when selecting a graduate program and completing training, you may feel that they are far removed from your position of beginning to consider clinical or counseling psychology as a career option. But be aware that there are also factors you should be attending to as an undergraduate because they will have bearing on your ability to enter graduate programs in these subfields.

Coursework. We have already established that clinical and counseling psychology programs differ considerably in their emphasis on research and applied training. As a result, absolute recommendations for the types of courses that best prepare you for these programs are not realistic. However, there are core courses in most undergraduate psychology curriculums that are judged to be vital for students aspiring to enter clinical or counseling psychology graduate programs. These courses, as well as relevant course areas outside of psychology, are listed in Box 10.4. Note that although courses pertaining to psychopathology and assessment are excellent choices, students also benefit from a background in the scientific foundations of the field and in various approaches to human behavior.

Activities. All students interested in graduate school are concerned about what types of experiences they should have that will prepare them and make their applications more desirable. There is much advice on this topic in the literature, and there are empirical studies that have surveyed graduate programs in psychology to determine what factors are most important when they are seeking new graduate students (e.g., see Norcross, Kohout, & Wicherski, 2006). Typically these graduate programs report that the most important components in a student's application are their letters of recommendation, personal statements, and GPA. From there, the student's interview, research experience, and GRE are the next group of important factors. Extracurricular activities and experience gained through internships and/or employment are typically the least valued components of a student's application. Although these

Box 10.4 Recommended Undergraduate Coursework for Clinical and Counseling Psychology

Courses Within Psychology
Research Methods
Experimental Psychology
Abnormal Psychology
Clinical or Counseling Psychology
Psychological Testing,
   Measurement, or Psychometrics
Ethics
Theories of Personality
Life-Span Developmental Psychology
Learning and Behavior

Course Areas Outside of Psychology
Statistics
Natural Sciences (Chemistry and Biology)
Business/Marketing/Accounting
Computer Science
Human Services

data reflect application components desired in all types of graduate programs in psychology, students interested in applying to clinical or counseling psychology programs should pay close attention to these findings. Those with limited time or resources to devote to preparing for graduate study will be best served by concentrating on their academic performance, developing a clear statement of their purpose and goals in pursuing graduate education, and cultivating relationships with faculty that might yield strong letters of support.

Working in Areas Related to Clinical or Counseling Psychology With a Bachelor's Degree

As discussed in earlier chapters, the bachelor's degree in psychology can be thought of as a liberal arts degree or a preprofessional degree. If you are interested in a career as a clinical psychologist or counseling psychologist, you should approach your undergraduate education as preparation for pursuing the doctoral degree. No matter how much coursework or exposure you have as an undergraduate to theories and applied practices of clinical and counseling psychologists, it is vital that you recognize that your education and expertise in this area is severely limited. As such, no undergraduate student in psychology should ever attempt to offer applied psychological services to another person. Few students would ever think of doing so. However, many others are far less cautious about casually attempting to diagnose disorders among friends and family, or offering recommendations about behavioral problems and treatment. Under no circumstance is such action appropriate. The potential for harm is substantial, and you must recognize the highly limited nature of your knowledge and experience base in these areas.

But what are undergraduate students who have interests in the clinical or counseling psychology subfields to do if they do not intend to pursue a graduate degree? Certainly there are excellent mental health career options at the master's level in other disciplines such as social work, counseling, and therapy. But what about those individuals who will seek employment with their bachelor's degree, either as a career or in preparation for later attending graduate school? There are a number of career and employment opportunities that tap aspects of clinical and counseling psychology. Some students are initially dissatisfied with them because they do not allow one to provide counseling or therapy. But once they understand that doing so always requires a graduate degree, they often are open to reevaluating these options. Many of these bachelor's level careers allow for working directly with individuals who are experiencing distress or difficulties in functioning, just not in providing treatment services. In addition, some of these careers involve interactions with individuals where the goal is to provide help and make a positive impact in another person's life. The most common options include mental health technicians/aides and human/social service specialists.

Mental Health Technician/Aide

Mental health technicians/aides often go by a variety of job titles, including psychiatric technician/aide or residential counselor/assistant. The work varies, but typically these positions involve large portions of time spent in direct contact with patients who are receiving mental health treatment, often in an inpatient or residential setting. Patients who are living at a treatment facility are experiencing the types of problems that require extensive supervision and assistance. Mental health technicians/aides are involved in the entire spectrum of the patient's daily routine. These professionals often know the patients well and are in the best position to monitor their behavior and response to treatment. Therefore, although mental health technicians/aides cannot provide treatment in the form of therapy or medication, they play an integral role in facilitating patients' overall care and advising the treatment teams. According to the U.S. Department of Labor (2007), the median salary estimate was $25,470 for psychiatric aides and $23,160 for nursing aides, orderlies, and attendants.

Human/Social Service Specialists

Human/social service specialists also go by a variety of job titles, including social worker, consultant, specialist, case manager, and patient liaison. The work varies, but most of these individuals are involved in some type of coordination of services between a patient or client and an agency that serves them. Some human/social service specialists are in nonprofit settings and may be involved in community outreach, management of charitable cases, and coordination of services for individuals in need. Others are employed by local and state governments to ensure that services are being adequately delivered to the public. This might involve direct work with clients who are in need of services that government agencies can provide. But it might also involve monitoring the performance of businesses that provide these services, such as the regulation of childcare centers. According to the U.S. Department of Labor (2007), the median salary estimate was $26,630 for human service assistants and $36,420 for community and social service specialists.

A Science of Heart and Mind

Robert McGrath, PhD
Fairleigh Dickinson University

People are sometimes surprised when they learn that even though I am a clinical psychologist I no longer provide clinical services. This is not because I do not value what psychotherapy can do for people. It can be a magical and moving experience, and I am proud that in some cases I profoundly affected another person's life for the better. Since early in my education, though, I was always drawn primarily to the potential for clinical psychology as a science.

The biggest problem I faced when I first began to develop a research program was how to pick just one topic to study. Clinical psychologists study a host of interesting issues. Just thinking of the colleagues with whom I work now, they are investigating topics as varied as the role mood plays in college students' alcohol abuse, how to improve treatment for eating disorders,

and the best methods for predicting whether incarcerated criminals are likely to offend again.

My own research focuses on how best to measure psychological concepts. Perhaps that seems like a dry topic to settle on, but it depends how you look at it. For me, it combines an intellectual interest in science with a romantic notion that we can learn how to read and understand what is in another person's heart and mind more effectively. That strikes me as pretty fascinating.

That is what I find special about a career as a researcher in clinical psychology: bringing the techniques of science to bear on questions about what it means to be human, and how to improve the human condition. Thanks to recent advances in genetics, brain imaging, and cognitive research, I think we are on the verge of a new era in terms of understanding the causes of unhappiness and discontent, and how to help those people who need it. I do not know how clinical psychology will evolve in response to this new knowledge, but I am proud that it will be guided by the research that is being done by research clinical psychologists.

Note. Dr. Robert McGrath is a clinical psychologist and professor of psychology in the School of Psychology at Fairleigh Dickinson University in Teaneck, NJ, where he is the Director of the PhD Program in Clinical Psychology and the MS Program in Clinical Psychopharmacology. Dr. McGrath has authored over 40 peer reviewed journal articles and is a past president of the American Society for the Advancement of Pharmacotherapy (APA Division 55).

Professional Spotlight

Kimberlyn Leary, PhD, ABPP

Education:
- Bachelor of Arts (BA) in Psychology from Amherst College
- Master of Arts (MA) in Psychology from the University of Michigan
- Doctor of Philosophy (PhD) in Clinical Psychology from the University of Michigan
- Graduate of the Michigan Psychoanalytic Institute
- Masters in Public Administration (MPA) from the Kennedy School of Government, Harvard University

Position:
Director of Psychology and Psychology Training at Cambridge Health Alliance; Associate Professor of Psychology at Harvard Medical School.

Description of Position:
I direct the Division of Psychology in a large, urban medical center that is also a teaching hospital, where I work with our psychology faculty to design and implement clinical training experiences for practicum students, interns, and postdoctoral fellows. As a professor, I teach both psychology interns and fellows (as well as medical students), and engage in research and writing, present at conferences, and work collaboratively with colleagues.

Most Significant Professional Accomplishment:
I feel honored to have the opportunity to serve as a leader. Leadership is an activity and consists of mobilizing others to engage in collaborative work towards shared goals. Thus, the most significant work I am doing now is engaging the psychologists in our system to do the work that is most meaningful towards our goal of teaching and training psychologists to care for patients who need help.

Favorite Publication:
Leary, K. (1999). Passing, posing and "keeping it real." *Constellations: An International Journal of Critical & Democratic Theory, 6*, 85–96.

Areas of Research:
My scholarly work is at the intersection of leadership, negotiation, and clinical psychology. I am researching and writing on collaborative, relational problem solving across different sectors. This work aims to be attentive to the multicultural contexts in which problem solving occurs. I am interested in helping people to resolve conflict more effectively – whether that conflict is within a person, between neighborhoods, or among international players.

Areas of Practice:
In my private practice, I offer psychoanalysis, psychodynamic therapy, and integrative therapies aimed at helping people with focal problems.

Professional Memberships:
As a member of the American Psychoanalytic Association, I sit on the Program Committee and the Committee on Racial and Ethnic Diversity. I co-coordinate the seminars for trainees program

and the Ticho Award process. As a member of American Psychological Association, I have served as Treasurer of the Section on Women in Division 39.

Most Rewarding Aspect of Your Career:
The most wonderful part of my professional life is the chance to learn with and from very talented, creative, and inspiring people – among them my colleagues, my students, and my patients. I love that being an effective psychologist obliges you to keep learning.

Words of Advice to the Student Who Is Interested in Your Subfield:
Think big, follow your heart, but remember real work takes place one-step at a time! Over the course of a career – if you are lucky – your interests will change. Listen to what your heart tells you and allow yourself to take reasonable chances. It is not possible to do everything that interests you all at once, but it may well be that you do many different things over the course of your career. Treat your career as an adventure.

Suggested Exercises

1. Obtain the perspective of a current graduate student who is pursuing a doctorate in clinical or counseling psychology. Many graduate programs provide e-mail addresses for their graduate students, and many of these students are willing to answer specific questions that a potential applicant might have.
2. Interview a clinical or counseling psychologist who is working in a setting you have not previously considered as part of your career goals (e.g., hospital, prison, university). Think about your particular interests in clinical and counseling psychology and what settings these interests could be applied to.
3. Investigate a research opportunity within your undergraduate program or one at a neighboring institution. Contact a faculty member whose research interests you and have a conversation with them about what they look for in an undergraduate research assistant. Use the information they provide you to consider the following two questions:
   • Would you be willing to work with them?
   • What do you need to do to ensure that they would want you to work for them?
4. Investigate a volunteer opportunity within an area hospital or residential treatment center. Larger hospitals often have volunteer centers and allow some choice in the areas you work (e.g., psychiatric unit or mental health outpatient clinic). These experiences can often help focus your career goals.

Suggested Readings by Topic Area

Clinical Psychology and Counseling Psychology Careers

Kuther, T. L. (2005). *Your career in psychology: Clinical and counseling psychology*. Belmont, CA: Wadsworth Publishing.

Graduate School in Clinical and Counseling Psychology

Norcross, J. C., Sayette, M. A., & Mayne, T. J. (2009). *Insider's guide to graduate programs in clinical and counseling psychology*. New York: Guilford Press.

Mental Health Care Issues

Mechanic, D. (2007). *Mental health and social policy: Beyond managed care* (5th ed.). Allyn & Bacon.

References

American Psychological Association. (2005). *2005 doctorate employment survey*. Washington, DC: Author.

APPIC Board of Directors. (2008). *2008 APPIC match statistics*. Retrieved from http://www.appic.org/match/5_2_2_match_about_statistics.html

Gaddy, C. D., Charlot-Swilley, D., Nelson, P. D., & Reich, J. N. (1995). Selected outcomes of accredited programs. *Professional Psychology: Research and Practice, 26*, 507–513.

Gallucci, N. T. (1997). An evaluation of the characteristics of undergraduate psychology majors. *Psychological Reports, 81*, 879–889.

Hayes, S. C., Barlow, D. H., & Nelson-Gray, R. O. (1999). *The scientist practitioner: Research and accountability in the age of managed care* (2nd ed.). Needham Heights, MA: Allyn & Bacon.

Hershey, J. M., Kopplin, D. A., & Cornell, J. E. (1991). Doctors of psychology: Their career experiences and attitudes toward degree and training. *Professional Psychology: Research and Practice, 22*, 351–356.

Kaslow, N. J., & Keilin, W. G. (2006). Internship training in clinical psychology: Looking into our crystal ball. *Clinical Psychology Science and Practice, 13*, 242–248.

National Science Foundation. (2006). Science and engineering doctorate awards: 2005 (NSF 07-305). Arlington, VA: Division of Science Resources Statistics. Retrieved from http://www.nsf.gov/statistics/nsf07305

Norcross, J. C., Castle, P. H., Sayette, M. A., & Mayne, T. J. (2004). The PsyD: Heterogeneity in practitioner training. *Professional Psychology: Research and Practice, 35*, 412–419.

Norcross, J. C., Kohout, J. L., & Wicherski, M. (2006). Graduate admissions in psychology I: The application process. *Eye on Psi Chi, 10*(2), 28–29, 42–43.

Phelps, R., Eisman, E. J., & Kohout, J. (1998). Psychological practice and managed care: Results of the CAPP practitioner survey. *Professional Psychology: Research and Practice, 29*, 31–36.

Rupert, P. A., & Baird, K. A. (2004). Managed care and the independent practice of psychology. *Professional Psychology: Research and Practice, 35*, 185–193.

U.S. Department of Labor. (2007). *May 2007 national occupational employment and wage estimates*. Retrieved from http://www.bls.gov/oes/current/oes_nat.htm

Webb, A. R., & Speer, J. R. (1985). The public image of psychologists. *American Psychologist, 40*, 1063–1064.

Resources

Society of Clinical Psychology – Division 12 of the APA
    http://www.apa.org/divisions/div12
Society of Counseling Psychology – Division 17 of the APA
    http://www.div17.org
Division of Psychotherapy – Division 29 of the APA
    http://www.divisionofpsychotherapy.org
Psychologists in Independent Practice – Division 42 of the APA
    http://www.division42.org
Association of Psychology Postdoctoral and Internship Centers (APPIC)
    http://www.appic.org
Association of State and Provincial Psychology Boards
    http://www.asppb.org

11

Careers in Educational and School Psychology

Introduction

Consider for a moment how much of your life has been spent in the pursuit of education. From kindergarten to 12th grade of high school, you likely spent 30–40 hours per week at school with additional time at home devoted to reading, studying, and completing assignments. Some of you even began your formal education earlier by attending programs such as pre-K and Head Start. Now that you are in college, the hours spent in the classroom have decreased but the time devoted to learning remains high. In fact, many of you may feel as though the time you have to devote to your families, friends, and work is constantly being consumed by the demands of your education. For those of you contemplating earning a graduate or professional degree, this could take an additional 2–8 years and often requires your full attention and devotion. With education playing such an enormous role in the lives of so many, it seems as though the field of psychology would have much to contribute to our understanding of the education process and the experiences of those involved. In fact, the field has been and continues to be closely involved in these educational endeavors, particularly through the work of educational and school psychologists.

The subfields of educational and school psychology are popular career options for students. Approximately 6.8% of all doctoral degrees granted in psychology in the United States are in one of these two subfields (American Psychological Association [APA], 2008). In a recent survey of educational and school psychologists, many indicated that personal experiences with an educational or school psychologist during their childhood or adolescence helped shape their interest (Graves & Wright, 2007). Others noted that the opportunity to work closely with student populations was an important factor in their decision to pursue this career.

Defining the Subfields

Educational and school psychologists share a common overall focus. The foundation of their work centers on situations in which learning takes place. However, these subfields diverge when choosing what areas and topics to address within the learning process.

Educational Psychology

The subfield of educational psychology is defined by its focus on the educational process. Educational psychologists are interested in how humans learn in educational settings. This includes an interest in both the teaching, or instructional, side of the process and the learning side. For the most part, educational psychologists approach these topics as researchers and theorists. They seek to generate new knowledge that can address psychological factors in the educational process.

Psychology in the United States has always been linked to the topics of learning and teaching. Many of the founding figures in American psychology, such as William James, G. Stanley Hall, Edward Thorndike, and John Dewey, offered research, observations, and contributions to our knowledge of educational processes. Outside of the United States, other leading figures in the field, such as Alfred Binet and Jean Piaget, viewed educational processes as fertile ground for developing their ideas about human learning, intelligence, and development.

Educational psychologists address a wide array of topics in their efforts to expand our knowledge of the teaching and learning process. Much of their work has been heavily influenced by dramatic shifts over the last 50 years in our understanding of human cognition. Currently educational psychologists examine factors in student learning such as motivation, intelligence, study habits, organization, perseverance, and response to success or failure. Others investigate aspects of instructional methods such as learning outcomes, teaching materials, curriculums, assessment methods, and the use of technology and media. Still other educational psychologists study the impact of environmental variables such as student-teacher ratios, class composition, and classroom management.

School Psychology

The subfield of school psychology is defined by its focus on assisting students with particular needs. School psychologists work to improve students' well-being by addressing developmental, emotional, social, and academic problems that interfere with their education. Unlike educational psychologists who tend to approach educational issues as researchers and theorists, school psychologists are more likely to serve in the role of practitioners who work directly with individual students. School psychology differs from school counseling or guidance counseling in its emphasis on helping those students who are experiencing the greatest number of problems relative to their education.

School psychology in large part developed out of the applied work of clinical and counseling psychologists and the focus of educational psychologists. Perhaps the single most influential event on the current state of school psychology occurred in 1975 when the Education for All Handicapped Children Act was put into place (Fagan & Wise, 2000). This piece of federal legislation led to the emergence of special education in the public school systems. The requirements placed new demands on schools to assess and respond to the needs of students experiencing a variety of disabilities. As a result, school districts across the country worked in the years that followed to implement requirements for providing special education resources to qualifying students. One result of these events was a doubling of the number of school psychologists between 1970 and 1980, and another doubling by the early 1990s (Reschly, 2000).

The topics of focus for school psychologists have expanded in recent decades as the laws guiding schools' handling of students with special needs have evolved. Many school psychologists concentrate on factors that contribute to student difficulties such as adjusting to school, academic achievement, mental health, substance abuse, social relationships, and life stress. But by far the single biggest issue that school psychologists address is students with special needs such as physical, emotional, and learning disabilities. School psychologists are involved in the assessment of these students and the coordination of special education programs designed to assist them. Although their primary focus is the needs of children who are experiencing these problems, school psychologists often consult with teachers and administrators about issues such as managing classroom behavior and structuring school environments.

The Work

Core Activities

Educational and school psychologists engage in activities consistent with their positions and responsibilities. Typically these activities are defined by the nature of the position and the setting in which the work is done. But much of this work falls into one of five categories: research, intervention, assessment, program evaluation, and consultation. To provide a glimpse into the diversity of career opportunities available, Box 11.1 provides a summary of several recent job advertisements in the education and school psychology subfields.

Research. The subfields of educational and school psychology are engaged in conducting research and applying the findings of this research to real world settings. In general, educational psychologists tend to pursue research careers, and school psychologists tend to pursue applied careers. Because educational psychologists are experts in teaching and learning processes, their research focuses on the design and evaluation of educational programs. They often evaluate methods of instruction and learning, develop new instructional techniques, and influence theories and approaches to the learning process. School psychologists are experts in assessment and intervention for individual students experiencing difficulties in educational settings. Given this, their

Box 11.1 Recent Openings in the Educational and School Psychology Subfields

Position:	School Psychologist
Setting:	Johnston County Schools, North Carolina
Responsibilities:	Serve on Response to Intervention teams, conduct assessments, serve on intervention teams, provide teacher consultation, assist with program implementation, counsel students, provide teaching training.
Position:	Assistant Professor, Educational Psychology
Setting:	University of New Mexico – Department of Individual, Family, and Community Education
Responsibilities:	Collaborate with educational psychology faculty; teach graduate courses in educational psychology, especially in advanced educational statistics and research methods; conduct research; advise graduate students; and provide support to students and faculty in the use and application of statistical and research methods.
Position:	Faculty Developer
Setting:	University of Michigan – Center for Research on Learning and Teaching
Responsibilities:	Develop and implement programs and activities to improve teaching; consult with graduate students, faculty, and academic units about teaching, curricular development and program evaluation; and assist with the infusion of multiculturalism into the curriculum and the dissemination of pedagogical methods appropriate for a diverse student body.
Position:	Assistant Professor, School Psychology
Setting:	University of South Carolina – Department of Psychology
Responsibilities:	Conduct research that meshes with departmental strengths with desirable expertise in either multicultural issues, internalizing disorders, small n designs, academic interventions, school-wide behavioral interventions, school-based mental health, school-based health and wellness, and system interventions. Contribute to the training mission of the School Psychology Graduate Training Program. Certification or eligibility for licensure desired.

research concentrates on creating new techniques of assessment, evaluating the effectiveness of interventions, and investigating the nature of student difficulties. For educational and school psychologists engaged in research, the dissemination of this information through publications is essential to having new information influence future research and educational practices. Box 11.2 lists several journals that publish research in these subfields.

Box 11.2 Journals That Publish Educational and School Psychology Research

Educational Psychology	*School Psychology*
Educational Psychologist	Journal of School Psychology
Journal of the Learning Sciences	School Psychology Review
Learning and Individual Differences	School Psychology Quarterly
Review of Educational Research	School Psychology International
Journal of Educational Psychology	Journal of Psychoeducational Assessment
Learning and Instruction	

Assessment and interventions.   Educational and school psychologists place great value in the careful assessment and evaluation of situations before intervening. School psychologists are more likely to conduct assessments at the individual level by working with a student to evaluate the nature of her or his current academic, social, emotional, and/or physical difficulties. Given their focus on students with special needs, school psychologists spend a large portion of their time conducting assessments to determine what, if any, special services are needed in order for a child to succeed in the school setting. This includes assessing intellectual abilities, aptitudes for learning, achievement, social and emotional functioning, and mental health status.

Because school psychologists so frequently engage in applied work, they are more likely than educational psychologists to provide direct interventions in educational settings. These interventions include such activities as providing counseling to students struggling with academic, social, emotional, and family problems. Typically these problems come to the attention of school psychologists because they impact the student's academic performance. Other interventions include creating behavioral management plans that teachers and parents can use to help a student decrease problematic behaviors and increase desired behaviors. Interventions that occur on a larger scale include workshops and courses provided to groups of students on topics such as social skills, anger management, study habits, and coping. Some school psychologists also play a key role in the event of a crisis in the school, community, or life of a student. They often guide administrators, teachers, and parents on how to best assist students in understanding and coping with such events.

Program evaluation.   Given their focus on teaching and learning processes, educational psychologists are more likely to conduct evaluations at a program level. These evaluations consist of investigating the nature of instructional and learning programs and determining their effectiveness. The results can be used to identify and implement appropriate strategies to improve educational processes. School psychologists engage in program evaluations as well, but typically only in situations where gathering information about an academic program or environment will help serve individual students. This might include evaluating the effectiveness of a special education or behavior management program in terms of its ability to address particular needs of a student.

Consultation. Educational psychologists often serve in the role of consultants given their broad expertise in instructional and learning methods. Schools, businesses with education and training centers, and companies that develop educational materials, frequently seek consultation regarding their practices and products. The educational psychologist's role is to help the organization understand what is effective in the design and delivery of instructional information and in the learning process. For school psychologists, consultation often comes in the form of collaborating with other professionals regarding the well-being of a student. They consult with teachers, administrators, parents, physicians, and mental health providers about the nature of a child's difficulties and the recommended interventions. Their goal is to find effective solutions to learning and behavior problems by gathering as much information as possible and strengthening working relationships between important figures in the child's life. School psychologists also consult with educational staff to address and prevent student difficulties. Prevention efforts often involve implementing programs to address bullying, tolerance of diversity, substance abuse, and peer relationships.

Settings

Educational and school psychologists are employed in a variety of settings. Data on employment settings for new school and educational psychologists are presented in Table 11.1 (APA, 2005). Note that these data do not include the large numbers of school psychologists who earn the specialist's degree (discussed later). However, previous research has indicated that the employment settings of all school psychologists are comparable (Curtis, Grier, Abshier, Sutton, & Hunley, 2002).

Salaries

In reporting data on the salaries of school psychologists, the U.S. Department of Labor (2007) groups this career in with clinical and counseling psychology. The data indicate that 80% of school psychologists earned an estimated annual salary between $37,300 and $104,520, with the median income for these psychologists being $62,210. Several factors contribute to the variations in salary, including the type of school and its funding source. School psychologists' level of education, as well as the level of administrative responsibilities in their positions, also helps determine salary. Valid salary information for educational psychologists alone is difficult to obtain, but given the

Table 11.1 Employment Settings for Educational and School Psychologists

	Educational Psychologists	School Psychologists
Universities, Colleges, Medical Schools	46.3%	8.7%
Schools and Other Educational Settings	31.7%	79.3%
Independent Practice	0%	1.1%
Direct/Human Services (hospitals, clinics)	9.8%	6.5%
Government and Business	9.8%	3.3%

settings in which they typically work, the median salary of non-clinical, counseling, and I/O psychologists in university and college settings provides a reasonable estimate at $67,020 (U.S. Department of Labor, 2007).

Employment Issues

Educational psychologists engage in work that often requires funding to support the evaluation and development of new programs and instructional techniques. As funding sources for such research rise and fall with changes in the economy and mission of funding agencies, educational psychologists may find that the feasibility of their work also changes. Those who work in school settings or provide direct services may face additional pressure of needing to select and implement educational procedures that produce positive results. An additional issue that has shaped the careers of educational psychologists in recent years has been the enormous influence of technology on instructional and learning methods. The ways in which teachers and students present, consume, and generate information has changed radically with the advancement of computer technology, the internet, and digital media. Most educational psychologists have welcomed this exciting shift in educational research and theory given its potential to transform instructional and learning processes.

Because school psychologists' activities are determined by current legislation and requirements placed on schools, their positions are often tied to funding for these services. Some school systems and districts look to save money by expanding the caseloads of school psychologists. Although some schools may have one or more school psychologists dedicated to serving their students, often these positions are shared across several schools in a district. Less populated areas may be limited to a single school psychologist across a county. These high case loads and shifting environments can at times contribute to a sense of isolation from fellow professionals. Despite efforts to spread their responsibilities, many schools and districts are in dire need of psychologists to provide services to students. In fact, a severe shortage of school psychologists has existed for some time and is expected to continue into the near future (Curtis, Hunley, & Grier, 2004). This shortage has come at a time when student populations have been changing dramatically along demographic variables such as race, ethnicity, and socio-economic status. The difficulties of responding to these changes have been further exacerbated by a lack of diversity among school psychologists, who in recent years have been predominantly Caucasian and female (Curtis, Grier, & Hunley, 2004).

Training and Preparation

Degree Options, Certification, and Licensure

The path to becoming an educational psychologist is fairly straightforward in that a doctoral degree is required. In contrast, school psychologists can hold degrees at the master's, specialist, or doctoral degree levels. Because most careers in psychology require a specific degree, the presence of these options is often a source of confusion for students.

In particular, many have never been exposed to the specialist level degree. The specialist level is not unique to the discipline of school psychology. It typically represents an intermediate level of training that falls between the master's and doctoral levels.

Because the APA has always asserted that the doctoral degree must be earned for entry into any type of professional practice in the field, it only gives accreditation to school psychology programs offering a doctoral degree. The APA does not provide training standards or evaluate programs at the master's or specialist level. However, the National Association of School Psychologists (NASP) provides scenarios for entry into school psychology with either a doctoral or a specialist level degree. As a result, NASP accredits programs that grant both levels of degrees.

To work in public school settings, school psychologists must be certified by the states in which they work. Most states now only provide certification to school psychologists that have already earned national certification. National certification as a school psychologist is granted by the NASP and requires a minimum of the specialist level degree along with successful completion of the Praxis School Psychology Exam. This creates a situation in which working as a school psychologist in most states requires at least a specialist level degree. As a result, students pursuing training in school psychology are increasingly viewing the specialist degree as the shortest path to their careers. Recent research found equal numbers of school psychologists seeking specialist and doctoral level degrees, with a strong trend towards increased numbers seeking the specialist level degree (Curtis et al., 2002). As a result, the number of school psychologists with a doctoral degree is expected to continue declining (Curtis, Hunley, et al., 2004).

As discussed in the Careers in Clinical Psychology and Counseling Psychology chapter and the Careers in Industrial/Organizational Psychology chapter, careers that involve the applied practice of psychology in working with the public typically require a license. For this reason, any educational or school psychologist who seeks to establish a private practice or provide services to the general public that are psychological in nature must be licensed. Since most states only allow those individuals with a doctorate to be licensed as psychologists, the work of school psychologists with training at the specialist level is typically limited to the school setting. However, some states have created licenses for school psychologists that require a specialist level degree. Although educational and school psychologists can theoretically offer in private practice many of the same services they provide in educational settings, state laws prohibit such work unless the practitioner is licensed. As a result, few educational and school psychologists operate independent practices, and these numbers appear to be shrinking as more school psychologists choose the specialist degree option.

Variations in Graduate Programs

Doctoral programs in educational psychology and school psychology vary in their focus and the nature of training they offer. Therefore, they produce graduates with distinct areas of expertise. Programs in educational psychology even differ in their titles, using names such as learning and motivation, instructional psychology and technology, and evaluation and measurement. Doctoral programs in school psychology tend to adhere to either a scientist-practitioner or an applied professional training model (Jackson,

1997). These two approaches to training are similar to the training models in clinical psychology and counseling psychology programs. The scientist-practitioner programs emphasize a traditional, broad base training with strong empirical/statistical components. The applied professional programs emphasize training in applied endeavors. In fact, school psychology still shares much in common with the clinical and counseling psychology subfields as all three degrees are viewed as general practice specialties that result in careers as health service providers. This means that these psychologists are trained specifically in applied techniques and interventions, often with enough breadth to allow them to work with a variety of different populations on a variety of different issues. The curriculums and training standards across these three subfields have much more in common than different (Cobb et al., 2004).

Specialist-level training in school psychology presents additional types of variations in graduate programs. Many programs require a combined master's and specialist's degree. Students typically must successfully complete the master's program before being admitted to the specialist's program. Other graduate programs in school psychology offer the specialist degree by itself. Both program types are often similar in their overall requirements of coursework and practicum/internship experience. The combined master's and specialist programs sometimes require more coursework, practicum, or research experience.

Earning the Degree

As with most graduate degrees, doctoral and specialist degrees in the subfields of educational and school psychology involve various components of training. Formal coursework is a foundation of all programs. In addition, most doctoral programs in educational psychology, and some of those in school psychology, place emphasis on training in both research (e.g., methods, experimentation, statistical analysis) and applied intervention (e.g., assessment, evaluation, counseling). Other doctoral and specialist programs in school psychology will place most of the emphasis on applied endeavors. Advancing in these programs will result in less coursework and greater supervised experience and independent study. Students in programs with a heavier research emphasis can expect to spend time conducting research as well as gaining applied experience. Students in programs that emphasize applied training will spend much of their time outside of class engaged in closely supervised intervention activities in educational and school settings.

Preparing for Graduate Training as an Undergraduate

As an undergraduate student considering the possibility of pursuing graduate training in the educational or school psychology subfields, it is important to keep in mind that there are things you can and should be doing now to prepare. In particular, the coursework and activities you engage in now can affect graduate programs' interest in you in the future.

Coursework.   Given the variations we have discussed within programs in the educational and school psychology subfields, it is difficult to establish absolute recommendations

Box 11.3 Recommended Undergraduate Coursework
for Educational and School Psychology

Courses Within Psychology
Developmental Psychology
Child/Adolescent Psychology
Family Psychology
Research Methods
Experimental Psychology
Psychological Testing
Cross-Cultural Psychology
Ethnic Minority Psychology
Ethics
Learning and Behavior

Course Areas Outside of Psychology
Statistics
Education (instruction and curriculum)
Special Education

for undergraduate coursework that will best prepare you for graduate level training. However, there are core courses in most undergraduate psychology curriculums that are vital for students aspiring to enter education and school psychology graduate programs. These courses, as well as relevant course areas outside of psychology, are listed in Box 11.3. Notice that while courses in development, research, and education are important, students also benefit from a solid background in psychological testing and diversity.

Activities.   The nature of the career you desire should shape the graduate programs to which you apply. In turn, the nature of these programs should shape the types of activities you engage in to prepare yourself for this training and establish yourself as a worthy applicant. Programs with greater emphasis on research skills and training (e.g., doctoral programs in educational psychology, scientist-practitioner doctoral programs in school psychology) will value applicants who have strong research skills and experiences as undergraduates. Although this experience will not be a disadvantage for students applying to more applied programs, these programs may also value direct experience with student populations in educational settings. Direct experience working with an educational or school psychologist can be difficult to come by, but general experience in school systems working with student populations is also helpful.

Working in Areas Related to Educational and School Psychology With a Bachelor's Degree

As discussed in earlier chapters, the bachelor's degree in psychology can be thought of as a liberal arts or preprofessional degree. It does not automatically qualify you to enter a particular career field, nor does it provide you with a defined set of skills that employers easily recognize. Instead, your ability to secure employment in an area related to educational or school psychology with only a bachelor's degree will in large part depend upon you gaining relevant experience as an undergraduate, identifying positions for which you qualify, and effectively conveying your knowledge and skills to potential employers. There are several career and employment opportunities that tap aspects of educational and school psychology. Many of these bachelor's level careers allow for working directly with students and instructors. The most common options include teaching and human services positions.

Human/Social Service Specialists

The careers of human/social service specialists are as varied as their job titles. Whether working in the capacity of a case manager, patient representative, or consultant, these individuals often serve as a liaison between their clients and an agency that can provide services to them. These positions typically exist in state and county government as well as nonprofit organizations. Although the responsibilities vary greatly, many human/social service specialists deal directly with children, and often this includes emphasis on their education and access to educational resources. Other human/social service specialists work to ensure that the agencies and institutions that provide services to these individuals do so in accordance with laws and regulations. According to the U.S. Department of Labor (2007), the median salary estimate was $26,630 for human service assistants and $36,420 for community and social service specialists.

Teachers

Psychology students who find the educational and school psychology subfields of interest but who will seek employment with a bachelor's degree might want to consider teaching. Teachers have the opportunity to work closely with students, parents, and other school staff to support the education and overall well-being of the students. Although teachers may not conduct research or articulate theory on educational processes, they are on the front lines of putting such research and theory into practice. Teachers who are well versed in educational research and its implications are involved daily in working to improve the learning of their students and the materials and techniques used to accomplish this goal. And although teachers do not provide counseling, intervention, or assessment services directly to students and families, they often play a vital role in the success of these services. In other words, the work of educational and school psychologists often depends heavily on the support and applied skills of teachers. Teaching positions thus provide an opportunity to be involved in this work and interact with students. Keep in mind that even though undergraduate psychology programs do not prepare students to earn a teaching certification, many school districts allow individuals to teach while they work to earn their certification. According to the U.S. Department of Labor (2007), the median salary estimate was $47,900 for middle school teachers and $49,420 for secondary school teachers.

The Science of People

A Career in School Psychology

William Pfohl, PsyD, NCSP
Western Kentucky University

Most who enter an applied area of psychology (e.g., school psychology, clinical psychology, industrial/organizational psychology) want to *make a difference.* They want a hands-on career with "real people" in real settings. School psychology is that profession. Making a difference is done in direct and indirect services. Working with a teacher who is having classroom discipline problems, working with a parent to help them understand the impact of autism on education and family, or developing a school safety program to prevent bullying are all within the activities and daily practice of a school psychologist.

School psychologists work in school settings with a wide range of ages, potentially birth to 22 years of age. They work with children, parents, administrators, educators, and outside agencies, all in an effort to address students' academic and emotional needs. They help enhance students' learning environments, emotional well-being, and capacity to cope with life events. School psychologists' careers are varied, never boring. Many provide assessment and treatment of those with disabilities and handicapping conditions. Others counsel parents and students about personal and emotional issues. Others consult by providing an array of academic and mental health services or helping to prevent the emergence of problems. Others write grants and conduct program evaluations, many currently emphasizing school safety issues and the prevention of school violence. Others train future school psychologists in university graduate programs.

I started college as a biochemistry major due to my love of science in high school. Quickly I discovered my passion was people, not labs and studying plants or animals. After visiting with a career counselor, I selected psychology as my major. I have never regretted it – studying the Science of People. School psychology as a career was nurtured by one of my professors since I had never heard of "school psychology." After completing my graduate training, I joined a statewide school psychology organization. An experienced school psychologist took me under her wing and introduced me to the world of professional school psychology organizations. While I worked as a practitioner in public schools, I became the newsletter editor, then president of the group. I re-entered graduate school 6 years later for my doctorate and then became a trainer of future school psychologists in a university setting. I still find the occupation rewarding and interesting to this day. While you may go to work each day at the same site, the days are varied, fast paced, and at times stressful. The job is typically not routine. I have also maintained my professional leadership involvement in professional organizations including twice being elected as president of the National Association of School Psychologists. I also served as President of the International School Psychology Association. These positions allow me to make a difference for children *and* the profession in practice, policy, and training.

A career that makes a difference is what school psychology is, and I have the opportunity to apply daily what I know about the "Science of People."

Note. Dr. William Pfohl is a school psychologist and a professor of psychology at Western Kentucky University, where he previously served as coordinator of the school psychology program. Dr. Pfohl has twice served as president of the National Association of School Psychologists and is a former president of the International School Psychologists Association. In addition to teaching courses on assessment, psychopathology, and child behavior, Dr. Pfohl maintains a private practice specializing in child and family issues.

Professional Spotlight

Rebecca S. Martínez, PhD, NCSP

Education:
- Bachelor of Science (BS) in Psychology from the University of Florida, Gainesville (1993)
- Master of Science (MS) in Program Evaluation from the University of Texas at Austin (2001)
- Doctor of Philosophy (PhD) in Educational Psychology from the University of Texas at Austin (2002)

Position:
Assistant Professor and Director of the Academic Well-Check Program (http://www.awcpindiana.org), Department of Counseling and Educational Psychology, School Psychology Program

Description of Position:
My job duties are equally split among research, teaching, and service.

Most Significant Professional Accomplishment:
I received the Bloomington Chamber of Commerce *2008 Leading Light Award* at the 7th Annual Franklin Initiative's Monroe County Educators of the Year Award Ceremony for my work in developing the Academic Well-Check Program (AWCP).

Favorite Publication:
Martínez, R. S. (2006). Social support in inclusive middle schools: Perceptions of youth with learning disabilities. *Psychology in the Schools, 43*, 197–209.

Areas of Research:
I investigate prevention and early intervention of reading and math difficulties, Response-to-Intervention (RTI), and ways to create school-wide supports for English language learners.

Professional Memberships:
- National Association of School Psychologists (NASP)
- Indiana Association of School Psychologists (IASP)
- Council of Directors of School Psychology Programs (CDSPP)

Most Rewarding Aspect of Your Career:
The most rewarding aspect of my career is having a widespread positive influence on children's school experiences because I have the opportunity to teach and train future school psychologists who will directly impact thousands of children, teachers, and parents.

Words of Advice to the Student Who Is Interested in Your Subfield:
First, learn all about school psychology by visiting the National Association of School Psychologists' website (http://www.nasponline.org). Next, find a local school psychologist and contact him or her about your interest in the field. Ask if you can shadow him or her for a day to see if school psychology is for you. Then, do well in your undergraduate courses so you will be competitive when you apply to school psychology graduate programs. Finally, if you decide to go into school psychology, know that you are embarking on a wonderfully challenging yet equally rewarding career path!

Suggested Exercises

1. Investigate graduate programs in either educational or school psychology. Once you find a program that fits your interests, identify a faculty member whose work appeals to you. Read a recent publication by this faculty member and generate questions about this work. Consider contacting this individual with your questions after having a trusted faculty member in your undergraduate program provide guidance and feedback on how best to initiate this conversation.

2. Contact a school psychologist within a school or school district that you previously attended as a student. Inquire about the possibility of interviewing him or her, either in person, by phone, or by email, to gain a better understanding of the nature of their work and their career

choice. Interviewing a school psychologist in a setting that is familiar to you will allow your questions and their responses to be more meaningful as you seek to learn about the career.

3. Think of an aspect of your learning or functioning in a school setting that has been a source of difficulty (e.g., reading comprehension, social relationships, stress management, study habits). Conduct a literature search to find articles in education and school psychology journals that address this topic. As you read these articles, think both about how the authors are working with this subject as part of their careers and how their findings might be of benefit to you in your educational pursuits.

Suggested Readings by Topic Area

School Psychology

Merrell, K. W., Ervin, R. A., & Gimpel, G. (2006). *School psychology for the 21st century: Foundations and practices.* New York: Guilford Press.

Reynolds, C. R., & Gutkin, T. B. (Eds.) (1999). *The handbook of school psychology* (3rd ed.). Hoboken, NJ: Wiley.

Educational Psychology

O'Donnell, A. M., Reeve, J., & Smith, J. K. (2008). *Educational psychology: Reflection for action* (2nd ed.). Hoboken, NJ: Wiley.

Slavin, R. E. (2008). *Educational psychology: Theory and practice* (9th ed.). Boston: Allyn and Bacon.

References

American Psychological Association. (2005). *2005 doctorate employment survey.* Washington, DC: Author.

American Psychological Association. (2008). *2008 graduate study in psychology.* Washington, DC: Author.

Cobb, H. C., Reeve, R. E., Shealy, C. N., Norcross, J. C., Schare, M. L., Rodolfa, E. R., et al. (2004). Overlap among clinical, counseling, and school psychology: Implications for the profession and combined-integrated training. *Journal of Clinical Psychology, 60,* 939–955.

Curtis, M. J., Grier, J. E. C., Abshier, D. W., Sutton, N. T., & Hunley, S. A. (2002). School psychology: Turning the corner into the twenty-first century. *Communiqué, 30*(8), 1–5.

Curtis, M. J., Grier, J. E. C., & Hunley, S. A. (2004). The changing face of school psychology: Trends in data and projections for the future. *School Psychology Review, 33,* 49–66.

Curtis, M. J., Hunley, S. A., & Grier, J. E. C. (2004). The status of school psychology: Implications of a major personnel shortage. *Psychology in the Schools, 41,* 431–442.

Fagan, T. K., & Wise, P. S. (2000). *School psychology: Past, present, and future.* Bethesda, MD: National Association of School Psychologists.

Graves, S. L., Jr., & Wright, L. B. (2007). Comparison of individual factors in school psychology graduate students: Why do students pursue a degree in school psychology? *Psychology in the Schools, 44,* 865–872.

Jackson, K. A. (1997). School psychology. *Eye on Psi Chi, 1*, 26–27, 30.

Reschly, D. J. (2000). The present and future status of school psychology in the United States. *School Psychology Review, 29*, 507–522.

U.S. Department of Labor. (2007). *May 2007 national occupational employment and wage estimates.* Retrieved from http://www.bls.gov/oes/current/oes_nat.htm

Resources

Educational Psychology – Division 15 of APA
   http://www.apa.org/divisions/div15
School Psychology – Division 16 of APA
   http://www.indiana.edu/~div16/index.html
National Association of School Psychologists
   http://www.nasponline.org

12

Careers in Exercise and Sport Psychology

Exercise and Sport Psychology Defined

Division 47 of the American Psychological Association (APA) is devoted to exercise and sport psychology (2008a; www.apa47.org). Division 47 (2008b) defines exercise and sport psychology as "the scientific study of the psychological factors that are associated with participation and performance in sport, exercise, and other types of physical activity" (http://www.apa47.org/studInfo.php). According to Division 47 (2008b), two broad themes run through the subfield of exercise and sport psychology. The first includes the use of psychological principles to help athletes "achieve optimal mental health and . . . improve performance (performance enhancement)" (http://www.apa47. org/studInfo.php). The second theme focuses on "understanding how participation in sport, exercise, and physical activity affects an individual's psychological development, health, and well-being throughout the life span" (http://www.apa47.org/studInfo.php). It is important to note here that the field of exercise and sport psychology is not exclusively applied to athletes. Rather, the field makes significant contributions to understanding and helping all individuals who engage in any form of physical activity.

Another major organization contributing to and helping define the field is the Association for Applied Sport Psychology (AASP; http://appliedsportpsych.org). In describing exercise and sport psychology, AASP (2008a) divides the subfield into three interrelated areas: Social Psychology, Performance Enhancement/Intervention, and Health and Exercise Psychology.

- The *social psychology area* "focuses on individual and group processes in sport and exercise settings. This area applies social psychological principles in examining factors related to the sport participant, coach, team, and spectator" (http://appliedsportpsych.org/about).
- The *performance enhancement/intervention area* "focuses on research, theory, and practice intended to improve performance in exercise and sport. This area is also

concerned with the effects of sport psychology interventions on the well-being of participants in exercise and sport" (http://appliedsportpsych.org/about).

- Whether it be in the professional, amateur, or leisure arena, the *health and exercise psychology area* "focuses on the application of psychological principles to the promotion and maintenance of health-enhancing behaviors over the lifespan, including play, leisure physical activity and structured exercise, and the psychological and emotional consequences of those behaviors. Researchers in this area also investigate the role of exercise in disease remediation, injury rehabilitation, and stress reduction" (http://appliedsportpsych.org/about).

The Work

Core Activities

As you can probably guess from the descriptions from Division 47 and the AASP, professionals in the exercise and sport psychology subfield contribute to psychology in a number of ways. These contributions can be categorized into the following three broad areas: research, practice, and teaching/training.

Research.   Developing and testing new ideas is the foundation upon which exercise and sport psychology rests. It is no overstatement to say that this subfield is founded on and grows as the result of rigorous empirical research. Given that these new developments withstand the rigor of peer review, dissemination follows so that others in the field may benefit. The primary method of disseminating information on new developments in the subfield is through publication in scholarly peer-reviewed journals. The growth in the subfield as well as its interconnections with other disciplines outside of psychology can be readily seen via some of the major publications in the field. Box 12.1 provides a list of some of the major publications in the area. Note that the titles do not always use the term *psychology*. For example, some of the journals use terms like *physical activity*, *biomechanics*, *movement science*, and *health science*.

As can be seen in Box 12.1, the range of publication outlets is broad. However, research topic areas covered by the various journals may not be as readily apparent. As an illustration and to give you an idea of the research areas studied by exercise and sport psychology professionals, here are some topics recently covered by articles published in the journals listed in Box 12.1:

- Adapting exercise and physical activity for those persons with disabilities
- Alcohol and drug use among student athletes
- Coping with competitive pressure and sport performance anxiety
- Disordered eating in dance professionals
- Gambling by student and professional athletes
- Gay, lesbian, bisexual, and transgender issues in sport
- Working with athletes who dope
- Coaching and motivational behavior
- Psychological issues associated with officiating/refereeing
- Maintaining an exercise program.

Box 12.1 Sampling of Journals That Publish Exercise and Sport Psychology Research

Adapted Physical Activity Quarterly
Health Psychology
Human Movement Science
International Journal of Sport and Exercise Psychology
Journal of Aging and Physical Activity
Journal of Applied Biomechanics
Journal of Applied Sport Psychology
Journal of Clinical Sport Psychology
Journal of Experimental Psychology: Human Perception and Performance
Journal of Social, Behavioral, and Health Sciences
Journal of Sport and Exercise Psychology
Motor Control
Research Quarterly for Exercise and Sport
The Sport Journal
The Sport Psychologist

For exercise and sport psychologists focused on research as their primary pursuit and those housed in an academic environment, activities will be similar to those discussed in the Careers in Academe chapter (i.e., teaching, research, and professional service activities). Interestingly, many exercise and sport psychologists often consult with their home universities' athletic and exercise programs, even when their positions are not housed in the athletic departments. In other words, the university's sport teams and exercise programs make good use of these professionals' expertise regardless of where they may happen to be on campus. Of course, those that consult with their schools' programs possess the education, training, and licensure necessary to provide those services (even when the services are provided for no charge). Training and preparation requirements are covered later in the chapter.

Practice.   The second domain in which exercise and sport psychology professionals contribute is the practice arena (i.e., provision of psychological services to individuals, groups, and organizations). As part of the APA's original recognition of sport psychology as a proficiency area in 2003, populations and groups that would be served by sport psychologists were identified (APA, 2008). According to the proficiency designation, those served by the profession include:

- "Youth/junior sport participants and organizations
- High school athletes and athletic departments
- Intercollegiate athletes and athletic departments
- Professional athletes, teams, and leagues
- Masters/seniors sport participants and organizations
- Injured athletes

- Elite athletes and sports organizations (e.g., Olympic athletes and national governing bodies)
- Recreational athletes
- Athletes with permanent disabilities
- People who are involved with, but not directly participating in, sports (families, coaches, administrators, officials)" (APA; http://www.apa.org/crsppp/archsportpsych.html).

As can be seen from this long list of beneficiaries, the populations served are quite extensive and are not limited to professional athletes.

The types of services provided by exercise and sport psychology practitioners, along with an example of each service, include:

- Assessment – e.g., evaluating athletes for healthy coping strategies; assessing a potential player's emotional stability relative to the level of performance required (moving from the amateur to the professional level).
- Treatment – e.g., treating children involved in dance/ballet for eating disorders; treating performance anxiety.
- Consultation with Teams and Coaches – e.g., consulting with a coach on effective strategies for dealing with a problem player or the loss of a player due to a team trade.
- Research (even for practitioners) – e.g., evaluating the effectiveness of a stress reduction program for gymnasts.
- Program Development – e.g., developing an appropriate exercise program for individuals over the age of 65 who attend a senior community center; developing a program to address inappropriate parental involvement at children's sporting events.
- Policy Development, Analysis, and Implementation – e.g., assist high school athletic associations in developing policies on student-athlete gambling and doping.

Teaching and training. As is the case with all areas of psychology, one of the main areas in which exercise and sport psychologists contribute to the discipline is through teaching and training. As a result, a significant proportion of those who identify themselves as exercise and sport psychologists hold academic positions at colleges and universities. Additionally, exercise and sport psychologists often provide psychoeducation as part of their practices. This type of teaching/education is geared specifically toward impacting the psychological functioning of the audience (e.g., educating a group of people on ways to incorporate exercise into their daily lives).

Employment Settings and Salary Expectations

Employment settings for exercise and sport psychology professionals comprise academic positions at colleges/universities in psychology, exercise science, movement science, sport science, and kinesiology departments. Interestingly, McCullagh and Noble (2002) point out that a trend appears to be emerging in which more interest in exercise and sport psychology is being displayed in mainstream psychology. As a result, this trend may mean increasing opportunities for exercise and sport psychologists within psychology departments (as opposed to the dominance of opportunities in kinesiology/ physical education departments). However, providing services to the public (outside of academe) is still relegated to doctoral-level licensed psychologists and not the kinesiology-trained/research-oriented professionals who are almost exclusively situated in the research environment.

As you might have guessed, another employment setting is within the private clinical and/or consulting practice area. In this setting, licensed psychologists provide a myriad of applied services to a wide range of individuals. However, only a portion of their work is in the exercise and sport psychology domain. Practices fully devoted to exercise and sport psychology are extremely rare.

The private practice (where a portion of the work is related to exercise and sport psychology) and the academic setting are the most common employment settings. Other settings like working for the United States Olympic Committee and in sport rehabilitation facilities encompass very few positions. In fact, sport rehabilitation facilities will often refer clients/patients out for psychological services. Highlighting the rarity of positions in these particular settings is not meant to be discouraging but rather informative. Limited positions in these settings are another reason to make sure your training is broad. Both AASP and Division 47 have listings of current job openings in the field. AASP's listing may be found at http://appliedsportpsych.org/jobs, and Division 47's listing may be found at http://www.apa47.org/jobs.php.

In terms of salary, income varies by work setting, reputation, and experience. Salaries for academic positions will be consistent with those noted in the Careers in Academe chapter, and salaries for practitioners will be consistent with those noted in the Careers in Clinical Psychology and Counseling Psychology chapter.

Training and Preparation

Earning a Degree

For research and applied positions, a doctorate is typically the entry-level degree. Given what you have read so far, this fact probably is not a surprise given that, by its very nature, exercise and sport psychology is an interdisciplinary field requiring significant depth and breadth of knowledge. As a result of its interdisciplinary nature, training may take place in sport science departments, kinesiology departments, health science departments, and psychology departments to name a few. Regardless of where your training takes place, Van Raalte and Williams (1994) recommend that you seek additional training and coursework in the areas not represented in your home department. Furthermore, given the increasing interest in the field, competition may squeeze out master's-level practitioners in favor of doctoral-trained individuals (McCullagh & Noble, 2002). This becomes truer as states/jurisdictions move toward requiring licensure at the doctoral level in order to practice in the area.

Another issue that you will want to keep in mind when pursuing training in this area is the actual path of your training. Two distinct academic training paths prepare students for work in the broad subfield of exercise and sport psychology (McCullagh & Noble,

2002). These two paths are psychology and kinesiology (i.e., the study of movement, broadly defined). Choosing the kinesiology path will open additional opportunities in the research area (e.g., physiological and rehabilitation issues) but will close the doors associated with being a licensed psychologist (e.g., independent practice outside of an academic setting). Choosing the psychology path will open the doors associated with being able to practice more broadly because of the necessary licensure at the doctoral level. The broad training will allow the psychologist who has training in the mental health areas (as compared to the kinesiologist) to work with individuals including athletes who have complicating mental health problems (e.g., anxiety, depression, eating disorders). The additional skills that come from being trained via the psychology path will benefit you too in terms of employment opportunities since you will not be limited to work with athletes only or to work in an academic/research setting. Regardless of the path chosen, each has benefits and limitations. As a result, an understanding of *how* you want to work in the area will assist you greatly in the decision of which path to pursue.

In addition to the insight you gained via the self-assessment in the Assessing and Developing Career Goals chapter, understanding the training and qualifications that the typical exercise and sport psychologist brings to the table will also help in your selection of which path best fits you and your goals. AASP (2008b) specifies training needed to be eligible for their certification. Certification through AASP is the standard in the field. In addition to a doctoral degree in an exercise and sport psychology area, coursework and supervised practice must also be completed. The required coursework for AASP certification includes:

- "3 sport and exercise psychology courses (2 at the graduate level)
- One course from each of the following categories:
  - Professional Ethics and Standards
  - Biomechanical and/or Physiological Bases of Sport
  - Historical, Philosophical, Social, or Motor Behavior Bases
  - Psychopathology and its Assessment
  - Counseling Skills (a graduate course)
  - Research Design, Statistics, or Psychological Assessment
  - Biological Bases of Behavior
  - Cognitive-Affective Bases of Behavior
  - Individual Behavior
- Demonstrated competence within skills/techniques/analysis in sport or exercise and related experiences (e.g., coaching, clinics, participation in sport)
- 400 hours of supervised experience in Sport & Exercise Psychology" (http://www.appliedsportpsych.org/consultants/become-certified)

To a large extent and not surprisingly, the required graduate-level coursework parallels the coursework required of clinical psychology, school psychology, and counseling psychology doctoral programs that are APA-accredited. See the chapters devoted to these subfields for more information and associated accreditation issues.

Importantly, completion of certain coursework is not the only requirement. Supervised experience is also mandatory. The supervised experience required for certification by AASP (2008b) includes:

- "100 hours . . . in direct contact hours with the clients
- 40 hours of supervision by an AASP approved supervisor, and all 400 hours must be verified by this supervisor" (http://www.appliedsportpsych.org/consultants/become-certified).

Although master's-level applicants are allowed to pursue certification by AASP, the requirements are more extensive for obvious reasons. Additionally, individuals with doctorates in kinesiology likely will take significantly longer to get certified because of the lack of background in psychology in their degree programs. In other words, those individuals would likely have to spend significant additional time in order simply to meet the extensive (yet minimal by psychology's standards) coursework requirements.

Licensure Issues

In terms of state licensure, it is not typically required for researchers, educators, and policy specialists. However, those that practice (i.e., provide treatment, assessment, and diagnosis) do require licensure by the respective state board of psychology. Please see the Careers in Clinical Psychology and Counseling Psychology chapter for discussion of the licensure process. In short, you will want to seek an APA-accredited doctoral program in clinical, school, or counseling psychology that emphasizes, provides a track in, or conducts significant research in exercise and sport psychology. Additionally and as noted earlier, this subfield also recognizes and strongly encourages certification through the AASP.

AASP certified consultants agree to abide by the AASP Code of Ethics. Authored by James Whelan (2008), the code can be found at http://www.appliedsportpsych.org/about/ethics/code. As noted in the code, it draws heavily from the APA's *Code of Ethics* (2002; http://www.apa.org/ethics/), yet another overlap in their respective standards. Furthermore, although trained at the doctoral level, those who choose the kinesiology path mentioned earlier will be relegated mainly to academic careers given limitations associated with not being licensed as a psychologist.

Training Programs

Sachs, Burke, and Loughren (2006) provide information on both the subfield of applied sport psychology as well as information on over 100 programs that have some sport psychology component. Interestingly, the majority of the programs are in sport science or kinesiology with a specialization in sport psychology and not specifically in exercise and sport psychology. Fewer programs exist in psychology with this emphasis. As a result and given that the programs that exist are in counseling psychology and clinical psychology programs, admission is highly competitive. When reviewing any of the exercise and sport psychology programs, you are encouraged to be mindful of quality since this varies and changes over time. As a reminder, you will want to review the information relating to selecting graduate programs which can be found in the chapter devoted to applying to graduate school.

Preparing for Your Graduate Training

The first step to becoming an exercise and sport psychologist is to ensure a solid undergraduate education. This foundation will serve you well as you pursue graduate and postgraduate education in the field. In addition to your regular coursework in psychology (i.e., research methods, experimental psychology, physiological psychology, etc.), McCullagh and Noble (2002) recommend that basic courses in exercise physiology, biomechanics, motor learning and control, sport sociology, and exercise and sport psychology be included in your coursework. They note that prerequisite coursework may need to be completed in areas like biology, chemistry, mathematics, or other physical sciences prior to enrolling in these courses.

Galli (2008) offers three pieces of advice to undergraduate students who are interested in this field. First, he recommends double majoring in psychology and exercise science as well as including coursework in the related discipline areas (which is consistent with McCullagh and Noble's, 2002, advice). Second, he recommends getting experience by assisting faculty who are involved in the field with their research. This recommendation is consistent with advice offered by us in the chapter devoted to preparing for graduate school. To reiterate, research experience should be the cornerstone of your undergraduate experience. As part of getting experience, Galli also suggests volunteering as a coach or assistant coach and working in a sport environment. Third, Galli suggests that you make connections with exercise and sport psychology professionals. These connections can be made through faculty at your home institution, graduate schools you are considering, and conferences in the field.

Working in Areas Related to Exercise and Sport Psychology With a Bachelor's Degree

As you can see from the information provided throughout this chapter, working as an exercise and sport psychologist clearly involves work at the doctoral and postdoctoral level (i.e., after receiving your doctoral degree). However, if you have an interest in exercise and sport psychology there are opportunities to work in environments that value individual and team sports as well as exercise. Some of these include:

- Coaching youth sports in a school setting (e.g., a local middle school) or in a community setting (e.g., the Boys and Girls Clubs)
- Physical education teacher with a double major in psychology (which would require a teaching certificate)
- Research assistant in a sport and exercise psychology lab
- Recreational worker (e.g., within the National Park Service and state park associations)
- Recreational/activity therapist in a hospital setting where you would plan and implement recreational activities with patients
- Coaching assistant in a sport or exercise program
- Health fitness instructor, exercise specialist, and personal trainer (to learn more about these professions and certification visit the American College of Sports Medicine at http://www.acsm.org).

Bachelor's-level salaries vary widely. For example, the median salary for a fitness instructor in 2007 was $27,680 (Occupational Information Network [O*NET], 2008; http://online.onetcenter.org/link/summary/39-9031.00), and the median salary for school teachers (which would include physical education teachers) in 2007 was $49,420 (O*NET, 2008; http://online.onetcenter.org/link/summary/25-2031.00). As a result, we encourage you to visit the Occupational Information Network at http://online. onetcenter.org/ to learn more about your particular interest area.

A Counseling Sport Psychologist's Journey

Reflections and Observations

Christopher M. Carr, PhD
St. Vincent Sports
Performance Center,
Indianapolis, IN

When I began my doctoral studies, I knew that I wanted to be a "sport" psychologist. More specifically, I wanted to be a counseling psychologist that had a developed competency in the practice of applied sport psychology. I did not believe that my background as a 4-year collegiate football player or graduate assistant college football coach was sufficient in order to be competent. In fact, I found that my own athletic and coaching experience was unique to me and not necessarily transferable to any other athlete (even in football). What I have found is that my preparation in my counseling psychology doctoral program (which included a minor in sport/exercise psychology), in addition to my one-year clinical research assistantship in the Sport Psychology

Department of the United States Olympic Training Center in Colorado Springs (USOC), has led to my career growth, success, and professional satisfaction. In essence, I am doing exactly what I want to do for the rest of my career.

My first postdoctoral position was at Washington State University (WSU), where I was the full-time athletic department counseling sport psychologist. My role was to provide comprehensive psychological services for the athletes, coaches, and support staff at this PAC-10 athletics department. This position was a great "first" sport psychology position; the athletic department was competitive but lacked some of the external distractions of larger and more well-known programs. I learned here that the athletic director is the *most* important support system that a sport psychologist can have in this type of position. Without this support, coaches are more tentative to utilize the service, and there is often difficulty in program development opportunities (e.g., leadership seminars).

It was during my first year at WSU that I was contacted by USA Skiing and became the consulting sport psychologist for the US Men's Alpine Ski Team. This 10-year relationship was instrumental in my experiences and opportunities to grow in my development as a counseling sport psychologist. Attending on-hill camps, traveling to international competitions, coordinating sport psychology team/coaching programs, and consulting with individual athletes were all integral experiences that I believed I had prepared for well. I cannot imagine a psychologist with no sport psychology training (either academic or supervised experience) being able to optimize such a consultation with an elite Olympic-level team.

I spent one year at Arizona State University in a combined athletic department/university counseling center staff sport psychologist position before being hired at the Ohio State University (OSU) to become the full-time athletic department sport psychologist. My position was housed in the OSU Sports Medicine Department, and since that time (1995), I have built my practice either within or in consultation with sports medicine departments. During my five years at Ohio State, I was integrally involved with one of the largest NCAA Division I athletic departments, and within my first month of being there I realized that I would need help. Again, with the support of the OSU athletics director and the OSU administration, I was able to propose and create a postdoctoral fellowship in counseling and sport psychology. This position allowed me the opportunity (and privilege) of mentoring four postdoctoral fellows. These fellows were involved within the structure of the OSU Athletic Department and had their own individual case loads, team consultations, and involvement with sport psychology programs (e.g., coaching seminars). During my time at OSU, I found that my training as a counseling psychologist was most influential in creating my niche within the athletic department. Being able to navigate my roles as therapist, consultant, educator, group facilitator, and lecturer was necessary to impact the psychological health of the over 800 student-athletes. I have found that the ability to serve and function optimally in multiple roles can greatly add to successful career growth.

My family and I returned to central Indiana in 2000 as I moved my practice into an orthopedic sports medicine clinic. In 2006 I was hired by St. Vincent Healthcare to develop and coordinate a sport and performance psychology program. This program, housed within the St. Vincent Sports Performance Center, provides comprehensive sport and performance psychology services. I coordinate psychological services for collegiate athletic departments and serve as the Consulting Sport Psychologist for the Indiana University Athletics Department.

I believe that I will always be involved with collegiate athletics. The athletes' developmental challenges are unique and enjoyable to deal with from a psychological standpoint; I also very much enjoy the professionalism that most coaches and support staff demonstrate in their desire to be the best and provide the best care. It is a dynamic and energetic environment. However, the stigma toward psychology still exists. Regardless, I am optimistic and have seen (especially over the past 5 years) an increase in new hirings of sport psychologists within major NCAA Division I athletic departments. In all of these hires, the sport psychologist was a licensed psychologist with a demonstrated competency in the field of sport psychology. I think this model best provides for the comprehensive care of the athlete client. In fact, I spent one month in Beijing, China in 2008 as the USA Olympic Diving Team Sport Psychologist (having consulted with them since 2004). It was clear that most of my consultations with athletes and coaches dealt with more "personal" dynamics that could have directly or indirectly impacted their performance.

As I view the next 10–15 years of my career (with 18 years of experience in sport psychology behind me), I am optimistic about the growth of our field. Although I am biased toward the hiring of licensed psychologists for sport psychologist positions within collegiate and professional sports, I do see a future where the academic (i.e., kinesiology and sport science) and applied (e.g., counseling psychology) fields collaborate in a scientist-practitioner model of enhancing the care we provide for athletes. This combination of research, education, and applied interventions/counseling must evolve through collaboration and dialogue. I am hopeful that this future comes to fruition.

Note. Dr. Christopher Carr earned his PhD in Counseling Psychology with a minor in Sport and Exercise Psychology from Ball State University. In addition to his work with collegiate, professional, and Olympic athletes and sports organizations, he was president of APA's Division 47 – Exercise and Sport Psychology. His publications include numerous book chapters and academic articles predominantly in the area of sports medicine and physical medicine in the area of sport and performance psychology.

Professional Spotlight

Kate F. Hays, PhD

Education:
- Bachelor of Arts in Psychology from University of New Hampshire
- Master of Arts in Psychology from Boston University
- PhD in Clinical Psychology from Boston University

Position:
Owner/Director of "The Performing Edge" in Toronto, Canada

Description of Position:
I provide individual and small group consultation, coaching, therapy, and workshops to athletes, performing artists, and business people to optimize mental skills for performance.

Most Significant Professional Accomplishment:
I was a visiting scholar at Geelong Grammar School (Australia) by invitation of Martin E. P. Seligman, extending positive psychology to mental skills in optimal performance (in sport, performance, academics) for students, faculty, and community members.

Favorite Publication:
Hays, K. F. (Ed.). (2009). *Performance psychology in action: A casebook for working with athletes,* *performing artists, business leaders, and professionals in high-risk occupations.* Washington, DC: American Psychological Association.

Areas of Research:
My current areas of research are the applications of sport psychology to performing arts, the intersection of performance psychology and positive psychology, and the mental benefits of physical activity.

Areas of Practice:
My current areas of practice are sport and performance psychology and general outpatient clinical psychology.

Professional Memberships:
- American Psychological Association
  - Fellow of Divisions 29, 35, 42, and 47
  - President, Division 47 (Exercise & Sport Psychology): 1999–2004
- Association for Applied Sport Psychology
- Ontario Psychological Association
- Canadian Psychological Association
- International Positive Psychology Association

Most Rewarding Aspects of Your Career:
The most rewarding aspects of my career are being able to make connections between disparate elements of the profession in order to help the profession grow, offering quality services to people otherwise unserved or underserved, and finding a profession that has continued to interest me after 37 years of practice.

Words of Advice to the Student Who Is Interested in Your Subfield:
I encourage those with interest in the field to develop knowledge of the whole person (soma as well as psyche), keep learning, and obtain formal education to the highest degree possible in order to maximize options.

Web Address: www.theperformingedge.com

Suggested Exercises

1. Using your college's course catalog, identify courses that are related to exercise and sport psychology. Answer the following questions for each course.
   a. What department offers the course?
   b. Is it an undergraduate or graduate level course?
   c. Is it part of a concentration, minor, or major program?
   d. Which professor usually teaches it?
2. Using the consultant finder on the AASP website, find a certified consultant in your general geographic area. Answer the following questions based on his or her profile:
   a. Where is the person employed?
   b. What is the person's job title?
   c. What is the person's contact information?
   d. In what sports does the person consult?
   e. What age client does the person see?
   f. What subspecialties and specializations does the person list?
   g. Is the person a licensed psychologist?
3. Using an article from one of the exercise and sport psychology publications noted in the chapter, answer the following questions.
   a. What is the title of the article?
   b. Who are the authors?
   c. What are their affiliations?/Where do they work?
   d. In 3 or 4 sentences describe the article's findings.

Suggested Readings

Burton, D., & Raedeke, T. D. (2008). *Sport psychology for coaches*. Champaign, IL: Human Kinetics.

Murphy, S. M. (Ed.). (2004). *The sport psych handbook*. Champaign, IL: Human Kinetics.

Tenenbaum, G., & Eklund, R. C. (Eds.). (2007). *Handbook of sport psychology* (3rd ed.). New York: Wiley.

Van Raalte, J. L., & Brewer, B. W. (Eds.). (2002). *Exploring sport and exercise psychology* (2nd ed.).

Washington, DC: American Psychological Association.

Weinberg, R. S., & Gould, D. (2007). *Foundations of sport and exercise psychology* (4th ed.). Champaign, IL: Human Kinetics.

Williams, J. M. (Ed.). (2005). *Applied sport psychology: Personal growth to peak performance* (5th ed.). McGraw-Hill: Boston.

References

American Psychological Association. (2002). *Ethical principles of psychologists and code of conduct*. Retrieved from http://www.apa.org/ethics/code2002.html

American Psychological Association. (2008). *Summary: Sport psychology: A proficiency in professional psychology*. Retrieved from http://www.apa.org/crsppp/archsportpsych.html

American Psychological Association – Division 47 – Exercise and Sport Psychology. (2008a). Retrieved from http://www.apa47.org/

American Psychological Association – Division 47 – Exercise and Sport Psychology. (2008b). *Student membership information and benefits*. Retrieved from http://www.apa47.org/studInfo.php

Association for Applied Sport Psychology. (2008a). *About AASP*. Retrieved from http://appliedsportpsych.org/about

Association for Applied Sport Psychology. (2008b). *Become a certified consultant*. Retrieved from http://appliedsportpsych.org/consultants/become-certified

Galli, N. (2008). *Tips for undergraduate students interested in a career in sport and exercise psychology*. Retrieved from http://appliedsportpsych.org/resource-center/professionals/articles/undergrad-tips

McCullagh, P., & Noble, J. M. (2002). Education for becoming a sport psychologist. In J. L. Van Raalte & B. W. Brewer (Eds.), *Exploring sport and exercise psychology* (2nd ed., pp. 439–457). Washington, DC: American Psychological Association.

Occupational Information Network. (2008). *Summary report for: 25-2031.00 – Secondary school teachers, except special and vocational education.* Retrieved from http://online.onetcenter.org/link/summary/25-2031.00

Occupational Information Network. (2008). *Summary report for: 39-9031.00 – Fitness trainers and aerobics instructors.* Retrieved from http://online.onetcenter.org/link/summary/39-9031.00

Sachs, M. L., Burke, K. L., Loughren, E. A. (Eds.). (2006). *Directory of graduate programs in applied sport psychology* (8th ed.). Morgantown, WV: Fitness Information Technology.

Van Raalte, J. L., & Williams, J. M. (1994, June). *Graduate training and career possibilities in exercise and sport psychology.* Retrieved from http://www.apa47.org/pracGrad.php

Whelan, J. (2008). *Ethics code: AASP ethical principles and standards.* Retrieved from http://www.appliedsportpsych.org/about/ethics/code

Resources

Professional Organizations Fully or Partially Devoted to Exercise and Sport Psychology (and Related Areas)

- American Alliance for Health, Physical Education, Recreation, and Dance (AAHPERD): http://www.aahperd.org/
- American College of Sports Medicine: http://www.acsm.org/
- American Psychological Association's Division 47 – Exercise and Sport Psychology: http://www.apa47.org/
- Association for Applied Sport Psychology: http://www.appliedsportpsych.org/
- British Association of Sport and Exercise Sciences: http://www.bases.org.uk/home.asp
- Canadian Society for Psychomotor Learning and Sport Psychology: http://www.scapps.org/
- International Society for Sport Psychology: http://issponline.org/
- North American Society for the Psychology of Sport and Physical Activity: http://www.naspspa.org/

Other Web Resources

- Human Kinetics: http://www.humankinetics.com/
- SelfhelpMagazine.com (Brief and synopses of articles on sport performance and sport psychology): http://www.selfhelpmagazine.com/articles/sports-performance.php

13

Careers in Health Psychology

Health Psychology Defined

Historically, the field of psychology debated about the impact of nature (i.e., genetics) and nurture (i.e., environmental factors) on development and a host of other areas. The conversations eventually led to the understanding that both nature and nurture impact all aspects of who we are. A similar debate also took place within the field of health psychology. The debate centered on the influence of biological, psychological, and socio-cultural factors on health. Although researchers and practitioners may focus on one of these factors more than the other two factors, the impact of all three shapes the subfield of health psychology. In fact, the field of health psychology is guided by and rooted in a *biopsychosocial* framework. This framework ensures that all of the contributive factors to our health are considered. This is where health psychology shines as a subfield.

Division 38 of the American Psychological Association (APA) is devoted to the subfield of health psychology. The mission of Division 38 (n.d.) is:

- "to advance contributions of psychology as a discipline to the understanding of health and illness through basic and clinical research" and
- to encourage "the integration of biomedical information . . . with current psychological knowledge [in order] to promote education and services in the psychology of health and illness. . . ." (http://www.health-psych.org/mission.php#)

Division 38 (http://www.health-psych.org/mission.php#) notes that their mission is reinforced by reports from the U.S. Surgeon General's Office which state that mortality in the United States is significantly influenced by behavioral factors. They go on to note that "these reports recommend that behavioral risk factors (e.g., drug and alcohol use, high risk sexual behavior, smoking, diet, a sedentary lifestyle, stress) be the main focus of efforts in the area of health promotion and disease prevention" (http://www.health-psych.org/mission.php#).

In summary, health psychology is an interdisciplinary field devoted to promoting, improving, and maintaining healthy functioning as well as preventing and treating illness. The Committee on Education and Training of Division 38 (n.d.) emphasizes this point by highlighting that health psychologists "strive to understand how biological, behavioral, and social factors influence health and illness" (http://www.health-psych.org/articles/what_is.php).

The Work

Core Activities

According to Gurung (2010), the health psychology subfield can be divided into three broad areas of study. These three areas are:

- stress and coping;
- health behaviors;
- issues in health care.

Within each of these broad areas health psychologists contribute via their research, practice, and teaching/training.

Research. As is the case with all subfields of psychology, research is the foundation upon which all of health psychology is built. As such, it is imperative that new insights, findings, and advancements in the field be available to others in the field. Prior to their dissemination, rigorous peer-review must take place. Once the findings are reviewed, publication may then take place. Publication of health psychology research occurs in a myriad of publications in the fields of psychology, medicine, and health sciences, just to name a few. For a sampling of journals that publish health psychology-related research, see Box 13.1.

Box 13.1 Sampling of Journals That Publish Health Psychology Research

Annals of Behavioral Medicine
Health Psychology
International Journal of Behavioral Medicine
Journal of Behavioral Medicine
Journal of Clinical Psychology in Medical Settings
Journal of Pediatric Psychology
Pain
Psychology and Health
Psychosomatic Medicine
The Health Psychologist (newsletter)

The type of research pursued and eventually published in these outlets is as varied as the subfield itself. Some of the topics recently covered in these publications include:

- The impact of culture on health
- Eating, dieting, and exercise/physical activity
- Smoking, alcohol use, and drug use
- (Lack of) Access to healthcare and healthcare policy
- Coping with chronic pain
- Chronic illness (e.g., diabetes, asthma)
- Cardiovascular issues (e.g., hypertension and stroke)
- The impact of psychological and biological factors on the immune system (psychoneuroimmunology)
- Sexually transmitted infections (e.g., herpes, HIV, HPV).

For health psychologists primarily focused on research, including those housed in an academic environment, activities will be similar to those discussed in the Careers in Academe chapter. Notably, the activities of these academically- and research-oriented health psychologists often entail strong ties to local clinics and hospitals that can provide participants for their research studies. As a result, interdisciplinary collaboration with health care providers (as well as other researchers) is not strictly the purview of clinical health psychologists. It is also a necessary activity for the academic/experimental health psychologist. Establishing and maintaining these strong relationships with the medical community is very important to the viability of research programs.

Practice: Applying the research findings.   Although the roots of the general research area of health psychology go back to the mid 1900s, the practice area of health psychology (i.e., clinical health psychology) was not recognized as a specialty by APA until 1997 (2008b). As part of the recognition, the practice area was defined, populations served were acknowledged, problems typically addressed were delineated, and common practice procedures were noted.

According to the specialty designation by APA (2008a), the *practice* of clinical health psychology:

> . . . applies scientific knowledge of the interrelationships among behavioral, emotional, cognitive, social, and biological components in health and disease to the promotion and maintenance of health; the prevention, treatment, and rehabilitation of illness and disability; and the improvement of the health care system. The distinct focus of Clinical Health Psychology is on physical health problems. The specialty is dedicated to the development of knowledge regarding the interface between behavior and health, and to the delivery of high quality services based on that knowledge to individuals, families, and health care systems. (http://www.apa.org/crsppp/health.html)

Clinical health psychologists serve populations across the lifespan, from prenatal issues of expectant mothers to geriatric issues. In addition to working with patients' families and other health care providers, clinical health psychologists work with a variety of individuals including but not limited to persons diagnosed with diabetes mellitus, pain, HIV/AIDS, alcohol/drug problems, cardiovascular diseases, cancers, stroke, eating disorders, weight problems/obesity, premenstrual syndrome, infertility and reproductive issues, sickle cell disease, dental disease, hypertension, and stress related problems. Because of their keen awareness of the impact of the environment on health problems, health psychologists work not only with the patients and their immediate families but also with communities. In working with all of these various stakeholders, clinical health psychologists can address multifaceted health problems both at the prevention stages and at the treatment stages (APA, 2008a).

As might be guessed from the types of patients noted in the previous section, the range of problems addressed by clinical health psychologists is very broad. APA's (2008a) description of the specialty lists 10 examples of the problems addressed:

"(1)   psychological conditions secondary to diseases/injury/disability (e.g., post myocardial infarction depression, family issues in chronic illness or death, body image concerns secondary to burns, amputation, surgery)

(2)   somatic presentations of psychological dysfunction (e.g., chest pain in panic attack, somatization disorders)

(3)   psychophysiological disorders (e.g., tension and migraine headache, irritable bowel syndrome)

(4)   physical symptoms/conditions responsive to behavioral interventions (e.g., vasospasms, urinary and fecal incontinence, anticipatory nausea)

(5)   somatic complications associated with behavioral factors (e.g., mismanagement of diabetes, noncompliance with medical regimens)

(6)   psychological presentation of organic disease (e.g., hypothyroidism presenting as depression, steroid induced psychosis)

(7)   psychological and behavioral aspects of stressful medical procedures (e.g., pain, lumbar puncture, wound debridement, cardiac catheterization)

(8)   behavioral risk actors for disease/injury/disability (e.g., smoking weight, substance abuse, risk-taking)

(9)   problems of health care providers and health care systems (e.g., physician-patient relationships, staff burn out, care delivery systems)

(10)   preferences for learning the development and maintenance of healthy lifestyles"
http://www.apa.org/crsppp/health.html

Like all psychologists who provide health care services to the public, health psychologists possess a broad range of skills. These skills include psychological assessment, intervention, and consultation skills. However, health psychologists build on these basic general clinical skills. For example, health psychologists specialize their consultation skills so that they can provide services to other health care providers and staff. In fact, the level of interdisciplinary collaboration is high within the field (APA, 2008a). Health-focused intervention strategies (e.g., biofeedback, hypnosis, relaxation training) and assessment instruments (e.g., tests assessing a person's behavioral health, readiness for transplant surgery, or experience of post-operative pain) are other examples of the specialization of their general clinical abilities. Importantly and because of their appreciation for environmental influences, health psychologists often utilize family therapy in their practices (APA, 2008a).

For applied/practicing health psychologists, major figures in the subfield of health psychology convened in 2007 to consider, formulate, and endorse "the foundational and functional competencies expected of a well-trained, entry level clinical health psychologist" (APA Division 38, 2007, p. 7). The resulting document (referred to as the Tempe Summit Report) outlined six capacities that all health psychologists that provide services to the public (i.e., individuals, families, groups, organizations) must possess. These six competencies are:

1. Assessment (e.g., evaluating a person's psychological readiness for gastric bypass surgery)
2. Intervention (e.g., helping an individual develop exercises that will decrease his experience of pain)
3. Consultation with other health care providers (e.g., physicians, rehabilitative specialists, dietitians)
4. Research (even for practitioners)
5. Supervision and training
6. Management/administration – including:
   • Program Development (e.g., healthy lifestyle programs, smoking cessation programs)
   • Policy Development, Analysis, and Implementation (e.g., policies about healthcare access and insurance coverage).

Teaching and training. As is the case with all areas of psychology, one of the main areas in which health psychologists contribute to the discipline is through teaching and training. As a result, a significant proportion of those who identify themselves as health psychologists hold academic positions at colleges and universities. Additionally, health psychologists often provide psychoeducational activities as part of their practices. These psychoeducational activities are geared specifically toward impacting the healthy functioning of the audience (e.g., educating a group of people at the local community center on ways to adjust their diet and lifestyles to reduce the risks of heart problems and diabetes in later life).

Focusing on the Future

It is important to highlight that none of these contributions exist in a stagnant field. In fact, the subfield of health psychology is very active as can be seen in the research areas noted previously. In addition, the subfield of health psychology is future driven. Health psychology envisions a very bright future that is full of positive contributions to our everyday lives. In looking toward the future with hope, Straub (2007) notes the following five challenges for the subfield:

• Increasing the healthy lifespan of all people
• Reducing health discrepancies based on gender, race, and socioeconomic status

- Providing equal access to preventive health care services
- Applying evidence-based approaches to healthy living
- Supporting and spearheading health care policy reform.

Employment Settings and Salary Expectations

For those health psychologists who focus their careers on conducting research, colleges and universities will be the primary setting for their work. Affiliations within a university may include appointments in the psychology department, health science department, and medical school. Research-oriented health psychologists also find employment in research institutes within universities as well as within government agencies (e.g., the National Institutes of Health and the Centers for Disease Control).

For those health psychologists who focus on providing direct health care services, clinical settings predominate. These settings include private practices and hospital settings. For those in private practices, most will perform a myriad of activities both within and outside of the health psychology domain (i.e., practice both general clinical and health psychology). It is important to note that many individuals practicing in the clinical health psychology area do so in group practices. That is, they work alongside physicians, nurses, and other healthcare workers to provide the full spectrum of services patients need. This is akin to a one-stop shopping for your health care needs.

A recent search using PsycCareers – APA's Online Career Center (http://jobs.psyccareers.com/) produced 64 advertisements under the "health psychology" category. Both research-oriented and applied/clinical health psychologist positions were represented. Box 13.2 provides a sampling of those openings.

Salaries of health psychologists vary by work setting, reputation, and experience. Salaries for academic positions will be consistent with those noted in the Careers in Academe chapter. Academic positions within medical school settings will be

Box 13.2 Recent Openings in the Health Psychology Field

- Assistant or Associate Professor of Experimental Health Psychology
- Behavioral Medicine Psychologist
- Eating Disorders Clinic Manager
- Health Outcomes Researcher
- HIV/AIDS Community Care and Prevention Advisor
- Psychologist at a Medical Center
- Public Health and Environment Researcher
- Research Associate
- Rehabilitation Psychologist in a Medical School
- Pain Psychologist (Assistant Professor)

somewhat higher than traditional university settings. Salaries for practitioners will be consistent with those noted in the Careers in Clinical Psychology and Counseling Psychology chapter. In short, the median annual wage in 2007 for clinical, counseling, and school psychologists was $62,210 (Occupational Information Network [O*NET], 2008a).

Training and Preparation

Earning a Degree

Given the information presented about the breadth of this subfield, including the research and practice areas addressed in the preceding section, it should come as no surprise that a doctoral degree is typically the entry-level degree for both research and applied positions. This is due in no small part to the interdisciplinary nature of the field. Although specific to the applied area of clinical health psychology, APA's recognition of the specialty (2008a) highlights the advanced knowledge necessary and distinctive to the subfield. In particular it notes that the "biological, cognitive, affective, social, and psychological bases of health and disease are bodies of knowledge that, when integrated with knowledge of biological, cognitive-affective, social, and psychological bases of behavior, constitute the distinctive knowledge base" (http://www.apa.org/crsppp/health.html). It goes on to note that a specialty in health psychology denotes/signifies extensive knowledge in such diverse areas as biology, motivation and learning, and psychoneuroimmunology. The extensive knowledge base also includes such topics as physician-patient relationships, health policy and care delivery, and diversity issues in health care.

Licensure Issues

It is important to note that those who deliver health care services must be licensed by their respective state board of psychology. However, state licensure is not typically required for researchers, educators, and policy specialists. Please see the Careers in Clinical Psychology and Counseling Psychology chapter for a discussion of the licensure process. In short, you will want to seek an APA-accredited doctoral program in clinical or counseling psychology that emphasizes, provides a track in, or conducts significant research in health psychology if you want to practice (i.e., do applied work) in this area. Additionally, this subfield also recognizes and encourages post-licensure board certification through the American Board of Clinical Health Psychology which is a part of the American Board of Professional Psychology (http://www.abpp.org/).

Training Programs

Graduate Study in Psychology (GSP; APA, 2010) provides information on graduate programs offering an emphasis in health psychology. Currently, the GSP index lists 19 programs that self-identify as having this emphasis area. Another resource compiled by Norcross, Sayette, and Mayne (2008) list 62 programs that self-identify as having a concentration or track in health psychology/behavioral medicine. A searchable database for information on graduate training programs is provided on Division 38's website (www.health-psych.org). Looking to the more distant future, the Association of Psychology Postdoctoral and Internship Centers (APPIC; 2008) lists 213 predoctoral internships with major rotations in health psychology and 399 sites with minor rotations in the area. For postdoctoral training (often required for licensure), APPIC listed 60 sites with a health psychology emphasis.

In reporting these resources and information, it is important to note that much of the information provided in GSP and Division 38's website databases is based on self-reports by individual graduate programs. As such and when reviewing any health psychology programs, you are encouraged to be mindful of quality since this varies and changes over time. In fact, we encourage you to review the information on selecting graduate programs that can be found in the chapter on applying to graduate school. In brief and to reiterate an earlier point, you will want to ensure that the graduate program is at a *minimum* APA-accredited if in the applied area and that those in the non-service delivery area have strong track records for research.

Preparing for Your Graduate Training

The first step to becoming a health psychologist is to ensure a solid undergraduate foundation in psychology. This foundation will serve you well as you pursue graduate and postgraduate education in the field. As alluded to in APA's recognition of the specialty (2008a), coursework in the areas of biology, pharmacology, anatomy and physiology, and pathophysiology will be helpful. Note that many of these courses and areas of study may require prerequisite coursework (i.e., completion of lower level biology, chemistry, mathematics, or other physical sciences prior to enrollment). Keep this in mind as you plan your coursework! Additional coursework in statistics is also not a bad idea since most good graduate training programs in health psychology have a strong research foundation (including the applied clinical programs). Again, though, this coursework is above and beyond that required by your psychology major (e.g., experimental psychology, physiological psychology, psychopharmacology).

Your undergraduate preparation should also include research experience. This suggestion is a reiteration of an earlier recommendation by us. In fact, we encourage you to revisit The Preprofessional Degree: Preparing for Graduate School chapter as it would be redundant to provide that general information again here.

Working in Areas Related to Health Psychology With a Bachelor's Degree

As you can see from the information provided, a specialty in the subfield of health psychology clearly involves training at the doctoral and postdoctoral levels. However, if you have an interest in health psychology there are opportunities to work in environments that value many of the same principles as those found in the subfield of health psychology. Some of these include occupational therapy assistant, research assistant in health settings, and medical-surgical hospital support staff/health educator.

- Occupational therapy assistant/aide. These individuals assist occupational therapists in the delivery of rehabilitative services to patients who have health impairments (e.g., post-stroke). They can assist patients in learning independent living skills so that they can return to the community or to lower levels of care. (O*NET, 2008c).
- Research assistant in health settings. These individuals assist with the protocols associated with drug trials, assist with data collection and analysis, and other supervised research activities. (O*NET, 2008d).
- Medical-surgical hospital support staff/health educator. These individuals assist in educational programs for the patients and public including providing families with information on support systems available in the community (e.g., diabetes support groups). (O*NET, 2008b).

Bachelor's-level salaries vary based on the type of position. As a result, you are encouraged to take a look at the O*NET (http://online.onetcenter.org/) for current salary information. Additionally, because students who are interested in health psychology are often similar to students who are interested in neuropsychology, you are encouraged to review the Careers in Neuropsychology chapter.

Health Psychology and Culture

An Exciting Area of Study

Regan A. R. Gurung, PhD
University of Wisconsin –
Green Bay

What is one of the hottest areas of research in the subfield of health psychology? The answer is "studying cultural differences." Culture is more important now than it has ever been. The United States is more culturally diverse now than it has even been. World politics is rife with the clashing of cultural factions (e.g., Shias and Shiites in the Middle East; caste and tribal genocide in Africa). Through this all, the disparities between different cultural groups – especially the rich and the poor – map onto significant health disparities. How does the culture that we come from and surround ourselves with influence our health and behaviors? Answering this question with a concerted look at sources of influence outside a person (i.e., not just his or her biology or psychology) is a distinctive feature of the approach taken by many health psychologists today. Most behaviors that influence health – whether healthy ones such as physical activity and eating nutritionally balanced diets or unhealthy ones such as smoking or drinking excessively – depend heavily on the culture in which we grew up.

We often ignore the importance of culture, partly because we rarely acknowledge its many dimensions. For example, what do your parents, your best friends, and your spiritual/religious beliefs have in common? Answer: They each constitute the major socialization forces of culture. Take parents for example. Whether we do something because they told us to (e.g., "Eat your greens!") or exactly because they told us *not to* (e.g., "Don't smoke!"), parents have a strong influence on us. In the same way, if our friends exercise, we are more likely to exercise also. As another example, consider religions, which have different prescriptions for what individuals should or should not do. Muslims cannot eat pork or drink alcohol. Hindus cannot eat beef. Unfortunately, discussions of culture are often limited to just race or ethnicity, when a broader discussion is required to understand fully the precedents of health and health behaviors. Culture is not just race or ethnicity; it also includes religion, age, gender, family values, the region of the country in which a person was raised, and many other features. Understanding the dynamic interplay of the cultural forces acting on us can greatly enhance how we face the world and how we optimize our way of life.

There are many examples of cultural health disparities: the infant death rate among African-Americans is still more than double that of European-Americans, heart disease death rates are more than 40% higher for African-Americans than for European-Americans. In general, health care and disease incidence (e.g., tuberculosis) rates vary significantly across ethnic groups.

Individuals in Wisconsin are more likely to be heavy drinkers (sadly Wisconsin is the number one state in the United States in regard to drinking rates). Individuals in California, Utah, and Hawaii are less likely to smoke. American Indians/Native Americans are more likely to die from diabetes and be obese than many other ethnic groups. Men are more likely to have lung cancer than women. These are just some of the many cultural differences in health.

One of the most pressing needs for health psychology is to spend more time and energy on examining how cultural differences influence health and behavior. The plot thickens because culture can play multiple roles within an investigation. For example, a certain ethnic group may have biological predispositions for a certain illness (a biological component), and they may also experience more stress from prejudice or discrimination (a psychological component), but they may also have stronger social networks (a social component). Consequently, the researcher has to balance multiple systems, variables, and levels. A number of health psychologists have drawn attention to this problem, but there is a lot more to be done and a great need for culturally educated health psychologists.

Note. Dr. Gurung is Professor of Psychology and Chair of the Department of Human Development at the University of Wisconsin – Green Bay. He is the author or editor of five books including the second edition of *Health Psychology: A Cultural Approach* (2010). In addition to his books, he has authored or co-authored 15 book chapters, over 25 peer-reviewed journal articles, and 12 invited journal articles. Dr. Gurung is a Fellow of the American Psychological Association and is actively involved in several divisions including Division 2 (Society for the Teaching of Psychology) and Division 38 (Health Psychology).

Professional Spotlight

Chris Dunkel Schetter, PhD

Education:
- Bachelor of Arts in Psychology from Connecticut College (1974)
- Master of Arts and Doctor of Philosophy (PhD) in Social Psychology from Northwestern University (1982)
- Postdoctoral Fellowship – National Science Foundation (1982–1983)
  - University of California, Berkeley – Department of Psychology
  - Sponsor: Richard Lazarus

Employer:
Department of Psychology, University of California, Los Angeles.

Position:
Professor of Psychology, Director of UCLA's Health Psychology Program.

Description of Position:
My job duties involve research, teaching, administration, and professional service. I teach and mentor graduate and undergraduate students and postdoctoral fellows.

Most Significant Professional Accomplishments:
My most significant professional accomplishments include the UCLA Distinguished Teaching Award and the American Psychological Association's Division 38 Senior Investigator Award for Outstanding Contributions to Health Psychology.

Favorite Publication:
Dunkel-Schetter, C. (1998). Maternal stress and preterm delivery. *Prenatal and Neonatal Medicine, 3,* 39–42.

Areas of Research:
My primary program of research at present is on stress processes in pregnancy. In this work, my students and I examine various aspects of prenatal maternal stress including exposure to and perceptions of stress, emotions, and effects on preterm birth and low birth weight. We also study social relationships, race and ethnicity, and cultural factors as they modify or are associated with stress or outcomes. My current research is focused mainly on unique risk factors and mechanisms involving African-American and Latina women, the role of social support and other resilience factors in pregnancy, and on preventive interventions. I am also involved as a Co-Principal Investigator in the Community Child Health Network, which is a study about stress and resilience and their influences on maternal allostatic load as a mediator of birth outcomes and child health and development.

Most Rewarding Aspect of Your Career:
Rewards come from teaching those who really want to learn and see the world differently by understanding science, and from conducting research; the process and outcomes of scientific discovery are still a big thrill for me after many years in this career. It is also rewarding to help build programs and organizations to do excellent training and research, and to use psychological science to address society's problems, especially in areas of health.

Words of Advice to the Student Who Is Interested in Your Subfield:
Have a multifaceted approach to research, and explore as much as you can of all kinds of psychological science. Read with an open and inquiring mind!

Suggested Exercises

1. Using your college's course catalog, identify courses that are related to health psychology. Answer the following questions for each course.
   a. What department offers the course?
   b. Is it an undergraduate or graduate level course?
   c. Are there any prerequisites for the course?
   d. Is it part of a concentration, minor, or major program?
2. Using the online directory of programs on Division 38's web page or *Graduate Study in Psychology* (APA, 2010), locate a health psychology graduate program that interests you and answer the following questions:
   a. What is the name of the university?
   b. Who is the program director?
   c. What type of degree does it offer?
   d. Is the program accredited?
   e. What are the program's research and clinical focus areas?
3. Using an article from one of the health psychology publications noted in the chapter, answer the following questions:
   a. What is the title of the article?
   b. Who are the authors?
   c. What are their affiliations?/Where do they work?
   d. In 3 or 4 sentences describe the article's findings.
4. Using PsycCareers – APA's Online Career Center (http://jobs.psyccareers.com/), search for a health psychology-related position opening. Answer the following questions.
   a. What is the title of the position?
   b. Where is it located (hospital, research institute, university)?
   c. What are the job responsibilities?
   d. Does it specify a particular area of health psychology (e.g., pain management, smoking cessation, obesity)?
   e. What are the requirements for the position (e.g., doctorate, research experience, licensure)?
   f. How do you apply for the position?

Suggested Readings

Belar, C. D., & Deardorff, W. W. (2008). *Clinical health psychology in medical settings: A practitioner's guidebook* (2nd ed.). Washington, DC: American Psychological Association.

Boll, T. (Senior Ed.). (2002–2004). *Handbook of clinical health psychology* (Vols. 1–3). Washington, DC: American Psychological Association.

Frank, R. G., McDaniel, S. H., Bray, J. H., & Heldring, M. (Eds.). (2003). *Primary care psychology*. Washington, DC: American Psychological Association.

Gatchel, R. J. (2004). *Clinical essentials of pain management*. Washington, DC: American Psychological Association.

Miller, S. M., Bowen, D. J., Croyle, R. T., & Rowland, J. H. (Eds.). (2008). *Handbook of cancer control and behavioral science: A resource for researchers, practitioners, and policymakers*. Washington, DC: American Psychological Association.

Phelps, L. (Ed.). (2006). *Chronic health-related disorders in children: Collaborative medical and psychoeducational interventions*. Washington, DC: American Psychological Association.

Stroebe, W. (Ed.). (2008). *Dieting, overweight, and obesity: Self-regulation in a food-rich environment*. Washington, DC: American Psychological Association.

Sutton, S. R., Baum, A., & Johnston, M. (Eds.). (2004). *The Sage handbook of health psychology*. London: Sage.

Taylor, S. E. (2008). *Health psychology* (5th ed.). Boston: McGraw-Hill.

References

American Psychological Association. (2008a). *Archival description of clinical health psychology.* Retrieved from http://www.apa.org/crsppp/health.html

American Psychological Association. (2008b). *Recognized specialties and proficiencies in professional psychology.* Retrieved from http://www.apa.org/crsppp/rsp.html

American Psychological Association. (2010). *Graduate study in psychology: 2010.* Washington, DC: Author.

American Psychological Association – Division 38 – Health Psychology. (2007). *Tempe summit report: Application of the competency model to clinical health psychology.* Retrieved from http://www.health-psych.org/educ_trng/TempeSummitReport_Draft070207.pdf

American Psychological Association – Division 38 – Health Psychology. (n.d.). *Mission statement.* Retrieved from http://www.health-psych.org/mission.php

Association of Psychology Postdoctoral and Internship Centers. (2008). *APPIC online directory.* Retrieved from http://www.appic.org/directory/4_1_directory_online.asp

Committee on Education and Training – American Psychological Association – Division 38 – Health

Psychology. (n.d.). What a health psychologist does and how to become one. Retrieved from http://www.health-psych.org/articles/what_is.php

Gurung, R. A. R. (2010). *Health psychology: A cultural approach* (2nd ed.). Belmont, CA: Cengage.

Norcross, J. C., Sayette, M. A., & Mayne, T. J. (2008). *Insider's guide to graduate programs in clinical and counseling psychology* (2008/2009 ed.). New York: Guilford.

Occupational Information Network. (2008a). *Summary report for: 19-3031.02 – Clinical psychologists.* Retrieved from http://online.onetcenter.org/link/summary/19-3031.02

Occupational Information Network. (2008b). *Summary report for: 21-1091.00 – Health educators.* Retrieved from http://online.onetcenter.org/link/summary/21-1091.00

Occupational Information Network. (2008c). *Summary report for: 31-2012.00 – Occupational therapist aides.* Retrieved from http://online.onetcenter.org/link/summary/31-2012.00

Occupational Information Network. (2008d). *Summary report for: 19-4061.00 – Social science research assistants.* Retrieved from http://online.onetcenter.org/link/summary/19-4061.00

Straub, R. O. (2007). *Health psychology: A biopsychosocial approach* (2nd ed.). New York: Worth.

Resources

Health Psychology and Related Professional Organizations

- American Psychosomatic Society: http://www.psychosomatic.org/
- British Psychological Society's Division of Health Psychology: http://www.health-psychology.org.uk/
- European Health Psychology Society: http://www.ehps.net/
- Health Psychology (American Psychological Association – Division 38): http://www.health-psych.org/
- International Association for the Study of Pain: http://www.iasp-pain.org
- International Society of Behavioral Medicine: http://www.isbm.info/
- Rehabilitation Psychology (American Psychological Association – Division 22): http://www.div22.org/
- Society of Behavioral Medicine: http://www.sbm.org/

Other Internet Resources

- Centers for Disease Control and Prevention: http://www.cdc.gov/
- Health Psychology and Rehabilitation: http://www.healthpsych.com/
- U.S. Department of Health and Human Services – National Institutes of Health: http://www.nih.gov/
- U.S. Department of Health and Human Services: http://www.healthfinder.gov/
- World Health Organization: http://www.who.int/en/

14

Careers in Neuropsychology

Neuropsychology Defined

Although the subfield of neuropsychology has been around since at least the mid 1900s (Boake & Bieliauskas, 2007), the clinical/applied area of neuropsychology was not recognized by the American Psychological Association (APA) as a specialty area of practice until 1996 (APA, 2008). According to APA's recognition, the specialty area of clinical neuropsychology:

> . . . applies principles of assessment and intervention based upon the scientific study of human behavior as it relates to normal and abnormal functioning of the central nervous system. The specialty is dedicated to enhancing the understanding of brain-behavior relationships and the application of such knowledge to human problems. (http://www.apa.org/crsppp/neuro.html)

In other words, experimental neuropsychology develops and clinical neuropsychology applies knowledge of brain-behavior relationships to human problems. It is important to note that although the bulk of the chapter focuses on the applied clinical area of neuropsychology, it could not exist without the experimental area of neuropsychology. Both complement each other. In fact, without the experimental area of neuropsychology, there would be no applied clinical area of neuropsychology.

The Work

Core Activities

As is the case with all subfields of psychology, neuropsychologists contribute to the discipline via their activities in the areas of research, practice, and teaching/training. Each of these activities is described here.

Research.   As noted in the opening to the chapter, before clinical neuropsychologists can apply scientific knowledge to human problems (i.e., practice), there must first be research to support/develop the application. As a result, scientific research is the foundation on which both experimental neuropsychology and clinical neuropsychology are built. Given the intradisciplinary and interdisciplinary nature of the field, it is not surprising that, in addition to the field of neuropsychology, the fields of neuroscience, cognitive psychology, rehabilitative psychology, medicine, and gerontology, among others, produce excellent research on which neuropsychological practice relies. All of these fields, including applied (i.e., clinical) neuropsychologists, are known for their research expertise and the production and dissemination of high quality neuropsychological research.

Once the research is complete (and given that it withstands the rigor of the peer review process), it may be disseminated in one of the journals that publish neuropsychological findings. A host of publications provide outlets for neuropsychological research. However, keep in mind that the neuropsychologist will be reading research from the closely related fields mentioned in the earlier paragraph in order to keep on top of the ever-changing field. Regardless, some of the publications in the field that you may find helpful as you explore this career are noted in Box 14.1. As noted throughout the book, journals are an excellent resource to explore current happenings in a field.

Box 14.1   Sampling of Journals That Publish Neuropsychological Research

Aging, Neuropsychology, and Cognition: A Journal on Normal and Dysfunctional Development
Applied Neuropsychology
Archives of Clinical Neuropsychology
Child Neuropsychology
Cognitive Neuropsychology
Developmental Neuropsychology
Journal of Clinical and Experimental Neuropsychology
Memory
Neuropsychological Rehabilitation
Neuropsychology
The Clinical Neuropsychologist

Although the journal titles noted in Box 14.1 give a small glimpse into the area, a sampling of topics studied (i.e., researched) by neuropsychologists may prove more useful. Here are some topics that recently appeared in some of the journals listed in the box:

• Developing culturally sensitive neuropsychological tests
• Cognitive functioning in adults with autism
• Memory functioning in individuals diagnosed with schizophrenia
• The impact of Alzheimer's disease on language

- The neuropsychological components of dyslexia
- Recovery from brain infections in persons diagnosed with HIV
- Long-term outcome for individuals who suffer a traumatic brain injury
- Effectiveness of educational programs that encourage use of helmets when cycling
- Stroke rehabilitation issues
- Neuropsychological effects of toxin exposure in industrial and military settings.

For neuropsychologists primarily focused on research and those housed in an academic environment, activities will be similar to those discussed in the Careers in Academe chapter. In addition, careers associated with experimental psychology, physiological psychology, and cognitive psychology are covered in the Careers in Research chapter. Given the obvious overlap neuropsychology has with these areas and to eliminate redundancy, we encourage you to visit or revisit those chapters.

Practice.   As part of the recognition of the specialty by APA in 1996, the practice area was defined, populations served were acknowledged, problems typically addressed were delineated, and common practice procedures were noted. The specialty designation defined the practice domain in the following way:

> The practice of clinical neuropsychology encompasses roles that address psychological or behavioral manifestations of neurological, neuropathological, pathophysiological, and neurochemical changes in brain disease and the full range of aberrations in the central nervous system that may arise during development. (http://www.apa.org/crsppp/ neuro.html)

In general, clinical neuropsychologists serve all populations at all phases of the developmental life cycle. They serve both children and adults, including those in medical-surgical and rehabilitation contexts. In terms of services for children, pediatric neuropsychologists work with children who have learning disabilities and developmental disabilities. APA's specialty recognition (2008) notes that these pediatric neuropsychologists are increasingly receiving referrals from other pediatric care providers for such issues as drug abuse and dependence, HIV/AIDS, and toxin exposure.

Although overlap exists in treatment issues, the practice of neuropsychology with adults can be quite different than clinical practice with a pediatric population. Even though certain types of neuropsychological traumas are common in the two groups (e.g., accidents), APA's specialty recognition (2008) acknowledges that adult populations often present for services with quite different issues. Based on the specialty recognition description, these issues appear to fall into two broad categories:

- *Neurological problems.* This category includes issues like dementias due to disease processes like Alzheimer's and Parkinson's diseases, cerebrovascular accidents, tumors, infectious diseases that affect the central nervous system, and degenerative and demyelinating diseases (e.g., multiple sclerosis).
- *Psychiatric problems.* This category includes problems like differential diagnostic issues for dementia and depression, somatoform disorders that appear to have a neurological component, and psychotic symptoms related to neurological problems.

Because of the nature of their expertise, APA (2008) notes that clinical neuropsychologists also work with individuals who have general medical and surgical issues. These individuals may include:

- geriatric populations whose health status is complicated by dementia, making management more difficult;
- candidates for surgery (e.g., potential kidney and heart transplant recipients); and
- persons who have chronic pain subsequent to a neurological incident.

APA's specialty recognition notes that referrals from other health professionals often focus on requesting assistance in differential diagnosis (i.e., determining if a situation is due to one disorder or another or both) and the untangling of the psychological and medical components to a presenting problem. Neuropsychologists are also extremely helpful in establishing a baseline of functioning for patients. This baseline can be used in the future to judge disease and recovery rates. Neuropsychologists also get their fair share of referrals for behavioral and rehabilitative interventions geared toward addressing a patient's limitations due to impaired neurological functioning (APA, 2008).

The 1996 specialty designation by APA noted common practice procedures, including: "neuropsychological assessment, cognitive remediation and intervention, agency and institutional consultation, education and counseling for individuals and families, and selected psychotherapies or behavior therapies as appropriate for neurologically involved individuals" (http://www.apa.org/crsppp/neuro.html). These common practice procedures were described in more depth in the report from the Houston Conference on Specialty Education and Training in Clinical Neuropsychology (Houston Conference Report; Hannay et al., 1998). Consistent with the core domains articulated by APA's Commission for the Recognition of Specialties and Proficiencies in Professional Psychology (CRSPPP), the seven core professional activities of neuropsychologists (along with an example of each) include:

- Assessment – e.g., assessment of memory functioning in individuals diagnosed with dementias
- Intervention – e.g., development of rehabilitative programs for individuals who have suffered a traumatic brain injury
- Consultation – e.g., consultation with physicians and rehabilitative specialists when neuropsychological issues are suspected; help other professionals differentiate between a dementing process and depression
- Supervision and Training – e.g., supervision of future neuropsychologists as well as assistants and aides; supervise trainees in the administration and interpretation of neuropsychological tests
- Research and Inquiry (even for practitioners) – e.g., evaluating an intervention program that a practitioner developed for use with individuals adjusting to the aftermath of a stroke or to see if interventions to improve memory functioning have helped
- Consumer Protection – e.g., assuring patients are receiving the care necessary to address all of their respective deficits, not just medical issues

- Professional Development – e.g., continuing education to stay on top of a rapidly (almost daily) changing field, learning new assessment and intervention tools.

Teaching and training.   As is the case with all areas of psychology, one of the main ways in which neuropsychologists contribute to the discipline is through teaching and training. As a result, many of those who identify themselves as neuropsychologists hold academic positions at colleges and universities, including medical schools. Additionally, neuropsychologists often provide psychoeducational activities as part of their practices. These psychoeducational (i.e., teaching) activities can include such things as educating caregivers on the neuropsychological problems associated with stroke, dementias, and traumatic brain injuries.

Employment Settings

Because of the strong scientific foundation of this area of psychology and as noted earlier, many neuropsychologists contribute to the subfield in the college/university setting (i.e., academic positions). Within the college or university setting, neuro-psychologists are found in psychology departments, health science departments, and medical schools. Also as noted previously, the fields of neuroscience and gerontology (among others) contribute significantly to the subfield of neuropsychology and have significant scientific overlap. As a result of the overlap, neuropsychologists also return the favor in terms of contributions and as such are valued members in these academic disciplines as well. Due to the common characteristics shared with academe, we encourage you to review the information in the Careers in Academe chapter.

Another setting where neuropsychologists contribute to the subfield is the applied setting (e.g., a clinical or consulting practice). As noted in APA's recognition of the specialty (2008):

> Clinical neuropsychologists function primarily on referral from health, education, and legal professionals; agencies and institutions; and in response to needs of other service systems (e.g., courts, schools, extended rehabilitation facilities and general care facilities, military installations, and chemical treatment facilities). Primary employment settings are estimated to be almost equally divided between hospital-medical centers, private practice, and a combination of (salaried) hospital or clinic-based employment, and private practice. (http://www.apa.org/crsppp/neuro.html)

For those neuropsychologists even more aligned with the neurosciences, positions at research institutes also provide employment opportunities. Such positions can be found in government agencies like the National Institutes of Health (NIH; http://www.nih.gov/). Some of the member institutes of the NIH that are of particular interest to those in the neuropsychological subfield include:

- National Institute on Aging: http://www.nia.nih.gov/
- National Institute on Alcohol Abuse and Alcoholism: http://www.niaaa.nih.gov/
- National Institute on Drug Abuse: http://www.nida.nih.gov/

- National Institute of Mental Health: http://www.nimh.nih.gov/
- National Institute of Neurological Disorders and Stroke: http://www.ninds.nih.gov/

Salaries

Needless to say, salaries vary by work setting, reputation, and experience. Salaries for academic positions will be consistent with those noted in the Careers in Academe chapter. Academic positions within medical school settings will pay somewhat higher than traditional university settings (e.g., departments of psychology, neuroscience departments). Salaries for practitioners will be consistent with those noted in the Careers in Clinical Psychology and Counseling Psychology chapter. In short, the median annual wage in 2007 for clinical, counseling, and school psychologists was $62,210 (Occupational Information Network [O*NET], 2008a). O*NET also reports that projected growth in these areas is likely to be faster than average over the next 10 years. However, a neuropsychology specialty, including board certification, is very likely to command salaries significantly higher than the median wages noted for all clinical, school, and counseling psychologists as lumped together in O*NET.

The projected growth estimated by O*NET is supported by a recent search using PsycCareers – APA's Online Career Center (http://jobs.psyccareers.com/). That search produced 57 advertisements under the "neuroscience" category for fulltime positions. Some of the positions available included:

- Assistant Professor of Neuroscience
- Chair of Neuroimaging Research
- Pediatric Neuropsychologist at a Medical School
- Licensed Neuropsychologist at an Adult Rehabilitation Hospital
- Lead Scientist – Children's Brain Function Lab

Training and Preparation

Earning a Degree

Given the information presented about the breadth and depth of this subfield, including both the research and practice areas addressed, it should come as no surprise that a doctoral degree is typically the *base* entry-level degree for both research and applied positions. This fact is due in no small part to the interdisciplinary nature of the subfield that combines the disciplines of psychology, biology, chemistry, and health science, among others. Furthermore, the Houston Conference Report puts forth an expectation that postdoctoral education and training in clinical neuropsychology be equal to at least two fulltime years (Hannay et al., 1998). In other words, the *general* clinical skills associated with basic neuropsychological training begin in the doctoral program with the neuropsychological component growing stronger during the predoctoral internship. However, and building upon these prior aspects of training, a *specialty* in clinical neuropsychology requires extensive postdoctoral training. APA's recognition of the specialty supports this perspective on training and highlights the advanced knowledge necessary and distinctive to the field (http://www.apa.org/crsppp/neuro.html).

The Houston Conference Report (Hannay et al., 1998), supported by many in the field, offered specifics when it comes to the knowledge base required for specialization in clinical neuropsychology. The report noted that neuropsychologists possess knowledge in the general psychological area (e.g., statistics, biological bases of behavior, cognitive psychology, human development), the general clinical psychological area (e.g., tests and measures, interviewing and diagnostic techniques, ethics), general brain-behavior area (e.g., neuroanatomy, neurological disorders, neuroimaging, neurochemistry), and clinical neuropsychology area (e.g., neuropsychological assessment and interventions, ethics related to neuropsychology, neuropsychological research skills). As a result, a "short" doctoral program rarely has enough time to cover all of these necessary pieces, leaving it to postdoctoral residency and continuing education to complete the *base-level* training.

Licensure Issues

It is important to note that although state licensure is not typically required for researchers and educators within academic environments (e.g., experimental neuropsychologists), licensure by the respective state board of psychology is required to practice in the applied neuropsychological area (i.e., those that provide treatment, assessment, and diagnosis). Please see the Careers in Clinical Psychology and Counseling Psychology chapter for a discussion of the licensure process. In short, you will want to seek an APA-accredited doctoral program in clinical, school, or counseling psychology that emphasizes, provides a track in, or conducts significant research in neuropsychology if you want to practice (i.e., do applied work) in this area. Additionally, this subfield also recognizes and encourages board certification through the American Board of Clinical Neuropsychology (http://www.theabcn.org/) which is a part of the American Board of Professional Psychology (http://www.abpp.org/).

Training Programs

The APA's Division 40 (Clinical Neuropsychology) has a website that provides a searchable database for graduate, internship, and postdoctoral training programs in clinical neuropsychology. It can be found at http://www.div40.org/training/index.html. Another place to get information on training programs is *Graduate Study in Psychology* (GSP; APA, 2010). GSP provides information on graduate programs offering an emphasis in clinical neuropsychology, neuropsychology, and neuroscience. Currently, and with some minimal overlap in the categories, the GSP index lists seven programs in the clinical neuropsychology category, nine programs in the neuropsychology category, and 19 programs in the neuroscience category.

In reporting these pieces of information, it is important to note that GSP (2010) and Division 40's website databases are based on self-reports by individual graduate programs. As such and when reviewing any neuropsychology program, you are encouraged to be mindful of quality since this varies and changes over time. Before starting your search, we encourage you to review the information in the Applying to Graduate School chapter.

Preparing for Graduate Training

The first step to becoming a neuropsychologist is to ensure a solid undergraduate foundation in psychology. This foundation will serve you well as you pursue graduate and postgraduate education in the field. As alluded to in APA's recognition of the specialty and in the Houston Conference Report (Hannay et al., 1998), coursework in the areas of biology, pharmacology, anatomy and physiology, and pathophysiology will be helpful. Note that many of these courses and areas of study may require prerequisite coursework (i.e., completion of lower-level biology, chemistry, mathematics, or other physical sciences prior to enrollment). Keep this in mind as you plan your coursework. Additional coursework in statistics is also not a bad idea. Again though, this coursework is above and beyond that required by your psychology major. In fact, you are strongly encouraged to take and excel in experimental psychology, psychometrics, perception, cognitive psychology, physiological psychology, and psychopharmacology when these courses are available.

Your undergraduate preparation should also include research experience. This suggestion is a reiteration of one of the chief recommendations we give throughout the book. In fact, we encourage you to visit or revisit The Preprofessional Degree: Preparing for Graduate School chapter as it would be redundant to provide that general information again here.

Working in Areas Related to Neuropsychology With a Bachelor's Degree

As you can see from the information provided, a specialty in the neuropsychology subfield clearly involves substantial training at the doctoral and postdoctoral levels, as well as licensure if professional practice is involved. However, if you have an interest in neuropsychology there are opportunities to work in environments that value the same principles as those found in the subfield of neuropsychology. Some of these include social science research assistants, occupational therapist aides, rehabilitation counselors, and health educators.

Social Science Research Assistants

According to the O*NET (2008e), social science research assistants are supervised by social scientists (e.g., neuropsychologists, neuroscientists). Social science research assistants help with "laboratory, survey, and other social research [and] may perform publication activities, laboratory analysis, quality control, or data management" (http://online.onetcenter.org/link/summary/19-4061.00). This assistance is typically provided for activities that are "more routine" according to the O*NET. Duties can include communicating with supervisors and research participants and collecting, processing, and analyzing research data. O*NET reported that median wages in 2007 were approximately $35,870 and projected that growth in the field over the next 10 years would be about average.

Occupational Therapist Aides

Occupational therapist aides assist occupational therapists (OTs) in "planning, implementing, and administering therapy programs to restore, reinforce, and enhance performance" (O*NET, 2008c; http://online.onetcenter.org/link/summary/31-2012.00). OTs are used extensively with individuals recovering from neurological events like strokes and head injuries (e.g., from motor vehicle accidents). The O*NET reported that the 2007 median annual salary was $26,080 and that projected growth in the field would be much faster than average over the next 10 years.

Rehabilitation Counselors

According to O*NET (2008d), rehabilitation counselors "counsel individuals to maximize the independence and employability of persons coping with personal, social, and vocational difficulties that result from birth defects, illness, disease, accidents, or the stress of daily life" (http://online.onetcenter.org/link/summary/21-1015.00). When working in a rehabilitation hospital or center, these counselors help coordinate patients' activities as well as assist in evaluating patients' needs. They also may help execute rehabilitation programs developed by the patients' physicians and psychologists. According to the O*NET, the median annual salary for rehabilitation counselors in 2007 was $29,630. O*NET projects growth in this field to be much faster than average over the next 10 years with a need of an additional 60,000 employees.

Health Educators

According to O*NET (2008b), health educators:

- "Promote, maintain, and improve individual and community health by assisting individuals and communities to adopt healthy behaviors,
- Collect and analyze data to identify community needs prior to planning, implementing, monitoring, and evaluating programs designed to encourage healthy lifestyles, policies, and environments, and
- May also serve as a resource to assist individuals, other professionals, or the community, and may administer fiscal resources for health education programs."
(http://online.onetcenter.org/link/summary/21-1091.00)

More specific to the field of neuropsychology, these individuals may assist in educational programs for patients and the public (e.g., helmet safety and car seat safety programs) and provide families with information on support systems available in the community (e.g., Alzheimer's support groups). In terms of wages, the 2007 median annual salary was $42,920 (O*NET). The O*NET also projects a growth rate much faster than average over the next 10 years.

Clinical Neuropsychology

Expanding our Borders

Maria T. Schultheis, PhD
Drexel University

By definition clinical neuropsychology is the study of the relationship between the brain and behavior. In this sense we often think of neuropsychologists as individuals who work with clinical populations that have cognitive impairment as a result of neurological (e.g., stroke, multiple sclerosis), psychiatric (e.g., dementia, schizophrenia) or other compromise (e.g., traumatic brain injury). In this role, neuropsychologists rely on assessment tools that evaluate cognition, and these tools are traditionally paper-and-pencil-based tasks. However, if we expand our thinking about the subfield of neuropsychology, new opportunities abound as a result of advancements in science, medicine, and technology.

First, consider the opportunity to advance our current assessment methodologies. Technologies, such as neuroimaging, have revolutionized our understanding of brain structure and functioning. As a result, it is reasonable that neuropsychologists will play a significant role in continuing to use this technology for improving our understanding of brain-behavior relationships. Other innovative technologies such as virtual reality simulation, the Internet, and wire-

less communication may also afford new creative techniques for evaluating human behavior. In particular these new methods may help address one of the biggest challenges faced by neuropsychologists, which is the evaluation of cognition in everyday tasks (e.g., driving, working, etc.). The application of these technologies offers future neuropsychologists an opportunity to work with a wide variety of experts (e.g., engineers, neuroscientists, clinicians) in the development of new techniques for understanding the brain-behavior relationship.

Second, consider the new integrated approach to medicine. Although many clinical specialty areas functioned independently in the past, the new focus on interdisciplinary approaches and translational clinical research has encouraged the true integration of the science and practice of neuropsychology. Future neuropsychologists will have the opportunity to study the human brain-behavior relationship across the spectrum, including incorporating the genetics of disorders, defining the natural course of the aging brain, defining the pharmacological needs of different disorders, and creating uniquely tailored clinical interventions for individuals. The growing knowledge base gained by the various sciences can only serve to expand the role and contributions that neuropsychologists can bring in the future.

Indeed, in addition to traditional roles of clinical assessment and treatment of cognitive disorders, neuropsychologists are now in the role of defining the application and integration of this growing knowledge. As experts in brain-behavior relationships, future neuropsychologists can serve to answer the new questions that will be raised, such as the appropriate development of new methodologies, the validation of these approaches, and the clinical application of the scientific findings. As such, opportunities for neuropsychologists expand well beyond the clinical setting and into work within laboratories, universities, businesses, and medicine. Natural collaborations with cognitive neuroscience, genetics, biomedical engineering, and neuro-pharmacokinetics all offer innovative environments for future neuropsychologists.

Finally, given the diverse options available in neuropsychology, one of the greatest advantages of this training is the opportunity to be involved and contribute in more than one area. That is, a career in neuropsychology can offer great variability in one's career, which can include clinical, research, industry, and academic work individually or in combination. As a result, stagnation can be minimized, and opportunities for innovation and creativity can be maximized. In sum, future neuropsychologists have a great opportunity to redefine the field and contribute to the larger goal of understanding brain-behavior relationships.

Note. Dr. Maria T. Schultheis earned her master's degree in Biological Science and her PhD in Clinical Psychology with a concentration in Neuropsychology. She is currently a Research Associate Professor in the Department of Psychology and in the School of Biomedical Engineering, Science, and Health Systems at Drexel University in Philadelphia, PA. Her research centers on the application of technology to psychology, driving behavior after brain injury, and neurorehabilitation. Her research has been supported by grants from organizations like the National Multiple Sclerosis Society, the National Institutes of Health, and the National Institute for Disability and Rehabilitation Research. Her work has resulted in dozens of publications and presentations and was acknowledged by APA Division 40 – Clinical Neuropsychology with the Early Career Award in 2007.

Professional Spotlight

Antonio E. Puente, PhD

Education:
- Bachelor's Degree in Psychology from University of Florida (1973)
- Master of Science Degree (MS) in Bio-psychology and Clinical Psychology from University of Georgia (1978)

- Doctor of Philosophy (PhD) in Bio-psychology from University of Georgia (1978)
- Postdoctoral Training at Northeast Florida State Hospital (1979–1981)
- Licensed Psychologist in North Carolina

Position:
Professor of Psychology at the University of North Carolina, Wilmington

Description of Position:
My job duties include:
- Teaching (from the undergraduate level to the post-doctoral level),
- Research (primarily in neuropsychology),
- Service (within the university and with various organizations outside the university),
- Clinical service (neuropsychology practice), and
- Public policy development (e.g., Medicare).

Most Significant Professional Accomplishment:
My most significant professional accomplishment actually relates to my family. I was fortunate enough to present colloquia at each of my three children's undergraduate and graduate schools (when they were students there). In fact, two of my children are in the field of psychology. My daughter attended the PsyD program at the Florida Institute of Technology, and my son attended the PhD program in Clinical Psychology at the University of Georgia.

Favorite Publications:
Puente, A. E., Matthews, J., & Brewer, C. (Eds.). (1992). *Teaching psychology in America: A history.* Washington, DC: American Psychological Association.

Puente, A. E., & McCaffrey, R. (Eds.). (1992). *Handbook of neuropsychological assessment: A biopsychosocial perspective.* New York: Plenum Press.

Research Area:
My primary area of research is the interface between culture and clinical neuropsychology.

Practice Areas:
My current area of practice is within the broad area of clinical neuropsychology. As part of my practice I conduct both clinical and forensic neuropsychological assessments as well as provide rehabilitation therapy.

Professional Memberships:
- American Psychological Association

- Member of Divisions 1, 2, 6, 26, 38, 40, 45, and 52
- Fellow of Divisions 1, 2, 6, 26, 40, and 52
- President of Division 40 (2002–2003)
- International Neuropsychological Society (member; 1995–present)
- Latin American Neuropsychological Society (member; 1991–present)
- National Academy of Neuropsychology
  - Founding Member, Fellow, and Past President
- North Carolina Psychological Association
  - Board of Directors (1985–1991) and Past President (1989–1990)
- Sociedad Interamericana de Psicología (1993–present)
- Hispanic Neuropsychological Society
  - Founding Board Member and Past President

Most Rewarding Aspect of Your Career:
The most rewarding aspect of my career is the evolution of balance between my family life and career. Within the profession itself, the most rewarding aspect is my ability to strike a balance among pedagogy, investigation, and service.

Words of Advice to the Student Who Is Interested in Your Subfield:
My advice to the undergraduate is to develop a vision, enact a trajectory, pursue it with diligence and perseverance while remaining flexible, enjoy the fruits of your success, share it with those seeking to understand and serve, and, above all, do not forget why you got involved with psychology.

Suggested Exercises

1. Using the online directory of training programs on Division 40's web page (http://www.div40.org/) or the GSP publication, locate a neuropsychology or neuroscience program that interests you and answer the following questions.
   a. What is the name of the university?
   b. Who is the program director?
   c. What type of degree does it offer?
   d. Is the program accredited?
   e. What are the program's research and/or clinical focus areas?

2. Using an article from one of the neuropsychology publications noted in the chapter, answer the following questions.
   a. What is the title of the article?
   b. Who are the authors?

c. What are their affiliations?/Where do they work?

d. In 3 or 4 sentences describe the article's findings.

3. Using PsycCareers – APA's Online Career Center (http://jobs.psyccareers.com/), search for a neuropsychology-related position opening. Answer the following questions.

a. What is the title of the position?

b. Where is it located (hospital, research institute, university)?

c. What are the job responsibilities?

d. Does it specify a particular area of neuropsychology (e.g., brain injury, geriatric, pediatric)?

e. What are the requirements for the position (e.g., doctorate, research experience, licensure)?

f. How do you apply for the position?

Suggested Readings

Attix, D. K., & Welsh-Bohmer, K. A. (Eds.). (2005). *Geriatric neuropsychology: Assessment and intervention*. New York: Guilford Press.

Banich, M. T. (2004). *Cognitive neuroscience and neuropsychology* (2nd ed.). Boston: Houghton-Mifflin.

D'Amato, R. C., Fletcher-Janzen, E., & Reynolds, C. R. (Eds.). (2005). *Handbook of school neuropsychology*. New York: Wiley.

Elias, L., & Saucier, D. (2005). *Neuropsychology: Clinical and experimental foundations*. Boston: Allyn & Bacon.

Kolb, B., & Whishaw, I. Q. (2008). *Fundamentals of human neuropsychology* (6th ed.). New York: Worth.

Lezak, M. D., Howieson, D. B., Loring, D. W., Hannay, H. J., & Fischer, J. S. (2004). *Neuropsychological assessment* (4th ed.). New York: Oxford University Press.

Morgan, J. E., & Ricker, J. H. (Eds.). (2008). *Textbook of clinical neuropsychology: Studies on neuropsychology, neurology, and cognition*. London: Taylor and Francis.

References

American Psychological Association. (2008). *Archival description of clinical neuropsychology*. Retrieved from http://www.apa.org/crsppp/neuro.html

American Psychological Association. (2010). *Graduate study in psychology: 2010*. Washington, DC: Author.

American Psychological Association – Division 40 – Clinical Neuropsychology. (n.d.). *Listing of training programs in clinical neuropsychology*. Retrieved from http://www.div40.org/training/index.html

Boake, C., & Bieliauskas, L. A. (2007, Summer). Development of clinical neuropsychology as a psychological specialty: A timeline of major events. *The ABPP Specialist*, 42–43.

Hannay, H. J., Bieliauskas, L. A., Crosson, B. A., Hammeke, T. A., Hamsher, K. deS., & Koffler, S. P. (1998). Proceedings of the Houston Conference on Specialty Education and Training in Clinical Neuropsychology. *Archives of Clinical Neuropsychology*, 13.

Occupational Information Network. (2008a). *Summary report for: 19-3031.02 – Clinical psychologists*. Retrieved from http://online.onetcenter.org/link/summary/19-3031.02

Occupational Information Network. (2008b). *Summary report for: 21-1091.00 – Health educators*. Retrieved from http://online.onetcenter.org/link/summary/21-1091.00

Occupational Information Network. (2008c). *Summary report for: 31-2012.00 – Occupational therapist aides*. Retrieved from http://online.onetcenter.org/link/summary/31-2012.00

Occupational Information Network. (2008d). *Summary report for: 21-1015.00 – Rehabilitation counselors*. Retrieved from http://online.onetcenter.org/link/summary/21-1015.00

Occupational Information Network. (2008e). *Summary report for: 19-4061.00 – Social science research assistants*. Retrieved from http://online.onetcenter.org/link/summary/19-4061.00

Resources

Neuropsychology and Related Organizations

- American Academy of Clinical Neuropsychology: http://www.theaacn.org/
- American Board of Clinical Neuropsychology: http://www.theabcn.org/
- American Board of Pediatric Neuropsychology: http://www.abpdn.org/
- American Board of Professional Neuropsychology: http://abpn.net/
- American Psychological Association – Division 6 – Behavioral Neuroscience and Comparative Psychology: http://www.apa.org/divisions/div6/
- American Psychological Association – Division 40 – Clinical Neuropsychology: http://www.div40.org/
- American Psychological Association – Division 22 – Rehabilitation Psychology: http://www.div22.org/
- Association for Neuropsychology Students in Training: http://www.div40.org/ANST/
- British Psychological Society – Division of Neuropsychology: http://www.bps.org.uk/don/
- International Neuropsychological Society: http://www.the-ins.org/
- National Academy of Neuropsychology: http://www.nanonline.org/

Other Neuropsychology Resources on the Web

- Neuropsychology Central: http://www.neuropsychologycentral.com/
- Annenberg Media: www.learner.org
    - The Brain – An online series of 32 videos on such topics as memory, Alzheimer's disease, aggression/violence, and neurorehabiliation. http://www.learner.org/resources/series142.html

15

Careers in Forensic Psychology

Forensic Psychology Defined

The field of forensic psychology is a much broader area than most people think. Bartol and Bartol (1999) defined forensic psychology as:

> ...both (a) the research endeavor that examines aspects of human behavior directly related to the legal process...and (b) the professional practice of psychology within, or in consultation with, a legal system that encompasses both criminal and civil law and the numerous areas where they interact. Therefore, forensic psychology refers broadly to the *production* and *application* of psychological knowledge to the civil and criminal justice systems. (p. 3, italics in original)

On the application side, forensic psychology is one of the newest subfields officially recognized by the American Psychological Association's (APA) Commission for the Recognition of Specialties and Proficiencies in Professional Psychology (2003). As part of the recognition (initially occurring in 2001), the APA defined the applied side of forensic psychology as:

> the professional practice by psychologists who foreseeably and regularly provide professional psychological expertise to the judicial system. Such professional practice is generally within the areas of clinical psychology, counseling psychology, neuropsychology, and school psychology, or other applied areas within psychology involving the delivery of human services, by psychologists who have additional expertise in law and the application of applied psychology to legal proceedings. (http://www.apa.org/crsppp/archivforensic.html)

However, as Bartol and Bartol (1999) noted, application is only one of the two broad aspects of forensic psychology with the other being production (i.e., research). Because of these different aspects and areas within forensic psychology, this subfield of psychology is often referred to by different names. These names include: Legal Psychology, Criminal Psychology, Psychology and Law, Police Psychology, Correctional Psychology, and Investigative Psychology. For reading ease, we will use the term Forensic Psychology when referring to any and all of these areas.

Additionally and by the very nature of the field and its relationship to the legal system, forensic psychology is often broken down further. The breakdown mirrors that of the American judicial system. The two broad divisions within forensic psychology are criminal forensic psychology and civil forensic psychology. Criminal forensic psychology interacts with the criminal legal system. In short, forensic psychology brings its skills to bear on processes involved in how criminal law establishes law, investigates and adjudicates suspects, and punishes offenders. Civil forensic psychology interacts with the civil legal system (e.g., family and administrative courts). While criminal law focuses its energies on punishment, civil law focuses its energies on redress of wrongs. Redress typically occurs via compensation or restitution (e.g., malpractice claims). These two divisions will become clearer when activities in the respective areas are discussed.

As might be guessed based on the description of the field, tension exists in the relationship between psychology and the legal system. The tension highlights the challenges inherent in the subfield of forensic psychology. While the legal system deals in absolutes (e.g., guilt vs. innocence; legal vs. illegal), psychology is based on and the opinions we offer spring out of research (e.g., statistical analyses of group data). As a result, the dichotomous field of law sometimes clashes with the statistically rooted, scientific field of psychology. This does not mean that value is not derived from our involvement. It is actually the exact opposite. High value is placed on our involvement because we consider all the variables and circumstances that impact a situation and offer expert opinions, reports, treatment, etc. based on research findings as opposed to non-scientific personal opinions or beliefs.

Contributions to the Discipline of Psychology

As might be guessed from the description of the breadth of this subfield, forensic psychologists contribute to the discipline in a number of ways. The four main ways are research, public policy development and analysis, education, and clinical practice. In terms of research, some of the topics studied include jury selection, domestic violence, eyewitness testimony, police lineups, confession, stalking, child abuse, guardianship, and child custody. For readers curious about what topics are currently being researched and published, you are encouraged to obtain a copy of one of the top journals in the field and peruse the table of contents. See Box 15.1 for a list of the top five journals that publish forensic psychology research.

Forensic psychologists also assist in the development of policy including analyzing a policy's effects. For example, a forensic psychologist may evaluate the impact of a new policy that diverts people from prison to drug treatment when warranted. This information can then be used by policymakers (e.g., legislators) to remedy any issues with the new policy.

Box 15.1 Top Journals That Publish Forensic
Psychology Research (Helms, 2009)

Law and Human Behavior
Psychology, Public Policy, and Law
Behavioral Sciences and the Law
Criminal Justice and Behavior
Applied Cognitive Psychology

In terms of education, forensic psychologists teach, train, and mentor the next generation of forensic psychologists. Contributions are made to the field via teaching specialized courses in forensic psychology in an undergraduate or graduate program, supervising residents on a postdoctoral fellowship, and collaborating with colleagues newly interested in the field.

Last but not least are the contributions made in the clinical practice domain. The forensic psychologist who works in the clinical practice area provides assessments/evaluations, treatment, and consultation to and for the courts, attorneys, and other legally involved parties (e.g., defendants). Because clinical practice is arguably the largest area within forensic psychology, an upcoming section provides more information.

Although clinical practice is the largest area, significant contributions are made to forensic psychology from a myriad of other subfields of psychology. Here are some examples of topics in the respective psychology subfields that are forensically related:

- Developmental psychology:
  - Effects of divorce and custody arrangements on children
  - Elder maltreatment and abuse
- Social psychology:
  - Racial profiling
  - Jury decision-making research
- Cognitive psychology:
  - Eyewitness evidence
  - False memories and recovered memories
- Neuropsychology:
  - Malingering and feigning memory problems
  - The effect of brain development on juvenile delinquency
- Industrial-organizational psychology:
  - Workplace harassment
  - Workplace violence
- School psychology:
  - Bullying
  - School violence

Core Activities of the Forensic Psychologist

For forensic psychologists focused on research and those housed in an academic environment, activities are similar to those discussed in the Careers in Academe chapter. As a result, the focus of this section is predominantly on the applied areas of forensic psychology. For practitioners who provide services to the public (i.e., individuals, attorneys, courts), activities include: assessment; treatment; consultation with attorneys, courts and insurance companies; trial consultation testimony; and program development and administration.

Assessment

As noted in the chapter on Careers in Clinical Psychology and Counseling Psychology, assessment is one of the main distinctions between psychology and the other mental health professions. This distinction, based in part on our abilities to develop reliable and valid tests and testing procedures, carries over to the forensic psychology subfield as well. Forensic psychologists use psychological tests, interviews, observations, and review of records to provide these assessments. The assessments can be requested by the court, an individual, an organization, or an attorney. Because of the number of potential referral sources and the value placed on the forensic psychologist's work, hundreds of thousands of forensic psychological assessments are provided each year. The assessments that forensic psychologists provide are divided into the two broad areas noted earlier, civil and criminal forensic psychology areas. Here are some common types of assessments in the two areas.

- Civil forensic psychological assessment
  Child custody: These assessments assist the court in determining the best living arrangements for a child.
  Guardianship: These assessments assist the court in determining if a person can care for himself/herself or if the person needs someone to help with providing the care.
  Competency to make treatment decisions: These assessments help the court determine if a person is capable of making sound treatment decisions (e.g., accepting/refusing psychoactive medications).
  Personal injury evaluations: These evaluations help determine if an injury (e.g., depression, brain injury) is due to another's negligence (e.g., auto accident) or if it is preexisting.
- Criminal forensic psychological assessment
  Competency to stand trial/Competency to be adjudicated: These assessments help the court determine if a defendant is able to understand the charges, understand the legal issues and procedures in the case, understand the dispositions and penalties possible, etc. (*Dusky v. United States*, 1960).
  Competency to waive Miranda *rights*: These evaluations help the court determine if a person knowingly, intelligently, and voluntarily waived the right to silence and assistance of an attorney (*Miranda v. Arizona*, 1966).

Transfer evaluations: These evaluations assist the court in determining if a juvenile should remain in the juvenile court system for treatment and rehabilitation or if he/she should be transferred to the adult court system.

Competency to be sentenced and executed: These assist the court in determining if a person understands what is being done to them and why.

Violence risk assessment: These assessments assist the court, parole boards, schools, and other entities in determining the risk of violence of an individual given certain circumstances and contexts (e.g., inpatient vs. outpatient; community placement vs. incarcerated).

Treatment

Another common activity of forensic psychologists is treatment. Treatment can be defined as the provision of psychological therapeutic techniques to change behavior, thoughts, and emotions. Forensically relevant treatment can be self-initiated or court ordered. As is the case with assessment, treatment in the forensic area is divided into civil and criminal domains. The following is a list of some common treatment circumstances seen by forensic psychologists.

- Civil forensic psychological treatment
  Victim treatment: This treatment includes children and adults as well as domestic and stranger violence. Treatment of those individuals that have been victimized is one of the larger areas of practice for some forensic psychologists.
  Treatment of law enforcement professionals: This type of treatment assists law enforcement professionals in coping with the stressors associated with their jobs (e.g., working in a prison setting, killing someone in the line of duty, witnessing violence).
  Divorce mediation/dispute resolution: This type of treatment (or intervention) assists families and parties in resolving conflict due to differing goals and needs.
- Criminal forensic psychological treatment:
  Sex offender treatment: This type of treatment works with individuals who have been adjudicated (i.e., convicted) of a sex offense and has the goal of eliminating or reducing recidivism.
  Drug dependence treatment: This type of treatment focuses on individuals (usually referred by the court) with drug dependence problems. Psychological treatments have been shown to be significantly more effective than incarceration in reducing recidivism.
  Multisystemic therapy: This is an empirically validated community-based treatment program used with juveniles who have histories significant for delinquency, including violent offenses and drug use (Henggeler et al., 1999).

Consultation with Attorneys, Courts, and Insurance Companies

Because of forensic psychologists' expertise in human behavior, they are often sought out by attorneys, courts, and insurance companies for their perspectives. Although these consultations may lead to a referral for an assessment or treatment, they are often used to clarify issues in a particular case. Here are some circumstances when a consultation may be sought.

- An insurance company consults with a forensic psychologist regarding an insurance claim that may involve fraud (e.g., malingering pain to increase insurance payment/settlement).
- An attorney seeks out a forensic psychologist for a consultation on what treatments are available in the community for a particular problem that the attorney's client has.
- An attorney hires a forensic psychologist to review a client's medical and treatment records subsequent to filing a malpractice lawsuit.

Trial Consultation

Due to the adversarial nature of our justice system, there is, by definition, a winner and a loser when all is finished. Depending on the circumstances, the "loser" can potentially lose his/her freedom (in criminal court) or large sums of money (in civil court). As a result of the high stakes nature of the legal process, both parties involved sometimes use trial consultants. Trial consultants can help with jury selection as well as case theme development and strategies. For example, trial consultants can conduct a survey of the community (i.e., potential jurors) to learn what type of juror is likely to be more favorable to their side (e.g., more or less likely to convict). Based on the results of the survey, attorneys can make decisions about who they would like to have as jurors during the *voir dire* process (i.e., the examination to determine the suitability of a potential juror). Due to the nature of this work, trial consultants are methodologically sophisticated (i.e., they have excellent skills in research methods and applied statistics).

Testimony

Due to the nature of the work, forensic psychologists are often called to testify in court or give a deposition. Sometimes, forensic psychologists are specifically hired as experts to provide this testimony. For example, a forensic psychologist may have a specialty in the treatment of posttraumatic stress disorder (PTSD) in battered women. An attorney that knows of this expertise may retain (i.e., hire) the psychologist to provide testimony regarding PTSD. Other times forensic psychologists provide testimony regarding the findings in their psychological assessments or during the course of treatment. Regardless of the circumstances or who retained you (the court, the prosecution/

plaintiff, or the defense) and given the adversarial nature of the process, testifying in court is stressful.

Program Development and Administration

Another area of practice for the forensic psychologist is program development and administration. Due to the breadth and depth of training and knowledge in human behavior, forensic psychologists are equipped to develop effective programs that address particular problems encountered by individuals entangled in the justice system. These programs are in such areas as treatment for battered women, abused children, sex offenders, and at-risk youth. Once developed, forensic psychologists often are hired specifically to administer the program. The activities involved in administering (i.e., running) a program include hiring qualified staff, supervising staff, evaluating the effectiveness of the program, and changing the program to meet the needs of those it serves.

A Note About Criminal Profiling

Criminal profiling is the development of a description of the likely perpetrator of a crime that has yet to be apprehended. A profile may include information on the personality and psychological characteristics of the offender as well as physical attributes (e.g., sex, race, height, weight). The primary purpose of the profile is to focus the investigation and shorten the time to apprehension of the offender. Unfortunately, profiling is an art and not a science. As such, psychology and in particular forensic psychology, steers clear of this area. In addition to being an art and not a science, other reasons that criminal profiling is routinely not included in the forensic psychology domain are:

- Training in profiling has typically fallen under the domain of the Federal Bureau of Investigation (FBI). As such, it is rarely available to those outside the FBI. Forensic psychology programs do *not* train students in criminal profiling.
- The job market for profilers is almost nonexistent. There is little need for these types of jobs.
- Criminal profiling often utilizes stereotypes about populations to derive the description. The use of stereotypes by law enforcement officials has contributed to disproportionate representation of minorities in the justice system in this country.

Training Required to Be a Forensic Psychologist

For research and academic positions, a doctorate is typically the entry level degree, although some master's-level research positions are available in large agencies (e.g., the Department of Justice, the Office of Juvenile Justice and Delinquency Prevention). As noted earlier, forensically oriented topics are addressed by many of the subfields of psychology including experimental, social, developmental, and cognitive psychology. As such, students interested in the forensic topics typically addressed by these subfields of psychology are encouraged to identify particular researchers in these fields, the university programs where the researchers work, and information regarding application and admission to graduate training in those programs. For more information on the application procedure, please see the Applying to Graduate School chapter.

For applied positions, a master's degree is likely sufficient for many treatment provider positions in correctional environments. According to a survey of master's-level psychology practitioners, approximately 31% worked within the state's department of corrections (MacKain, Tedeschi, Durham, & Goldman, 2002). In a study presented at the 2008 American Psychology-Law Society (APLS) conference, DiCataldo et al. reported that the main activity of the master's-level practitioner is the provision of treatment. In fact, the study indicated that almost half (46.3%) of the master's-level practitioner's work week is spent providing therapy.

However, the Forensic Specialty Council (2007), the group responsible for developing and submitting to APA the education and training guidelines used to establish the specialty, recommends a different path to forensic specialization and training. Specifically, the Forensic Specialty Council clearly states that to function as an applied forensic psychologist, postdoctoral training is required. The Council and others suggest:

- general broad training at the doctoral level in clinical, counseling, or school psychology including supervised practica;
- postdoctoral training in a forensically oriented environment under a forensic psychologist;
- licensure as a psychologist in the respective jurisdiction; and
- board certification by the American Board of Forensic Psychology. (This aspect is preferred but not required.)

It is important to note that state licensure is not typically required for researchers, educators, and policy specialists, including those researchers, educators, and policy specialists that give expert testimony. However, those that provide treatment, assessment, and diagnosis do require licensure. (Please see the Careers in Clinical Psychology and Counseling Psychology chapter for discussion of the licensure process.) This requirement, along with laws and statutes excluding the involvement of non-doctoral-level practitioners in some areas of forensic practice (e.g., assessment, some expert roles), makes it imperative that students understand the limitations associated with different degree levels.

Additionally, one question that is asked routinely is whether or not a law degree is needed to practice in the forensic psychology subfield, especially given the overlapping nature of the areas and the knowledge required to practice effectively. It is true that some psychologists chose to attend law school (JD degree) or attain a Masters of Legal Studies degree (MLS). As a matter of fact, several joint degree programs exist. These joint degree programs allow the student to simultaneously pursue a graduate psychology degree and the law degree (e.g., JD/PhD programs). Although excellent training, these are not necessary to be a forensic psychologist. What is necessary is an understanding of and familiarity with the law as it applies to your particular area of practice whether it is research endeavors, assessment, or treatment.

Forensic Psychology Training Programs

There are a number of graduate programs that train individuals in forensic psychology. The two best resources that list programs along with a link to the respective graduate program's web page are:

- The American Psychology-Law Society Student Section web page: http://www.aplsstudentsection.com/Programs.htm
- Helms and Mayhew's (2006) *Undergraduate preparation for graduate training in forensic psychology*: http://teachpsych.org/otrp/resources/helms06.pdf

Although both of these resources provide excellent starting points, the interested student is cautioned because program quality varies widely. Because of the wide disparity between programs, this book's first author (Helms) initiated a program rankings study that was presented at the 2008 APLS conference. The survey was e-mailed to those individuals who were actively involved in the field of forensic psychology. The top clinically oriented and top research-oriented doctoral programs are listed in Box 15.2.

Box 15.2 Top Programs in Forensic Psychology (Helms, 2008)

Top Clinically Oriented Forensic Programs
1. Simon Fraser University
2. University of Nebraska – Lincoln
3. University of Alabama
4*. John Jay College of Criminal Justice
4*. Sam Houston State University

* Denotes a tie

Top Research-Oriented Forensic Programs
1. University of Nebraska – Lincoln
2. John Jay College of Criminal Justice
3. Simon Fraser University
4. Florida International University
5. University of Arizona

Preparing for Graduate Training in Forensic Psychology

For those students interested in increasing their chances of getting accepted into a graduate program that emphasizes forensic psychology, a study by this book's first author and a colleague (Helms & Mayhew, 2006) can provide some help. For the study, Helms and Mayhew surveyed individuals involved in selecting students for graduate study in forensic psychology and complemented these findings with information provided by forensic psychology graduate programs. Based on a three-point scale where 1 was "optional," 2 was "recommend," and 3 was "require," mean ratings placed six courses in the "recommend" to "require" range. These are shown in Table 15.1.

As can be seen from the mean ratings, it is clear that high value is placed on the scientific basis of psychology. As a result, those students interested in pursuing graduate training with an emphasis in forensic psychology are strongly encouraged to take and excel in the more research-oriented coursework in the undergraduate curriculum.

As noted in the first part of the book, there is more to getting accepted to graduate school than good grades. As a result, Helms and Mayhew (2006) also asked people involved in the selection of graduate students for forensic psychology programs

Table 15.1 Mean Ratings for Undergraduate Courses Required or Recommended for Graduate Training in Forensic Psychology (Helms & Mayhew, 2006)

Course	Mean (SD)
Research Methods	2.98 (.14)
Statistics	2.96 (.20)
Abnormal Psychology	2.44 (.71)
Experimental Psychology	2.29 (.71)
Introduction to Forensic Psychology	2.24 (.69)
Social Psychology	2.18 (.70)

Table 15.2 Activities Rating Means and Percentages for People Involved in Forensic Psychology Graduate Student Selection (Helms & Mayhew, 2006)

Activity	M (SD)	High	Medium	Low
Previous research activity	2.94 (.24)	93.9	6.1	0.0
Letters of recommendation	2.82 (.44)	84.0	14.0	2.0
Statement of goals and objectives	2.70 (.46)	70.0	30.0	0.0
Interview	2.38 (.67)	48.0	42.0	10.0
Work experience	1.96 (.64)	18.0	60.0	22.0
Clinically related public service	1.84 (.59)	10.2	63.3	26.5
Extracurricular activity	1.36 (.56)	4.0	28.0	68.0

Note. Means based on High = 3, Medium = 2, and Low = 1.

to rate the importance of some common activities. Table 15.2 presents the results. It is clear from the results (and complements the ratings of the coursework noted earlier) that research activity is highly valued. Additionally, letters of recommendation, the applicant's statement of goals and objectives, and an interview received mean ratings in the "medium" to "high" ranges. It is also important to mention those activities that were not rated as high. Work experience, clinically related public service, and extracurricular activity received mean ratings in the "low" to "medium" range. Although this does not mean they are not valued, it does mean that other activities are valued more. Given that most students have limited time, this information can assist you in making the most of the time that is available, especially if the goal is gaining admission to a graduate program with an emphasis in forensic psychology.

Employment in the Forensic Psychology Subfield

Settings

As you probably guessed based on the variety of activities, there are a myriad of employment opportunities in the subfield of forensic psychology. Box 15.3 provides some examples of recent position openings in forensic psychology. In terms of research-oriented positions, opportunities in research institutes and government agencies like the Department of Justice and the Office of Juvenile Justice and Delinquency Prevention are possible. Of course, the main employment setting for those interested in research is academe. As such, colleges and universities that have a commitment to research are likely places, and most academic environments encourage (or even require) the expansion of knowledge in a person's field of expertise via research and publication. For those interested in more of the training side of education, professional schools and medical schools provide opportunities.

As noted in the study by MacKain et al. (2002), many master's-level practitioners work in correctional settings, especially at the local and state level. When it comes to the federal level, most openings are for those at the doctoral level because licensure to practice independently is often required. Prisons at both the state and federal level also typically provide training opportunities for those in need of supervised experience prior to licensure. Additionally, the pay tends to be quite good, and positions tend to be plentiful. Unfortunately, the reasons for the good pay and plentiful positions tend to correlate with retention issues. Stress is a big factor in these settings and often leads to individuals seeking out different employment (i.e., quitting). Regardless, most agree that the training and learning opportunities in these environments are excellent for the forensic psychologist.

If the correctional setting (i.e., jails and prisons) is not a good fit or interesting to you, opportunities inside law enforcement agencies may be a better fit. Opportunities with probation and parole departments are available to those with forensic psychology expertise. For example, a recent advertisement recruiting doctoral-level licensed forensic

Box 15.3 Recent Forensic Psychology Position Openings

Forensic Psychologist at a Secure Medical Facility (Alabama)
- Forensic evaluation and treatment of criminally-committed patients
- Salary range is $53,455–$81,427

Forensic Psychologist at a Forensic Hospital (Nova Scotia)
- Assessment, treatment, and consultation as well as active involvement in program planning and evaluation, ongoing research, clinical supervision, and various administration and operational activities
- Salary range is $75,809–$89,259

Forensic Psychologist at a Sex Offender Treatment Center (Minnesota)
- Provide services to patients civilly committed as mentally ill and dangerous or sexually dangerous persons, and individuals with cognitive disabilities who have sexually offended
- Salary is described as highly competitive

Forensic Psychologist at a State Hospital (California)
- Provide substance abuse treatment, treat seriously mentally ill individuals, design behavior plans, provide behavior therapy
- Starting salary pre-licensure is $78,000. Salary for licensed psychologists is approximately $97,000

Master's-Level Practitioner at State Youth Commission School (Texas)
- Provide group, family, and individual therapy; administration and interpretation of psychological evaluations of youth at-risk of suicide or in need of special treatment services
- Salary range is $36,043–$43,609

Note. Information was extracted from job advertisements posted on the APLS and APA websites.

psychologists for the California Board of Parole Hearings indicated multiple openings in the state with salaries starting around $100,000, significantly greater than almost all other areas of psychology. Individuals in these settings provide assessments of individuals coming up for parole for the parole boards. Police departments also hire forensic psychologists. Although most outsource their forensic psychological needs (i.e., hire consultants on an "as needed" basis), some police agencies hire forensic psychologists to treat stress reactions in officers, evaluate officers for fitness for duty after a traumatic incident, and evaluate potential police recruits for jobs.

Another setting for forensic psychologists is court clinics. In order to avoid or limit delays in the judicial process, some court systems hire forensic psychologists to evaluate defendants on site instead of transporting them to the local state hospital. Keeping defendants on site saves both time and money. However, the services are not limited to evaluation, although it is the main function. Forensic psychologists in the court clinic have the opportunity routinely to consult with judges and attorneys as well as to provide brief therapy and crisis intervention services.

Other settings that employ forensic psychologists include hospitals (especially state psychiatric hospitals). When an individual is found not guilty by reason of insanity or an individual is found to be a danger to himself/herself or other, that individual is most often hospitalized at a state psychiatric facility. In order to remain hospitalized, the person must continue to meet certain legal criteria. These criteria include having a mental illness, being a danger to self or others, benefitting from treatment, and the hospital being the least restrictive environment necessary to accomplish the treatment. Forensic psychologists via assessment and testimony help the courts determine whether or not a person should remain in the hospital. Some state hospitals also house individuals that are found incompetent to stand trial. Depending on the state, these hospitals provide competency restoration programs (i.e., programs designed to help an individual become competent so that he/she can go to trial or resolve the legal issues at hand). Forensic psychologists often develop and administer these programs.

Last but not least, some forensic psychologists are self-employed. In other words, they have their own private forensic psychology practices. Because forensic psychologists in this environment are generally free to pick and choose the types of cases they accept, the work they do is quite broad sometimes. For example, although a forensic psychologist in private practice may specialize in custody evaluations while another forensic psychologist specializes in trial consultation and jury selection, both forensic psychologists will likely work on cases in other forensic areas as well. Along these same lines, it is important to note that most private practitioners incorporate nonforensic areas into the practice. This is done in part to limit the stress involved as well as continue to keep their skills fresh in other areas (e.g., general clinical skills like psychotherapy).

Salaries

As alluded to earlier with the California Board of Parole Hearings example and as can be seen in Box 15.3, salaries tend to be quite good relative to other subfields of psychology. Starting salaries at the doctoral level for those in the clinically oriented area generally start around $65,000 to $70,000. However, this is dependent on the area of the country, the work setting, and the forensic psychologist's reputation and experience. Certainly a forensic psychologist with more experience and who is well known in his/her practicing community will likely command higher pay than someone who is just getting licensed.

Special Employment Issues

Although each employment area has idiosyncrasies related to hiring procedures, there are several issues specific to employment in the field of forensic psychology that warrant mentioning. First, background checks (along with fingerprinting) are routine. The thoroughness of the check varies (with federal positions requiring significantly more, including interviews of associates, family, etc.). Regardless, all background checks will certainly reveal arrests as well as convictions including misdemeanors (e.g., public intoxication). Traffic violations also can cause problems since they can be interpreted as risk-taking behavior. Second, drug screening preemployment (and postemployment) is also routinely done. With regard to this issue, it is important to emphasize that agents and detectives who interview friends, former friends, family, teachers, roommates, ex-boyfriends/girlfriends/wives/husbands, etc. will ask about current and past drug use. Any drug use can prevent employment in many federal positions (e.g., federal prisons). These issues are not meant to scare but to inform and prepare the person interested in working in settings that require security clearance (e.g., prisons).

Working in Areas Related to Forensic Psychology With a Bachelor's Degree

As noted earlier, opportunities to practice forensic psychology are generally limited to those individuals with advanced graduate training, likely at the doctoral level. After reading the chapter, it makes sense that the breadth and depth of knowledge required to practice adequately in this area would require such training, hence why many state and federal statutes require that doctoral-level psychologists perform many of the tasks and activities noted. For example, would you want someone with a bachelor's degree consulting on jury selection with your attorney if you were on trial for murder? We wouldn't!

Although many activities are outside the skill set of a bachelor's-level person, there are many that are not. As a matter of fact, there are quite a few opportunities for individuals who have a bachelor's degree including those who are stopping at that educational level and those who are taking some time off prior to applying for graduate school (e.g., trying the field out to see if it might be a good fit). Some of the more common ways to get involved in the forensic psychology subfield with a bachelor's degree are discussed below.

Police or Law Enforcement Officers

Although this career does not always require a bachelor's degree, the degree will put an applicant significantly ahead of those without one. Even with a bachelor's degree, officer training is required in order to learn law enforcement procedures, gun use, vehicle use, etc. Regardless, this type of position will allow intimate involvement with the justice system from arrest through incarceration. One of the benefits for an individual who may be considering this as an interim position prior to applying to graduate school, is that the duties of a police officer, including court appearances, will increase comfort with the judicial process and judicial players (e.g., judges, clerks, and attorneys). As a result, anxieties related to being in the adversarial climate will diminish, thereby making you a better witness in the future. According to the

Occupational Outlook Handbook (OOH; U.S. Department of Labor, 2008–2009), median salary was approximately $50,000 for local and state governments and $45,000 for the federal government.

Correctional Officers

According to the OOH (2008–2009), "correctional officers, also known as detention officers, are responsible for overseeing individuals who have been arrested and are awaiting trial or who have been convicted of a crime and sentenced to serve time in a jail, reformatory, or penitentiary." The OOH also indicates that salaries are relatively competitive. The median salary for correctional officers at the state and local level is approximately $35,000. Because the positions are more competitive, the median salary at the federal government level is approximately $50,000.

Adult and Juvenile Probation and Parole Officers

According to the OOH (2008–2009):

> Probation officers, who are called community supervision officers in some states, supervise people who have been placed on probation . . . . Parole officers perform many of the same duties that probation officers perform. The difference is that parole officers supervise offenders who have been released from prison, whereas probation officers work with those who are sentenced to probation instead of prison. (http://www.bls.gov/oco/ocos265.htm)

According to the OOH, the median salary for professionals in this area is approximately $45,000.

Other Positions

Some other positions that are available to applicants with a bachelor's degree in psychology include caseworker/case manager, program assistant, and mental health technician. Prior to and after being released on parole or released from the hospital, individuals can benefit from the additional support provided by a caseworker or case manager. In fact, it can be instrumental in the person remaining on the outside. Such support can include assistance in identifying mental health services, employment, medication assistance, and housing.

Another possible position at the bachelor's level is program assistant. Program assistants provide support to professional staff at shelters, domestic violence prevention programs, at-risk youth programs, etc. Regardless of the type of program, the program assistant is on the front line in serving the program's clients. This is also true of mental health technicians in the forensic hospital setting. Due to other duties and responsibilities, nurses, psychologists, and psychiatrists can not provide most of the moment-to-moment care of patients in these settings throughout the course of the day. These professionals rely heavily on mental health technicians to carry out specific activities and programs as well as provide front line and back up support to the medical staff.

Why Become a Forensic Psychologist?

Matthew T. Huss
Creighton University

Forensic psychology is one of the fastest growing fields in psychology, and much of this growth is fueled by increasing media attention. Books, movies, and television shows are making it more and more interesting to become a forensic psychologist. Although the media sometimes focuses on the more sensational and less than realistic aspects of the field, there are many genuine reasons for students interested in the area to pursue it as a career. Here are three of them.

First, one of the most interesting aspects of forensic psychology is that it is the intersection of two very different disciplines, the law and psychology. The two disciplines are inter-dependent but hold very different viewpoints, often making the intersection somewhat messy. Although forensic psychologists do not have to be psychologists *and* attorneys, you do have to be well versed in both the law and psychology. Becoming an expert in one field is difficult enough, but the additional challenge of inte-grating the law into psychology is very attractive to many people.

Second, forensic psychology offers a diversity of job opportunities. Depending on the person's training, there are many settings in which a forensic psychologist can work, including law enforcement agencies, hospitals, juvenile deten-tion facilities, government agencies, and mental health centers. A forensic psychologist can even open his or her own private practice or teach and conduct research at a college or university. This variety allows for a person to pursue many dif-ferent paths either simultaneously or consecutively during a career.

Last but not least, there is no denying the sensational aspects that attract many people to forensic psychology. These aspects are even interesting to forensic psychologists who are around them on a regular basis. Simply put, forensic psychology is *sexy*. Forensic psychologists get to meet and evaluate some of the most notorious criminals of our time such as Ted Kaczynski, Charles Manson, and Jeffrey Dahmer. Through the use of jury selection techniques, they assist attorneys in influencing the outcome of famous trials such as O. J. Simpson's criminal trial for murder and Oprah Winfrey's civil trial for defamation of the beef industry in Texas. However, even the less public cases are inherently interesting to almost anyone.

In summary, these three potential reasons to become a forensic psychologist barely scratch the surface of possibilities within the profession. However, it should excite anyone with an interest in the field and encourage them to pursue more information.

Note. Currently an associate professor of psychology at Creighton University, Dr. Matthew Huss received his doctorate in clinical psychology and a master's in legal studies from the University of Nebraska-Lincoln. He has published dozens of journal articles and book chapters and has given over 70 professional research presentations. One of his most recent publications is his book titled *Forensic Psychology: Research, Clinical Practice, and Applications* (2009). His involvement with students in their research interests has resulted in numer-ous student publications and presentations. Dr. Huss's primary research interests focus on prediction of violence, domestic violence, sex offenders, and the admissibility of scientific evidence in court.

Professional Spotlight

Gina M. Vincent, PhD

Education:
- Bachelor of Arts in Psychology from the University of Alaska – Anchorage
- Master of Arts in Law and Psychology from Simon Fraser University
- PhD in Experimental Psychology, Law and Psychology Specialization from Simon Fraser University

Employer:
University of Massachusetts Medical School – Center for Mental Health Services Research

Position:
Assistant Professor of Psychiatry

Description of Position:
My academic position is funded primarily by research grants. As a result, the duties involve writing grants, conducting grant-funded research, some mentoring and limited teaching for various psychiatry divisions (e.g., Child and Adolescent Psychiatry, Law & Psychiatry), and service activities.

Most Significant Professional Accomplishment:
My most significant professional accomplishment is receiving grants from the MacArthur Foundation and the National Institute of Mental Health for my research with juvenile offender populations.

Favorite Publication:
Vincent, G. M., Vitacco, M. J., Grisso, T., & Corrado, R. R. (2003). Subtypes of adolescent offenders: Affective traits and antisocial behavior patterns [Special issue: Juvenile psychopathy]. *Behavioral Sciences and the Law*, *21*, 695–712.

Area of Research:
My area of research is where psychology interfaces with the law pertaining to juveniles; namely, the impact of implementing risk for recidivism assessment in juvenile probation, identification of psychopathic personality disorder in youth, and mental disorder in juvenile justice.

Professional Memberships:
- American Psychology-Law Society
  - Psychopathy Specialty Reviewer (Chair)
  - APLS Conference Co-chair (2009)
- International Association of Forensic Mental Health Services
  - Scientific Review Committee
- Society for the Scientific Study of Psychopathy (SSSP)
- American Psychological Association

Most Rewarding Aspect of Your Career:
The most rewarding aspect of my career is working with juvenile justice agencies to put research findings into practice and change juvenile justice policy in a manner that is in line with adolescent development.

Words of Advice to the Student Who Is Interested in Your Subfield:
If you are interested in the psychology and law field, I recommend going to one of the graduate universities that has a specialized program in this area. If you do not pursue a clinical degree, most likely you will end up in academe or in a policy-related position. Given where these fields are headed, I strongly recommend getting grant writing experience during graduate school.

Suggested Exercises

1. The APLS website (www.ap-ls.org) has a "Job Listings" page that gives information on academic, nonacademic, and training opportunities. Choose one position opening from each category and answer the following questions.
   - What type of position is it (academic, nonacademic, postdoctoral fellowship)?
   - Where is the position?
   - How does an applicant apply?
   - What does a person include in his/her application?
   - What training is required for the position?
2. Locate an issue of one of the top journals listed in this chapter. Answer the following questions.
   - What are some of the topics studied?
   - Where do the authors work?
   - Were any of the authors students?
3. For one of the authors cited in this chapter or on the APLS web page, do a web search for information on him/her. Answer the following questions:
   - Where does the person work?
   - What is the person's job (e.g., professor, student, clinician)?
   - What other publications/presentations does the person have?

- If the person is a professor, what courses do they teach?
- What are some of the topics they study?

4. Research one of the forensically oriented graduate programs listed in the article by Helms and Mayhew (2006) or on the APLS Student Section web page. Answer the following questions:
   - What is the name of the program?
   - What degrees does the program offer?
   - What are the application procedures?
   - When is the application deadline?
   - Do they require entrance exams (e.g., the GRE)? If so, what are the minimum scores? More importantly, what are the average scores of recent students?
   - What other requirements do they have for admission?
   - What, if any, financial support do they provide their students?
   - What do their students end up doing when they graduate?
   - What is their acceptance rate? How many people apply? How many people do they accept? How many people actually come to the program?

Suggested Readings

Case Examples in Forensic Psychology

Ewing, C. P. (2008). *Trials of a forensic psychologist: A casebook*. New York: John Wiley & Sons.

Meyer, R. G., & Weaver, C. M. (2006). *Law and mental health: A case-based approach*. New York: Guilford Press.

General Forensic Psychology

Fulero, S. M., & Wrightsman, L. S. (2008). *Forensic psychology* (3rd ed.). Belmont, CA: Wadsworth.

Goldstein, A. M. (Ed.). (2006). *Forensic psychology: Emerging topics and expanding roles*. New York: John Wiley & Sons.

Kuther, T. L. (2004). *Your career in psychology: Psychology and the law*. Belmont, CA: Thomson/ Wadsworth.

Weiner, I. B., & Hess, A. K. (Eds.). (2005). *The handbook of forensic psychology* (3rd ed.). New York: John Wiley & Sons. (This book also contains information relevant to the civil forensic psychology domain.)

Interrogations and Confessions

Gudjonsson, G. H. (2003). *The psychology of interrogations and confessions: A handbook*. West Sussex, England: John Wiley & Sons.

Juvenile Forensic Psychology

Grisso, T., & Schwartz, R. (Eds.). (2001). *Youth on trial: A developmental perspective on juvenile justice*. Chicago: University of Chicago Press.

Heilbrun, K., Goldstein, N. E. S., & Redding, R. E. (Eds.). (2005). *Juvenile delinquency: Prevention, assessment, and intervention.* New York: Oxford University Press.

Trial Consultation

Posey, A. J., & Wrightsman, L. S. (2005). *Trial consulting.* New York: Oxford University Press.

References

American Psychological Association. (2003). *Archival description: Specialty of forensic psychology.* Retrieved from http://www.apa.org/crsppp/archivforensic.html

Bartol, C. R., & Bartol, A. M. (1999). History of forensic psychology. In A. K. Hess & I. B. Weiner (Eds.), *Handbook of forensic psychology* (2nd ed., pp. 3–23). New York: John Wiley & Sons.

DiCataldo, F., Whitworth, D., Russo, R., Hanigan, B., MacHardy, M., Berman, G., et al. (2008, March). *A survey of forensic mental health directors on the clinical role and duties of master's-level forensic psychology professionals.* Paper presented at the American Psychology – Law Society annual conference, Jacksonville, FL.

Dusky v. United States, 362 U.S. 402 (1960).

Forensic Specialty Council. (2007). *Education and training guidelines for forensic psychology.*

Helms, J. L. (2008, March). *Forensic psychology program rankings.* Poster session presented at the American Psychology – Law Society annual conference, Jacksonville, FL.

Helms, J. L. (2009, March). *Forensic psychology journal rankings.* Poster session presented at the American Psychology – Law Society annual conference, San Antonio, TX.

Helms, J. L., & Mayhew, L. L. (2006). *Undergraduate preparation for graduate training in forensic psychology.* APA Division 2–Society for the Teaching of Psychology's Office of Teaching Resources in Psychology. Retrieved from http://teachpsych.org/otrp/resources/helms06.pdf

Henggeler, S. W., Rowland, M. R., Randall, J., Ward, D., Pickrel, S. G., Cunningham, P. B., et al. (1999). Home-based multisystemic therapy as an alternative to the hospitalization of youth in psychiatric crisis: Clinical outcomes. *Journal of the American Academy of Child & Adolescent Psychiatry, 38,* 1331–1339.

Huss, M. T. (2009). *Forensic psychology: Research, clinical practice, and applications.* Boston: Wiley-Blackwell.

MacKain, S. J., Tedeschi, R. G., Durham, T. W., & Goldman, V. J. (2002). So what are master's-level psychology practitioners doing? Surveys of employers and recent graduates in North Carolina. *Professional Psychology: Research and Practice, 33,* 408–412.

Miranda v. Arizona, 384 US 436 (1966).

U.S. Department of Labor, Bureau of Labor Statistics. (2008–2009). Occupational outlook handbook. Retrieved from http://www.bls.gov/oco/

Resources

American Psychology-Law Society – Division 41 of the American Psychological Association
• http://www.ap-ls.org/
American Board of Forensic Psychology
• http://www.abfp.com/

16

Careers in Academe

Academe Defined

Academe refers to the academic (i.e., higher education) community and environment. Careers in this area include not only the traditional profession of university professor but also administrative positions like institute directors, department chairs, deans, and university presidents. According to the U.S. Department of Labor, Bureau of Labor Statistics' Occupational Outlook Handbook (OOH; 2008–2009), there were approximately 37,000 postsecondary (i.e., college/university) psychology teaching jobs in 2006. This is not surprising given that the leading employment setting for those with a doctorate in psychology is a college or university (Wicherski & Kohout, 2007). In fact, the majority of recipients of doctoral degrees in the non-health service provider areas of psychology (e.g., Cognitive Psychology, Social Psychology, Experimental Psychology) pursue academic-related employment upon graduation (Wicherski & Kohout). Additionally, the OOH indicates that the outlook for employment of all postsecondary teachers is positive and increasing. As such this is an excellent career to consider pursuing.

Employment Settings

Types of Settings

Although the types of settings for academic employment vary, many are already familiar to you. The main settings for psychologists in academe are technical schools, community/junior colleges, 4-year colleges, universities, professional psychology schools, and medical schools (Wicherski & Kohout, 2007).

Technical schools typically have a very limited psychology curriculum, oftentimes only offering General Psychology and Developmental Psychology. This limited curriculum makes sense given that the major areas of study in this setting will be more in line with employment-related skill areas like practical nursing, culinary arts, respiratory therapy, and automotive repair. Programs offered in technical schools are often geared toward certification in a particular skill area (e.g., computer programming) and are time-limited (i.e., 2 years or less).

Community colleges (sometimes called junior colleges) are similar to the technical schools in that they offer many of the same vocational training programs. However, community colleges also offer 2-year programs of study that often result in an associate's degree. These 2-year degrees almost always focus on general education requirements (e.g., English, Math, and Science). As a result, the psychology curriculum is also usually very limited since the focus is on what are referred to as foundational courses associated with the first 2 years of college.

Four-year colleges confer bachelor's degrees, including psychology degrees. These colleges rarely have graduate programs but instead focus the overwhelming part of their energies and resources on undergraduate education. Most 4-year colleges have a psychology program, including a full curriculum.

Universities are similar to 4-year colleges in that they also have a wide variety of undergraduate degree programs, including psychology. However, in addition to the undergraduate programs, universities have extensive graduate program offerings, sometimes including psychology.

Professional psychology schools can be within a university setting or freestanding (i.e., not affiliated with a university). These programs focus exclusively on graduate training in psychology and are usually private (i.e., not state/government funded). As a result, these institutions (especially freestanding schools) derive most of their operating expenses from tuition, which is usually significantly higher than state-supported schools. These schools also tend to have lower admission standards and higher acceptance rates (Norcross, Kohout, & Wicherski, 2005). University-based professional psychology schools have less of these issues. (Note: Be careful! The terms "college" and "university" are not legally protected terms. This lack of protection means that anyone can refer to the school that offers even one degree program as a college or university. This is common among professional schools and can be misleading to students.) Faculty at professional psychology schools focus almost exclusively on teaching required course-work and training activities (e.g., supervising students learning psychological tests).

Medical schools are similar to professional schools in that psychology faculty in this setting are predominantly involved in training activities. Additionally, faculty may be conducting research in hospital clinics, training predoctoral interns, or supervising postdoctoral residents. Regardless, their function is predominantly applied.

Setting Matters

Although the actual activities are described in the Professorial Activities section later in the chapter, it deserves mentioning here that setting does matter. Relative emphasis on the major activities (i.e., teaching, professional service, and research) varies significantly. In technical schools, community colleges, and professional psychology schools, the emphasis is heavily weighted toward teaching. As a result, there is limited and sometimes no expectation to contribute to the discipline in other ways (e.g., research). At 4-year colleges and universities emphasis on teaching relative to research varies. At research-intensive universities there are high expectations regarding research productivity (i.e., publishing research and garnering grant money) and lower expectations regarding teaching. Approximately 25% of academic positions are in this type of setting (Berger, Kirshstein, & Rowe, 2001). Less emphasis on research productivity is seen at 4-year colleges and more teaching-focused universities. However, keep in mind that the term "less" does not mean "none." In fact, most 4-year colleges and almost all universities expect that a portion of a professor's time will be devoted to research activities and publishing.

Because of the emphasis on research, universities typically require less teaching. It is not unusual at very research-intensive universities for faculty to teach only two or three courses during an academic year, sometimes less. At 4-year colleges and less research-intensive universities, the teaching load can hover around six to eight courses per year. At community colleges and technical schools where research expectations generally do not exist, teaching loads can be around 10 to 12 courses per year.

Professorial Activities

Professorial activities fall into three major domains. These domains are teaching, supervision, and mentoring; research; and professional service. In addition to addressing each of these domains separately, Box 16.1 provides a list of the top tasks associated with being a psychology professor.

Teaching, Supervision, and Mentoring

As the name suggests, the major activities in this domain center on direct interaction with students. These activities are typically the ones that students and outside observers use to describe a career in academe. Interestingly, being inside the classroom and having direct contact with students are relatively small parts of the work week for a faculty member. However, the activities that lead up to and follow being in the classroom and meeting with students devour a large portion of the faculty member's time. One of these activities is course preparation. Although some material changes little from year to year at the undergraduate level (e.g., elementary statistics), other material changes considerably. Developments in the respective subfields of psychology occur almost daily. As a result, the professor must keep up to date on the recent research in the field as well as new texts that become available. Once the professor is up to date in her/his respective area, the materials used in the course must be updated. Depending on the developments, these updates can take weeks of preparation prior to the semester starting along with significant amounts of time during the semester. This preparation is done with the specific intent of making time in front of the class as enriching as possible. In short, the syllabus, presentation slides, movie clips, handouts, activities, etc. are the culmination of significant effort by the professor, effort that is rarely seen by the students and outside observers.

In addition to course preparation activities, the professor also has evaluative responsibilities. Making and grading tests, essays, homework assignments, and term papers

Box 16.1 Top Tasks Associated With Being a Psychology Professor

1. Develop and give lectures to students
2. Evaluate and grade students' work (laboratory work, assignments, term papers)
3. Initiate, facilitate, and moderate class discussions
4. Develop, administer, and grade examinations
5. Keep up to date on developments in the respective field (e.g., reading the current literature, attending professional conferences)
6. Prepare course materials (e.g., assignments, syllabi)
7. Revise curriculum, course content, and course materials
8. Maintain student records (e.g., grades)
9. Supervise students' laboratory work
10. Supervise students' field and research work
11. Maintain office hours for student advising
12. Conduct and publish research in the field of expertise
13. Provide career and academic advisement to students
14. Select and obtain materials (e.g., textbooks)
15. Work with colleagues to address problems that arise in teaching and research
16. Serve on departmental and university committees
17. Perform administrative duties (e.g., serving as department chair)
18. Develop materials for reading assignments
19. Participate in new student recruitment and orientation activities
20. Advise student organizations
21. Write grants to secure external funding for research activities
22. Participate in campus and community events
23. Consult with government and businesses

Note. Information comes from Occupational Information Network (O*NET; 2005).

take significant chunks of a professor's time. Once you "do the math" it becomes quite clear. Let's take an abnormal psychology term paper. If a professor spends 30 minutes reading/grading/giving feedback on each student's term paper, then grading papers for a class of 30 students would take 15 hours to complete. Since most professors would be teaching a couple of other courses alongside this one, a completion time of 45 hours would not be unrealistic. Remember, this estimate is for only one assignment. Of course, we know what the student is thinking. "Don't assign term papers!" As you will learn in the Careers in Clinical Psychology and Counseling Psychology chapter, one of the skills that set us apart from other professions is our assessment skills (i.e., our ability to develop reliable and valid tests and measures). As such we know that measuring student learning in more than one way is better than giving only one opportunity or one type of measure. As a result, students will often have term papers, exams that have different types of questions (e.g., multiple choice, short answer, and essay), participation points, group activity grades, and homework assignments as part of a course. Rest assured; for most of us professors, grading is our least favorite activity.

Professors also spend time supervising and mentoring. The supervision piece includes activities like observing a graduate student administering a psychological test or working with a patient that is depressed for the first time. Supervision also occurs with undergraduate students who participate in research and field practicum activities, valuable experiences for all involved. Mentoring of students often occurs informally but can also have more formal aspects. The more formal aspects include meeting with an advisor and completing a directed study with a professor. Interestingly, for some professors, supervision and mentoring activities often involve other faculty members as the supervisee or mentee. For faculty members just beginning their careers it is important that colleagues be there to support the transition from graduate student to faculty member.

Research

Although many different words can be used to describe the activities in this area (e.g., scholarship, creative activities), the bottom line is that careers in academe generally require research activity. Research activities include developing research protocols and procedures, administering tests, entering data, statistically analyzing data, interpreting the results, and presenting the results to the broader community. Even though more time will be spent in the process leading up to this presentation, making the findings available to a wider audience is often the defining aspect of this professorial activity. As a result, significant quantities of time are spent writing. Once the writing is complete, the paper/article can be submitted to conferences for possible inclusion in the presentation schedules. The paper/article is also often submitted for publication in a peer-reviewed journal, keeping in mind that most articles submitted for publication are rejected.

An additional piece to research activities is the cost involved in some faculty member's research activities. Although some faculty members are fully financially supported by the university (an extremely rare circumstance) and some faculty do not require significant financial support for his/her particular research activities, many faculty require financial support to accomplish the research that is required for their academic position. As such, many faculty seek funding from external sources (i.e., grants). Grants can come from federal, state, and local governments as well as private philanthropic organizations or foundations. Regardless of the grant's origin, they are extremely competitive. However, the grant received may provide for a faculty member's salary over the summer months when not under contract or being paid. It may also pay for trips to conferences to present research findings. These trips are often not fully covered by the university, although they are often required as part of the job.

Professional Service

Last but not least, professional service is the third major domain of professional activities for those with a career in academe. Professional service can be broken down into two broad areas, university-based and community-based. University-based professional service includes activities in the faculty member's own department and outside the department. These activities include serving on committees and advising student organizations. Some committees that a faculty may serve on include committees that revise the curriculum, committees that select applicants to interview for position openings, and committees that address student academic concerns (e.g., plagiarism and cheating). This type of service ensures the smooth operation of the faculty member's department and the university as a whole.

Community-based professional service includes activities that center on the larger profession as well as the community outside the university (local, state, and beyond). Professional service to the larger profession may include such activities as serving as editor of a professional journal as well as serving as president, secretary, etc. of a professional association (e.g., one of the divisions of the American Psychological Association; http://www.apa.org/about/division.html). Professional service also may include providing expertise to the community. This service can include having a small private practice, serving on the board of directors of an organization, helping a nonprofit agency evaluate their services, etc. Regardless of the setting, the intent of the service is to help move that person, group, or organization closer to a defined goal (e.g., reaching more people in need of services). The service itself springs out of the expertise the faculty member has relative to her/his educational background and training. It is important to note that professional service activities also require a large portion of the faculty member's time.

Relative Emphasis

Relative emphasis of each of the three domains of activities varies significantly from university to university. As noted in the previous section, research intensive universities (e.g., University of Georgia, University of California–Los Angeles) value research productivity and garnering external funding (i.e., grants) the most. As a result, significantly less emphasis is given to activities in the teaching and service areas. However, this does not equate to *no* emphasis. In more teaching-focused academic settings, teaching comes first, meaning that the bulk of a professor's time, energy, and evaluation is spent in teaching, supervision, and mentoring activities. However, this does not mean that research and professional service are not valued or expected. That interpretation is not correct. It is all relative.

Working Conditions

Although the term "working conditions" typically refers to the actual work space (e.g., lighting, air quality), it is used here to describe the environmental, intangible, and relationship components of the academic profession that are not as easily quantified as salary and benefit packages. Although not easily quantifiable, these conditions significantly contribute to a person's quality of life. Box 16.2 lists some of these factors.

As emphasis on particular activities varies from one academic setting to another so too do working conditions vary. Some of the variability can be due to collegiality

> **Box 16.2** Top 10 Physical and Social Factors That Influence the Nature of the Work for Psychology Professors
>
> 1. Allows freedom to make decisions
> 2. Involves significant use of electronic mail
> 3. Involves face-to-face discussions
> 4. Significantly more unstructured than structured
> 5. Involves working indoors
> 6. Involves telephone conversations
> 7. Involves public speaking
> 8. Involves significant amounts of interaction with others
> 9. Long work week
> 10. Time pressure
>
> *Note.* Information comes from O*NET (2005).

issues (i.e., how well the coworkers get along with one another). Collegiality is difficult to determine as an outsider. That is, by the time a person finds out there is little collegiality it is often too late and the person has already accepted the position and started working. However, there are working conditions that can be explored prior to employment.

Academic Freedom

One of the cornerstones to academe is the concept of academic freedom. In defining academic freedom, the American Association of University Professors (AAUP; 1940/1970) states that "Teachers are entitled to full freedom in research and in the publication of the results. . . . Teachers are entitled to freedom in the classroom in discussing their subject . . ." (http://www.aaup.org/AAUP/pubsres/policydocs/contents/1940statement. htm). Without an environment that embraces this freedom, advances in the respective fields are potentially prevented. As a result, more than 200 education and scientific groups endorse the statement and principles underlying it. These organizations include the American Psychological Association's endorsement in 1961 and the Association for Psychological Science's endorsement in 1989. For a list of those colleges and universities that are currently censured (i.e., "unsatisfactory conditions of academic freedom and tenure have been found to prevail at these institutions") by the AAUP, please see their website at http://www.aaup.org/AAUP/censuredadmins/

Facilities and Support

Facilities and support are additional pieces that contribute to the working conditions in academe. Typically, fulltime professors get their own offices, computer equipment, phone, and furniture. Office supplies and some office support (i.e., secretarial help) are also common. However, updating existing equipment and office space rarely happens. As a result, it is not uncommon for a newly hired faculty member to receive a new computer and for that faculty member to have that same computer, monitor, printer, etc. five, ten, or more years. Student computer labs, university resources (e.g., faculty gyms), and laboratory space varies considerably in amount and quality. In short, facilities differ from institution to institution. For those of you who have transferred colleges, we guess that there are some significant differences between the buildings, computer labs, etc. in your current school compared to your last school.

Work Schedule

One of the most attractive parts of a career in academe is the flexibility in the work schedule. Although there are limits to the flexibility, as long as a faculty member "gets the job done," that member is often free to set her/his own office hours and also can have a voice in choosing the times of course offerings (e.g., days, evenings). The reason that the flexibility works relatively well is that faculty members typically work long hours and take work home with them, including over holiday/semester breaks. For example, as I (Helms) am writing this section it is 12:30 on a Saturday afternoon in June. The important piece to take away from the flexibility is that in order to be successful in a career in academe, a person has to be a self-starter and self-motivated. There is not a lot of supervision (i.e., someone looking over your shoulder). Instead, there is the expectation that a faculty member will seek out opportunities and direction as needed. On this same note it is important to point out that the career in academe is not really a job or a career but rather a lifestyle. By lifestyle it is meant that the boundaries between work and home are often blurred, which may not fit for some people. Boundaries are blurred in the sense that not only do almost all faculty take work home with them in the evenings or on weekends/holidays but also many of their outside work activities involve fellow faculty members and their families. In other words, faculty members often spend social time together outside of work, not out of obligation but out of a genuine desire and interest to do so.

Educational Degree and Training Needed

Although a master's degree is sufficient for many community and technical colleges, competition is increasing. As a result, a doctoral degree will put you in a better place as an applicant. However, for colleges and universities the entry-level degree is the doctorate. More specifically, the doctor of philosophy degree (PhD) in psychology is the degree of choice. The particular area within psychology is less of an issue in that it depends on a hiring department's needs. For example, a recent advertisement for a job opening at our university did not indicate a specific area within psychology. Instead, the advertisement indicated the need for a person with experience in teaching Research Methods and Experimental Psychology. This specified need of our department left the field open. As a result, we received applications from every subfield of psychology including Social Psychology, Clinical Psychology, Experimental Psychology, Cognitive Psychology, Health Psychology, etc.

There is an important note to be made regarding the emphasis on the PhD degree relative to other doctoral degrees, specifically the doctor of psychology degree (PsyD). Discrimination is still rampant in the academic community relative to the PsyD degree. As a result, it is more difficult to get an academic position with the PsyD degree relative to the PhD degree. The discrimination is based on the inaccurate belief that individuals with PsyD degrees are incapable of doing the quality or quantity of research necessary for the position. Of course, this is a stereotype. As with most stereotypes, examples are available to bolster the argument for discrimination. Additionally, self-selection into a PsyD program usually means a desire to practice in a clinical setting, not teach and do research, meaning that few with the PsyD degree will pursue careers in academe.

Interestingly, the majority of doctoral programs provide no formal training in teaching skills. In fact, most "training" occurs on the job. That is, graduate students are assigned a course to teach as part of a teaching assistantship. The belief is that since a student has been a student for most of his/her life the student will naturally know what to do when confronted with the tasks involved. Of course, the same is not said for the research activities required in the position where graduate students spend most of their graduate training learning how to do good research. Regardless, some graduate programs are beginning to incorporate courses on teaching. In fact, a program, Preparing Future Faculty, was developed in 1993 that begins to address the inadequacies for preparing future faculty members.

> The Preparing Future Faculty (PFF) program is a national movement to transform the way aspiring faculty members are prepared for their careers. PFF programs provide doctoral students, as well as some master's and postdoctoral students, with opportunities to observe and experience faculty responsibilities at a variety of academic institutions with varying missions, diverse student bodies, and different expectations for faculty. (http://www.preparing-faculty.org/)

As part of the PFF program, a graduate student will have the opportunity to learn strategies to increase success as a future faculty member in the three main domains described earlier (i.e., teaching, supervision, and mentoring; research; and professional service). Given the traditional emphasis on research mentoring in graduate school (and assuming the students are already receiving sufficient mentoring in that area), many of the university programs participating in the PFF program and similar programs spend relatively more time mentoring future faculty in the domain of teaching compared to universities that do not participate. Some of the universities that have participated in the PFF program or have similar types of programs include Miami University (OH), University of Colorado-Boulder, University of Georgia, and University of New Hampshire. Sponsored by the Society for the Teaching of Psychology (Division 2 of the American Psychological Association), Howard, Buskist, and Stowell (2007) developed a resource guide to graduate student training in the teaching of psychology. The guide lists almost 50 graduate programs in psychology in 25 states that provide students with the opportunity to receive training in the domain of teaching.

Rank

As is the case with many careers, there are designated ranks associated with faculty positions. Here are some of the most common position rank/status designations.

Part-time/Adjunct Faculty

Part-time/adjunct faculty are contracted to teach typically only one or two courses for a particular semester. As a result of their part-time status, they do not receive benefits. There are also no expectations to provide professional service or engage in research activities. In addition, there is no expectation that an adjunct faculty member will teach the following semester or year.

Visiting Faculty

Visiting faculty are also contracted for a specified length of time, typically one or two years. Although duties vary, visiting faculty usually teach heavy loads. There is usually low or no expectations regarding professional service and research productivity. Due to the fulltime status of the position, visiting faculty receive benefits. However, once the contract is finished there is no opportunity to continue in the position.

Research and Clinical Faculty

Research and clinical faculty members' duties focus on the respective role. For research faculty, they were hired specifically to conduct research or supervise student research. For clinical faculty, they were hired specifically to train students in clinical skills and supervise their work with patients. As such, research and clinical faculty typically do not "teach" in the traditional sense but rather supervise. Depending on the nature of their duties, research and clinical faculty can be fulltime or part-time. Additionally, their positions may be time-limited (i.e., only for a specific length of time) or continuing (i.e., ongoing with no definite stop date to the contract).

Fulltime Faculty

These faculty are traditionally the ones most often encountered by students. Fulltime faculty include instructors, assistant professors, associate professors, and full professors. Instructors typically hold only the master's degree. As such, depending on the institution, they are not eligible for promotion to the professorial ranks. Instructors typically are utilized in lower-level courses like Introduction to Psychology. The typical entry point to a career in academe is the assistant professor level. Promotion to the ranks of associate professor and full professor are not automatic. This process is described later in the chapter. Regardless, the typical progress when promotion occurs is from assistant professor to associate professor to full professor.

Due to the fulltime nature of the position, all fulltime faculty enjoy benefit packages (e.g., retirement and insurance). However, until tenured, fulltime faculty still
operate under a contractual system that typically runs one year at a time. Because of
the uncertainty this creates, tenure is briefly described later in the chapter.

Salaries

The mean salary for all postsecondary psychology teachers in 2006 was $64,580
(http://www.bls.gov/oes/current/oes251066.htm; U.S. Department of Labor, Bureau
of Labor Statistics, 2007). This mean includes all ranks. As a result, it may be more
illustrative to look at the entry-level rank of the assistant professor. Table 16.1 lists the
mean salaries of assistant professors based on setting.

It is important to remember that salaries vary based in part on location. For example,
the mean salary in 2006 for a psychology professor (all ranks) was $71,760 in
Massachusetts and $45,170 in Arizona (U.S. Department of Labor, Bureau of Labor
Statistics, 2007). The reason that the starting point is so important is that salaries in
academe are very slow to rise. Given that there are typically only two promotions
in a professor's lifetime (i.e., from assistant to associate and from associate to full
professor) and neither are guaranteed, starting salary becomes even more important.
Some people suggest that the lower salary and sparse raises are offset by the fact that
most faculty contracts are for 9–10 months (i.e., faculty have their summers "off").
Although it is true that many elementary, middle, and high school teachers have
summers off from work, this is not the case with faculty for the most part. Although
faculty do not get paid during the summer (unless they teach summer school which
is not always available or guaranteed and is not paid at the same rate as salary), faculty
generally are in their offices catching up on research and preparing for the following
semester, activities they are not able to complete during their contract due to other
pressures on their time. Although faculty can sometimes supplement their salaries with
consulting work and grants at some schools (not all schools allow outside consulting),

Table 16.1 Mean Salaries of Assistant Professors Based on Setting

Setting	Mean Salary
University Psychology Department	55,097
University Education Department	56,164
University Business School	104,231
4-year College – Psychology Department	49,162
4-year College – Education Department	64,500
2-year College	53,143
Medical School – Psychiatry Department	64,741
University-Affiliated Professional School of Psychology	58,250
Other Professional School of Psychology	64,250

Note. Information comes from Center for Psychology Workforce Analysis and Research (2007).

as is the case with most careers, the "best" way to increase salary is to leave for a better/higher paying position. Unlike other jobs, finding employment is not easy, and when employment is found, it almost always requires moving to another state. This fact, obviously, is a significant disincentive to moving, especially once "roots are planted."

Finding Employment

Finding employment in academe can be tough. As noted in the previous section, the job seeker should be prepared to move. It is a rarity when a person does not have to make several significant moves to accomplish the goal of becoming a psychology professor and working in academe. Although there are lots of positions available, they are not typically next door, across town, or at the local university. As a matter of fact, most universities will not hire their own graduates for positions. Universities often want to bring in people with different backgrounds, training, and perspectives. As a result, the job search is typically at least regional if not national/international.

In terms of obtaining employment, Wicherski and Kohout's (2007) doctoral employment survey indicates that the most often used job search strategies included informal strategies (71.7%), use of the Internet/electronic resources (32.4%), advertisements in APA's *Monitor on Psychology* (26.6%), faculty advisors (26.9%), newspaper classified advertisements (20.5%), and *Chronicle of Higher Education* advertisements (16.5%). This same survey found that the most successful method was informal channels (i.e., friends, colleagues, and professors). Box 16.3 provides a list of websites that post academic position openings in psychology.

As noted previously, careers in academe are more consistent with a lifestyle than a 9-to-5 job. As such the interview process for a faculty position is often quite different from other careers. Interviews tend to be significantly longer, up to three days in some situations. This makes sense given that most interviewees will not be local and will need to fly. In addition to the process being longer due to travel requirements, the process is also longer due to the incorporation of one or two presentations that are typically required. One presentation is typically a lecture on a course topic, and the other presentation is on the applicant's research program. In addition to interviews with those in administration (e.g., the department chair, dean, vice president, provost), interviews with the current faculty also occur. These interviews occur both formally

---

Box 16.3   Websites That Post Academic Position Openings in Psychology

American Psychological Association	http://jobs.psyccareers.com/
Association for Psychological Science	http://www.psychologicalscience.org/jobs/
Chronicle of Higher Education	http://chronicle.com/
HigherEdJobs.com	http://www.higheredjobs.com/

and informally. The informal interviews take place on the ride to and from the airport and hotel and discussions over breakfast, lunch, and dinner. During the process, the department may also set up time for you to meet with a realtor in order to learn about housing, schools, etc. In all, it is a long and generally intense process.

Many applicants do not even get interviews. In the broad search we mentioned that our department recently completed, we received over 170 applications for one position. Obviously, some positions at some schools receive far fewer applications. Additionally, and unlike other careers, academic positions almost always start in the Fall semester (i.e., August/September). As such, the interview season starts with application for positions in the Fall, interview for positions in the Spring, acceptance of a position/offer in February/March/April, relocation in the Summer, and initiation of the faculty position in the Fall. In other words, a very long process.

You Do Not Just Get to Stay!

Given the length of training, the accompanying educational background, and a grueling interview process, it would seem that a deep sigh of relief could be released upon securing that faculty position. The reality is that the work then begins because you do not just get to stay. A faculty member must demonstrate effectiveness in each of the three major domains noted earlier (i.e., teaching, supervision, and mentoring; research; and professional service). Effectiveness is evaluated by the department chair typically on an annual basis. A third-year review also takes place typically and incorporates feedback on a faculty member's work since his/her arrival. This feedback is provided not only by the department chair but also by peers/colleagues. In the fifth or sixth year of employment, the faculty member must apply for tenure. The application includes evidence of effectiveness in each of the three major domains and is typically submitted in the form of portfolios. Promotion to the associate professor level is usually addressed at this time as well. The tenure decision is made by the department chair, tenured department faculty, the college dean, the vice president of academic affairs or the provost, and the president of the university. Generally, all levels of review must be favorable for a faculty member to receive tenure and promotion. If it is not a favorable review, the faculty member is given a year to find another position (i.e., enough time to go through one academic job search cycle). Prior to tenure, there is no guarantee of another year of employment (i.e., a contract renewal). This is why the annual reviews and demonstrating effectiveness are so important. Tenure guarantees a contract renewal (except in the most unusual and extreme circumstances).

After tenure, posttenure review is typically done every 5 years. This process is less strenuous but gives an opportunity for the faculty member to receive critical feedback on his/her work. Annual reviews continue for all faculty members typically. Eligibility for promotion from associate to full professor typically requires 5 years in the associate rank prior to application for promotion. It is important to note that many professional psychology schools (especially the private freestanding ones) do not have a tenure process. As such, employment is most often in the form of a contract, resulting in significantly less stable employment over the course of time.

Working in the Teaching Area With a Bachelor's Degree

As mentioned previously, teaching at the college level requires a minimum of a master's degree due in part to accreditation standards. However, a doctorate is really the entry-level degree. As a result, for someone interested in the teaching domain who does not want to pursue a graduate degree, teaching psychology at the high school level is the best alternative. Teaching at the high school level requires a teaching certificate from the respective state's board of education. Students interested in this route are encouraged to seek guidance from their university's education department. In fact, many students choose to double major in Education and Psychology, typically adding only one semester to their bachelor's degree program. For those farther into their under-graduate education or those nearing graduation, many states offer a program for people interested in teaching that have degrees outside of education. These programs allow a person to complete the training necessary to get a teaching certificate usually in a relatively brief period of time (e.g., 12 months). Additionally, some states will allow you to teach in the meantime on an "emergency" or temporary license (particularly in underserved areas). Again, students interested in this option are encouraged to contact an advisor in their education department.

Teaching psychology courses at the high school level is competitive since it is often viewed as an elective (and fun!). However, most high schools do offer an introductory psychology course. Some even have Advanced Placement courses, meaning if a student passes an exam the student will get college credit for it. As a result, these courses are usually very rigorous. As a matter of fact, there is an entire organization within the American Psychological Association devoted to teaching psychology in high school! Information can be found at http://www.apa.org/ed/topss/homepage.html.

Being an Academic Psychologist

A Great Career Choice

Randolph A. Smith
Lamar University

In many ways, being an academic psychologist is like an extension of being a student. If you really enjoy the student role and lifestyle, then academe may be a good career choice for you. Here are three questions to consider.

1. *Do you enjoy learning?* Academic psychologists are constantly learning. The negative stereo-type of a professor involves someone who pulls out old, yellowed lecture notes and goes to class teaching the same thing year after year. Nothing could be farther from the truth! In 30+ years of teaching, many "facts" that I used to teach are no longer factual. My experience illustrates why it is so important to never

stop learning and why academic psychologists value life-long learning so highly. It is our job to keep up on the latest research and discoveries in our field so that we can share it with students like you.

2. *Do you enjoy research?* As the book's authors point out, staying active in research is also part of the job for professors. Professors have the job not only of spreading knowledge through teaching but also of creating new knowledge through research activity. The majority of research produced in psychology comes not from psychologists who are fulltime researchers but from the labs of academic psychologists. Although they may not have a laboratory full of rats, they do have classrooms full of waiting psychology students, who are most often the participants in psychology experiments—you may have even had that opportunity. Academic psychologists conduct research on virtually every topic represented in your introductory psychology class, so teaching is not a barrier for any research specialization a faculty member may want to pursue.

3. *Do you enjoy working with people?* Psychology professors have the opportunity (and responsibility) to work with a variety of different people including students, other faculty, administrators, and the public. Although it may be obvious that professors teach students, they may also serve as mentors to students. Faculty work with other faculty a great deal – often on committees at the department, college, or university level (some of the service the book's authors mentioned). Professors also interact with administrators (e.g., deans, directors, vice presidents) to varying degrees. These interactions tend to take on importance because the faculty member is representing the department to the higher administration.

Being able to get along with, work well with, and enjoy working with a variety of people is an important trait for psychology professors.

If you answered these questions positively, take the next step. Find a mentor—a faculty member who will take a special interest in you, your education, and career goals. Often, someone who supervises you in a research project is a good candidate for a mentor. Perhaps your department has a shadowing program in which you spend a day (or longer) with a faculty member, learning what they do in their job. Perhaps your department has an undergraduate assistantship program in which you could serve as a teaching or research assistant to a faculty member. If none of these situations fit you, choose a faculty member to approach and ask if you can work in his or her research lab. Securing a mentor *and* obtaining research experience is a double bonus! If you ask most faculty, I believe that they will be able to mention a faculty member who was instrumental in helping them get on track or inspiring them as an undergraduate. Best wishes as you pursue your dream!

Note. Dr. Smith is chair of and professor of psychology in the Department of Psychology at Lamar University. Dr. Smith has over 60 publications and nearly 100 professional presentations, many centering on teaching issues. He spent 12 years as editor of the premier scholarly teaching journal, *Teaching of Psychology*. Dr. Smith is a Fellow of both APA Division One (General Psychology) and Division Two (Society for the Teaching of Psychology). His significant contributions to the field were recognized in 2006 when he was awarded the highest teaching award in the profession of psychology, the American Psychological Foundation's Charles L. Brewer Distinguished Teaching of Psychology Award.

Professional Spotlight

Janie H. Wilson, PhD

Education:
- Bachelor of Science in Psychology from the College of Charleston
- Instead of a master's degree, I completed a qualifying project (much like a master's thesis) to move forward in the PhD program.
- PhD in Experimental Psychology from the University of South Carolina

Employer:
Georgia Southern University (Statesboro, GA)

Position:
Professor of Psychology

Description of Position:
I teach both graduates and undergraduates in Psychology. I also conduct research and am active in service.

Most Significant Professional Accomplishment:
It is a tie between the Georgia Southern University *Award for Excellence in Contributions to Instruction* and a grant from the National Institute of Mental Health for rat research.

Favorite Publications:
Wilson, J. H. (2001). Prolactin in rats is attenuated by conspecific touch in a novel environment. *Cognitive, Affective, and Behavioral Neuroscience, 1,* 199–205.
Wilson, J. H. (2006). Predicting student attitudes and grades from perceptions of instructors' attitudes. *Teaching of Psychology, 33,* 91–94.

Areas of Research:
For over 15 years, I conducted research on social buffering in rats with a physiological component. I have recently transitioned to social buffering in humans. In addition, I study social aspects of teaching, focusing on rapport between teachers and students.

Professional Memberships/Activities:
- Society for the Teaching of Psychology, Program Director, 2008–2013
- Governor's Teaching Fellowship Program, 2006–2007
- *Who's Who Among America's Teachers,* 2004–2006 (nominated by students)
- *Teaching of Psychology,* Consulting Editor, 2004–2007
- Southeastern Psychological Association, 1998–present

Most Rewarding Aspect of Your Career:
My favorite activity is teaching, including teaching in the classroom and research on teaching.

Words of Advice to the Student Who Is Interested in Your Subfield:
Since my training is in Experimental Psychology, I would tell students that they should get involved in any type of research. Research of any kind will teach so much. After gaining some experience, focus on conducting research in an area of personal interest.

Suggested Exercises

1. Find an advertisement for a faculty position from one of the resources listed in the chapter. Answer the following questions:
   - Where is the position?
   - What rank is the position (visiting, instructor, assistant, associate, full)?
   - Is it tenure-track, tenured, or something other designation?
   - What are the responsibilities of the position?
   - Does the position seem more focused on teaching, research, or administration?
   - What must a person do to apply?
   - When is the deadline?
2. Research one of the faculty member's in your department.
   - Does the person have a web page?

- Does the person have her/his vita posted?
- What research interests does the faculty member have?
- What publications does the faculty member have? (Do a literature search.)
- List one of the faculty's publications in APA style.
- Where did the faculty member get his/her education? What field?
- What courses does he/she teach?
- What committees does the person serve on?
- Did the faculty member teach elsewhere before coming to your school?
- Is the faculty member a member of a professional organization? If so, which one(s)?

Suggested Readings

Adams, K. A. (2002). *What colleges and universities want in new faculty*. Washington, DC: Association of American Colleges and Universities. Retrieved from http://www.aacu.org/pff/pdfs/PFF_Adams.PDF

Buskist, W., Beins, B. C., & Hevern, V. W. (Eds.). (2004). *Preparing the new psychology professoriate: Helping graduate students become competent teachers*. Retrieved from http://teachpsych.org/resources/e-books/pnpp/rtf/pnpp.rtf

Darley, J. M., Zanna, M. P., & Roediger, H. L., III (Eds.). (2003). *The compleat academic: A career guide* (2nd ed.). Washington, DC: American Psychological Association.

Davis, S. F., & Buskist, W. (Eds.). (2002). *The teaching of psychology: Essays in honor of Wilbert J. McKeachie and Charles L. Brewer*. Mahwah, NJ: Lawrence Erlbaum Associates.

Forsyth, D. R. (2003). *The professor's guide to teaching: Psychological principles and practices*. Washington, DC: American Psychological Association.

Gaff, J. G., Pruitt-Logan, A. S., Sims, L. B., & Denecke, D. D. (2003). *Preparing future faculty in the humanities and social sciences: A guide for change*. Washington, DC: Association of American Colleges and Universities. Retrieved from http://www.preparing-faculty.org/PFFWeb.PFF4Manual.pdf

McKeachie, W. J., & Svinicki, M. (2006). *McKeachie's teaching tips: Strategies, research, and theory for college and university teachers* (12th ed.). Belmont, CA: Wadsworth.

References

American Association of University Professors. (1940/1970). *1940 statement of principles on academic freedom and tenure with 1970 interpretive comments*. Retrieved from http://www.aaup.org/AAUP/pubsres/policydocs/contents/1940statement.htm

Berger, A., Kirshstein, R., & Rowe, E. (2001). *Institutional policies and practices: Results from the 1999 National Study of Postsecondary Faculty, Institution Survey*. Washington, DC: U.S. Department of Education, National Center for Education Statistics (NCES).

Center for Psychology Workforce Analysis and Research. (2007). *2007 salaries in psychology: Preliminary data.* Washington, DC: American Psychological Association. Retrieved from http://research.apa.org/t1salaries07.pdf

Howard, C., Buskist, W., & Stowell, J. (Eds.). (2007). *The STP guide to graduate student training in the teaching of psychology.* Retrieved from http://teachpsych.org/resources/e-books/gst2007/gst07.php

Norcross, J. C., Kohout, J. L., & Wicherski, M. (2005). Graduate study in psychology. *American Psychologist, 60,* 959–975.

Occupational Information Network. (2005). *Details report for 25-1066.00 – Psychology teachers, post-secondary.* Retrieved from http://online.onetcenter.org/link/details/25-1066.00

Preparing Future Faculty. (n.d.). *The preparing future faculty program.* Retrieved from http://www.preparing-faculty.org/

U.S. Department of Labor, Bureau of Labor Statistics. (2007). *Occupational employment and wages, May 2006: 25-1066 psychology teachers, postsecondary.* Retrieved from http://www.bls.gov/oes/current/oes251066.htm

U.S. Department of Labor, Bureau of Labor Statistics. (2008–2009). *Occupational outlook handbook.* Retrieved from http://www.bls.gov/oco/

Wicherski, M., & Kohout, J. (2007). *2005 doctorate employment suvey.* Washington, DC: American Psychological Association's Center for Psychology Workforce Analysis and Research. Retrieved from http://research.apa.org/des05.html

Resources

America's Career InfoNet
* http://www.careerinfonet.org/
* Contains videos about higher education administrators, professors, teachers, and special education teachers: http://www.careerinfonet.org/videos_by_cluster.asp?id=27&nodeid=28&cluster=5

Preparing Future Faculty
* http://www.preparing-faculty.org/

Teachers of Psychology in Secondary Schools (TOPSS)
* http://www.apa.org/ed/topss/homepage.html
* Contains information for those interested in and those already teaching high school

Society for the Teaching of Psychology (STP)
* Division 2 of the American Psychological Association
* http://teachpsych.org/

17

Assessing the Career Outlook for the Psychology Major

Introduction

As a student of psychology, you have a vested interest in the future of the field. The various directions it takes will have a substantial impact on your professional career. Thinking of the future likely brings several questions to mind regarding your career goals. Will you be able to access the education and training you need? Will you be able to have the career you want, and in that career will you be able to engage in the work you want to do? Will you be financially secure in your career? What will your sense of professional identity be? How will society view your profession and accomplishments? In the coming years, forces at work within and outside of the field will play a large role in determining the answers to these questions. As we have seen throughout this book, being knowledgeable about these forces and their potential impact on you is the first step in ensuring that you succeed in achieving your career goals.

Predicting the future of a career is never easy. It becomes even more complicated if you are still contemplating several options in a field. However, you can gain an overall sense of the career outlook for psychology majors by assessing factors likely to guide the field as a whole in coming years. In this chapter, we provide a brief assessment of several of these factors that are already impacting psychology careers. Our discussion is organized into considerations of psychology's strengths, weaknesses, threats, and opportunities, as well as what these factors might mean for bachelor's and graduate level students in the field.

Psychology's Strengths

Psychology has numerous strengths that establish a strong foundation for the field. Although change is certain to occur as the various subfields evolve, these strengths are unlikely to transform significantly in a short period of time. Among psychology's strengths, its scientific basis, ethical rigor, and recent growth are noteworthy for their likely influence on a variety of psychology careers.

Beginning with the early work of figures like Wilhelm Wundt, G. Stanley Hall, and William James, psychology has established itself to be a scientific discipline. Today the field addresses a staggering array of topics that fall under the broad definition of behavior and mental processes. This is evidenced by the numerous subfields that have emerged in recent decades. Yet despite the diversity among psychologists in terms of their subject matter and professional activities, their work remains rooted in science. They understand and appreciate the role played by theory, research methodology, experimentation, data collection and analysis, and the dissemination of findings. Certainly some careers in the field may not engage in the active production of scientific knowledge, but these psychologists will continue to be trained to understand scientific approaches and to use the findings of research in their careers.

Psychologists in all subfields conduct their work with ethical rigor. They emphasize ethics in all of their activities for two reasons. First, ethics forms a cornerstone of all psychologists' education and training. This is because they work directly with human and nonhuman animals as participants, subjects, patients, clients, and students, and their work has direct bearing on the well-being of others. Second, ethical standards and responsibilities are embedded in the professional activities of all psychologists. Although the American Psychological Association's "Ethical Principles of Psychologists and Code of Conduct" often serves as the ethical guide for psychologists, it also provides an excellent model for how psychologists view ethics. In this code, ethics are conceptualized both as rules or guidelines that are to be followed and as aspirational, general principles that all psychologists strive to uphold throughout their professional work. In other words, psychologists both adhere to clear ethical standards and uphold guiding values in their work in order to ensure that their actions promote well-being and do not cause harm.

Psychology has experienced substantial growth over the past two decades. Data from the National Center for Education Statistics (Snyder, Dillow, & Hoffman, 2008) reveals that between 1985 and 2005, the number of psychology bachelor's degrees granted in the United States rose 117%. During the same time period, the number of master's degrees granted in psychology rose 101%. This growth has resulted in psychology being consistently among the top two or three undergraduate majors in U.S. colleges and universities. In addition, the number, diversity, and size of master's level programs have expanded. Importantly, the growth in the number of doctoral degrees granted during this time period has also increased, but at a much lower rate of 37%. These figures indicate that much of the expansion in career areas in the field has been at master's and bachelor's levels.

Psychology's strengths have several implications for your career outlook. At the bachelor's level, expect your coursework to emphasize both the scientific and ethical principles of psychology. Recognize that these strengths in your education will become part of the expertise and skills you will possess. Familiarity with research methods, experimentation, statistical analysis, and scientific writing, as well as sensitivity to ethical issues in specific career settings, are core components of what psychology majors can offer potential employers. The increasing popularity of the psychology major means increased competition for employment at the bachelor's level. As a result, you should strive to identify your career goals and then work to distinguish yourself in your under-graduate education and experiences. At the graduate level, you should expect to witness increasing emphasis on scientific training and research productivity, especially at the doctoral level. The ethical principles of psychologists will continue to play a significant role in the education and training of graduate students as the field evolves. You should prepare yourself to conduct your graduate training and careers in ways that conform to these principles. The growth in the field at the master's level has not been as significant at the doctoral level. Some subfields have witnessed substantial growth while others have declined. To ensure your career success, remain cognizant of these trends and how they might be affecting graduate admissions, training, and career opportunities.

Psychology's Weaknesses

Although typically outshone by its strengths, there are several areas of weakness within the field of psychology that have been identified and discussed in recent years. Despite efforts to address these issues, each continues to affect the standing of the field and is likely to play an ongoing role in its career outlook. The viability of some careers may hinge on your ability to address the roles these weaknesses play in your particular career.

As indicated in the previous chapters on careers in the field, psychology is an incredibly broad discipline. In fact, many large universities in the United States have multiple psychology degree programs housed in separate academic divisions (e.g., clinical psychology in arts and sciences, school psychology in education, industrial/ organizational psychology in business). In addition to having two large professional organizations in the United States, psychologists within these organizations have furthered divided themselves into dozens of divisions based on their specific interests. Remarkably, many of these divisions are divided even further into smaller sections. This breadth is a testament to the far reaching applications of psychological science, yet it also poses several problems. First, such diversity can at times contribute to a lack of cohesion. Psychologists sometimes struggle to communicate with each other when their expertise and interests differ. Schisms have emerged within the field along theoretical lines (e.g., behaviorism versus cognitivism) or between those who engage in varied professional careers (e.g., practitioners vs. academics). Second, those outside the field may at times struggle to understand who psychologists are and what they contribute. A student taking a first psychology course, a patient seeking mental healthcare, and an organization looking to grant research funding, may all struggle to identify what exactly psychology is.

As a field and area of study, psychology has had mixed experiences with promoting the diversity of its members. In terms of gender, the field has experienced a strong trend towards higher numbers of female students over the past two decades. In the 2005–2006 academic year, women were the recipients of 77% of the bachelor's, 79% of the master's, and 73% of the doctoral degrees in psychology (Snyder et al., 2008). In fact at the graduate level, women earned more degrees than men in each of the subfields of psychology. In terms of racial composition, psychology has experienced an underrepresentation of minority students at the undergraduate level and has seen this trend become even more pronounced at the master's and doctoral levels. Maton, Kohout, Wicherski, Leary, and Vinokurov (2006) reported that despite comprising 32% of the population in the United States in 2002, minorities earned only 24% of bachelor's, 22% of master's, 19% of PsyD, and 16% of PhD degrees in psychology. These percentages for bachelor's and master's degrees reflect steady increases in minority students since the late 1980s. In contrast, the percentages for doctoral degrees reflect limited growth since the late 1990s.

Psychology has often failed to demonstrate the real world applications of its theoretical and research developments. Despite the fact that some subfields concentrate on researching and providing direct applications to society, there remains a general sense in the field that we do not do enough to communicate the benefits of progress in psychological science. In particular, concerns have been voiced that the general public has limited understanding of what psychologists do and how psychologists' work impacts their daily lives. Such understanding on the part of the average citizen is critical. Individuals are more inclined to seek the beneficial services of applied psychologists when they are familiar with their expertise and offerings. In addition, individuals are more inclined to be supportive of funding for psychological research when they have an appreciation for how this science contributes to their well-being. Finally, information gleaned from psychological science can have an immediate positive impact on the lives of these individuals if it is properly explained and contextualized.

Psychology's weaknesses have several implications for your career outlook. At the bachelor's level, you might sometimes feel overwhelmed at the number of subfields and career options available. This can lead to uncertainty about career goals given that the bachelor's degree does not offer highly specialized knowledge and skills in an easily defined area. If you pursue training at the graduate level, you may find yourself having to select a subfield of focus before you feel ready given the need to apply to specialized programs of study. You should also be aware of how your gender and race may play a role in your education and training. At the bachelor's and master's levels, minority students are likely to find many opportunities and a level of diversity that is beginning to better approximate the population. At the doctoral level, underrepresentation of minority students will be more prominent. At all levels, students are likely to notice the overrepresentation of women in each subfield. Although you may not directly feel the effects of psychology's struggle to educate the general public about our field, the viability of the field is in part dependent upon the perception of psychology as a useful contributor to society and the well-being of its members.

Psychology's Threats

Threats to the field of psychology come in varied forms. By threats we do not mean to invoke images of other disciplines plotting to bring down the field. Instead, we wish to convey that certain issues in society, such as higher education, healthcare, and legislation, have the potential to negatively impact the field. Often such issues are shaped by invariable shifts in the economy, public interest, and government, so they can be difficult to predict. Yet, they can have far reaching implications for the career outlook of many psychologists.

As described earlier, psychology has experienced substantial growth, particularly at the undergraduate level, over the past two decades. Unfortunately, funding of psychology programs, and higher education in general, has lagged behind. As a result, many departments of psychology have struggled to hire faculty, offer courses, and provide student resources to meet new demands. At the graduate level, psychology programs have expanded relatively little over this period of time with the exception of a few emerging subfields with strong research funding. In fact, much of the growth in graduate education has been concentrated in psychology professional school programs and in master's degrees in other mental health fields. Because these professional schools and master's level programs often generate their funding largely through student tuition, they are less susceptible to shifts in funding for education and research. Therefore, this trend is not without consequences. For example, Wicherski and Kohout (2005) reported that in 2003, students earning a PsyD in clinical psychology reported a median education debt of $90,000. By comparison, students earning a PhD in clinical psychology reported a median debt of $50,000, and students earning a PhD in all of the research subfields combined reported a median debt of $21,500. In addition, sharp increases in the number of master's level mental health practitioners in non-psychology fields have led to increased competition for outpatient mental health careers and patients.

As previously discussed in the Careers in Clinical Psychology and Counseling Psychology chapter, developments in insurance and managed care pose a specific threat to practitioners in these subfields. The most substantial threats have been to patients' ability to access affordable, quality mental health care, and to psychologists' ability to receive adequate compensation for providing these services. Although the picture has become increasingly bleak in recent years, legislative developments in 2008 brought renewed hope to patients and psychologists. The passage of the Paul Wellstone and Pete Dominici Mental Health and Addiction Equity Act opened the door to the possibility that insurance and managed care organizations will begin to cover medical and mental health care on equal terms. The regulatory success of such a law will certainly face many hurdles, but there is optimism that the restrictions these organizations have been placing on mental health coverage may begin to lessen.

Another potential threat to the field is reduced funding for psychological research. The majority of funding for behavioral and social sciences research comes from government agencies, particularly the National Science Foundation (NSF) and National Institutes of Health (NIH). Although funding for behavioral and social science research typically falls well below that for other fields, flat budgets in recent years for NSF and NIH have only amplified this problem (Silver, Sharpe, Kelly, Kobor, & Sroufe, 2008). In recent years, NSF has increased its emphasis on engineering and physical sciences, and NIH budgets for behavioral and social sciences have experienced limited growth. While some gains have been made in funding for health and neuropsychological research, much promising research still remains unfunded.

In terms of career outlook, the threats to psychology pose several implications for you at the bachelor's and graduate level. The increasing popularity of the undergraduate psychology major, coupled with slower growth in funding for higher education and research, creates a situation in which resources may be insufficient to ensure adequate education and training. Be mindful of how this situation might be affecting the psychology department at your institution and any others that you are considering attending. At the graduate level, if you decide to pursue a degree in a research-focused subfield, be aware of how the state of research funding might impact your graduate training and early career efforts. In addition, if you are considering academic careers or careers in the clinical or counseling psychology subfields, you must be mindful of how changes in insurance, higher education, and research funding might impact the availability of jobs and earning potentials.

Psychology's Opportunities

As you continue to formulate your career goals and progress through your education, it is vital to recognize some of the opportunities that psychology is poised to capitalize on. The U.S. Department of Labor (2008) has projected varied growth for subfields of psychology between 2006 and 2016. Industrial/organizational (I/O) psychology is expected to grow at 21.3%, clinical/counseling/school psychology at 15.8%, and all other subfields combined at 7.9%. New psychologists will play a key role in shaping and guiding the growing and emerging areas. In addition, these are the most likely areas to generate new career opportunities.

The potential for growth within I/O psychology stems from two factors. First, this area is relatively new in the field, particularly in its efforts to provide increasingly varied types of services to businesses. Second, as businesses rapidly change in response to shifts in technology, the workforce, and increased globalization, the need for services from I/O psychologists is continually being renewed. For additional information on this subfield, refer to the Careers in Industrial Organizational Psychology chapter.

As already discussed in earlier chapters, health psychology and neuropsychology are among the fastest growing subfields. Their growth is in part due to their newness and need for expansion, but other factors have contributed as well. Health psychology and neuropsychology have both research and applied emphases. On the research side, improvements in imaging technology and assessment techniques have expanded the types of information these psychologists can gather. In addition, funding for this research has often exceeded that of other subfields in psychology. On the applied side, both health and neuropsychologists are involved in work that has a direct impact on the lives of patients. Often they are working to address issues that are of major concern to individuals and society at large such as obesity, brain injury, smoking cessation, attention-deficit/hyperactivity disorder, and dementia.

Other growth areas cross multiple subfields. For example, psychologists with expertise in cross-cultural and ethnic minority issues have become increasingly in demand as global and societal changes necessitate increasing knowledge about these issues and competence for them in research and practice. For psychologists with careers involving applied work, proficiency in multiple languages will likely continue to be a substantial asset. Most of the growth areas focus on issues that are by their nature interdisciplinary. For example, a movement in recent years known as positive psychology has investigated how individuals and groups flourish and lead fulfilling existences. Although psychologists have been heavily involved in this new way of thinking about behavior and mental processes, other disciplines have contributed substantially. Psychologists engaged in this and similar endeavors are capitalizing on the growing trend to share knowledge and expertise across disciplines in order to answer research questions and solve applied problems. The subfields of psychology that succeed as cultivating and capitalizing on these and other interdisciplinary collaborations stand the best chance of sustaining growth.

Psychology's opportunities have several implications for your training as well as your career outlook. At the bachelor's level, you should seek to be as informed as possible about emerging and growing areas in the field. Take coursework and secure research opportunities in these areas when they are available. This will provide excellent experience and assist you in deciding if these subfields fit your interests. At the graduate level, be aware of what career fields are poised for the greatest growth and consider how changes in funding might affect the availability and viability of graduate programs in these areas.

Conclusion

Psychology remains a fascinating and vibrant field of study that offers a diverse array of career options and experiences. Learning about the process of obtaining an education in the field and pursuing career goals can at times be daunting. At points you may feel that keeping up with your current academic responsibilities allows little time for implementing new study skills, assessing your career goals, or preparing for employment or graduate school. It is our intention that the information contained in this book be empowering rather than overwhelming or intimidating. Understanding the vast career options available to you and the various steps required to obtain these careers is vital. We hope that by formulating your career goals, and making educational and occupational decisions that will support these goals, you will place yourself on the surest path to success.

References

Maton, K. I., Kohout, J. L., Wicherski, M., Leary, G. E., & Vinokurov, A. (2006). Minority students of color and the psychology graduate pipeline: Disquieting and encouraging trends, 1989–2003. *American Psychologist, 61,* 117–131.

Silver, H. J., Sharpe, A. L., Kelly, H., Kobor, P., & Sroufe, G. (2008). Behavioral and social science research in the administration's FY 2009 budget. In Intersociety Working Group, *AAAS report XXXIII: Research and development FY 2009* (pp. 195–202). Washington, DC: American Association for the Advancement of Science.

Snyder, T. D., Dillow, S. A., & Hoffman, C. M. (2008). *Digest of education statistics: 2007* (NCES 2008-022). Washington, DC: National Center for Education Statistics, Institute of Education Sciences, U.S. Department of Education. Retrieved from http://nces.ed.gov/pubsearch/pubsinfo.asp?pubid =2008022

U.S. Department of Labor. (2008). *Occupational projections and training data: 2008–09 edition* (Bulletin 2702). Washington, DC: Author.

Wicherski, M., & Kohout, J. (2005). *2003 doctorate employment survey.* Retrieved from http://research. apa.org/des03.html

Appendix

Divisions of the American Psychological Association

Division Number	Division	Web Address*
1	Society for General Psychology	www.apa.org/divisions/div1
2	Society for the Teaching of Psychology	www.teachpsych.org
3	Experimental Psychology	www.apa.org/divisions/div3
4	No Division	n/a
5	Evaluation, Measurement, and Statistics	www.apa.org/divisions/div5
6	Behavioral Neuroscience and Comparative Psychology	www.apa.org/divisions/div6
7	Developmental Psychology	ecp.fiu.edu/APA/div7
8	Society for Personality and Social Psychology	www.spsp.org
9	Society for the Psychological Study of Social Issues	www.spssi.org
10	Society for the Psychology of Aesthetics, Creativity, and the Arts	www.apa.org/divisions/div10
11	No Division	n/a
12	Society of Clinical Psychology	www.apa.org/divisions/div12
13	Society of Consulting Psychology	www.div13.org
14	Society for Industrial and Organizational Psychology	www.siop.org
15	Educational Psychology	www.apa.org/divisions/div15
16	School Psychology	www.indiana.edu/~div16
17	Society of Counseling Psychology	www.div17.org
18	Psychologists in Public Service	www.apa.org/divisions/div18
19	Society for Military Psychology	www.apa.org/divisions/div19
20	Adult Development and Aging	apadiv20.phhp.ufl.edu

Appendix *Cont'd*

Division Number	Division	Web Address*
21	Applied Experimental and Engineering Psychology	www.apa21.org
22	Rehabilitation Psychology	www.div22.org
23	Society for Consumer Psychology	www.myscp.org
24	Society for Theoretical and Philosophical Psychology	www1.indstate.edu/coe/div24
25	Behavior Analysis	www.auburn.edu/~newlamc/apa_div25
26	Society for the History of Psychology	www.hood.edu/shp
27	Society for Community Research and Action: Division of Community Psychology	www.scra27.org
28	Psychopharmacology and Substance Abuse	www.apa.org/divisions/div28
29	Psychotherapy	www.divisionofpsychotherapy.org
30	Society of Psychological Hypnosis	www.apa.org/divisions/div30
31	State, Provincial, Territorial Psychological Association Affairs	www.apadiv31.org
32	Society for Humanistic Psychology	www.apa.org/divisions/div32
33	Intellectual and Developmental Disabilities	www.apa.org/divisions/div33
34	Population and Environmental Psychology	apa34.cos.ucf.edu
35	Society for the Psychology of Women	www.apa.org/divisions/div35
36	Psychology of Religion	www.apa.org/divisions/div36
37	Society for Child and Family Policy and Practice	www.apa.org/divisions/div37
38	Health Psychology	www.health-psych.org
39	Psychoanalysis	www.division39.org
40	Clinical Neuropsychology	www.div40.org
41	American Psychology-Law Society	www.ap-ls.org
42	Psychologists in Independent Practice	www.division42.org
43	Society for Family Psychology	www.apa.org/divisions/div43
44	Society for the Psychological Study of Lesbian, Gay, and Bisexual Issues	www.apadivision44.org
45	Society for the Psychological Study of Ethnic Minority Issues	www.apa.org/divisions/div45
46	Media Psychology	www.apa.org/divisions/div46
47	Exercise and Sport Psychology	www.apa47.org
48	Society for the Study of Peace, Conflict, and Violence: Peace Psychology Division	www.webster.edu/peacepsychology
49	Group Psychology and Group Psychotherapy	www.apa49.org

Appendix   *Cont'd*

Division Number	Division	Web Address*
50	Addictions	www.apa.org/divisions/div50
51	Society for the Psychological Study of Men and Masculinity	www.apa.org/divisions/div51
52	International Psychology	www.internationalpsychology.net
53	Society of Clinical Child and Adolescent Psychology	www.clinicalchildpsychology.org
54	Society of Pediatric Psychology	www.societyofpediatricpsychology.org
55	American Society for the Advancement of Pharmacotherapy	www.division55.org
56	Trauma Psychology	www.apatraumadivision.org

* If a web address is not listed or is no longer active, check the APA website at http://www.apa.org/about/division.html for information about the division.

Index